Self-Regulated Learning Interventions With At-Risk Youth

SCHOOL PSYCHOLOGY BOOK SERIES

Health-Related Disorders in Children and Adolescents: A Guidebook for Understanding and Educating
   Edited by LeAdelle Phelps

Enhancing Relationships Between Children and Teachers
   Robert C. Pianta

Working With Parents of Aggressive Children: A Practitioner's Guide
   Timothy A. Cavell

Empowered Families, Successful Children: Early Intervention Programs That Work
   Susan Epps and Barbara J. Jackson

School-Based Mental Health Services: Creating Comprehensive and Culturally Specific Programs
   Bonnie Kaul Nastasi, Rachel Bernstein Moore, and Kristen M. Varjas

Working With Parents of Noncompliant Children: A Guide to Evidence-Based Parent Training for Practitioners and Students
   Mark D. Shriver and Keith D. Allen

Behavioral Interventions in Schools: Evidence-Based Positive Strategies
   Edited by Angeleque Akin-Little, Steven G. Little, Melissa A. Bray, and Thomas J. Kehle

Healthy Eating in Schools: Evidence-Based Interventions to Help Kids Thrive
   Catherine P. Cook-Cottone, Evelyn Tribole, and Tracy L. Tylka

Treatment Integrity: A Foundation for Evidence-Based Practice in Applied Psychology
   Edited by Lisa M. Hagermoser Sanetti and Thomas R. Kratochwill

Assessing Bilingual Children in Context: An Integrated Approach
   Edited by Amanda B. Clinton

Universal Screening in Educational Settings: Evidence-Based Decision Making for Schools
   Edited by Ryan J. Kettler, Todd A. Glover, Craig A. Albers, and Kelly A. Feeney-Kettler

Autism Spectrum Disorder in Children and Adolescents: Evidence-Based Assessment and Intervention in Schools
   Edited by Lee A. Wilkinson

Single-Case Intervention Research: Methodological and Statistical Advances
   Edited by Thomas R. Kratochwill and Joel R. Levin

Testing Accommodations for Students With Disabilities: Research-Based Practice
   Benjamin J. Lovett and Lawrence J. Lewandowski

Self-Regulated Learning Interventions With At-Risk Youth: Enhancing Adaptability, Performance, and Well-Being
   Edited by Timothy J. Cleary

Self-Regulated Learning Interventions With At-Risk Youth

Enhancing Adaptability, Performance, and Well-Being

Edited by Timothy J. Cleary

American Psychological Association
WASHINGTON, DC

Copyright © 2015 by the American Psychological Association. All rights reserved. Except as permitted under the United States Copyright Act of 1976, no part of this publication may be reproduced or distributed in any form or by any means, including, but not limited to, the process of scanning and digitization, or stored in a database or retrieval system, without the prior written permission of the publisher.

Published by
American Psychological Association
750 First Street, NE
Washington, DC 20002
www.apa.org

To order
APA Order Department
P.O. Box 92984
Washington, DC 20090-2984
Tel: (800) 374-2721; Direct: (202) 336-5510
Fax: (202) 336-5502; TDD/TTY: (202) 336-6123
Online: www.apa.org/pubs/books
E-mail: order@apa.org

In the U.K., Europe, Africa, and the Middle East, copies may be ordered from
American Psychological Association
3 Henrietta Street
Covent Garden, London
WC2E 8LU England

Typeset in Goudy by Circle Graphics, Inc., Columbia, MD

Printer: Edwards Brothers, Inc., Lillington, NC
Cover Designer: Beth Schlenoff Design, Bethesda, MD

The opinions and statements published are the responsibility of the authors, and such opinions and statements do not necessarily represent the policies of the American Psychological Association.

Library of Congress Cataloging-in-Publication Data

Self-regulated learning interventions with at-risk youth : enhancing adaptability, performance, and well-being / editor, Timothy J. Cleary.
    pages cm. — (School psychology book series)
  Includes bibliographical references and index.
  ISBN 978-1-4338-1987-2 — ISBN 1-4338-1987-2 1. Children with social disabilities—Education—United States. 2. Children with disabilities—Education—United States. 3. Learning. 4. Self-control. 5. Emotional problems of children. 6. Behavior modification. 7. Behavioral assessment. 8. Classroom management. 9. School psychology. I. Cleary, Timothy J.
  LC4091.S44 2015
  371.90973—dc23
                                  2014041622

British Library Cataloguing-in-Publication Data
A CIP record is available from the British Library.

Printed in the United States of America
First Edition

http://dx.doi.org/10.1037/14641-000

Noreen M. Clark, a visionary leader in the management of chronic disease, died on November 23, 2013. She leaves an outstanding legacy, and her chapter in this series edition is just one example. Central to her therapeutic mission was her firm belief that 99% of disease management is in the hands of individuals and their families, and she was a pioneer in applying self-regulation theory to empower afflicted families. Because of her exemplary research and program development, Noreen was elected to the board of directors and Leadership Council of the American Lung Association, chaired the behavioral science section of the American Thoracic Society, and served as president of the Society for Public Health Education.

Noreen held important academic leadership positions, including dean of the School of Public Health at the University of Michigan, Ann Arbor, from 1995 to 2005. She also was the Myron E. Wegman Distinguished University Professor of Public Health at the University of Michigan, where she founded and directed the Center for Managing Chronic Disease. Among the many honors in her storied career, she was a Distinguished Fellow of the Society for Public Health Education, a Derryberry Award recipient of the American Public Health Association, and a Health Education Research Award honoree of the National Asthma Education and Prevention Program. She also was a member of the Institute of Medicine of the National Academy of Sciences.

A brilliant scholar, dedicated health educator, inspiring mentor, and public health leader, Noreen was also a precious friend. She was broadly known as a wise, caring mentor to countless students and colleagues throughout her career. She is greatly missed.

—Barry J. Zimmerman and Minal R. Patel

CONTENTS

Contributors xi

Series Foreword xiii
Barry J. Zimmerman

Acknowledgments xv

Introduction: An Overview of Applications of Self-Regulated Learning 3
Timothy J. Cleary

I. Self-Regulated Learning Interventions Targeting Academic and Behavioral Skills 13

Chapter 1. Use of Self-Regulated Learning for Children With ADHD: Research and Practice Opportunities 15
Linda A. Reddy, Erik Newman, and Arielle Verdesco

Chapter 2. Self-Management Interventions to Reduce Disruptive Classroom Behavior 45
Amy M. Briesch and Jacquelyn M. Briesch

| Chapter 3. | Self-Regulated Learning Interventions for Motivationally Disengaged College Students 67
Christopher A. Wolters and Leah D. Hoops |

| Chapter 4. | Success for Students With Learning Disabilities: What Does Self-Regulation Have To Do With It? 89
Deborah L. Butler and Leyton Schnellert |

| Chapter 5. | Supporting Self-Regulated Reading for English Language Learners in Middle Schools 113
Ana Taboada Barber and Melissa A. Gallagher |

II. Self-Regulated Learning Interventions Targeting Mental and Physical Health 135

| Chapter 6. | Emotion Regulation Interventions for Youth With Anxiety Disorders 137
Cynthia Suveg, Molly Davis, and Anna Jones |

| Chapter 7. | Emotion Regulation Interventions and Childhood Depression 157
Jill Ehrenreich-May, Sarah M. Kennedy, and Cara S. Remmes |

| Chapter 8. | Self-Regulation–Based Interventions for Children and Adolescents With Asthma 181
Noreen M. Clark and Minal R. Patel |

III. Self-Regulated Learning Interventions Across Diverse Contexts 203

| Chapter 9. | Professional Development Contexts That Promote Self-Regulated Learning and Content Learning in Trainees 205
Erin E. Peters-Burton, Timothy J. Cleary, and Susan G. Forman |

| Chapter 10. | Using Teacher Learning Teams as a Framework for Bridging Theory and Practice in Self-Regulated Learning 229
Nancy E. Perry, Charlotte A. Brenner, and Nicole MacPherson |

Chapter 11.	Contexts Supporting Self-Regulated Learning at School Transitions 251
	Wendy S. Grolnick and Jacquelyn N. Raftery-Helmer
Chapter 12.	Learning Technologies as Supportive Contexts for Promoting College Student Self-Regulated Learning 277
	Anastasia Kitsantas, Nada Dabbagh, Suzanne E. Hiller, and Brian Mandell

Index 295

About the Editor 305

CONTRIBUTORS

Ana Taboada Barber, PhD, University of Maryland, College Park
Charlotte A. Brenner, MEd, The University of British Columbia, Vancouver, Canada
Amy M. Briesch, PhD, Northeastern University, Boston, MA
Jacquelyn M. Briesch, MS, Northeastern University, Boston, MA
Deborah L. Butler, PhD, The University of British Columbia, Vancouver, Canada
Noreen M. Clark, PhD, University of Michigan, Ann Arbor
Timothy J. Cleary, PhD, Rutgers, The State University of New Jersey, New Brunswick
Nada Dabbagh, PhD, George Mason University, Fairfax, VA
Molly Davis, BA, University of Georgia, Athens
Jill Ehrenreich-May, PhD, University of Miami, Coral Gables, FL
Susan G. Forman, PhD, Rutgers, The State University of New Jersey, New Brunswick
Melissa A. Gallagher, MA, George Mason University, Fairfax, VA
Wendy S. Grolnick, PhD, Clark University, Worcester, MA
Suzanne E. Hiller, PhD, George Mason University, Fairfax, VA
Leah D. Hoops, MEd, The Ohio State University, Columbus

Anna Jones, BS, University of Georgia, Athens
Sarah M. Kennedy, MA, University of Miami, Coral Gables, FL
Anastasia Kitsantas, PhD, George Mason University, Fairfax, VA
Nicole MacPherson, MEd, The University of British Columbia, Vancouver, Canada
Brian Mandell, PhD, George Mason University, Fairfax, VA
Erik Newman, PhD, University of California, San Diego, and Integrative Psychotherapy Services of San Diego, Carlsbad
Minal R. Patel, PhD, MPH, University of Michigan, Ann Arbor
Nancy E. Perry, PhD, The University of British Columbia, Vancouver, Canada
Erin E. Peters-Burton, PhD, NBCT, George Mason University, Fairfax, VA
Jacquelyn N. Raftery-Helmer, MA, Clark University, Worcester, MA
Linda A. Reddy, PhD, Rutgers, The State University of New Jersey, New Brunswick
Cara S. Remmes, MS, University of Miami, Coral Gables, FL
Leyton Schnellert, PhD, The University of British Columbia, Kelowna, Canada
Cynthia Suveg, PhD, University of Georgia, Athens
Arielle Verdesco, BS, Rutgers, The State University of New Jersey, New Brunswick
Christopher A. Wolters, PhD, The Ohio State University, Columbus
Barry J. Zimmerman, PhD, The Graduate Center, City University of New York, New York

SERIES FOREWORD

BARRY J. ZIMMERMAN

Outside of their homes, children spend more time in schools than in any other setting. Tragedies such as the Sandy Hook Elementary School and Columbine High School shootings, and more hopeful developments, such as the movement toward improved mental health, physical health, and academic achievement, all illustrate the ongoing need for high-quality writing that explains how children, families, and communities associated with schools worldwide can be supported through the application of sound psychological research, theory, and practice.

For the past several years, the American Psychological Association (APA) Books program and APA Division of School Psychology (Division 16) have partnered to produce the School Psychology Book Series. The mission of this series is to increase the visibility of psychological science, practice, and policy for children and adolescents in schools and communities. The result has been a strong collection of scholarly work that appeals not only to psychologists but to individuals from all fields who have reason to seek and use what psychology has to offer in schools.

This book continues that tradition by discussing interventions that can make a significant difference in the well-being and academic performance of children who are at risk of school failure. Research on self-regulation of learning and performance has grown exponentially during the past three decades. This topic has attracted attention because of the widespread belief that problems in school and life can be overcome if one has the appropriate tools. This book documents how entrenched human problems can be modified through intervention programs that target deficits in self-regulatory skills, such as goal setting, strategy use, and self-monitoring, and because of the authors' focus on teaching self-regulatory skills to at-risk students on diverse tasks, the text makes a unique contribution to the application literature. These problems constitute a challenging test of a theory because of their severity and the need to overcome the adverse effects of the students' environmental context. Of particular concern to the authors was the challenge of creating effective feedback loops in settings that are difficult to self-regulate.

The chapter authors are nationally known for their research in the field; collectively, their chapters reveal that at-risk students can be taught to self-regulate cognitive disorders (e.g., attention-deficit/hyperactivity disorder, learning disabilities); mental health problems (e.g., anxiety, depression); physical health problems (e.g., asthma); and academic problems (e.g., class disruptions, English language learning). This range of topics makes the book suitable for use in graduate courses in education, special education, school psychology, clinical psychology, and health education. To develop a book that could function as a cohesive text, the volume editor, Timothy J. Cleary, provided the authors with a common organizational structure for their chapters, and the effect is impressive. Despite the diversity of their tasks, the authors' compelling accounts can be readily compared, integrated, and applied. Readers will appreciate how self-regulatory training can make a difference—even with protracted human problems.

I owe thanks to the many individuals who have made significant contributions to the School Psychology Book Series. I would like to acknowledge the dedication of past series editors: Sandra L. Christenson, Jan Hughes, R. Steve McCallum, LeAdelle Phelps, Susan Sheridan, Christopher H. Skinner, and Linda Reddy. I also would like to acknowledge the outstanding editorial vision of the scholars who have edited or authored books for the series. The work of these scholars has significantly advanced psychological science and practice for children and adolescents worldwide. We welcome your comments about this volume and other topics you would like to see explored in this series. Visit the Division 16 website at http://www.apadivisions.org/division-16 to share your thoughts.

ACKNOWLEDGMENTS

I appreciate the individuals who made important contributions to this published book, including Barry Zimmerman, who served as series editor, and the APA Books support staff. I am also very much indebted to the chapter authors, whose strong scholarship and outstanding chapters serve as the backbone of this book.

Of greatest importance, I want express my gratitude and love to my wife, Deborah, and my two boys, Benjamin and Maximillian, for the amazing amount of patience, positive energy, and support that they provide me on a daily basis. You are the story of my life.

Self-Regulated Learning Interventions With At-Risk Youth

INTRODUCTION: AN OVERVIEW OF APPLICATIONS OF SELF-REGULATED LEARNING

TIMOTHY J. CLEARY

The primary role of many professionals and service providers, such as teachers, therapists, counselors, and school psychologists is to enhance the competencies, performance outcomes, and/or well-being of children and adolescents. In addition to serving as exemplary models and empowering sources of support for the individuals with whom they work, these professionals often have the greatest influence on youth who are vulnerable or at risk for suboptimal performance and other types of dysfunction. Although many at-risk youth can learn how to adapt and function more effectively over time, particularly when immersed in positive support systems, the unfortunate reality is that not all children and adolescents are able to overcome challenging circumstances and experiences. Rather, many become stuck in negative cycles of poor performance and display self-handicapping behaviors that persist throughout their development.

---

http://dx.doi.org/10.1037/14641-001
Self-Regulated Learning Interventions With At-Risk Youth: Enhancing Adaptability, Performance, and Well-Being, T. J. Cleary (Editor)
Copyright © 2015 by the American Psychological Association. All rights reserved.

At the outset of this book, it is critical to underscore that no universally accepted definition of the term *at risk* exists. Children and adolescents frequently are labeled in this fashion if they exhibit one or more maladaptive outcomes (e.g., failing grades in school, depression, disruptive behaviors); possess within-person deficits (e.g., disability status, poor self-regulation skills); and/or attempt to learn or function in challenging contexts (e.g., unstable home environments, schools with poor instructional resources). Because a goal of this book is to address an array of at-risk populations across distinct areas of functioning and contexts, the term *at risk* is used in a relatively global and broad manner.

VIEWPOINT OF THIS BOOK

This book offers the viewpoint that self-regulated learning (SRL) research and theory can serve as a useful platform for analyzing and understanding why many at-risk children and adolescents struggle to overcome challenging circumstances and fail to break out of destructive patterns of action and thought (Boekaerts, Pintrich, & Zeidner, 2000; Zimmerman & Schunk, 2011). Although several SRL paradigms are referenced in this book, many of the chapter authors emphasize social-cognitive principles (see, e.g., Chapters 1, 5, 6, 9, and 12). From this perspective, *SRL* is defined as a process through which individuals self-generate thoughts and actions that are planned, monitored, and refined as they pursue personal goals. Zimmerman (2000) described SRL in terms of a cyclical loop involving three related phases: forethought (i.e., processes that precede learning: goal setting, planning); performance (i.e., processes that occur during learning: self-control, self-monitoring); and self-reflection (i.e., processes that come after learning: self-evaluation, attributions). Many of the struggles that individuals experience often can be traced to deficits in regulatory processes embedded within one or more of these phases (Bembenutty, Cleary, & Kitsantas, 2013). That is, some individuals possess a limited knowledge or repertoire of strategies to improve specific aspects of their lives and thus frequently will plan or approach situations in a relatively simplistic and circumscribed manner (i.e., poor forethought planning). For example, a 10th-grade student may struggle to improve his or her failing test grades in chemistry because the student does not know how to adequately take class notes or to plan or manage study time, and because his or her repertoire of study strategies consists only of rehearsal strategies (e.g., rereading class notes).

Conversely, other youth may struggle to use effective coping methods when under stress, not because they lack strategic knowledge or effective planning skills but because they have not developed the necessary self-control or performance phase skills to effectively apply and use previously learned strategies in appropriate ways during authentic situations. For example, a preadolescent boy who has learned to successfully identify and manage feelings of anger and frustration in individual counseling sessions may continue to find himself in contentious situations with teachers and peers until he has practiced and refined his newly developed skills enough to apply them in situations that elicit high levels of anger or frustration.

Successfully overcoming challenging circumstances, however, goes beyond strategic planning and the use of effective task-specific strategies. Individuals must also be sufficiently motivated to reflect on and manage these situations. Many researchers have shown that students who exhibit self-defeating patterns of motivation beliefs, such as poor self-efficacy or outcome expectations, and self-reflective judgments, such as uncontrollable attributions following failure, are at greater risk for displaying avoidance or other forms of negative regulatory behaviors (Bandura, 1997; Schunk, 2008; Zimmerman, 2000). Furthermore, when individuals perceive that engaging in effortful regulatory behaviors is not personally meaningful or has greater costs than benefits, or if they are offered minimal autonomy to decide when and how to engage in those behaviors, it is highly likely that they will not put forth the needed effort to improve (Reeve & Jang, 2006; Wigfield, Hoa, & Klauda, 2008).

In a general sense, sophisticated self-regulated learners tend to possess the strategic and metacognitive skills (e.g., planning, monitoring, evaluation) to succeed and the motivational will to persevere through discouraging and frustrating situations. They are intentional and purposeful individuals who, because they are empowered with a strong belief in their personal competency and skills, actively seek to transform their environments, adapt their thinking or ways of approaching a task, and sustain their motivation to accomplish personally meaningful goals (Zimmerman, 2000).

Of importance, however, and consistent with a key underlying theme of this book, is that individuals can only realistically engage in efficient cycles of regulation and adaptation when they have accurate information about their skills or performance levels—whether they gather that information through their self-observations and monitoring or via feedback provided by external sources, such as a teacher or therapist. *Feedback* is broadly defined as information related to performance or task understanding. It represents data that individuals can use to modify their thinking, affect, and behavior as they seek to improve their functioning or to reach goals (Butler & Winne, 1995; Hattie & Timperley, 2007; Shute, 2008).

SRL researchers often discuss feedback in terms of a *cyclical feedback loop*, a general process through which individuals evaluate their behavior or performance relative to a predetermined level as defined by a standard, comparator, or goal. Although different types of feedback loops have been discussed in the literature, such as closed versus open loops and negative versus positive loops (Carver & Scheier, 1990; Miller, Galanter, & Pribram, 1960; Winne & Hadwin, 1998; Zimmerman, 2000), the basic premise is that sophisticated self-regulated learners will use both internally generated and external sources of feedback to guide their strategic behaviors as they seek to reduce the discrepancy between current behaviors or performance and a predetermined benchmark. When given in an optimal manner, feedback has the potential to enhance the quality with which individuals evaluate goal attainment, identify patterns of errors or misunderstandings, and enable conclusions about how best to restrategize when they do not realize performance goals. Akin to the computer science concept of "garbage in, garbage out," when feedback is faulty, lacking, or erroneous (i.e., an ineffective input), the quality of individuals' reflective judgments and their subsequent emotional, cognitive, and behavioral reactions (i.e., a maladaptive output) will be severely comprised and undermined. Most SRL scholars would agree with the premise that teaching children and adolescents how to self-generate their own feedback is instrumental in promoting healthy levels of independent functioning and adaptation. Furthermore, because many youth exhibit poor self-awareness and struggle to accurately track their thoughts and actions, and because feedback provided by others is often lacking or inadequate, it is essential that support services and intervention programs empower youth to improve their self-monitoring and feedback-generation skills (Hattie & Timperley, 2007).

During my years as a school psychologist in the early 2000s, I was struck by the relative infrequency with which SRL-oriented principles were embedded within the school curriculum and resource support services. Recent survey research with different types of school personnel (i.e., regular education teachers, special education teachers, school psychologists) has supported these anecdotal observations. Research has shown that educators perceive motivation and SRL processes to be key enablers of student success, but they do not systematically incorporate SRL-related principles into their professional work and interactions with students because, in part, they do not feel adequately trained and prepared to work with students exhibiting regulatory deficits (Cleary, 2009; Cleary, Gubi, & Prescott, 2010; Cleary & Zimmerman, 2006; Coalition for Psychology in Schools and Education, 2006; Grigal, Neubert, Moon, & Graham, 2003; Wehmeyer, Agran, & Hughes, 2000). When key service providers do not possess the knowledge and capacity to effectively help children and adolescents improve their regulatory and feedback-generation skills, these youth will become more likely to exhibit maladaptive outcomes, particularly as the demands for self-sufficiency and self-management naturally increase during development.

PURPOSE AND ORGANIZATION OF THE BOOK

This book was grounded, in part, on the basic premise that although SRL skill deficits—poor planning and goal setting, ineffective selection and use of task strategies, inconsistent self-monitoring, and maladaptive reflection—are central to the academic, behavioral, and emotional challenges experienced by children and adolescents, these skills can be modified through targeted SRL intervention programs and optimally structured environments. More specifically, the book has three primary objectives:

- to delineate the self-regulatory challenges exhibited by diverse groups of children and adolescents;
- to illustrate how different contexts can facilitate or inhibit healthy forms of regulatory functioning; and
- to discuss and illustrate the key components of empirically based SRL interventions and adaptive contexts, with a particular focus on the central role of feedback loops.

To accomplish these objectives, I invited a diverse group of nationally recognized scholars with expertise in applying SRL interventions with at-risk youth and young adults. Contributors to this book come from diverse theoretical backgrounds and fields, including school psychology, educational psychology, developmental psychology, and clinical psychology. Including a kaleidoscope of theoretical perspectives and viewpoints helps this volume to provide a robust account of SRL interventions and a strong foundation from which to identify the many commonalities that exist across distinct lines of research and domains of functioning.

To ensure uniformity across chapters, all authors were asked to address the following topics relative to at-risk populations and/or SRL contexts: (a) theory, (b) interventions and applications, (c) research, and (d) future directions. Furthermore, many of the chapters provide compelling case scenarios to illustrate how SRL principles can be applied with specific populations and in diverse contexts. The names and identities of individuals used in the case scenarios have been disguised to protect confidentiality. It is my hope that this collection of chapters will underscore the unique and common elements of applying SRL principles in research and applied settings.

The chapters in this volume are organized into three parts. Part I includes five chapters that focus primarily on academic performance and behavioral problems often exhibited in school contexts. The chapter authors explicitly link SRL processes to a specific at-risk population and discuss and illustrate empirically supported interventions designed to optimize regulation. The first three chapters address the regulatory mechanisms underlying disruptive or maladaptive behaviors, such as poor attention, weak impulse control, oppositional or lack of compliance tendencies, and disengagement from academic work. In Chapter 1, Reddy, Newman, and Verdesco focus on school-age students diagnosed with attention-deficit/hyperactivity disorder (ADHD) and underscore the role of executive control deficits in the students' struggles to regulate or control school-based behaviors. In addition to providing a comprehensive review of the literature examining the efficacy of SRL interventions with ADHD youth, Reddy and colleagues propose a best practices model that integrates regulatory feedback loop mechanisms, evidence-based behavioral strategies, and attention to neuropsychological processes. In Chapter 2, Briesch and Briesch adhere to a behavioral perspective to examine the link between SRL and a range of disruptive behaviors observed in school contexts. They provide compelling evidence that self-management interventions are effective in reducing disruptive behaviors and in promoting engagement, and they underscore the need for practitioners and researchers to use feedback loops to help students manage or direct their own behaviors, instead of using such loops as a form of external management. In Chapter 3, Wolters and Hoops present a model of motivational engagement that places primary importance on the role of motivational beliefs and self-control tactics in understanding student behaviors and engagement in school. This chapter also serves as an effective complement to Chapters 1 and 2 because it focuses primarily on college-age populations. Chapters 4 and 5 focus on the link between SRL interventions and learning outcomes for academically at-risk students, such as those with learning disabilities (LD) and students identified as English language learners (ELLs). In Chapter 4, Butler and Schnellert identify the core regulatory deficiencies exhibited by students with LD and provide empirical support for intervention programs that systematically engage such students in cycles of strategic action. These authors emphasize that data-generating mechanisms are essential for helping students and teachers become more independent in evaluating student learning progress and for optimizing decisions about how a student can learn most effectively. In Chapter 5, Taboada Barber and Gallagher examine the link between SRL processes and ELLs. They ground their chapter in social-cognitive theory and research and provide impressive case scenarios to illustrate how teachers can improve ELLs' reading comprehension skills by integrating content-area instruction, cognitive strategy training, and motivation and SRL principles.

Part II consists of three chapters primarily concerned with youth who exhibit emotional difficulties, such as anxiety and depression, or chronic health conditions, such as asthma. Collectively, these chapters focus on how to use dynamic feedback loops to empower students to exert greater strategic control over their emotions and physical ailments. In Chapter 6, Suveg, Davis, and Jones argue that feedback loops are naturally embedded within empirically supported treatments for youth with anxiety difficulties and that by enhancing the capacity of youth to effectively regulate emotion one can improve the broader skill of self-regulation. These authors also establish the empirical link between anxiety and emotion-regulation deficits and illustrate how a cognitive–behavioral treatment engages students in empowering cycles of regulated action. Ehrenreich-May, Kennedy, and Remmes approach Chapter 7 with similar goals in mind but focus specifically on the link between emotion-regulation deficits and youth depression and comorbid conditions. These authors review empirical evidence for a manual-based, emotion-regulation intervention program and present a case study illustrating how practitioners can create data-based feedback loops that directly affect children and adolescents' emotion-regulation and self-regulation skills. In Chapter 8, Clark and Patel provide compelling empirical data supporting the efficacy of SRL interventions that target mental health and disease management outcomes of economically disadvantaged youth with chronic asthma conditions. Central to their chapter is an illustration of the core theoretical and logistical or procedural components of their SRL intervention programs.

Although the chapters in Part III also underscore the importance of SRL in human functioning, they focus primarily on how different types of contexts support or inhibit adaptive regulatory skills. In Chapter 9, Peters-Burton, Cleary, and Forman use a social-cognitive model of SRL as the framework for a multilevel professional development (PD) training program. They also review research showing how PD trainers can use contextualized SRL measures as formative assessment tools to guide PD activities and, ultimately, to enhance trainees' competencies and skills. In Chapter 10, Perry, Brenner, and MacPherson illustrate a participatory model PD framework that describes how researchers and practitioners can effectively collaborate to produce high-quality SRL interventions and school-based student supports. The authors provide extensive case scenarios of teacher learning teams that illustrate how researchers' use of cyclical feedback mechanisms can lead to more adaptive researcher–teacher interactions and teacher instructional behaviors.

The final two chapters address important contexts that affect student functioning in schools. In Chapter 11, Grolnick and Raftery-Helmer adopt a self-determination theoretical perspective to explore the interplay between student SRL and the key transitions students experience as they progress from primary through secondary school. The authors underscore the reciprocal nature of the relations between transition contexts and SRL, and they provide extensive information about empirically based contextual supports that enhance SRL processes and student success during these transitions. In Chapter 12, Kitsantas, Dabbagh, Hiller, and Mandell provide empirical support for linking learning technologies and academic success, and discuss how to structure learning technologies to directly affect students' skills in self-directing their behaviors. In viewing learning technologies as a modifiable SRL context, the authors create a road map for how future research can most efficiently explore and address this emergent issue.

REFERENCES

Bandura, A. (1997). *Self-efficacy: The exercise of control.* New York, NY: Freeman.

Bembenutty, H., Cleary, T. J., & Kitsantas, A. (Eds.). (2013). *Applications of self-regulated learning across diverse disciplines: A tribute to Barry J. Zimmerman.* Charlotte, NC: Information Age.

Boekaerts, M., Pintrich, P. R., & Zeidner, M. (Eds.). (2000). *Handbook of self-regulation.* San Diego, CA: Academic Press.

Butler, D. L., & Winne, P. H. (1995). Feedback and self-regulated learning: A theoretical synthesis. *Review of Educational Research, 65,* 245–281. doi:10.3102/00346543065003245

Carver, C. S., & Scheier, M. F. (1990). Origins and functions of positive and negative affect: A control-process view. *Psychological Review, 97,* 19–35. doi:10.1037/0033-295X.97.1.19

Cleary, T. J. (2009). School-based motivation and self-regulation assessments: An examination of school psychologist beliefs and practices. *Journal of Applied School Psychology, 25,* 71–94. doi:10.1080/15377900802484190

Cleary, T. J., Gubi, A., & Prescott, M. V. (2010). Motivation and self-regulation assessments: Professional practices and needs of school psychologists. *Psychology in the Schools, 47,* 985–1002. doi:10.1002/pits.20519

Cleary, T. J., & Zimmerman, B. J. (2006). Teachers' perceived usefulness of strategy microanalytic assessment information. *Psychology in the Schools, 43,* 149–155. doi:10.1002/pits.20141

Coalition for Psychology in Schools and Education. (2006, August). *Report on the Teacher Needs Survey.* Washington, DC: American Psychological Association, Center for Psychology in Schools and Education.

Grigal, M., Neubert, D. A., Moon, S. M., & Graham, S. (2003). Self-determination for students with disabilities: Views of parents and teachers. *Exceptional Children, 70,* 97–112.

Hattie, J., & Timperley, H. (2007). The power of feedback. *Review of Educational Research, 77,* 81–112. doi:10.3102/003465430298487

Miller, G. A., Galanter, E., & Pribram, K. H. (1960). *Plans and the structure of behavior.* New York, NY: Henry Holt. doi:10.1037/10039-000

Reeve, J., & Jang, H. (2006). What teachers say and do to support students' autonomy during a learning activity. *Journal of Educational Psychology, 98,* 209–218. doi:10.1037/0022-0663.98.1.209

Schunk, D. H. (2008). Attributions as motivators of self-regulated learning. In D. H. Schunk & B. J. Zimmerman (Eds.), *Motivation and self-regulated learning: Theory, research, and applications* (pp. 245–266). New York, NY: Erlbaum.

Shute, V. J. (2008). Focus on formative feedback. *Review of Educational Research, 78,* 153–189. doi:10.3102/0034654307313795

Wehmeyer, M. L., Agran, M., & Hughes, C. (2000). A national survey of teachers' promotion of self-determination and student-directed learning. *Journal of Special Education, 34*(2), 58–68. doi:10.1177/002246690003400201

Wigfield, A., Hoa, L. W., & Klauda, S. L. (2008). The role of achievement values in the regulation of achievement behaviors. In D. H. Schunk & B. J. Zimmerman (Eds.), *Motivation and self-regulated learning: Theory, research, and applications* (pp. 169–196). New York, NY: Erlbaum.

Winne, P. H., & Hadwin, A. F. (1998). Studying as self-regulated learning. In D. J. Hacker, J. Dunlosky, & A. C. Graesser (Eds.), *Metacognition in educational theory and practice* (pp. 279–306). Hillsdale, NJ: Erlbaum.

Zimmerman, B. J. (2000). Attaining self-regulation: A social cognitive perspective. In M. Boekaerts, P. R. Pintrich, & M. Zeidner (Eds.), *Handbook of self-regulation* (pp. 13–39). San Diego, CA: Academic Press. doi:10.1016/B978-012109890-2/50031-7

Zimmerman, B. J., & Schunk, D. H. (Eds.). (2011). *Handbook of self-regulation of learning and performance.* New York, NY: Routledge.

I

SELF-REGULATED LEARNING INTERVENTIONS TARGETING ACADEMIC AND BEHAVIORAL SKILLS

1

USE OF SELF-REGULATED LEARNING FOR CHILDREN WITH ADHD: RESEARCH AND PRACTICE OPPORTUNITIES

LINDA A. REDDY, ERIK NEWMAN, AND ARIELLE VERDESCO

Attention-deficit/hyperactivity disorder (ADHD) is a neurocognitive disorder that manifests as impairments in attention, hyperactivity, impulsivity, planning, organization, and evaluation skills across settings (Douglas, 2005; Reddy & Hale, 2007). These neurocognitive deficits result in a heterogeneous mix of cognitive, behavioral, and social problems. Most scholars assert that the core deficits in ADHD are in *executive functioning* (EF), the cognitive abilities necessary for implementing and adapting goal-directed behavior and self-regulation (e.g., Barkley, 1997; Castellanos & Tannock, 2002; Douglas, 2005). Children with deficits in EF typically experience difficulties with planning, self-monitoring, and problem-solving skills (Hale et al., 2011). Other neuropsychological findings

---

The research reported here was supported by the Institute of Education Sciences, U.S. Department of Education, through Grant R305A080337 and the U.S. Department of Education's Teacher Incentive Fund Program through Grant S374A120060 to Rutgers, The State University of New Jersey. The opinions expressed are those of the authors and do not represent the views of the institute or the U.S. Department of Education.

http://dx.doi.org/10.1037/14641-002
Self-Regulated Learning Interventions With At-Risk Youth: Enhancing Adaptability, Performance, and Well-Being, T. J. Cleary (Editor)
Copyright © 2015 by the American Psychological Association. All rights reserved.

suggest that underlying deficits in response inhibition and delay aversion may also result in symptoms of ADHD (Barkley, 1997; Krain & Castellanos, 2006).

According to the *Diagnostic and Statistical Manual of Mental Disorders, Fifth Edition* (DSM–5; American Psychiatric Association, 2013), ADHD is defined by persistent patterns of inattention and/or hyperactivity/impulsivity, more than would be observed in individuals of a comparable developmental level. ADHD is broken down into three symptom categories, inattention, hyperactivity, and impulsivity, which are associated with impairments in social and/or academic functioning across settings (e.g., American Psychiatric Association, 2013; Vile Junod, DuPaul, Jitendra, Volpe, & Cleary, 2006). Inattentive children appear distracted and withdrawn, whereas hyperactive and impulsive children tend to display high levels of activity and act without thinking. These three symptom categories are used, in part, for differentiating three ADHD subtypes: ADHD-inattention, ADHD-hyperactivity/impulsivity, and ADHD-combined. Overall, annually between 2007 and 2009, ADHD was diagnosed on average in 9.0% of children ages 5 through 17 years and, annually between 1998 and 2000, in 6.9% (Centers for Disease Control and Prevention, 2011).

The assessment and intervention process for ADHD is complex because of the heterogeneity of the population. The comorbidity rate for ADHD is high: Approximately 66% of children diagnosed with ADHD have at least one additional psychiatric diagnosis (Elia, Ambrosini, & Berrettini, 2008). Furthermore, symptoms of ADHD often overlap with other related childhood disorders (e.g., learning disabilities [LD], language-based disorders, disruptive behavior disorders) or conditions (e.g., medical, familial, environmental). Comorbidity and overlapping symptom dimensions with ADHD vary across disorder, gender, and age. For example, reading disabilities may appear in 25% to 40% of youth with ADHD-inattention or ADHD-combined type (Reddy & Hale, 2007; Willcutt & Pennington, 2000), whereas LD, in general, may appear in up to 70% of youth with ADHD (Kellner, Houghton, & Douglas, 2003). Other common comorbidities include written expression disorder, auditory processing disorder, disruptive behavior disorders, anxiety, and depression. In addition, medical conditions and familial and environmental factors can lead to behaviors that frequently resemble ADHD symptoms (e.g., inattentiveness, hyperactivity, impulsivity; Cushman & Johnson, 2001; Reddy & Hale, 2007).

The expression of ADHD symptoms also changes across development. Those symptoms can be identified at a young age, and fewer symptoms have been associated with more positive trajectories (e.g., Galéra et al., 2011; White, 1999), which highlights the importance of early identification and intervention. Symptoms of hyperactivity and impulsivity tend to decrease with age, whereas difficulties with inattention markedly increase up to age 6 years (Galéra et al., 2011). Although ADHD symptoms may change form throughout development, the severity and extensity of the disorder often remain (APA, 2013). Differences are also seen across gender: The number of boys diagnosed with ADHD outnumbers girls by at least 4 to 1 (Barkley, 2012). Females typically experience internalizing symptoms related to mood, affect, emotion, and inattentiveness, whereas males are more likely to exhibit externalizing symptoms, including hyperactivity and aggression.

ADHD poses many challenges for assessing and intervening. It is imperative that practitioners are aware of the unique neurocognitive strengths and weaknesses for individual children. Levels of EF impairment can vary widely: A child with moderate or severe deficits will require assistance and support from a well-informed adult to benefit from an intervention. The symptoms of ADHD often present differently within and across settings such as the home (morning vs. evening routines), classrooms (e.g., mathematics, language arts, gym, art), and lunch/recess periods. Interventions should be tailored to a child's cognitive and behavioral abilities, settings, and adult's skills to successfully implement the intervention in context(s). Practitioners must recognize that this population includes high rates of comorbidity and the possibility of symptom overlap with other disorders and conditions, which may lead to misdiagnosis and perhaps less than optimal intervention planning.

The literature fails to provide a precise definition for EF, which is an imperative construct in any discussion on ADHD. For the purpose of this chapter, EF refers to the self-directed cognitive abilities that contribute to self-regulation (e.g., Barkley, 1997; Castellanos & Tannock, 2002; Douglas, 2005). *Self-regulation* is any response by an individual that will alter that person's behavior to influence the likelihood of a future consequence or goal attainment (Barkley, 1997, 2012). Self-regulation is an integrated learning process; in this chapter, we refer to the application of this method as *self-regulated learning* (SRL).

The present chapter provides a brief overview of SRL and EF for youth with ADHD. It also offers a synthesis of the current outcome research on self-regulated interventions for ADHD. A proposed training/intervention framework is outlined that integrates evidence-based behavioral techniques, neuropsychological research, and feedback loop mechanisms for adults (e.g., teachers, caregivers) and children for this population. Directions for research are briefly presented.

THEORETICAL FOUNDATION OF SELF-REGULATED LEARNING AND EXECUTIVE FUNCTIONING

Many scholars agree that the neurocognitive makeup of ADHD is complex and includes a range of EF impairments, such as attention, planning, organization, memory, self-control, and goal-directedness (e.g., Barkley, 1997;

Pennington & Ozonoff, 1996). According to Lezak (1995), "The executive functions consist of those capacities that enable a person to engage successfully in independent, purposive, self-serving behavior" (p. 42). However, scholars continue to disagree on a specific operational definition for EF. According to Barkley (2012), EF can be operationally defined as "self-regulation across time for the attainment of one's goals (self-interests), often in the context of others" (p. 13). Therefore, EFs, such as working memory, internalization of speech, and regulation of affect, allow people to regulate toward the attainment of goals. EFs are subsumed under the broader umbrella of self-regulation.

Self-regulation is typically considered the means by which individuals manage themselves to attain goals. It appears that self-regulation and EF consist of similar cognitive and behavioral processes, including goal-directed, future-oriented actions, sustaining actions over time to achieve a goal, and problem-solving as a part of the goal-directed actions. An EF is a specific process (action) directed at the self for self-regulatory purposes (Barkley, 2012). Thus, each EF can be redefined as a specific type of self-directed action, consisting of inhibition, self-directed sensory-motor actions (e.g., hindsight, sense of time), self-directed attention (e.g., self-monitoring), working memory (e.g., self-imagery, self-speech), planning and problem solving (e.g., self-directed play), self-motivation, and emotional self-regulation (Barkley, 2012).

Existing research paradigms and assumptions have challenged the notion that EF and self-regulation are corresponding processes. EF tends to focus on fixed cognitive abilities, whereas self-regulation models pay greater attention to the malleable cognitive processes, behaviors, and beliefs. For example, Kaplan and Berman (2010) defined EF as a high-level cognitive mechanism and self-regulation as a mechanism that involves the capacity to behave oneself and resist temptation. This chapter refers to EF as the self-directed, cognitive abilities that contribute to self-regulation. For example, a child may use the EF of working memory as a way to self-regulate in that the child's working memory will help him or her to achieve a long-term goal. Directing executive attention to goal-related information has been viewed as a primary mechanism by which self-regulated goals are shielded from competing goals and distractions in working memory (Shah, Friedman, & Kruglanski, 2002).

Self-regulation has been identified as a key enabler of student academic and social–emotional competence (Cleary, Platten, & Nelson, 2008). SRL involves self-generated thoughts, feelings, and behaviors that, to attain self-set goals, are planned and cyclically adapted on the basis of performance feedback (Zimmerman, 2000). In academic contexts, several models of SRL have been developed to explain how individuals use regulatory strategies to manage their motivation, cognition, and metacognition as they attempt to learn (see Boekaerts, Pintrich, & Zeidner, 2000; Zimmerman & Schunk, 2011). In general, models of SRL are similar to Barkley's (2012) notion of self-regulation in that SRL is conceptualized as goal-directed actions. Although many of these SRL theories are viable, the focus in this chapter is on a social-cognitive account of SRL, given its extensive research foundation and because of the clarity of its delineation of SRL subprocesses. From this perspective, SRL is viewed as a malleable process consisting of teachable skills that help a person to plan or approach academic tasks, engage in self-control during these activities, and reflect on and evaluate his or her performance following task performance.

The social-cognitive perspective views SRL as a cyclical process involving a feedback loop that consists of three interdependent sequential phases: forethought, performance control, and self-reflection (Cleary et al., 2008). *Forethought* generally involves processes that guide learning, such as goal setting and strategic planning. *Performance control* is influenced by forethought, and includes processes such as the use of task/learning strategies (e.g., note-taking, rehearsal) and comprehension monitoring. A variety of important *self-reflection* processes, such as self-evaluation, causal attributions, and adaptive inferences, are used (Cleary et al., 2008). Self-regulated learners actively manage their learning activities as they engage in a task and flexibly adjust their approaches as necessary (Butler, 1998). For more information on SRL, see Zimmerman (2002) and Cleary et al. (2008).

Synthesis of Research Evidence for SRL Training/Intervention Approaches for ADHD

Because children with ADHD often have impairments in self-regulation because of the overlap between models of academic SRL and EF (i.e., goal-directed behavior, self-monitoring, sustained effort), practitioners would benefit from knowledge of SRL principles and training in SRL techniques. Although school-based SRL training programs have been developed for general use (e.g., Self-Regulation Empowerment Program, Moodle Format SRL Training), the research on SRL training and interventions for children diagnosed with ADHD is limited, yet emerging. We conducted a comprehensive literature search on reviews and studies from 1998 to 2013 that examined the effectiveness of SRL[1] training/interventions with children at risk for or diagnosed with ADHD. The SRL training/interventions involve techniques targeting one or more of the aforementioned SRL phases.

Our search yielded two published reviews that included studies with SRL training and/or interventions for ADHD-related populations (i.e., Reid, Trout, & Schartz, 2005; Trout, Lienemann, Reid, & Epstein, 2007). Reid et al. (2005) reviewed 16 studies using SRL, as defined across four

---

[1]*SRL training* is techniques and interventions using self-regulation.

areas—self-monitoring, self-monitoring plus reinforcement, self-management, and self-reinforcement—that resembled the performance control phase of SRL but placed little importance on the rest of the feedback loop. Trout et al.'s (2007) meta-analysis involved 41 studies, 11 of which included SRL training/interventions. Collectively, those two reviews contained 22 SRL studies from 1979 to 2002. Since the publication of those two reviews, only three additional studies have been published on the use of SRL with ADHD populations (2003–2013). According to our review, 25 studies have examined the effectiveness of SRL training/interventions on ADHD populations. Those studies have been conducted across a variety of settings, such as classrooms (21 studies), clinics (two studies), residential treatment facilities (one study), and inpatient psychiatric hospitals (one study). Table 1.1 presents a synthesis of the literature.

Taken together, the 25 studies reflect some methodological limitations, yet potentially promising results. The studies included samples of one to 24 subjects, thus offering limited power for statistical testing. Many studies used single-case designs, which do not meet acceptable design or evidence standards as set forth by the Institute of Education Sciences' What Works Clearinghouse single-case design standards (e.g., Kratochwill & Levin, 2014). Four out of the 25 studies used an experimental design with randomization to a control group. Across the literature, limited use of parametric statistics (four studies) and effect sizes (three studies) was found. Our search revealed that the extant literature has focused on self-monitoring but has seldom included information about how the monitoring is used to create a behavior plan and execute, evaluate, and modify it. This search suggests that current literature linking SRL and ADHD has focused on the performance control phase of SRL, with much less attention devoted to forethought (e.g., goal setting, task analysis) and reflection phase processes (e.g., attributions). Overall, the SRL interventions were broadly described as child focused within many studies that included trained adults using verbal and nonverbal prompts and rewards to redirect and encourage children on the SRL techniques. Despite these conceptual and methodological limitations (including the limited literature over the past 10 years), the authors described practical and innovative applications of SRL. Results, in general, suggested improvements in student academic performance, on-task behavior, hyperactivity, and inappropriate verbalizations and behaviors.

Consensus and evidence exist for the use of multimodal interventions for children with ADHD (Reddy, Newman, & Verdesco, 2014). Across 14 reviews and meta-analyses published from 1998 to 2012, children with ADHD profited most from targeted combined interventions that included the training of adults (i.e., teachers, parents, coaches) as key agents for codesigning and implementing interventions, and supportively facilitating child

TABLE 1.1
Review of the Literature on Self-Regulated Learning with Attention-Deficit/Hyperactivity Disorder, $n = 25$ Studies

Study	Sample characteristics	Research design	Interventions	Outcomes
Friedling & O'Leary (1979)	$n = 8$ (1 female, 7 males) Age 7–8 Hyperactive	Assigned to self-instructional training group or control group	Self-instruction taught in training sessions and on-task behavior and classroom performance measured	Some improvements seen in math but generalization from training session to on-task behavior in the classroom not replicable
Varni & Henker (1979)	$n = 3$ (0 females, 3 males) Age 8–10 Hyperactive and disruptive	Not specified	Combination of self-instruction, self-monitoring, and self-reinforcement techniques used in the absence of adult supervision	Self-instructional training and self-monitoring did not significantly improve performance; combination of self-monitoring and self-reinforcement resulted in improved academic performance and decreased hyperactivity
Barkley, Copeland, & Sivage (1980)	$n = 6$ (0 females, 6 males) Age 7–10 Hyperactive	Within-subjects ABAB reversal design	Package of self-control procedures applied; participants asked to self-assess behavior and self-record results; reinforcement provided for accuracy[a]	Self-control package effective in improving misbehavior and attention to tasks during individual work but not during group instruction
Denkowski, Denkowski, & Omizo (1983)	$n = 24$ (0 females, 24 males) Age 11–14 Hyperactive	Experimental design	EMG-assisted relaxation training included six biweekly sessions of EMG digital and self-monitoring to determine effects on academic performance, locus of control, and self-esteem[a]	EMG self-monitoring promoted academic performance in reading and language, but no effects seen in math; an internal shift in locus of control observed[b]

(*continues*)

TABLE 1.1
Review of the Literature on Self-Regulated Learning with Attention-Deficit/Hyperactivity Disorder, n = 25 Studies (Continued)

Study	Sample characteristics	Research design	Interventions	Outcomes
Horn, Chatoor, & Conners (1983)	n = 1 (0 females, 1 male) Age 9 Hyperactive	Single-case experimental design	Dexedrine systematically applied and withdrawn during presence and absence of self-control training; training consisted of self-monitoring behaviors and reinforcement provided[a]	Combination of Dexedrine and self-control training more effective than either method alone to increase on-task behavior in class and decrease teacher reports of hyperactivity and distractibility
Christie, Hiss, & Lozanoff (1984)	n = 3 (0 females, 3 males) Hyperactive	Single-case design	Training program taught students to self-monitor behavior at intervals of time when signaled by teacher[a]	Signaled self-recording reduced inattentive and inappropriate classroom behavior and increased on-task behavior
Denkowski & Denkowski (1984)	n = 13 (0 females, 13 males) Grade 3–5 Hyperactive	Experimental design	Examined if group progressive relaxation training was as effective as individual EMG biofeedback training in facilitating the academic achievement and self-control of children[a]	Findings revealed some improvements but no significant academic improvement due to EMG biofeedback[b]
Abikoff & Gittelman (1985)	n = 21 (2 females, 19 males) Age 6–12 ADHD	Experimental design	All children maintained on stimulant treatment; cognitive training and self-instruction emphasized reflective and social problem-solving skills; control groups included attention control treatment and no training[a]	Cognitive training did not improve behavior or academic performance or facilitate withdrawal of medication[b,c]

Bowers, Clement, Fantuzzo, & Sorensen (1985)	n = 6 (0 females, 6 males) Age 8–11 Learning disability, included children with ADHD	Counterbalanced reversal design with six counterbalanced, crossover, intensive studies	Compared effects of teacher-administered reinforcers to baseline and self-monitoring/reinforcement conditions; students taught to self-monitor their attentive behaviors and self-administer reinforcement when on task[a]	Both conditions increased attention to task and academic accuracy, but improvement was greater during self-monitoring/reinforcement condition[c]
Chase & Clement (1985)	n = 6 (0 females, 6 males) Age 9–12 ADHD	Series of single-subject studies using a combined operant/inverted design	Treatment phases consisted of Ritalin (plus non-contingent reinforcement), self-reinforcement (plus a drug placebo), and Ritalin plus self-reinforcement; self-reinforcement included self-cuing methods and behavior recording; no additional prompts, but participation was rewarded[a]	Academic performance measured, and self-reinforcement was better than Ritalin alone, but combination of both was most effective
Abikoff et al. (1988)	n = 11 (0 females, 11 males) Age 7–12 ADHD	Experimental design	All children maintained on stimulant medication; children randomly assigned to academic cognitive training plus medication, remedial tutoring plus medication, or medication alone; academic cognitive training incorporated self-instructional training, self-monitoring, self-reinforcement, and strategy training[a]	Results for academic cognitive training indicated some gains in academic growth[b]

(*continues*)

TABLE 1.1
Review of the Literature on Self-Regulated Learning with Attention-Deficit/Hyperactivity Disorder, $n = 25$ Studies *(Continued)*

Study	Sample characteristics	Research design	Interventions	Outcomes
De Haas-Warner (1992)	$n = 2$ (1 female, 1 male) Grade: Preschool Poor on-task behavior	Multiple baseline across-subjects design	Self-monitoring used to increase on-task behavior during independent tasks and to maintain behavior when external prompts were removed; students rewarded for appropriate behavior[a]	Self-monitoring learned as strategy to increase on-task behavior and maintained after prompts removed
Stewart & McLaughlin (1993)	$n = 1$ (0 females, 1 male) Grade: High school ADHD	ABAB single-subject replication design	Student trained in self-monitoring of off-task behaviors; student received reinforcement for appropriately self-monitoring behaviors[a]	Results indicated an increase in off-task behavior in the classroom and perceived lack of generalization; however, student observer noted a decrease in severity of disruption during self-monitoring phase
Ajibola & Clement (1995)	$n = 6$ (0 females, 6 males) Age 9–12 ADHD	Modified Latin-square design	Medication titration with non-contingent reinforcement or self-reinforcement; for self-reinforcement, students asked to self-assess, self-record, and self-reinforce performance without prompts; participation was rewarded[a]	Academic performance measured; drug placebo and non-contingent reinforcers had no effect; methylphenidate had differential effects across behaviors; self-reinforcement improved academic performance, but combination of medication and self-reinforcement had greatest effect on performance[c]
Edwards, Salant, Howard, Brougher, & McLaughlin (1995)	$n = 3$ (0 females, 3 males) Grade: Elementary ADHD	ABABC with follow-up single-subject design	Students cued to record on-task attention at variable intervals and rewarded for being on-task and for performance[a]	On-task behavior increased during the self-management phases and reading comprehension accuracy improved

Mathes & Bender (1997)	n = 3 (0 females, 3 males) Age 8–11 ADHD	Multiple baseline design	Students already receiving pharmacological treatment were trained in self-monitoring procedures; they received prompts to self-assess and self-record, which were systematically withdrawn[a]	Combination of pharmacological intervention and self-monitoring procedures improved on-task behavior
Ervin, DuPaul, Kern, & Friman (1998)	n = 2 (0 females, 2 males) Age 13–14 Comorbid ADHD and ODD	Multiple baseline design	Teachers systematically manipulated environmental classroom variables and students used self-management by using a scale to rate appropriate behaviors[a]	Results indicated substantial reduction in problem behaviors within classroom setting
Hoff & DuPaul (1998)	n = 3 (1 female, 2 males) Age 9 ADHD or ODD	Multiple-probe across settings design	Students rated behaviors on scale to indicate their use of disruptive and appropriate behaviors; verbal praise and feedback initially provided[a]	Self-management resulted in decreased disruptive behavior, even in absence of teacher or in an unstructured setting
Shimabukuro, Prater, Jenkins, & Edelen-Smith (1999)	n = 3 (0 females, 3 males) Grade 6–7 Comorbid ADHD and LD	Single group, multiple baseline design	Students taught to self-monitor and self-graph their academic performance across three academic areas	Students made gains in academic productivity and accuracy, and their on-task behaviors improved
Davies & Witte (2000)	n = 4 (2 females, 2 males) Grade 3 ADHD	ABAB reversal design	Students trained to use self-management and peer-monitoring strategies, and were reinforced[a]	Self-management intervention substantially decreased inappropriate verbalizations
Kern, Ringdahl, Hilt, & Sterling-Turner (2001)	n = 3 (0 females, 3 males) Age 4–7 ADHD with problem behaviors	Not specified	Students taught to self-manage problematic behaviors and received a reward for appropriate behavior[a]	Results indicated decrease in maladaptive behaviors and increase in positive behaviors

(*continues*)

TABLE 1.1
Review of the Literature on Self-Regulated Learning with Attention-Deficit/Hyperactivity Disorder, n = 25 Studies (Continued)

Study	Sample characteristics	Research design	Interventions	Outcomes
Rossiter (2002)	n = 1 male (0 females, 1 male) Age 13 ADHD	Ratio feedback case study and tutorial	Neurofeedback conducted and protocols provided visual and auditory feedback based on ratio of slow wave activity divided by fast wave activity to be suppressed to be enhanced[a]	Improvements seen in reading performance, but not for spelling or math
Harris, Friedlander, Saddler, Frizzelle, & Graham (2005)	n = 6 (1 female, 5 males) Grades 3–5 ADHD	Counter-balanced, multiple-baseline, across-subjects design	Self-monitoring of attention and self-monitoring of performance effects on on-task and spelling study behavior	Self-monitoring of attention and performance led to improvements in on-task and spelling study behaviors
Reid & Lienemann (2006)	n = 3 (1 female, 2 males) Grades 3–4 ADHD with writing difficulties	Multiple baseline across-participants design with multiple probes during baseline	Self-regulated strategy development model used to improve self-monitoring and student independence during a story-writing task	Results indicated improvements on length, completeness, and holistic quality of narratives
Lienemann & Reid (2008)	n = 4 (2 females, 2 males) Grades 4–5 ADHD with writing difficulties	Multiple baseline across-participants design with multiple probes during baseline	Self-regulated strategy development model used to improve self-monitoring and student independence during an essay-writing task	Length, completeness, and quality of writing improved following strategy instruction

Note. ADHD = attention-deficit/hyperactivity disorder; EMG = electromyography; LD = learning disabilities; ODD = oppositional defiant disorder.
[a]Indicates use of a multimodal intervention, not solely child-based. [b]Indicates use of parametric statistics. [c]Indicates use of effect sizes.

engagement (adherence) in interventions (Reddy, Fabiano, Barbarasch, & Dudek, 2012; Reddy et al., 2014). We advocate that child-focused SRL interventions be used with adult-facilitated behavioral interventions for improving and sustaining outcomes. As shown in Table 1.1, 19 of the 25 published studies used a range of multimodal interventions. Among these 19 studies, six used SRL with medication; 12 used SRL with adult reinforcement, prompting, or other cognitive behavioral interventions; and three used electromyography-assisted training. The combination of medication with child-focused SRL was found to be more effective than child-focused SRL alone. In recognition of importance of adult participation in the treatment of ADHD, and the current lack of focus on the forethought and reflection phases of SRL for these children, we offer the following SRL training/intervention framework that builds on existing approaches to include these key treatment components.

Proposed Training/Intervention Framework

The overlap between SRL and EF presents a conundrum for the treatment of ADHD. On the one hand, these are often precisely the behavioral deficits that most need remediation in children with ADHD. On the other hand, the neurocognitive limitations that accompany ADHD make these skills the most difficult to not only acquire but also to use consistently and internalize. The inhibitory dysfunction associated with ADHD often limits the ability to attend to relevant stimuli, control interference, identify relevant behavioral response sequences, persist with goal-directed behavior, evaluate the outcome of that behavioral sequence, and modify future behavioral plans and actions accordingly. Furthermore, the extent of these limitations depends on the child's age and the level of neurocognitive impairment. Individualized attention from parents and teachers is critical to the success of ADHD interventions because it provides additional EF support to children that can act as scaffolding while the children are developing these skills. With this in mind, we propose a tri-part model for an SRL intervention to treat children with this disorder. This model consists of child training, teacher training, and parent training with a focus on consistent feedback and monitoring by teachers and parents to facilitate the growth of SRL skills for the child.

To illustrate the specific strategies used in this model and the value added by the teacher and parent components of treatment, we integrate into the description of this framework a case scenario of an 8-year-old boy, Max, who is struggling in math. Max underwent a comprehensive neuropsychological and behavioral assessment approximately a year ago and was diagnosed with ADHD-combined type. The testing report noted that Max had an average IQ but significant difficulty with planning, organization, and attention, and that he was very hyperactive and impulsive. At the recommendation of the psychologist who performed the assessment, Max's parents brought him to a psychiatrist for a medication evaluation. He subsequently began taking psychostimulant medication, which was reported to alleviate much of his hyperactivity and impulsivity. However, his teacher recently noted that Max seems unable to follow the math lessons in class and rarely turns in his math homework. As a result, his parents decided to begin adjunctive behavioral treatment from a psychologist, Dr. Smith, who used an SRL approach to teach Max to monitor his own behaviors, to become more aware of the feedback he was receiving, and to use that information to make adaptive changes to his behavior. Parent training and teacher consultation were also included as parts of this treatment.

Child Training

Child training in SRL strategies for children with ADHD is similar to most other SRL interventions in that it involves training children to use feedback loops to more thoughtfully plan and execute behaviors, evaluate the success of those plans and actions, and modify future behaviors on the basis of that evaluation. As with any technique or disorder, the key to a successful intervention for children with ADHD is to identify appropriate goals and strategies (i.e., the forethought phase of SRL training). Because children with ADHD are a heterogeneous group, these goals will vary widely. However, the following guidelines may help with this process.

Children are often motivated by success and frustrated and discouraged by failure. A key motivator of behavioral change in all people is self-efficacy (Bandura, 1997). When people believe they are powerless to affect behavioral change, they are unlikely to try. When experiences reinforce those beliefs, the beliefs are even more difficult to change and they are even more likely to elicit feelings of frustration and distress at the thought of trying, especially in children with ADHD, because of the emotion-regulation deficits frequently associated with the disorder. For this reason, it is important to set the children up for success by creating small, attainable goals rather than large, challenging ones. It can be useful to think of goals as having three distinct dimensions when trying to set children up for success: proximal versus distal, process versus outcome, and specific versus general. *Proximal* goals can be met and evaluated in the near future (e.g., this week), whereas a *distal* goal is longer term (e.g., this school year). Proximal goals can keep people on track in the short term by reinforcing self-efficacy and motivation (Stock & Cervone, 1990). *Process* goals, also called learning goals, focus on behavioral actions, such as studying, that can be taken en route to learning a skill set, whereas *outcome* goals, also called performance goals, focus on results, such as test scores (Dweck, 1986). *Specific* goals are concretely operationalized and measurable within a particular context, whereas *general* goals are often ambiguous or operationalized and measured differently in different contexts (Locke & Latham, 1990). Goals that are proximal, process oriented, and specific (e.g., number of hours spent practicing math problems this week) tend to be more useful than distal, outcome-oriented, and general goals (e.g., getting better grades in school this year) when trying improve functioning, because such goals are more tangible. This is not to say that improvement in academic performance should not be an ultimate goal. However, children with ADHD, even more so than typical children, tend to find it easier to focus on tangible goals. Furthermore, children can fail to meet academic expectations for any number of reasons beyond their control, which can be particularly frustrating. Instead, children with ADHD should be encouraged to focus on intermediate behavioral goals, with an awareness that the purpose of their behavioral goals is to improve performance down the road.

In the case of Max, his therapist, Dr. Smith, initially worked with Max to help him identify specific things he would need to do to achieve the distal outcome goal of getting better grades in math. Max initially identified general process goals such as "go to class," "do classwork," and "do homework." Although those goals were still not very specific, they represented an important shift away from ones that felt overwhelming and out of reach to specific behaviors that Max perceived to be more attainable and within his control.

Once intermediate behavioral goals are established, the last part of the forethought phase of SRL training is for the child to identify the specific steps necessary to achieve the goals that they can execute in the performance control phase of the intervention. It is particularly important for children with ADHD to explicitly identify these steps that are often approached implicitly by their typically developing peers. Because youth with ADHD often have impaired executive functions, such as working memory and organizational skills, it may be difficult for them to hold behavioral sequences in memory long enough to successfully follow through. Therefore, they should be encouraged to identify a limited number of simple steps (e.g., two steps) and to record them so they can refer to them later. In addition, it may help to set an alarm or use a similar strategy to cue the child to refer to the written list when it is time to perform a behavioral sequence. Doing these things provides a sort of safety net that can be used to buffer against tendencies for disorganization and forgetfulness by reducing the complexity and number of cognitive demands being placed on an already taxed system at one time.

In the case of Max, Dr. Smith discussed with him how each of his intermediate goals actually involved a number of more specific actions; Dr. Smith encouraged Max to identify specific sequences of behaviors required for each. For example, "go to class" became "place math books and pencils in backpack" and "take math books and pencils out of backpack during class." "Do classwork" was modified to "follow teacher instructions to open book" and "work on the problems assigned." "Do homework" was broken down into "write down homework in notebook," "pack math books in backpack," and "work on assigned problems at home." Once these more specific goals were set, a chart was created so Max could monitor each specific behavior every day for the next week. Although Max only completed this monitoring chart 3 out of the next 5 days (assisting children with follow-through is discussed later in this chapter in the sections on adult training), it became clear that Max consistently forgot key materials needed to do his work (e.g., forgot to bring his pencils and notebook to school, forgot to write down his homework assignment or bring his textbook home). However, Max was able to identify these as targets for treatment that were within his control and make a refined to-do list that consisted of "pack math books and pencils in backpack" to be executed at home, and "write down math homework" and "pack math books in backpack" to be executed at school. When asked how he would remember to look at these list items, Max said that he would make it part of his daily routine after completing his homework and at the end of his class, respectively. Although these solutions might not be effective, continuing to monitor his behavior chart allows for the constant gathering of new data that Max can use later to determine the effectiveness of the current strategy and the need for modifications.

Once a strategy is being executed, ongoing monitoring of the child's use of the strategy and its effectiveness is crucial. An important part of this phase of the intervention is comprehension monitoring. It is crucial that children with ADHD monitor not only their understanding of the academic material being taught (which relates more to performance outcomes) but also their understanding of the behavioral strategy being used to learn that material. For example, Max knew that he was supposed to bring home his "math books," but he had a few different books and did not always seem sure which ones were for math, so clarification was needed. Once it is clear the child understands what he or she is supposed to do, he or she can use cues to remember what to do and when to do it. Cues can also be used as a reminder to engage in the self-reflection phase of SRL training by reminding the child when to evaluate whether the plan was followed as intended and then determine if the strategy resulted in successful goal attainment. If the planned steps were self-recorded, the child has a visual aid to assist in this evaluation and does not need to rely as heavily on working memory and executive control. An alarm can also be used as a reminder to check the list.

Max's weekly monitoring charts (sparse as they were) indicated that, despite having the list of items to pack with him at home and at school, he was still occasionally forgetting to pack them. After talking with Max, Dr. Smith realized that Max was not consistently remembering to check the lists. However, Max had a wristwatch with an alarm, and Dr. Smith was able to help him set the alarm to vibrate at the end of class and in the evening as a cue to check his lists and also as a cue to later evaluate his preparedness for classwork and homework. Doing so resulted in less frustration and negative emotion at home and at school and therefore reinforced the strategy and also allowed Max to evaluate the steps in his plan that he missed when unable to participate. It was more salient and memorable when he forgot to set his alarm, which had the potential to highlight important steps that may have been overlooked when first identifying goals and problems. Although evaluation should primarily focus on attainment of the behavioral goal, comprehension of the material can also be monitored, and improved academic performance that results from these behavioral changes can further reinforce these behaviors through a sense of pride and increased self-efficacy.

Children with ADHD often have difficulty anticipating the consequences of their behavior. SRL strategies provide a venue for these children to go through the metacognitive process of thinking about their plans and actions. As such, it allows them an opportunity to reflect on the expectations and effective ways to manage future situations. In Max's case, the main barriers to success appeared, at least initially, to be primarily related to his lack of preparedness. However, similar behavioral strategies apply when the problem is more directly related to task performance (e.g., solving a math problem). That is, breaking tasks into a sequence of specific, proximal, and process-oriented steps that are explicitly delineated in a simple structure allows children with ADHD to practice tasks in a more manageable setting. This, in turn, allows them to devote the majority of their cognitive resources to performance, evaluation, and modification, rather than being overwhelmed by the process before they even begin.

Adult Training to Support SRL

Research on SRL training for children with ADHD shows promise. However, many of the studies supporting the benefits of SRL do so in the context of other intervention modalities (see Table 1.1). Deficits in EF that commonly accompany ADHD make it difficult for these children to remember what they are supposed to do and persist at it. Even with the lists and cues that help to reduce the cognitive demands that overwhelm them, they still typically need the assistance of adults to help keep them on track in different contexts. Furthermore, the younger the child is, the more assistance she or he is likely to need. The responsibility of acting as a "surrogate frontal lobe" typically falls on teachers in the school context and on parents in the home context (Greene & Ablon, 2005), thus often meaning helping these children find the inherent structure in a task and making it explicit and simple to follow. An added benefit of adjunctive adult interventions is that teachers and parents can monitor progress toward academic goals without frustrating the child and modify behavioral goals as necessary to increase the likelihood of meeting academic goals.

In the section that follows, we describe ways in which practitioners can help teachers and parents effect greater change within and across contexts using an SRL intervention framework. As such, the discussion reflects two levels of training: directly implementing strategies that enable children to successfully engage in SRL-related processes and indirectly benefitting children by helping teachers and parents to more effectively set goals for their own behavior.

Teacher Training. During the school day, teachers are in the best position to observe how their students are behaving and the types of academic difficulties they are experiencing. Teachers can provide verbal and nonverbal prompts and structure that children with ADHD need to remain on task during class. Without this adult assistance, these children often become distracted and/or misbehave instead of completing their assignments. Teachers can play a critical role in implementing SRL interventions by working with children and families to identify academic problems and behavioral goals that can help remediate problems, implementing child-focused and classroom-wide instructional and behavioral management strategies, helping children to monitor and evaluate their use of specific strategies, and communicating progress to children, parents, and/or other treatment providers (e.g., physicians, speech and language therapists, occupational therapists).

Teachers are in a great position to identify academic and behavioral problems in children. However, children with ADHD typically present with a large number of problems, and it may be unreasonable to expect progress toward goals in all these areas. A critical component of teacher training is helping teachers to prioritize goals and choose a few to focus on at a time. This prioritization may be particularly difficult when teachers have to consider the priorities of various stakeholders (e.g., themselves, children, parents, treatment providers). As a rule, teachers should be encouraged to target no more than two behaviors at a time. Behavioral targets should be specific, observable, and measurable, so that children can learn to monitor and evaluate their own behavior and so that teachers can track the extent to which children are meeting their behavioral goals. In addition, setting goals related to the child's classroom attention and on-task behavior can aid in monitoring progress without negatively influencing the child's ability to attend to tasks. In Max's case, his teacher was able to help him—and his parents and therapist—identify the supplies he was missing and the assignments he was not completing. Without this assistance, it would likely have taken Dr. Smith and Max much longer to identify the problem. Furthermore, the teacher was able to monitor Max's time-on-task and cue him as needed, and this support helped Max to stay focused on the task at hand when his vigilance and persistence began to wane.

After identifying child-specific goals, strategies must be implemented to achieve those goals. More traditional SRL interventions rely heavily on students' initiating the use of regulatory strategies (e.g., self-monitoring, self-reinforcement). However, given the difficulty that many children with ADHD have providing their own cognitive and behavioral structure, teachers are critical to the implementation of these strategies. Teachers can work with children to identify appropriate behavioral sequences, develop mnemonic devices and reminder strategies to implement these sequences, and help monitor the child's comprehension and use of these strategies. It is recommended that behavioral expectations and academic concepts are specific, step-by-step, and explicitly stated. Teachers can identify and implement reinforcement contingencies that work best for the child. Depending on the age of the child, reinforcers may be internal (e.g., praise) or external (e.g., prizes, points).

Two evidence-based tools that may be helpful for teachers when implementing classroom strategies are the Classroom Strategies Scale—Observer Form (CSS; Reddy, Fabiano, Dudek, & Hsu, 2013a, 2013b, 2013c) and the Daily Report Card (DRC; Volpe & Fabiano, 2013). The CSS is a multisource, multimethod approach for assessing teachers' use of empirically supported instructional and behavioral management strategies; it includes a number of academic and behavioral targets that can be used for classroom-wide interventions and supports. Teacher targets include providing frequent concept summaries in class to foster consolidation of important concepts through repetition; academic response opportunities for students to share their ideas and thoughts regarding the learning process; clear one- to two-step directives (rather than vague directives); specific praise and corrective feedback for academic performance; and specific praise and corrective feedback for children's behavior. The CSS has teacher and observer forms that foster the training of teachers by helping them monitor their own use of strategies and recognize when and how often they are using them in various contexts. For example, to reduce frustration, it is typically recommended that children with ADHD receive three to five praise statements for every corrective feedback statement; the CSS can help teachers track this ratio when providing feedback about the child's use of self-regulatory strategies. These strategies not only help teachers provide appropriate structure for optimal learning but also foster SRL in children with ADHD through consistent feedback and modeling of effective monitoring tools (Reddy et al., 2012).

The DRC provides a classroom-based visual aid for teachers to track the child's use of targeted behaviors. It should be a collaborative process between the teacher and child so that the child can learn to track his or her own use of target strategies, and it provides the foundation for external reinforcers. Points can be assigned and charted for the completion of behaviors on the DRC. Teachers can then work with children and families to determine how those points will be translated into rewards that are motivating for the child. An important aspect of the collaborative monitoring process is that, although teachers and students can work together to develop appropriate learning strategies, they can independently evaluate how well the students met the behavioral criteria specified. Points can also be assigned when the child's self-evaluation matches the teacher evaluation. This is crucial as an adjunct to an SRL intervention because it fosters accurate self-evaluation, which is an important factor in navigating the self-reflection component of SRL and ultimately improving performance (Hacker, Bol, & Bahbahani, 2008).

In terms of child-focused strategies, Max's teacher tracked his success at bringing his school supplies and also helped him track his own success by prompting him, when necessary. She used a supplies list as a visual cue for what was expected of him and helped him develop a mnemonic device to foster internalization of that list (e.g., use the mnemonic pen for pencils, erasers, and notebooks). She used a DRC to track and award points for meeting the goals on his list, and for accurate self-evaluation of those behaviors. Once she established these contingencies, she also adopted a teacher-focused classroom strategy that incorporated frequent concept summaries to consolidate key concepts. She also provided numerous opportunities for Max and other children to ask and answer questions, if necessary. She tracked changes in Max's academic performance that corresponded to his use of target behaviors and metacognitive strategies, and praised completion of behavioral targets and academic successes that corresponded to them; she provided direct and simple feedback, when necessary. Furthermore, she monitored her own use of the strategies, which allowed her to communicate the successes and failures of this approach to other key stakeholders and modify the process as necessary.

Parent Training. Parents are in the best position to ensure that behavior in the home furthers the academic and behavioral goals set by the teachers and other treatment providers, so they must be welcomed and active members of the intervention team. Parents play an important role in ensuring adherence to adjunctive treatments, implementing reinforcement systems for behaviors in home and school, allowing opportunities to practice strategies at home, monitoring and modeling the use of strategies in the home, and reinforcing the link between strategies and academic performance.

Many children with ADHD take stimulant medication, especially if their ADHD symptoms are more severe. In these cases, it is crucial for parents to ensure that the child is taking the medication as prescribed. Otherwise, the best attempts by the child, teacher, or other treatment provider may be thwarted. This was an important responsibility of Max's parents. Other types of adjunctive treatment may include social skills training, computer-based working memory training, neurofeedback, cognitive–behavioral therapy, and/or parent training. Parent training approaches (e.g., Anastopoulos & Farley, 2003) typically provide psychoeducation about ADHD and family dynamics, clear communication, problem solving, and the appropriate use of reward and punishment.

Although a discussion of the key components of cognitive–behavioral parent training for ADHD is beyond the scope of this chapter, the use of rewards warrants further discussion, because rewards reinforce and shape behaviors in the home and align efforts across the home and school. To visualize and track target behaviors in a manner that is consistent across contexts, parents are encouraged to use a behavior chart at home similar to the DRC used in school. Behaviors that foster school preparedness can be included in this chart. In Max's case, the chart was originally designed by Max and his therapist, Dr. Smith, and eventually was adopted for this purpose. Max was awarded points for packing his bag with supplies, bringing home the necessary homework materials, and completing his homework, which eventually led to more consistent monitoring of his own behavior and more consistent data from which Dr. Smith could work. To maximize the effectiveness of this strategy, parents should work with children to develop a menu of short-, medium-, and long-term rewards for meeting behavioral targets. Short-term rewards may include TV, parent, or computer times each day. Medium-term rewards may be nonmonetary or monetary ones, such as a weekly trip (e.g., to an arcade, movie, shop, restaurant) if a certain number of points are accumulated for the week. Long-term rewards may be a more expensive toy or trip to a theme park or other special place after a report card. These strategies increase children's extrinsic motivation to sustain appropriate behavior, which, in turn, increases the likelihood of academic success and increased self-esteem. Max turned out to be most motivated by 1 hour of video game time each day he met his targets and a weekly trip to Chuck E. Cheese's if he met his targets on at least 4 days. His parents also rewarded him with a new video game system when his report card showed that his preparedness, effort, and time-on-task had improved.

Parents can create opportunities to practice strategies at home. Regular communication with teachers should provide parents with a wealth of information about the strategies that work in school and the areas that require greater consistency from the child. Finding ways to practice these strategies during homework, other home tasks, or through games will reinforce the use of these strategies through repetition. Parents can even model the use of strategies across different simulated or real situations so the child can learn how to adapt strategies to be effective across similar contexts. This approach is especially helpful because it decreases frustration by allowing the learning and practice to occur without concern for the consequence of failure. Parents can reinforce links between strategies and academic outcomes. Sometimes it is difficult for children to reflect on the use and consequences of their strategies while they are expending so much energy trying to use them. However, students who attribute their successes and failures to their strategy choice are likely to show higher levels of self-efficacy and motivation, and better performance (Cleary, Zimmerman, & Keating, 2006; Zimmerman & Kitsantas, 1999). Although this metacognitive task is often difficult for children with ADHD, SRL interventions may be a useful method for developing this skill.

In addition to the child-focused goals outlined earlier, parents can also address goals of their own using strategies similar to those described earlier for teachers. Many parenting programs involve training in the use of clear and concrete directives, praise, and corrective feedback. In addition, many programs encourage structured play sessions between parent and child. These skills do not necessarily come naturally to parents, but using a structure similar to the CSS can help parents to not only set goals for their own behavior but also monitor and evaluate their progress.

Max's parents set up a home version of a behavioral chart, awarded points, and created a rewards menu. In addition, they worked toward their own use of clear directives to increase the likelihood of Max's success. Mnemonic devices and reminder strategies established in behavior therapy and in the classroom were simulated at home, and his parents monitored their use and the accuracy of Max's self-monitoring. The consistency of these targets across home and school settings helped Max internalize the monitoring and reflection processes. With the help of his parents, teachers, and therapist, Max gradually became more consistent in his use of these strategies, which led to more consistent preparedness and better overall performance. Perhaps the greatest testament to Max's success was that, with the help of the adults around him, he was also able to apply these principles to improve his performance in other subject areas.

FUTURE DIRECTIONS AND CONCLUSIONS

SRL training/intervention offers opportunities and challenges for future research and practice. The current body of research on SRL for youth with ADHD is limited, yet promising. The good news is that across the 25 reviewed published studies (see Table 1.1), SRL training/intervention yielded meaningful improvements for children's academic and behavior needs. However, practitioners are cautioned to not draw firm conclusions on the overall efficacy of SRL training/intervention for children with ADHD at this time because of the limited research and questionable methodological features in some of the studies.

The most notable gap in this literature is the absence of focus on the forethought and reflection phases of SRL training. As such, the literature provides some evidence for the effectiveness of self-monitoring but little guidance on the use of evaluation-based feedback loops to iteratively modify goals and plans. Another limitation is that the majority of 25 reviewed studies consisted of small sample sizes, many with fewer than 10 participants, and few used experimental designs (i.e., no control groups), which precluded the ability to eliminate alternative explanations for improvements. Likewise, outcomes were infrequently assessed with statistical tests and effect sizes, thus warranting further investigations on the reliable and practical changes yielded by SRL interventions. In addition, many of the studies reported vague diagnostic information (e.g., characteristics and process of diagnosis) and some included preexisting diagnoses of ADHD established from other providers. Given the heterogeneous nature of this population and high rates of comorbidity, future SRL intervention research would benefit from providing detailed information on the diagnostic process used for ADHD status and characteristics of ADHD subtypes. Another limitation is that the 25 studies did not include information on levels of EF impairment before and during training/intervention. Impairments in EF are a critical requisite for determining the overall fit and/or tailoring of SRL training/intervention to individual children. Research has found that neuropsychological assessment of EF levels can inform titration of stimulant medication and behavior intervention for maximizing outcomes (Hale et al., 2011). Likewise, EF level can serve as an independent variable and/or dependent variable (outcome) for assessing the efficacy of SRL training/intervention.

Although SRL training/intervention research would be advanced by more experimental design studies, single-case design studies can be particularly valuable in pinpointing mechanisms that foster or inhibit positive responses to SRL training/interventions for child, teachers, and parents (Kratochwill & Levin, 2014). Single-case design studies allow practitioners and researchers to distinguish children and adults who benefit (i.e., responders) from SRL training/interventions from those who do not benefit (i.e., nonresponders) from such methods. This line of research can further build SRL and EF theory specific to ADHD.

A small but emerging body of research exists on the overall effectiveness of SRL training/interventions for youth with ADHD. This line of inquiry offers promise for linking theory, science, and practice for this population. However, this literature has focused almost entirely on the performance control phase of SRL training (i.e., strategy implementation and self-monitoring), so it has not offered insights into the effectiveness of the entire feedback loop that constitutes SRL (i.e., forethought, performance control, and reflection).

In this chapter, we attempted to provide a framework for a more complete SRL intervention for children with ADHD that is consistent with the key findings of this limited body of work and the extant behavior intervention research for this population. However, much work remains to fully assess the efficacy of SRL training/interventions for specific subgroups of ADHD. The tailoring of SRL interventions in relation to levels of EF is critical to maximizing outcomes and the development of new intervention models for this population.

REFERENCES

*[2]Abikoff, H., Ganeles, D., Reiter, G., Blum, C., Foley, C., & Klein, R. G. (1988). Cognitive training in academically deficient ADDH boys receiving stimulant medication. *Journal of Abnormal Child Psychology, 16,* 411–432. doi:10.1007/BF00914172

*Abikoff, H., & Gittelman, R. (1985). Hyperactive children treated with stimulants. Is cognitive training a useful adjunct? *Archives of General Psychiatry, 42,* 953–961. doi:10.1001/archpsyc.1985.01790330033004

*Ajibola, O., & Clement, P. W. (1995). Differential effects of methylphenidate and self-reinforcement on attention-deficit hyperactivity disorder. *Behavior Modification, 19,* 211–233. doi:10.1177/01454455950192004

American Psychiatric Association. (2013). *Diagnostic and statistical manual of mental disorders* (5th ed.). Arlington, VA: American Psychiatric Publishing.

Anastopoulos, A. D., & Farley, S. E. (2003). A cognitive–behavioral training program for parents of children with attention-deficit/hyperactivity disorder. In A. E. Kazdin & J. R. Weisz (Eds.), *Evidence-based psychotherapies for children and adolescents* (pp. 187–203). New York, NY: Guilford Press.

Bandura, A. (1997). *Self-efficacy: The exercise of control.* New York, NY: W. H. Freeman.

Barkley, R. A. (1997). Behavioral inhibition, sustained attention, and executive functions: Constructing a unifying theory of ADHD. *Psychological Bulletin, 121,* 65–94. doi:10.1037/0033-2909.121.1.65

Barkley, R. A. (2012). *Executive functions: What they are, how they work, and why they evolved.* New York, NY: Guilford Press.

*Barkley, R. A., Copeland, A. P., & Sivage, C. (1980). A self-control classroom for hyperactive children. *Journal of Autism and Developmental Disorders, 10*(1), 75–89. doi:10.1007/BF02408435

Boekaerts, M., Pintrich, P. R., & Zeidner, M. (Eds.). (2000). *Handbook of self-regulation.* San Diego, CA: Academic Press.

*Bowers, D. S., Clement, P. W., Fantuzzo, J. W., & Sorensen, D. A. (1985). Effects of teacher-administered and self-administered reinforcers on learning disabled children. *Behavior Therapy, 16,* 357–369. doi:10.1016/S0005-7894(85)80003-4

---

[2]Asterisks indicate that the study was used in the review of the literature on SRL and ADHD.

Butler, R. (1998). Determinants of help seeking: Relations between perceived reasons for classroom help-avoidance and help-seeking behaviors in an experimental context. *Journal of Educational Psychology, 90,* 630–643. doi:10.1037/0022-0663.90.4.630

Castellanos, F. X., & Tannock, R. (2002). Neuroscience of attention-deficit/hyperactivity disorder: The search for endophenotypes. *Nature Reviews Neuroscience, 3,* 617–628.

Centers for Disease Control and Prevention. (2011). *National Health Interview Survey.* Retrieved from http://www.cdc.gov/nchs/nhis.htm

*Chase, S. N., & Clement, P. W. (1985). Effects of self-reinforcement and stimulants on academic performance in children with attention deficit disorder. *Journal of Clinical Child Psychology, 14,* 323–333. doi:10.1207/s15374424jccp1404_10

*Christie, D. J., Hiss, M., & Lozanoff, B. (1984). Modification of inattentive classroom behavior: Hyperactive children's use of self-recording with teacher guidance. *Behavior Modification, 8,* 391–406. doi:10.1177/01454455840083006

Cleary, T. J., Platten, P., & Nelson, A. (2008). Effectiveness of the Self-Regulation Empowerment Program (SREP) with urban high school youth: An initial investigation. *Journal of Advanced Academics, 20,* 70–107.

Cleary, T. J., Zimmerman, B. J., & Keating, T. (2006). Training physical education students to self-regulate during basketball free throw practice. *Research Quarterly for Exercise and Sport, 77,* 251–262. doi:10.1080/02701367.2006.10599358

Cushman, T. P., & Johnson, T. B. (2001). Understanding "inattention" in children and adolescents. *Ethical Human Sciences & Services, 3,* 107–125.

*Davies, S., & Witte, R. (2000). Self-management and peer-monitoring within a group contingency to decrease uncontrolled verbalizations of children with attention-deficit/hyperactivity disorder. *Psychology in the Schools, 37,* 135–147. doi:10.1002/(SICI)1520-6807(200003)37:2%3C135::AID-PITS5%3E3.3.CO;2-L

*De Haas-Warner, S. (1992). The utility of self-monitoring for preschool on-task behavior. *Topics in Early Childhood Special Education, 12,* 478–495. doi:10.1177/027112149201200406

*Denkowski, K. M., & Denkowski, G. C. (1984). Is group progressive relaxation training as effective with hyperactive children as individual EMG biofeedback treatment? *Biofeedback and Self-Regulation, 9,* 353–364. doi:10.1007/BF00998978

*Denkowski, K. M., Denkowski, G. C., & Omizo, M. M. (1983). The effects of EMG-assisted relaxation training on the academic performance, locus of control, and self-esteem of hyperactive boys. *Biofeedback & Self-Regulation, 8,* 363–375. doi:10.1007/BF00998746

Douglas, V. I. (2005). Cognitive deficits in children with attention deficit hyperactivity disorder: A long term follow-up. *Canadian Psychology/Psychologie Canadienne, 46*(1), 23–31. doi:10.1037/h0085821

Dweck, C. (1986). Motivational processes affecting learning. *American Psychologist, 41,* 1040–1048. doi:10.1037/0003-066X.41.10.1040

*Edwards, L., Salant, V., Howard, V. F., Brougher, J., & McLaughlin, T. F. (1995). Effectiveness of self-management on attentional behavior and reading comprehension for children with attention deficit disorder. *Child & Family Behavior Therapy, 17*(2), 1–17. doi:10.1300/J019v17n02_01

Elia, J., Ambrosini, P., & Berrettini, W. (2008). ADHD characteristics: I. Concurrent comorbidity patterns in children & adolescents. *Child and Adolescent Psychiatry and Mental Health, 2*(1), 15. doi:10.1186/1753-2000-2-15

*Ervin, R. A., DuPaul, G. J., Kern, L., & Friman, P. C. (1998). Classroom-based functional and adjunctive assessments: Proactive approaches to intervention selection for adolescents with attention deficit hyperactivity disorder. *Journal of Applied Behavior Analysis, 31*(1), 65–78. doi:10.1901/jaba.1998.31-65

*Friedling, C., & O'Leary, S. G. (1979). Effects of self-instructional training on second- and third-grade hyperactive children: A failure to replicate. *Journal of Applied Behavior Analysis, 12*, 211–219. doi:10.1901/jaba.1979.12-211

Galéra, C., Côté, S. M., Bouvard, M. P., Pingault, J. B., Melchior, M., Michel, G., . . . Tremblay, R. E. (2011). Early risk factors for hyperactivity-impulsivity and inattention trajectories from age 17 months to 8 years. *Archives of General Psychiatry, 68*, 1267–1275. doi:10.1001/archgenpsychiatry.2011.138

Greene, R., & Ablon, S. J. (2005). *Treating explosive kids: The collaborative problem-solving approach.* New York, NY: Guilford Press.

Hacker, D. J., Bol, L., & Bahbahani, K. (2008). Explaining calibration accuracy in classroom contexts: The effects of incentives, reflection, and explanatory style. *Metacognition and Learning, 3*, 101–121. doi:10.1007/s11409-008-9021-5

Hale, J. B., Reddy, L. A., Semrud-Clikeman, M., Hain, L. A., Whitaker, J., Morley, J., . . . Jones, N. (2011). Executive impairment determines ADHD medication response: Implications for academic achievement. *Journal of Learning Disabilities, 44*, 196–212. doi:10.1177/0022219410391191

*Harris, K. R., Friedlander, B. D., Saddler, B., Frizzelle, R., & Graham, S. (2005). Self-monitoring of attention versus self-monitoring of academic performance: Effects among students with ADHD in the general education classroom. *Journal of Special Education, 39*, 145–157. doi:10.1177/00224669050390030201

*Hoff, K. E., & DuPaul, G. J. (1998). Reducing disruptive behavior in general education classrooms: The use of self-management strategies. *School Psychology Review, 27*, 290–303.

*Horn, W. F., Chatoor, I., & Conners, C. K. (1983). Additive effects of Dexedrine and self-control training. A multiple assessment. *Behavior Modification, 7*, 383–402. doi:10.1177/01454455830073006

Kaplan, S., & Berman, M. G. (2010). Directed attention as a common resource for executive functioning and self-regulation. *Perspectives on Psychological Science, 5*, 43–57. doi:10.1177/1745691609356784

Kellner, R., Houghton, S., & Douglas, G. (2003). Peer-related personal experiences of children with attention-deficit/hyperactivity with and without comorbid learning disabilities. *International Journal of Disability, Development and Education, 50,* 119–136. doi:10.1080/1034912032000089639

*Kern, L., Ringdahl, J. E., Hilt, A., & Sterling-Turner, H. E. (2001). Linking self-management procedures to functional analysis results. *Behavioral Disorders, 26,* 214–226.

Krain, A. L., & Castellanos, F. X. (2006). Brain development and ADHD. *Clinical Psychology Review, 26,* 433–444. doi:10.1016/j.cpr.2006.01.005

Kratochwill, T., & Levin, J. R. (Eds.). (2014). *Single-case intervention research: Methodological and statistical advances.* Washington, DC: American Psychological Association. doi:10.1037/14376-000

Lezak, M. D. (1995). *Neuropsychological assessment* (3rd ed.). New York, NY: Oxford University Press.

*Lienemann, T. O., & Reid, R. (2008). Using self-regulated strategy development to improve expository writing with students with attention deficit hyperactivity disorder. *Exceptional Children, 74,* 471–486.

Locke, E. A., & Latham, G. P. (1990). *A theory of goal setting & task performance.* Englewood Cliffs, NJ: Prentice Hall.

*Mathes, M. Y., & Bender, W. N. (1997). The effects of self-monitoring on children with attention-deficit/hyperactivity disorder who are receiving pharmacological interventions. *Remedial and Special Education, 18,* 121–128. doi:10.1177/074193259701800206

Pennington, B. F., & Ozonoff, S. (1996). Executive functions and developmental psychopathology. *Child Psychology & Psychiatry & Allied Disciplines, 37,* 51–87. doi:10.1111/j.1469-7610.1996.tb01380.x

Reddy, L., Fabiano, G., Barbarasch, B., & Dudek, C. (2012). Behavior management of students with attention-deficit/hyperactivity disorders using teacher and student progress monitoring. In L. M. Crothers & J. B. Kolbert (Eds.), *Understanding and managing behaviors of children with psychological disorders: A reference for classroom teachers* (pp. 17–27). New York, NY: Continuum International.

Reddy, L. A., Fabiano, G., Dudek, C. M., & Hsu, L. (2013a). Development and construct validity of the Classroom Strategies Scale-Observer Form. *School Psychology Quarterly, 28,* 317–341. doi:10.1037/spq0000043

Reddy, L. A., Fabiano, G. A., Dudek, C. M., & Hsu, L. (2013b). Instructional and behavior management practices implemented by elementary general education teachers. *Journal of School Psychology, 51,* 683–700. doi:10.1016/j.jsp.2013.10.001

Reddy, L. A., Fabiano, G. A., Dudek, C. M., & Hsu, L. (2013c). Predictive validity of the classroom strategies scale-observer form on statewide testing scores: An initial investigation. *School Psychology Quarterly, 28,* 301–316. doi:10.1037/spq0000041

Reddy, L. A., & Hale, J. B. (2007). Inattentiveness. In A. R. Eisen (Ed.), *Treating childhood behavioral and emotional problems: A step-by-step evidence-based approach.* (pp. 156–211). New York, NY: Guilford Press.

Reddy, L. A., Newman, E., & Verdesco, A. (2014). Attention deficit hyperactivity disorder: Use of evidence-based assessments and interventions. In R. Flanagan, K. Allen, & E. Levine (Eds.), *A practical guide to cognitive–behavioral therapy in the schools*. New York, NY: Springer.

*Reid, R., & Lienemann, T. O. (2006). Self-regulated strategy development for written expression with students with attention deficit/hyperactivity disorder. *Exceptional Children, 73*, 53–68. doi:10.1177/001440290607300103

Reid, R., Trout, A. L., & Schartz, M. (2005). Self-regulation interventions for children with attention deficit/hyperactivity disorder. *Exceptional Children, 71*, 361–377.

*Rossiter, T. (2002). Neurofeedback for AD/HD: A ratio feedback case study and tutorial. *Journal of Neurotherapy, 6*(3), 9–35. doi:10.1300/J184v06n03_03

Shah, J. Y., Friedman, R., & Kruglanski, A. W. (2002). Forgetting all else: On the antecedents and consequences of goal shielding. *Journal of Personality and Social Psychology, 83*, 1261–1280.

*Shimabukuro, S. M., Prater, M. A., Jenkins, A., & Edelen-Smith, P. (1999). The effects of self-monitoring of academic performance on students with learning disabilities and ADD/ADHD. *Education & Treatment of Children, 22*, 397–414.

*Stewart, K. G., & McLaughlin, T. F. (1993). Self-recording: Effects on reducing off-task behavior with a high school student with an attention deficit hyperactivity disorder. *Child & Family Behavior Therapy, 14*(3), 53–59. doi:10.1300/J019v14n03_04

Stock, J., & Cervone, D. (1990). Proximal goal-setting and self-regulatory processes. *Cognitive Therapy and Research, 14*, 483–498. doi:10.1007/BF01172969

Trout, A. L., Lienemann, T. O., Reid, R., & Epstein, M. H. (2007). A review of nonmedication interventions to improve academic performance of children and youth with ADHD. *Remedial and Special Education, 28*, 207–226.

*Varni, J. W., & Henker, B. (1979). A self-regulation approach to the treatment of three hyperactive boys. *Child Behavior Therapy, 1*, 171–192. doi:10.1300/J473v01n02_04

Vile Junod, R. E., DuPaul, G. J., Jitendra, A. K., Volpe, R. J., & Cleary, K. S. (2006). Classroom observations of students with and without ADHD: Differences across types of engagement. *Journal of School Psychology, 44*, 87–104. doi:10.1016/j.jsp.2005.12.004

Volpe, R. J., & Fabiano, G. A. (2013). *Daily behavior report cards: An evidence-based system of assessment and intervention*. New York, NY: Guilford Press.

White, J. D. (1999). Personality, temperament and ADHD: A review of the literature. *Personality and Individual Differences, 7*, 589–598. doi:10.1016/S0191-8869(98)00273-6

Willcutt, E. G., & Pennington, B. F. (2000). Comorbidity of reading disability and attention-deficit/hyperactivity disorder: Differences by gender and subtype. *Journal of Learning Disabilities, 33*, 179–191. doi:10.1177/002221940003300206

Zimmerman, B. J. (2000). Attainment of self-regulation: A social cognitive perspective. In M. Boekaerts, P. R. Pintrich, & M. Zeidner (Eds.), *Handbook of self-regulation* (pp. 13–39). San Diego, CA: Academic Press. doi:10.1016/B978-012109890-2/50031-7

Zimmerman, B. J. (2002). Becoming a self-regulated learner: An overview. *Theory Into Practice, 41*(2), 64–70. doi:10.1207/s15430421tip4102_2

Zimmerman, B. J., & Kitsantas, A. (1999). Acquiring writing revision skill: Shifting from process to outcome self-regulatory goals. *Journal of Educational Psychology, 91*, 241–250. doi:10.1037/0022-0663.91.2.241

Zimmerman, B. J., & Schunk, D. H. (Eds.). (2011). *Handbook of self-regulation of learning and performance*. New York, NY: Routledge.

2

SELF-MANAGEMENT INTERVENTIONS TO REDUCE DISRUPTIVE CLASSROOM BEHAVIOR

AMY M. BRIESCH AND JACQUELYN M. BRIESCH

Calling out, engaging in side conversations with peers, getting out of one's seat, playing with objects—although common to many classroom settings, these types of disruptions can significantly interfere with the learning of the students involved and their larger community of peers (Walker et al., 1994). A 1995 poll conducted by the American Federation of Teachers found that 17% of classroom teachers reported losing 4 or more hours of instructional time each week due to disruptive behavior (Walker, Ramsey, & Gresham, 2003–2004). As such, a great deal of empirical attention has been paid over the past half century to the development and evaluation of teacher-directed strategies for reducing disruptive behavior; those strategies have ranged from the use of deliberate praise and ignoring to token economies and group contingencies (Stage & Quiroz, 1997). Although positive behavior change has been documented, a central limitation of teacher-directed interventions is that behavior remains externally managed. The importance

http://dx.doi.org/10.1037/14641-003
Self-Regulated Learning Interventions With At-Risk Youth: Enhancing Adaptability, Performance, and Well-Being, T. J. Cleary (Editor)
Copyright © 2015 by the American Psychological Association. All rights reserved.

of self-regulation, however, is clear: Research has repeatedly documented the relationship between students' ability to control their own emotions and behavior and both social and academic competence (Eisenberg, Valiente, & Eggum, 2010).

Rather than relying on teachers to manage disruptive behavior, one alternative involves the use of interventions designed to strengthen students' ability to self-regulate their own behavior. When explored within academic contexts, self-regulation has been conceptualized across different theoretical frameworks as a cyclical feedback loop consisting of multiple phases (Butler & Winne, 1995; Pintrich, 1999; Zimmerman, 2008). Although the different self-regulated learning (SRL) theories label the phases in distinct ways and have varying assumptions about human functioning, they differentiate between activities that occur before, during, and following a learning task. Before engaging in a learning task, students may attempt to obtain a better understanding of what the task entails, plan for how to approach the task, and set personal goals for performance. Next comes the active phase of learning in which students implement the plan they developed and monitor their performance by comparing what they actually did to the previously determined goals or plan. Reflection or adaptation occurs following the learning task; at this point, the student uses the information gained during monitoring to guide changes to future behavior. SRL is therefore believed to be a proactive process rather than a reactive response to external events and forces (Zimmerman, 2008).

When applying SRL specifically to the treatment of disruptive classroom behaviors (e.g., off-task, inappropriate verbalizations, out of seat), many researchers have attempted to teach students self-regulatory skills through what have been termed *self-management interventions*. Self-management and SRL are similar in that both aim to empower the individual to take control of his or her own learning or behavior by using self-generated feedback to drive changes to future performance. Most definitions of self-management, however, place greater emphasis on the behavioral activities of monitoring one's behavior and making changes in response to feedback (e.g., reinforcement, punishment) than the cognitive and metacognitive preparatory activities stressed in the SRL models.

At minimum, self-management interventions involve a two-stage process referred to as *self-monitoring*, in which students observe and record their own behavior (Nelson & Hayes, 1981). However, additional intervention components are often incorporated to potentially bolster treatment effects. In reviewing 42 studies targeting students' classroom behavior, Fantuzzo and Polite (1990) identified a total of 11 components that may be used within a self-management intervention in some combination: selecting a target behavior, operationally defining the target behavior, choosing rewards, determining performance goals, delivering prompt(s) to record behavior, observing the target behavior, recording the target behavior, evaluating effectiveness, administering points/tokens, administering rewards, and monitoring performance over time. A recent review of the literature indicated that the use of self-monitoring (i.e., observing and recording one's own behavior) components is consistent across self-management applications; however, the remaining components have been combined in a variety of ways (Briesch & Chafouleas, 2009).

Self-management interventions are particularly well suited for the treatment of disruptive behavior, given that disruptive behavior often stems from an individual's inability to regulate his or her own behavior and affect. Although one student may wander the classroom when he or she is supposed to be seated, whereas another student shoves a peer with whom he or she disagrees, both represent instances in which a student's inability to control his or her own behavior can result in significant disruption to the surrounding classroom environment. In this chapter, we discuss the use of self-management interventions to reduce disruptive classroom behavior in three parts. First, we present the theoretical underpinnings of self-management interventions, emphasizing Kanfer's (1970) three-stage model of behavioral self-regulation. Next, we use this three-stage model to describe the ways in which behavioral self-management interventions have been most commonly implemented and use examples from the extant literature to provide further illustration. Third, we present a case scenario to illustrate the practical application of this intervention approach. Last, we propose directions for future research in this area.

THEORETICAL FOUNDATIONS OF BEHAVIORAL SELF-MANAGEMENT

Although asking an individual to reflect on and record his or her own behavior is now considered to be an intervention technique in and of itself, self-monitoring began as a way for researchers and clinicians to collect information about behaviors that were more difficult to observe (e.g., calorie consumption, anxiety levels). It did not take long, however, before researchers came to realize that the simple act of observing and recording one's own behavior may lead to behavioral changes beyond those attributable to a unique intervention (e.g., Webb, Campbell, Schwartz, & Sechrest, 1966). Derived from the idea that individuals may change their behavior if they know they are being observed, this effect came to be known as the *reactivity of self-monitoring* (Nelson & Hayes, 1981). As McFall (1970) wrote,

> Nearly everyone has had the experience of becoming self-conscious about his behavior and, as a result, experiencing a change in that behavior. For example, if a person's attention is drawn to the way he walks,

holds his hands, or swings a golf club, it often makes it difficult for him to perform these activities naturally. (p. 140)

Self-monitoring interventions therefore attempt to harness the power of reactivity by explicitly teaching individuals to become more aware of their own behavior.

Within the literature, basic self-monitoring procedures have been used successfully to decrease disruptive behavior in classroom settings (e.g., Houghton, 1989), suggesting that simply increasing students' self-awareness may result in immediate behavioral change. Kanfer (1970), however, proposed that sustained behavior change occurs as the result of a feedback loop consisting of three distinct phases: self-monitoring, self-evaluation, and self-reinforcement (see Figure 2.1). During the first phase, the individual is prompted to observe his or her own behavior. The act of self-monitoring is then believed to automatically trigger a subsequent phase of self-evaluation. Self-evaluation involves comparing one's own behavior (as assessed during the self-monitoring stage) with established norms or other predetermined criteria. The final component in the three-stage model of behavioral self-regulation is that of self-reinforcement. Within Kanfer's (1970) conceptualization, some degree of self-reward or punishment is likely to result from comparing one's behavior to a criterion (i.e., self-evaluation). Kanfer (1971) posited that behavioral change results when an individual successfully moves through all three phases, because the information obtained during the self-evaluation phase drives changes made to current behavior. This feedback loop then begins anew when self-monitoring is used to observe any instances of future behavior. Kanfer's model is similar to the predominant models of SRL—mentioned at the outset of this chapter—in

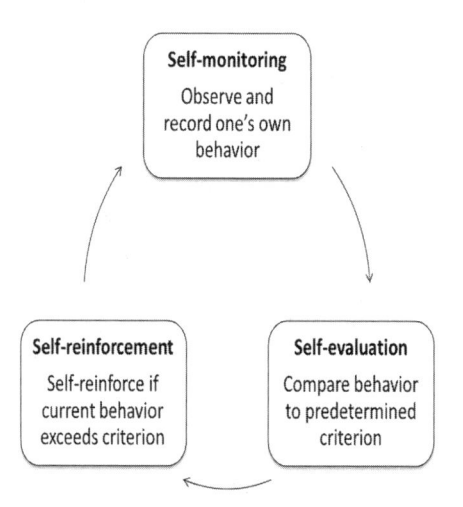

Figure 2.1. Kanfer's (1970) model of self-regulation.

that behavior change is seen as the result of monitoring and evaluating one's own behavior in relation to an established goal. However, Kanfer's model more heavily emphasizes behavioral elements than cognitive components, suggesting that behavior change occurs in response to both antecedent (i.e., self-monitoring) and consequence (i.e., self-administered reinforcement or punishment) stimuli.

CHARACTERISTICS AND RESEARCH EVIDENCE FOR KEY COMPONENTS OF SELF-MANAGEMENT INTERVENTIONS

In the following sections, we discuss how each of the three phases of Kanfer's (1970) model have been operationalized within self-management interventions designed to improve student behavior by either decreasing disruptive behavior or concomitantly increasing student engagement. Before self-monitoring can commence, though, it is essential that a target behavior be selected. Interestingly, one consistency across studies is the notable absence of student involvement in the identification of those behaviors that they are charged with assessing (Briesch & Chafouleas, 2009). Brownell (1978) suggested that "behavior change is virtually impossible to occasion without the knowledge and willingness of the subject involved" (p. 291), and the importance of perceived control in effecting behavioral change has been repeatedly noted in the clinical literature (Deci & Ryan, 1987; Taylor, Adelman, & Kaser-Boyd, 1983). With regard to self-monitoring in particular, researchers have suggested that reactivity may be greatly influenced by an individual's motivation to change his or her behavior (Gardner & Cole, 1988). That is, unless an individual is committed to reducing his or her cigarette usage or calorie consumption, it is unlikely that the self-monitoring process will be effective. Furthermore, research has shown that SRL strategies are more likely to be used by students who perceive a task to be important and personally meaningful (Pintrich, 1999) and that whether a student believes he or she can successfully change his or her behavior will affect the nature of the initial goals set and the persistence with which one moves toward those goals (Butler & Winne, 1995). Despite these findings, however, self-management training procedures have remained largely focused on logistical elements (e.g., how to conduct ratings) rather than working with students to ensure that they are sufficiently motivated to change aspects of their own behavior. This is of particular concern given that students who exhibit disruptive behavior are often the ones who are least aware that their behavior is problematic and therefore are least motivated to change it. Although some exceptions can be noted in the literature, such as when students assisted in the identification of those behaviors that were interfering with their classroom success (Barry & Messer, 2003), greater attention likely needs to be paid to determining how best to empower students to want to change those behaviors that are standing in the way of their success.

Self-Monitoring

Once a target behavior has been identified, the first stage of Kanfer's (1970) model of behavioral self-regulation involves self-monitoring, which requires the student to self-reflect and judge whether or not he or she was demonstrating an operationally defined target behavior. This stage may involve taking note of how frequently one is engaging in a particular behavior (e.g., out of seat) or how intense or problematic a behavior is (e.g., disruptive behavior). For example, a student who struggles with off-task behavior might stop to ask, "Was I paying attention?" and then answer the question either in his or her head or in writing. Despite the variability in implementation noted across studies, self-monitoring has remained the cornerstone of self-management interventions targeting problem behavior in classrooms (Briesch & Chafouleas, 2009). The effectiveness of simply teaching students how to self-monitor in improving on-task behavior has been demonstrated across studies involving students with intellectual disabilities (e.g., Boyle & Hughes, 1994), autism (e.g., Holifield, Goodman, Hazelkorn, & Heflin, 2010) and behavioral and learning disabilities (e.g., Amato Zech, Hoff, & Doepke, 2006; see also Chapter 4, this volume), and students without exceptionalities (e.g., Hoff & DuPaul, 1998).

Training

To ensure that the student has a clear understanding of the target behavior and is able to successfully conduct the self-ratings, the teacher would typically meet with the student to conduct some level of training. In most cases, this would involve providing the student with both examples (e.g., sitting quietly, listening to the teacher) and nonexamples (e.g., getting out of seat, talking to neighbors) of a target behavior and then allowing the student to practice rating while receiving feedback (e.g., structured discussions, role-playing). Across studies, however, the level of training provided to students has varied widely. Examples can be found in which training lasted as few as 10 minutes with general education students being taught to rate their on-task behavior each time that an audiotaped tone sounded (Moore, Prebble, Robertson, Waetford, & Anderson, 2001). Depending on the student's developmental level or the complexity of the self-management procedures, however, adequate training may require additional time. For example, in one study by McCarl, Svobodny, and Beare (1991), three elementary school students with mild to moderate intellectual disabilities were similarly taught to rate their on-task behavior according to a series of audiotaped tones; however, training took place across five 20- to 30-minute sessions. Although the content of these sessions was not fully described by the study authors, more practice opportunities were likely needed before students could accurately discriminate between examples of on- and off-task behavior.

Once a student has demonstrated an understanding of the target behavior in a training context, a period of in vivo practice with the rating procedures often follows. In some studies, researchers have required students to implement the self-monitoring procedures for a fixed number of days while receiving more intensive feedback before intervention data are collected (e.g., Barry & Messer, 2003; Dalton, Martella, & Marchand-Martella, 1999). In other cases, an accuracy criterion has been used to determine whether a student is ready to self-monitor independently. For example, in a study by Cavalier, Ferretti, and Hodges (1997), students were required to demonstrate 85% accuracy in recording inappropriate verbalizations for four consecutive sessions before moving into the active intervention phase.

Self-Recording

After learning to identify and reflect on his or her behavior, the student is most typically asked to record that behavior in some form. Although frequency counts may be used to record instances of discrete disruptive behaviors, such as calling out, interval sampling has been used much more frequently within classroom-based applications. That is, a kitchen timer or beep tape would be used to signal a student to observe his or her own behavior at either fixed or, more typically, random intervals. For example, students monitoring their attention may check "Yes" or "No" on a card on their desk, or rate their level of attention on a scale ranging from 1 *(not paying attention at all)* to 5 *(totally paying attention)* when a buzzer sounds. The determination of an appropriate scale of measurement must be made in consideration of the student's developmental level. That is, younger students or those with limited cognitive abilities may not be able to meaningfully distinguish between numbers on a multipoint scale and therefore may need to use a dichotomous (e.g., yes/no) or graphic (e.g., smiley face/frowning face) scale instead. Although responses are typically recorded using a paper-and-pencil sheet on the student's desk, some authors have used other recording devices, such as wrist counters, to target behaviors, such as being out of area (e.g., Noland, Arnold, & Clement, 1980).

Although it is not required that students keep a written record of their behavior, the importance of self-recording has been repeatedly demonstrated within the literature. In a study by J. W. Lloyd, Hallahan, Kosiewicz, and Kneedler (1982), students demonstrated consistently higher levels of on-task behavior when engaged in self-recording (i.e., marking the appropriate column to indicate whether the student was paying attention) than in self-assessment (i.e., asking themselves whether they had been paying attention) alone. Similarly, Maag, Rutherford, and DiGangi (1992) found that elementary school students demonstrated significantly higher levels of on-task behavior when they were asked to mark their answer on a form than when they were simply instructed to ask themselves the question "Am I working on the assignment?" Although the number of studies investigating this issue has been limited, the importance of maintaining a record of behavior is consistent with research that suggests that reactivity may be enhanced when behavioral feedback is made more readily available (e.g., Kazdin, 1974).

Furthermore, it may be possible to further harness the power of performance feedback by keeping a record of self-monitoring data over time. Across a small number of studies, students have kept track of their daily behavior by graphing it over time, such as charting the amount of time they were on-task each day on a summative graph for the duration of the intervention (Crawley, Lynch, & Vannest, 2006; Harris, Graham, Reid, McElroy, & Hamby, 1994). Monitoring progress over time has been suggested to increase motivation or behavior change and to increase the salience of feedback using a summative, visual representation (Harris et al., 1994); it therefore may hold promise for use in self-management applications.

Self-Evaluation

Kanfer (1970) posited that the process of self-monitoring triggers two subsequent phases of self-evaluation and reinforcement in which current performance is compared with some desired level of performance; then, either self-reward or punishment is delivered based on proximity to the goal. When working with adults, it is assumed that this feedback loop is being activated repeatedly as an individual continues to make small adjustments to his or her behavior based on obtained feedback until the gap between current and desired performance is no longer noticeable (Kanfer, 1971). Questions may be raised, however, regarding whether this metacognitive process is actually being activated and used when students are simply asked to self-observe and record their behavior independently (e.g., Holifield et al., 2010; Wood, Murdock, Cronin, Dawson, & Kirby, 1998). A recent meta-analysis found that nearly half (45%) of the self-management studies reviewed required students to self-monitor without engaging in any discussion with, or receiving feedback from, the classroom teacher (Briesch & Briesch, in press). Within the context of these studies, it becomes difficult to determine whether behavior change is truly the product of an activated internal feedback loop, given the covert nature of these processes.

This issue becomes even more salient when one considers the variable frequency with which self-monitoring has been conducted in the literature. Self-monitoring has occurred intermittently every 10 to 15 minutes (e.g., Barry & Messer, 2003; Levendoski & Cartledge, 2000), or even one time at the end of a class period (e.g., Clees, 1994–1995; Wood et al., 1998); however, prompts have also been delivered as frequently as every 45 seconds (e.g., Boyle & Hughes, 1994; McCarl et al., 1991). According to Kanfer's (1970) theoretical model, behavior change occurs when individuals not only stop to observe their own behavior but also to reinforce or punish themselves based on an evaluation of that behavior. In those studies in which students are asked to monitor very frequently (e.g., once every 45 seconds to 1 minute), it is possible that there may not be enough time to fully activate the three-phase metacognitive cycle that Kanfer described. Instead, each prompt to self-monitor may serve simply as an antecedent cue or as a push to encourage desired behavior (Reid, 1996). In contrast, when students are required to self-monitor less frequently (e.g., once at the end of the period), this may allow for a more thorough, meaningful self-evaluation to occur. Given Butler and Winne's (1995) argument that "for all self-regulated activities, feedback is an inherent catalyst" (p. 246), it appears that more empirical attention must be paid to understanding the mechanism by which behavior change occurs when using basic self-monitoring procedures with children and adolescents.

In light of these issues, many of the self-management studies within the school-based literature have relied on adults to scaffold the evaluative process. In these cases, the classroom teacher would typically meet with the student at the end of the rating period to discuss the student's ratings and administer reinforcement, as applicable. Depending on the study, however, the evaluation that takes place may focus on the student's level of performance, the accuracy of the student's ratings, or both.

A performance criterion has been used most often within the literature to evaluate student self-ratings (Briesch & Chafouleas, 2009), and students are required to meet or surpass a behavioral goal. For example, the number of times that a target student is out of his or her seat during class may be compared either with the number of times that the student's classmates, on average, are out of their seats (i.e., social comparison) or with the number of times that the student's teacher believes to be appropriate (i.e., predetermined goal). Researchers have highlighted the importance of involving students in the selection of performance goals to ensure that the selected standards are seen as meaningful and relevant (Cleary, 2011) and that students have a higher degree of commitment to obtaining the goal (Schunk, 1995). Although students have been involved in establishing these goals in a limited number of self-management studies (e.g., Gureasko-Moore, DuPaul, & White, 2006), a performance criterion has typically been determined by the teacher or researcher through examination of the student's current (i.e., baseline) level of behavior (e.g., Maag et al., 1992) or based on normative standards (e.g., the class average; Barry & Messer, 2003). Regardless of who establishes the goal, it is important that it be challenging but attainable so that the student has a reasonable chance of experiencing success (Moore et al., 2001).

The teacher then meets daily with the student to compare the student's actual level of performance with the predetermined goal. Consistent with Kanfer's (1970) theoretical model, any noted discrepancy between current and desired performance is used to trigger future adjustments to one's behavior. Although it may be assumed that this feedback loop is being activated independently, some level of adult scaffolding may be necessary, especially at the start of the intervention. When actual behavior falls short of the goal, for example, the adult may facilitate a discussion with the student that focuses on identifying concrete ways in which to change future behavior to achieve the goal (e.g., Briesch & Daniels, 2013). Once the initial performance goal is obtained, however, the level of the goal might then be systematically increased until an optimal level of performance is achieved (e.g., Callahan & Rademacher, 1999).

In contrast, accuracy evaluations involve the comparison of the student's ratings with those of another observer, such as the teacher or researcher. In some cases, the focus of the teacher–student meeting may be on assessing how accurately the student is self-monitoring, regardless of the student's actual level of behavior (e.g., Davies, Jones, & Rafoth, 2010; Peterson, Young, Salzberg, West, & Hill, 2006). Other examples can be found, however, in which students can earn bonus points for conducting accurate ratings in addition to points based on criterion-related performance (e.g., Hoff & DuPaul, 1998; O'Reilly et al., 2002). Interestingly, despite the incorporation of an accuracy-based evaluation across many studies, the importance of rating accuracy remains unclear. Whereas some research has shown that notable behavior change may occur even when students overestimate their performance (e.g., Broden, Hall, & Mitts, 1971), other researchers have argued that self-monitoring is only effective if ratings are accurate (e.g., Bolstad & Johnson, 1972). Although some evidence suggests that rating inaccuracies should not be a source of major concern, the use of additional strategies to improve accuracy, such as providing additional training (Ardoin & Martens, 2004) or delivering rewards for accurate recording (M. E. Lloyd & Hilliard, 1989), has been shown to have an incremental effect on behavior.

Self-Reinforcement

Within Kanfer's (1970) model, the final phase of self-regulation involves the application of either self-reward or self-punishment, depending on whether one's goal was met. That is, if an individual finds that the level of performance exceeds the criterion, that person is likely to either engage in positive self-talk (e.g., "I really did a great job") or administer some type of external reward (e.g., going out to dinner). Conversely, if an individual finds that the level of performance fell short of the criterion, the person is likely to verbally chastise (e.g., "I really messed up") or punish (e.g., staying home rather than going out) himself or herself. Although Kanfer's model stresses that consequences are self-imposed, within the school-based literature, self-reinforcement has been the exception rather than the norm. Instead, classroom teachers are typically charged with administering reinforcement to students in the form of primary (e.g., tangible items, activity rewards) or secondary (e.g., points) reinforcers.

In some studies, students directly received small rewards, such as snacks, small prizes, or other tangible items, for meeting their goals. However, because evaluations could potentially occur multiple times per day, students more typically earned points or tokens for meeting their goals, which could then be exchanged for primary reinforcers at predetermined intervals or point values (Briesch & Chafouleas, 2009). No studies have specifically investigated the independent effect of using rewards; however, many studies have incorporated rewards as part of a comprehensive package (e.g., Barry & Messer, 2003; Dalton et al., 1999).

Although the use of external reinforcement has been successful within the context of research studies, Bandura (1976) noted that reinforcement could only be truly self-managed if the individual determines the criteria needed for reinforcement, has unrestricted access to reinforcers, and administers reinforcers if and only if the performance criteria have been met. A limited number of examples can be found in the literature in which students have self-administered points based on performance in relation to a goal; however, those points were later exchanged with an adult for tangible reinforcers (e.g., Fantuzzo, Harrell, & McLeod, 1980; Noland et al., 1980). One of the most feasible ways for students to deliver self-reinforcement may be through the use of self-verbalizations. Although private speech has commonly been thought of as a strategy for navigating and solving problems (Schunk, 1986), students may instead be taught to self-deliver covert praise for meeting a goal (e.g., "Nice job paying attention") or critical feedback when goals are not met (e.g., "I shouldn't have been talking to my neighbor"). In this way, the use of self-reinforcement may be made more sustainable from a logistical standpoint and may also result in behavioral change that is more generalizable.

Completing the Loop

Once an individual has delivered either self-reward or punishment based on his or her performance in relation to the goal, the person then theoretically uses this feedback to make any necessary changes to future behavior. For example, a student who observed himself to be turned around talking to his neighbors when he was supposed to be quietly listening to instruction might make adjustments to his behavior, such as sitting forward and looking at the teacher. The loop then begins again when the student engages in self-monitoring of the adjusted behavior and self-evaluates and self-reinforces accordingly.

CASE SCENARIO OF A SELF-MANAGEMENT INTERVENTION

The following case scenario illustrates best practices in implementing a self-management intervention to decrease disruptive classroom behavior (see Table 2.1). Billy is a fourth-grade student; his teacher, Mr. Martin, reports

TABLE 2.1
Self-Management Components and Implementation Considerations

Component	Definition	Considerations
Self-monitoring	The process of observing and recording one's own behavior	What will training involve to teach self-monitoring skills? Will event recording or time sampling be used? How often will monitoring take place (e.g., every minute, end of class)? Will the student keep a written record of his or her behavior? Will this written record be maintained across time?
Self-evaluation	The process of establishing goals for one's own behavior and comparing actual performance to those goals	Will the established goal be based on actual performance (e.g., 80% on-task behavior) or rating accuracy (e.g., 80% of student ratings within one point of teacher ratings)? Will the student evaluate his or her performance independently or meet with an adult to evaluate goal attainment?
Self-reinforcement	The process of administering reinforcement based on goal attainment	Will praise, points, or rewards be administered or will the student be taught to self-administer contingencies?

that Billy is having difficulty remaining on-task during independent seatwork periods. Billy regularly engages in a number of disruptive behaviors, such as having side conversations with peers, wandering around the room, and calling out. In consultation with the school psychologist, Mr. Martin decides to implement a self-management intervention with Billy. First, he meets with Billy to teach him to become more aware of, and self-monitor, his level of on-task behavior. In one individual 20-minute training meeting, Mr. Martin teaches Billy what is meant by "disruptive behavior" (i.e., behavior that interferes with his own or other students' ability to work, such as getting out of seat, talking to peers, and calling out) and, using case examples, helps him to practice judging whether behavior is disruptive. During each independent seatwork period, Billy is taught to place a tally mark on his self-monitoring card each time he disrupts the classroom (i.e., self-monitoring). At the end of the period, he uses the number of tally marks to assign himself a point value (i.e., $0 = 5+$ *disruptions*, $1 = 3–4$ *disruptions*, $2 = 1–2$ *disruptions*, $3 = no$ *disruptions*). Through monitoring the number of disruptions, it is hoped that Billy will become more aware of his own behavior.

Once Billy has demonstrated an understanding of the procedural aspects of self-monitoring within a training context, he begins to practice self-monitoring during regular classroom instruction. Initially, Mr. Martin also observes and records Billy's behavior at the end of each independent work period, and they meet to compare and discuss their ratings during a daily check-in. Mr. Martin rewards Billy with points for any ratings that match, which he can exchange for prizes from a rewards menu (e.g., pencils, candy) at the end of the week. If any major discrepancies between their ratings exist, Mr. Martin facilitates a conversation about why the behaviors Billy demonstrated during the period may have justified a particular rating. If their ratings are consistent, Mr. Martin spends the time either praising Billy for his appropriate behavior or helping him brainstorm strategies for decreasing his disruptive behavior in the future. By the end of the first week, Billy's self-ratings consistently match Mr. Martin's ratings of his behavior, and he is ready to move on to independent monitoring.

The following week, Mr. Martin stops conducting ratings and, instead, uses daily meetings to set performance goals to decrease Billy's level of disruptive behavior. Together, the two of them review the monitoring cards completed during Week 1 and find that Billy has been earning an average of 50% of the possible points each day. They decide to set an initial goal for him to earn 65% of the points on his card each day. During each daily check-in, they meet to calculate the number of points Billy earned and to determine whether he met his goal (i.e., self-evaluation). Each time the goal is met, Billy receives points that he can continue to redeem for prizes. During these meetings Mr. Martin also provides him with feedback on his behavior, such as highlighting strategies that worked to increase his on-task behavior (e.g., keeping his eyes on his paper) or noting behaviors that reduced his attention to task (e.g., getting out of his seat).

After a couple of weeks, Billy has met his initial goal consistently and begins to evaluate and reinforce himself independently. At the end of each day, Billy calculates his level of on-task behavior and compares it to a more ambitious goal of 75% (i.e., self-evaluation). If he met his goal, Billy will use this feedback to award himself points (i.e., self-reinforcement). If he did not meet his goal, he may use this feedback to reflect on what may have impeded his goal achievement (e.g., sitting next to a chatty peer) and to identify strategies to improve his performance next time (e.g., choosing a seat away from his peers). Rather than exchanging his points for tangible items, Mr. Martin and Billy generate a list of activities that the student may use to reward himself if he meets his goal; they discuss this list with Billy's parents to ensure that they agree with any home-based rewards (e.g., an extra 20 minutes of video games at home). Although Mr. Martin makes himself available to problem solve whenever Billy would like, he only formally checks in with Billy once a week. Over time, Billy's increasingly independent self-evaluation and self-reinforcement deepen his self-awareness and complete the self-management feedback loop.

CONCLUSIONS, IMPLICATIONS, AND FUTURE DIRECTIONS

An extensive research base accumulated over the past four decades clearly supports the use of self-management interventions to reduce disruptive behavior and thereby promote engagement in school-age children (Maggin, Briesch, & Chafouleas, 2013; Stage & Quiroz, 1997). As first noted by Webber, Scheuermann, McCall, and Coleman (1993) more than 20 years ago, however, perhaps the biggest question that remains concerns the degree to which behavioral self-management interventions truly promote an internalized process of self-regulation. That is, although the goal of a self-management intervention is to teach students to use self-generated feedback to become more aware of, and better able to control, their own behavior, the degree to which behavior change may actually be externally managed remains unclear. Researchers have stressed the importance of ensuring that individuals believe that they can successfully regulate their own behavior before teaching such strategies (Pintrich, 1999). If self-efficacy is found to be sufficient, it is then also important that the individual be involved in the process of goal setting to ensure sufficient goal commitment (Schunk, 1995). Given that the majority of behavioral self-management studies conducted to date have neither assessed participant readiness nor involved students in the development of performance goals, students may be less likely to continue to self-monitor their behavior independently into the future. As another example, when a classroom teacher meets with a student to evaluate the student's behavior and administer points or rewards accordingly, it is difficult to determine the extent to which the student's internal self-regulatory feedback loop is actually being activated as opposed to the evaluation process simply being managed by the adult. Also problematic is the difficulty in determining the effectiveness of self-evaluation independent of the use of external reinforcement. Given that the evaluation component is often paired with reinforcement administered by teachers or other adults in the classroom environment, it becomes difficult to tease the two apart (e.g., Dalton et al., 1999; Edwards, Salant, Howard, Brougher, & McLaughlin, 1995).

An additional area of inquiry that warrants further attention concerns the maintenance of observed intervention effects. One of the primary advantages of self-management interventions is that students become more knowledgeable about their own behavior, which allows them to develop skills that they can take into future settings (Cole & Bambara, 1992). Unfortunately, however, few studies have investigated the maintenance of effects over time (i.e., only 26% of studies in a review by Briesch & Chafouleas, 2009) and, when included, these maintenance periods have tended to be fairly short in duration (e.g., 10 days; Maag, Reid, & DiGangi, 1993). Furthermore, several studies have used reversal (i.e., ABAB) designs (e.g., Edwards et al., 1995; Levendoski & Cartledge, 2000), implying that the effects of self-management are assumed to be temporary and reversible. Clearly, self-management procedures can have a notable effect on behavior when external rating prompts are delivered regularly; however, questions remain as to the degree to which these strategies are actually internalized for sustained use.

Research on behavioral self-management may need to move toward greater exploration of ways to promote stronger generalization of student skills. Given the finding that students tend to be involved in a minimal number of self-management intervention components (Briesch & Chafouleas, 2009), one possible way to accomplish this goal may be to involve them to a greater extent in intervention design and implementation. Through participation in decision making, it is anticipated that the student will develop an increased sense of responsibility and a concomitant increase in motivation to enact behavior change (Kanfer & Gaelick-Buys, 1991), which may ultimately lead to more sustainable behavior change. For example, students may be asked to brainstorm those behaviors that most interfere with their success in the classroom to identify the most appropriate targets for intervention. They may also be asked their preferences in terms of implementation logistics, such as how often behavior should be monitored or what materials should be used for recording. Furthermore, increased student management of the evaluation and reinforcement components may increase the likelihood that the student will engage in the internal metacognitive processes described by Kanfer, thereby practicing and internalizing this feedback loop to be applied again in the future. Although having an adult model and participate in the process of comparing current performance to an established goal will be helpful initially, over time, evaluation should become the student's sole responsibility. It is important that the student is able to conduct the evaluations accurately and independently. As described in the case scenario, students should also be taught ways to self-reinforce rather than relying on externally delivered points or tangibles. Self-reinforcement can include having the student engage in positive self-talk (e.g., "I did a great job of answering questions today!") or identifying activities that the student can easily access when a goal is met (e.g., playing a video game for 20 minutes). Given concerns regarding continued adult control over key intervention components (Briesch & Chafouleas, 2009), it may also be necessary to explore ways in which teacher involvement can be reduced without jeopardizing the effectiveness of the intervention. For example, rather than relying on the comparison of student to teacher ratings, students could be taught to assess the appropriateness of their own behavior in relation to that of the environment in which they are situated. Being able to discern between appropriate or inappropriate behavior within a particular context would certainly be an important skill for students to adapt to new situations and changing expectations as they enter adulthood. Thus, self-management interventions should strengthen important metacognitive skills, such as comparing self-awareness of behavior with self-generated standards and using feedback loops to support self-directed and adaptive behavior for the future.

REFERENCES

Amato Zech, N. A., Hoff, K. E., & Doepke, K. J. (2006). Increasing on-task behavior in the classroom: Extension of self-monitoring strategies. *Psychology in the Schools, 43*, 211–221. doi:10.1002/pits.20137

Ardoin, S. P., & Martens, B. K. (2004). Training children to make accurate self-evaluations: Effects on behavior and the quality of self-ratings. *Journal of Behavioral Education, 13*, 1–23. doi:10.1023/B:JOBE.0000011257.63085.88

Bandura, A. (1976). Self-reinforcement: Theoretical and methodological considerations. *Behaviorism, 4*, 135–155.

Barry, L. M., & Messer, J. J. (2003). A practical application of self-management for students diagnosed with attention-deficit/hyperactivity disorder. *Journal of Positive Behavior Interventions, 5*, 238–248. doi:10.1177/10983007030050040701

Bolstad, O. D., & Johnson, S. M. (1972). Self-regulation in the modification of disruptive classroom behavior. *Journal of Applied Behavior Analysis, 5*, 443–454. doi:10.1901/jaba.1972.5-443

Boyle, J. R., & Hughes, C. A. (1994). Effects of self-monitoring and subsequent fading of external prompts on the on-task behavior and task productivity of elementary students with moderate mental retardation. *Journal of Behavioral Education, 4*, 439–457. doi:10.1007/BF01539544

Briesch, A. M., & Briesch, J. M. (in press). A meta-analysis of self-management interventions targeting student behavior. *School Psychology Review.*

Briesch, A. M., & Chafouleas, S. M. (2009). Review and analysis of the literature on self-management interventions to promote appropriate classroom behaviors (1988–2008). *School Psychology Quarterly, 24*, 106–118.

Briesch, A. M., & Daniels, B. (2013). Using self-management interventions to address general education behavioral needs: Assessment of effectiveness and feasibility. *Psychology in the Schools, 50*, 366–381. doi:10.1002/pits.21679

Broden, M., Hall, R. V., & Mitts, B. (1971). The effect of self-recording on the classroom behavior of two eighth-grade students. *Journal of Applied Behavior Analysis, 4*, 191–199. doi:10.1901/jaba.1971.4-191

Brownell, K. D. (1978). Theoretical and applied issues in self-control. *The Psychological Record, 28*, 291–298.

Butler, D. L., & Winne, P. H. (1995). Feedback and self-regulated learning: A theoretical synthesis. *Review of Educational Research, 65*, 245–281. doi:10.3102/00346543065003245

Callahan, K., & Rademacher, J. A. (1999). Using self-management strategies to increase the on-task behavior of a student with autism. *Journal of Positive Behavior Interventions, 1*, 117–122. doi:10.1177/109830079900100206

Cavalier, A. R., Ferretti, R. P., & Hodges, A. E. (1997). Self-management within a classroom token economy for students with learning disabilities. *Research in Developmental Disabilities, 18*, 167–178. doi:10.1016/S0891-4222(96)00045-5

Cleary, T. J. (2011). Self-regulation in academic settings. In S. Goldstein & J. A. Naglieri (Eds.), *Encyclopedia of child behavior and development* (pp. 1313–1316). New York, NY: Springer.

Clees, T. J. (1994–1995). Self-recording of students' daily schedules of teachers' expectancies: Perspectives on reactivity, stimulus control, and generalization. *Exceptionality, 5*, 113–129. doi:10.1207/s15327035ex0503_1

Cole, C. L., & Bambara, L. M. (1992). Issues surrounding the use of self-management interventions in the schools. *School Psychology Review, 21*, 193–201.

Crawley, S. H., Lynch, P., & Vannest, K. (2006). The use of self-monitoring to reduce off-task behavior and cross-correlation examination of weekends and absences as an antecedent to off-task behavior. *Child & Family Behavior Therapy, 28*, 29–48. doi:10.1300/J019v28n02_03

Dalton, T., Martella, R. C., & Marchand-Martella, N. E. (1999). The effects of a self-management program in reducing off-task behavior. *Journal of Behavioral Education, 9*, 157–176. doi:10.1023/A:1022183430622

Davies, S. C., Jones, K. M., & Rafoth, M. A. (2010). Effects of a self-monitoring intervention on children with traumatic brain injury. *Journal of Applied School Psychology, 26*, 308–326. doi:10.1080/15377903.2010.518587

Deci, E. L., & Ryan, R. M. (1987). The support of autonomy and the control of behavior. *Journal of Personality and Social Psychology, 53*, 1024–1037. doi:10.1037/0022-3514.53.6.1024

Edwards, L., Salant, V., Howard, V. F., Brougher, J., & McLaughlin, T. F. (1995). Effectiveness of self-management on attentional behavior and reading comprehension for children with attention deficit disorder. *Child & Family Behavior Therapy, 17*, 1–17. doi:10.1300/J019v17n02_01

Eisenberg, N., Valiente, C., & Eggum, N. D. (2010). Self-regulation and school readiness. *Early Education and Development, 21*, 681–698. doi:10.1080/10409289.2010.497451

Fantuzzo, J., Harrell, K., & McLeod, M. (1980). Across-subject generalization of attending behavior as a function of self-regulation training. *Child Behavior Therapy, 1*, 313–321. doi:10.1300/J473v01n04_01

Fantuzzo, J. W., & Polite, K. (1990). School-based, behavioral self-management: A review and analysis. *School Psychology Quarterly, 5*, 180–198. doi:10.1037/h0090612

Gardner, W. I., & Cole, C. L. (1988). Self-monitoring. In E. S. Shapiro & T. R. Kratochwill (Eds.), *Behavioral assessment in schools: Conceptual foundations and practical applications* (pp. 206–246). New York, NY: Guilford Press.

Gureasko-Moore, S., DuPaul, G. J., & White, G. P. (2006). The effects of self-management in general education classrooms on the organizational skills of adolescents with ADHD. *Behavior Modification, 30*, 159–183. doi:10.1177/0145445503259387

Harris, K. R., Graham, S., Reid, R., McElroy, K., & Hamby, R. S. (1994). Self-monitoring of attention versus self-monitoring of performance: Replication and cross-task comparison studies. *Learning Disability Quarterly, 17*, 121–139. doi:10.2307/1511182

Hoff, K. E., & DuPaul, G. J. (1998). Reducing disruptive behavior in general education classrooms: The use of self-management strategies. *School Psychology Review, 27*, 290–303.

Holifield, C., Goodman, J., Hazelkorn, M., & Heflin, L. J. (2010). Using self-monitoring to increase attending to task and academic accuracy in children with autism. *Focus on Autism and Other Developmental Disabilities, 25*, 230–238. doi:10.1177/1088357610380137

Houghton, S. (1989). Improving social behaviour and academic performance of a secondary school pupil through self-recording: A replication of Merrett and

Blundell. *Educational Psychology: An International Journal of Experimental Educational Psychology, 9,* 239–245. doi:10.1080/0144341890090305

Kanfer, F. H. (1970). Self-regulation: Research, issues, and speculations. In C. Neuringer & J. L. Michael (Eds.), *Behavior modification in clinical psychology* (pp. 178–220). New York, NY: Appleton-Century-Crofts.

Kanfer, F. H. (1971). The maintenance of behavior by self-generated stimuli and reinforcement. In A. Jacobs & L. B. Sachs (Eds.), *The psychology of private events: Perspectives on covert response systems* (pp. 39–59). New York, NY: Academic Press. doi:10.1016/B978-0-12-379650-9.50009-5

Kanfer, F. H., & Gaelick-Buys, L. (1991). Self-management methods. In F. H. Kanfer & A. P. Goldstein (Eds.), *Helping people change: A textbook of methods* (4th ed., pp. 305–360). New York, NY: Pergamon Press.

Kazdin, A. E. (1974). Reactive self-monitoring: The effects of response desirability, goal setting, and feedback. *Journal of Consulting and Clinical Psychology, 42,* 704–716. doi:10.1037/h0037050

Levendoski, L. S., & Cartledge, G. (2000). Self-monitoring for elementary school children with serious emotional disturbances: Classroom applications for increased academic responding. *Behavioral Disorders, 25,* 211–224.

Lloyd, J. W., Hallahan, D. P., Kosiewicz, M. M., & Kneedler, R. D. (1982). Reactive effects of self-assessment and self-recording on attention to task and academic productivity. *Learning Disability Quarterly, 5,* 216–227. doi:10.2307/1510289

Lloyd, M. E., & Hilliard, A. M. (1989). Accuracy of self-recording as a function of repeated experience with different self-control contingencies. *Child & Family Behavior Therapy, 11,* 1–14. doi:10.1300/J019v11n02_01

Maag, J. W., Reid, R., & DiGangi, S. A. (1993). Differential effects of self-monitoring attention, accuracy, and productivity. *Journal of Applied Behavior Analysis, 26,* 329–344. doi:10.1901/jaba.1993.26-329

Maag, J. W., Rutherford, R. B., & DiGangi, S. A. (1992). Effects of self-monitoring and contingent reinforcement on on-task behavior and academic productivity of learning-disabled students: A social validation study. *Psychology in the Schools, 29,* 157–172. doi:10.1002/1520-6807(199204)29:2<157::AID-PITS2310290211>3.0.CO;2-F

Maggin, D. M., Briesch, A. M., & Chafoulas, S. M. (2013). An application of the What Works Clearinghouse standards for evaluating single-subject research: Synthesis of the self-management literature base. *Remedial and Special Education, 34,* 44–58. doi:10.1177/0741932511435176

McCarl, J. J., Svobodny, L., & Beare, P. L. (1991). Self-recording in a classroom for students with mild to moderate mental handicaps: Effects on productivity and on-task behavior. *Education & Training in Mental Retardation, 26,* 79–88.

McFall, R. M. (1970). Effects of self-monitoring on normal smoking behavior. *Journal of Consulting and Clinical Psychology, 35,* 135–142. doi:10.1037/h0030087

Moore, D. W., Prebble, S., Robertson, J., Waetford, R., & Anderson, A. (2001). Self-recording with goal setting: A self-management programme for the classroom. *Educational Psychology, 21*, 255–265. doi:10.1080/01443410123466

Nelson, R. O., & Hayes, S. C. (1981). Theoretical explanations for reactivity in self-monitoring. *Behavior Modification, 5*, 3–14. doi:10.1177/014544558151001

Noland, S. A., Arnold, J., & Clement, P. W. (1980). Self-reinforcement by under-achieving, under-controlled girls. *Psychological Reports, 47*, 671–678. doi:10.2466/pr0.1980.47.2.671

O'Reilly, M., Tiernan, R., Lancioni, G., Lacey, C., Hillery, J., & Gardiner, M. (2002). Use of self-monitoring and delayed feedback to increase on-task behavior in a post-institutionalized child within regular classroom settings. *Education & Treatment of Children, 25*, 91–102.

Peterson, L. D., Young, K. R., Salzberg, C. L., West, R. P., & Hill, M. (2006). Using self-management procedures to improve classroom social skills in multiple general education settings. *Education & Treatment of Children, 29*, 1–21.

Pintrich, P. R. (1999). The role of motivation in promoting and sustaining self-regulated learning. *International Journal of Educational Research, 31*, 459–470. doi:10.1016/S0883-0355(99)00015-4

Reid, R. (1996). Research in self-monitoring with students with learning disabilities: The present, the prospects, the pitfalls. *Journal of Learning Disabilities, 29*, 317–331. doi:10.1177/002221949602900311

Schunk, D. H. (1986). Verbalization and children's self-regulated learning. *Contemporary Educational Psychology, 11*, 347–369. doi:10.1016/0361-476X(86)90030-5

Schunk, D. H. (1995). Self-efficacy and education and instruction. In J. E. Maddux (Ed.), *Self-efficacy, adaptation, and adjustment: Theory, research, and application* (pp. 281–303). New York: Plenum Press. doi:10.1007/978-1-4419-6868-5_10

Stage, S. A., & Quiroz, D. R. (1997). A meta-analysis of interventions to decrease disruptive classroom behavior in public education settings. *School Psychology Review, 26*, 333–368.

Taylor, L., Adelman, H. S., & Kaser-Boyd, N. (1983). Perspectives of children regarding their participation in psychoeducational decisions. *Professional Psychology: Research and Practice, 14*, 882–894. doi:10.1037/0735-7028.14.6.882

Walker, H. W., Ramsey, E., & Gresham, F. M. (2003–2004, Winter). How early intervention can reduce defiant behavior—and win back teaching time. *American Educator*. Retrieved from http://www.aft.org/periodical/american-educator/winter-2003-2004/heading-disruptive-behavior

Walker, H. M., Severson, H. H., Nicholson, F., Kehle, T., Jenson, W. R., & Clark, E. (1994). Replication of the Systematic Screening for Behavior Disorders (SSBD) procedure for the identification of at-risk children. *Journal of Emotional and Behavioral Disorders, 2*, 66–77. doi:10.1177/106342669400200201

Webb, E. J., Campbell, D. T., Schwartz, R. D., & Sechrest, L. (1966). *Unobtrusive measures*. Chicago, IL: Rand McNally.

Webber, J., Scheuermann, B., McCall, C., & Coleman, M. (1993). Research on self-monitoring as a behavior management technique in special education classrooms: A descriptive review. *RASE: Remedial & Special Education, 14*, 38–56. doi:10.1177/074193259301400206

Wood, S. J., Murdock, J. Y., Cronin, M. E., Dawson, N. M., & Kirby, P. C. (1998). Effects of self-monitoring on-task behaviors of at-risk middle school students. *Journal of Behavioral Education, 8*, 263–279. doi:10.1023/A:1022891725732

Zimmerman, B. J. (2008). Investigating self-regulation and motivation: Historical background, methodological developments, and future prospects. *American Educational Research Journal, 45*, 166–183. doi:10.3102/0002831207312909

3

SELF-REGULATED LEARNING INTERVENTIONS FOR MOTIVATIONALLY DISENGAGED COLLEGE STUDENTS

CHRISTOPHER A. WOLTERS AND LEAH D. HOOPS

In the United States, higher or postsecondary education includes a diverse set of institutions and contexts that vary across a number of dimensions. For instance, these institutions can differ with regard to the academic programs they offer and the numbers and types of degrees they grant. Also, they range in size from smaller community colleges with enrollments below some secondary schools to land-grant universities with enrollments topping 50,000. The students served by particular institutions also vary widely. Some institutions are designed more for the needs of minority, immigrant, low-income, or lower achieving populations; others have costs and academic standards that limit their enrollments to wealthier or more elite students. As a whole, the system of higher education in the United States has been lauded as the best in world and routinely draws large numbers of students from other countries (Schmidtlein & Berdahl, 2011).

There also is an increasing recognition that too many students who begin a postsecondary education ultimately disengage and fail to complete

http://dx.doi.org/10.1037/14641-004
Self-Regulated Learning Interventions With At-Risk Youth: Enhancing Adaptability, Performance, and Well-Being, T. J. Cleary (Editor)
Copyright © 2015 by the American Psychological Association. All rights reserved.

any academic degree. Recent statistics, for instance, suggest that more than 40% of the first-time-in-college students who initially enrolled full-time in a 4-year institution failed to graduate within 6 years (National Center for Education Statistics, 2012). Within this context, withdrawing from enrollment and failing to graduate actually represents a final and critical step in a larger continuum of beliefs, attitudes, and behaviors that, together, reflect students' academic disengagement (Bean & Eaton, 2000; Tinto, 1993). Earlier indications of this disengagement can include receiving low grades, failing to complete assignments, skipping classes, dropping out of individual courses, or perhaps leaving a specific major. Motivational disengagement, such as decreases in students' self-confidence, interest, and value for the material they are learning, is an important factor that contributes to these poor academic outcomes. In two extensive reviews, for instance, self-efficacy was identified as a critical determinant of college students' academic success (Richardson, Abraham, & Bond, 2012; Robbins et al., 2004).

Disengagement and the failure of postsecondary students to complete an academic degree is a critical problem for many reasons. Obtaining a college degree remains an important pathway to individual economic success and well-being. In contrast, students who drop out of college can amass large amounts of debt that negatively influence their own outlook and the larger economy. College dropouts also consume institutional and financial resources that might otherwise support students who would persist and graduate. Disengagement of students from particular majors or academic programs is also an ongoing national concern. Combined, these issues point to a continuing and increasingly vital need to understand and ameliorate the factors that contribute to students' academic and motivational disengagement in postsecondary settings.

Self-regulated learning (SRL) is one model used to understand students' engagement and achievement in academic settings (Cleary & Zimmerman, 2012; Wolters & Taylor, 2012). Furthermore, SRL may be especially salient as students enter postsecondary contexts (Cohen, 2012; Park, Edmondson, & Lee, 2012; Pintrich & Zusho, 2007). One reason is that, for many students, beginning a higher education is accompanied by increased personal and social freedom, responsibility, and independence. Many students are—often for the first extended time—away from the direct supervision of parents. College typically presents students with additional opportunities and greater flexibility with regard to their social life and academic pursuits. The nature of instruction and academic demands can also shift dramatically. Compared with many academic requirements in high school, college courses are more rigorous and involve less time in class, fewer interactions with instructors, more long-term assignments and evaluations, and less direct oversight regarding when and how assignments get completed. Postsecondary educational contexts, therefore, are likely to present serious challenges to students' continuing motivation and active engagement in learning.

The purpose of this chapter is to evaluate SRL as one model for better understanding and addressing motivational aspects of college students' disengagement. Accordingly, the remainder of the chapter is divided into four major sections. We briefly describe our model of SRL and how it applies to motivational disengagement among college students. We then review three types of SRL interventions designed to prevent or ameliorate disengagement among college students. We recommend several instructional practices and policies that can be used to nurture students' SRL, especially with regard to their regulation of motivation. Last, we recommend future directions for the research linking college students' SRL and their engagement within academic contexts.

SRL AS A FRAMEWORK FOR UNDERSTANDING DISENGAGEMENT

Models of SRL have emerged from a diverse set of theoretical roots that incorporate research investigating cognitive and social development, metacognition, volition, and motivation (Zimmerman & Schunk, 2007). Despite this diversity, most models share several core assumptions and a goal of trying to understand and explain individuals' active management of their own academic functioning (Pintrich, 2004). In line with this perspective, we view college students' SRL as an active, constructive process through which they set academic goals and work to monitor and control dimensions of the learning process to accomplish those goals (Pintrich & Zusho, 2007; Wolters, 2003).

Dimensions

The dimensions of learning that students can actively manage during SRL include their own cognition, motivation, and behavior, and elements of the academic context (Pintrich & Zusho, 2007). Cognition concerns the various mental processes individuals use to encode, process, or learn when engaged in academic tasks (Pintrich, 2004; Winne & Hadwin, 1998). Students' cognitive and metacognitive learning strategies have most often been used to represent these processes. A second dimension of learning and engagement that students can self-regulate is their physical actions, overt conduct, or behavior. For example, students manage their time, including when and how much effort they devote toward completing academic tasks

(Zimmerman, Greenberg, & Weinstein, 1994). A third facet of their learning that students can self-regulate is the context or environment (Corno, 2001; Pintrich, 2004). Students, for instance, might monitor and control the lighting, temperature, and noise in their environment. They might manage interactions with their teachers, parents, and peers to promote their own learning (Corno, 2001; Wolters, 2003). Finally, students can self-regulate motivation (Pintrich, 2004; Wolters, 2003), including the direct influence of their motivational beliefs and attitudes (e.g., self-efficacy, value, interests) on their engagement in academic tasks. In addition, this dimension of SRL includes students' efforts to actively plan, monitor, and control their motivation (Wolters, 2003). Although these four dimensions are integrated and each is critical to the overall SRL, in the remainder of this chapter, we focus on students' self-regulation of their motivation.

Phases of SRL

In line with many others (Boekaerts, 1996; Greene & Azevedo, 2007; Pintrich & Zusho, 2007; Winne & Hadwin, 2008; Zimmerman, 2000), we also view SRL as involving multiple interdependent phases. One phase, often labeled *forethought* (Zimmerman, 2000; Zusho & Edwards, 2011), reflects students' planning, goal-setting, prior knowledge activation, and other processes that often occur as students initiate tasks. This phase incorporates students' activation of motivational attitudes and beliefs, such as the perceived importance or usefulness of what they will learn and the interestingness and difficulty of learning tasks, as well as their perceived control and self-efficacy for learning successfully. For instance, students waiting for a class lecture to start might think about how important the course is with regard to their major, but they also may consider how difficult it has been to understand the material and how worried they are about getting a good grade on the next exam. Forethought can also include forming intentions or goals about one's motivation, such as wanting to be interested, engaged, and effortful during the day's lecture.

A second phase, *monitoring* (Pintrich, Wolters, & Baxter, 2000; Winne & Hadwin, 2008), describes students' efforts to be aware of their ongoing processing, progress, or performance with regard to a task or learning activity. With regard to motivation, this phase includes students' awareness of the strength of their motivation for completing a task and recognition of the source(s) of that motivation. Students' understanding of problems, distractions, or other impediments that detract from their motivation may also be part of what they monitor. During class, for example, students might become aware that they are not really interested in the day's topic, that they are being distracted by alerts on their phone, or that the lack of visual aids makes them feel less confident in their ability to understand the material.

A third phase identified in most models of SRL has been labeled *control, management,* or *regulation* (Pintrich, 2004; Winne & Hadwin, 2008; Zimmerman, 2000). This process involves students' initial engagement and enactment of plans or strategies designed to complete academic tasks (Pintrich et al., 2000; Zimmerman, 2000). For instance, students might bring a cup of coffee to stay alert in a large lecture hall and sit away from perceived distractions. This phase also reflects learners' strategic efforts to change what they are doing to sustain or improve their motivation. After students realize their motivation is waning during a lecture, for instance, they might talk to themselves about how important understanding the material is for their future job, promise themselves a lunch out if they concentrate and take good notes, or try to make the material more immediately relevant by linking it to their own lives (Wolters, 1998, 2003).

A fourth phase incorporated within many models of SRL includes students' efforts to reflect on and respond to feedback generated through their own monitoring or from external reactions to their performance. Motivational aspects of this phase are embodied within the attributional process (Weiner, 2000) and when students update their beliefs about the interestingness, difficulty, and usefulness of particular activities, topics, or courses. After a class has finished, for example, students might conclude that being motivated in the course is challenging because the professor is boring, that sitting by the door makes it difficult to concentrate, or that making up personal examples to illustrate the material makes it more interesting.

Although conceptually distinct, these different phases do not represent a strict time-ordered sequence or a causally connected linear process (Pintrich & Zusho, 2007; Winne & Hadwin, 2008; Zimmerman, 2000). Rather, they provide a structure and emphasize that SRL is a function of students' active and adaptive engagement before, during, and after the completion of academic tasks. Furthermore, they highlight that SRL necessarily involves continuous feedback loops whereby students set goals, evaluate their progress, and modify their actions to advance toward those goals (Cleary & Zimmerman, 2012). As the review here highlights, college students can engage in this type of feedback loop to self-regulate their own motivational processes that are critical to engagement and learning.

INTERVENTIONS FOR IMPROVING COLLEGE STUDENTS' SRL

SRL has proven useful for understanding and predicting college students' academic functioning (Kitsantas, 2002; Pintrich & Zusho, 2007; Wolters, 1998). Students characterized as more frequently involved in SRL tend to be more successful and productive learners. As a result, some researchers have argued that a major goal of formal education should be to teach SRL skills so that students may become self-regulated learners (Bembenutty, 2008; Boekaerts, 1996). Critical to this viewpoint is the assumption that many of the underlying abilities, skills, beliefs, and dispositions necessary for SRL are amenable to improvement.

Advancements in students' SRL can result from personal experience, modeling, and trial and error (Schunk & Zimmerman, 1997; Winne, 1997; Wolters, 2011). In addition, SRL can be improved through purposeful interventions designed and directed by teachers, counselors, or other educators (Schunk & Zimmerman, 1998). We center our discussion on interventions designed to improve SRL within postsecondary populations, with particular attention to the motivational aspects of these interventions. Our focus is on adjunct interventions that have development of SRL as a primary goal rather than those embedded within regular content courses (Hofer, Yu, & Pintrich, 1998; Zimmerman, Moylan, Hudesman, White, & Flugman, 2011). We consider three types of interventions in our discussion: tutoring, workshops, and extended course work. For each, we identify potential strengths and weaknesses for fostering the motivational aspects of SRL among postsecondary students and consider the empirical evidence of their effectiveness. Table 3.1 presents a summary of the points in this discussion.

Tutoring

Academic counseling, tutoring, mentoring, or other one-on-one instructional experiences represent a common type of intervention used to improve college students' SRL. One defining feature of this type of intervention is the individualized nature of the experience. Unlike more traditional academic tutoring (Topping, 1996), individualized SRL interventions are not primarily geared toward improving students' knowledge or understanding within a particular content area. Instead, tutoring in SRL is focused on improving the more general underlying beliefs, attitudes, and skills necessary for SRL (see Chapter 4, this volume). As tutors work to improve content-specific learning skills and more domain-free strategies and beliefs, however, it can be difficult (and unnecessary) to make this distinction.

One advantage of this type of intervention is that skilled tutors are able to respond to an individual student's needs regarding academic course content and SRL skills (Hock, Deshler, & Schumaker, 1999). A well-skilled tutor can assess students' areas of need with regard to SRL and quickly work on one or more strategies to help them best reach their academic goals. A number of researchers have begun to develop computerized tutoring programs designed to achieve goals similar to this type of individualized tutoring

TABLE 3.1
Comparison of Postsecondary Self-Regulated Learning Intervention Types

Category	Tutoring	Workshops	Course work
Basic characteristics or description	Counseling, mentoring, or coaching Focused more on SRL and less on specific academic subjects, but interventions can include both	Offered through campus learning centers to general student population Often required for struggling or at-risk students	Learning to Learn (L2L), Student Success, or Learning and Motivation Strategies course Offered as elective credit or required for students enrolled in developmental education
Duration	Short-term (~30–90 minutes) Students can attend one or multiple sessions, so duration may vary by student	Short-term (~60–180 minutes) Not usually offered as a series (i.e., students only attend one session)	Longer term one academic session (e.g., semester, quarter)
Dimensions of SRL covered	Based on individual student need Could cover one or all dimensions	Typically focused on one or two specific dimensions or strategies (e.g., note-taking or mind-mapping)	All four areas can be covered, but not often equally Both theory and strategies of SRL
Strengths	Tutors able to assess individual student needs If multiple sessions, opportunity for students to receive and apply feedback	Quick "shot" of SRL instruction Able to focus on a specific strategy or area of SRL	More comprehensive approach to developing effective SRL engagement behaviors Multiple opportunities for feedback and data generation Empirical evidence of improved grades, retention, and SRL engagement of course takers
Weaknesses	Not typically comprehensive SRL interventions (i.e., theory behind strategies not typically discussed)	No guidance on how to modify behaviors after initial instruction	Minimal evidence of effectiveness in improving students' regulation of motivation
Nature of motivational feedback loop	Not present unless motivation is specific focus of intervention sessions	Not generally available	Present more in some courses than in others, depending on curriculum and focus of institution

(Azevedo, 2005; Hadwin & Winne, 2001). Improving students' motivational feedback loop or motivational regulation, however, is not a commonly cited goal of individual tutoring, regardless of how it is delivered.

Empirical evidence that personalized tutoring programs can improve student learning and performance is limited (Hock et al., 1999; Norton & Crowley, 1995). Evidence that these individualized interventions can be effective for improving attitudes, beliefs, or the planning, monitoring, and strategies necessary for motivational regulation is even rarer. In one of the few studies that have examined the effect of tutoring programs on students' SRL engagement, an individualized intervention developed by Butler (2003) proved successful for helping college students with a learning disability improve their ability to engage in SRL. In this system, students and the trained instructors jointly select what tasks they will complete; the instructor asks questions, promotes reflection, and prompts students' strategic thinking; and the student discusses, articulates, and makes final decisions about how tasks are to be completed (Butler, 2003). This work shows that supporting, developing, and improving the motivational and strategic aspects of SRL also can be incorporated into individual tutoring sessions.

Workshops

Workshops represent a second type of academic intervention geared toward improving SRL. Commonly offered through campus learning centers or other support units, this type of intervention is directed at improving one or two component skills within SRL (e.g., note taking, time management), often with a small group of students. Although they may be components of a larger program, workshops most often represent discrete experiences that are independent of other instructional supports (Norton & Crowley, 1995). As an example, a learning center might offer individual workshops, each covering a different aspect of SRL, with attendance voluntary (see Chapters 9 and 10, this volume, for details about professional development workshops).

Workshops or other similar short-term interventions can be appealing to students because the required level of commitment is relatively low and they can select experiences linked to their perceived needs. When these interventions are done well, students can receive a quick, focused "shot" of SRL instruction that they might otherwise not receive. Unless they attend sessions focused on motivation, however, these interventions may provide no help in developing students' motivational regulation. Another disadvantage of these programs is their duration: Although students may receive instruction to help them generate data to modify their behaviors, they often do not receive additional guidance in how to do so.

Moreover, there is little time for them to practice and receive feedback on any skills they are being taught.

Empirical research that has evaluated the effectiveness of actual workshops for improving students' SRL, engagement, and academic performance is minimal. However, early studies have found that the amount of time students spent receiving these short-term interventions at learning centers contributed to the academic success of high-risk college students (Abrams & Jernigan, 1984). In addition, students who received intervention services often outperformed those who did not (Norton & Crowley, 1995). To the extent that they reflect similar short-term experiences designed to improve a discrete set of skills, beliefs, or dispositions, evidence for the efficacy of instructional treatments within experimental studies also indicates that workshops can be effective. For instance, studies have consistently shown that short-term interventions can be used to train students of all ages to use more motivationally adaptive attributions (Perry, Hechter, Menec, & Weinberg, 1993; Weiner, 2012). These interventions can range from a single session to multiple sessions spread out over time and have been shown to help students generate more adaptive attributions (Haynes, Ruthig, Perry, Stupnisky, & Hall, 2006; Perry et al., 1993) and increase their likelihood of academic success (Haynes et al., 2006; Haynes Stewart et al., 2011; Van Overwalle & de Metsenaere, 1990).

Course Work

A third type of intervention designed to improve college students' SRL is a formal, semester-long, credit-bearing course. Colloquially termed Learning to Learn (L2L), these courses often are designed to help students improve their academic performance by instructing them in some of the theory behind the process and about specific strategies necessary for SRL. In general, course-takers may first be provided with a general overview of SRL and how the process affects academic outcomes. Then, throughout the semester, students are taught specific SRL strategies and provided opportunities to apply the strategies to current courses or assignments. These courses play an important role in providing academic support to undergraduate college students (Dembo, 2004) and thrive at a range of institutions (Forster, Swallow, Fodor, & Foulser, 1999; Petrie & Helmcamp, 1998; Simpson, Hynd, Nist, & Burrell, 1997). L2L courses are offered under many titles and descriptions (e.g., Student Success Course, Introduction to College, and College 101), with a curriculum that varies across institutions. The still expanding selection of textbooks (e.g., Dembo & Seli, 2013; Downing, 2010; Ellis, 2013; Tuckman, Abry, & Smith, 2008; Van Blerkom, 2012) intended for these courses is evidence of their popularity.

Despite the inherent variance in their particular features and requirements, many prototypical elements exist within these courses. For instance, many cover the cognitive, motivational or affective, behavioral, and contextual dimensions inherent in SRL (Bembenutty, 2008; Hofer et al., 1998). Specific topics often include time management, goal-setting, decision making, affect management, test-taking, and help-seeking, and specific information processing techniques based on cognitive psychology. Other aspects that contribute to students' success, including career planning and exposure to campus resources, such as academic advising and the campus learning center, also may be covered. Instruction that builds motivational strategies and feedback loops that focus on motivation are not uncommon within these courses (Hofer et al., 1998). In general, for-credit L2L courses appear to provide an effective context for SRL interventions because they provide motivational instruction and strategy instruction with metacognitive information, and some courses provide contextual support and feedback.

Empirical research that has documented the effectiveness of for-credit courses designed to foster SRL is limited but growing. For instance, course-takers have been found to earn higher semester grade point averages than non–course-taker comparison students in both the semesters of enrollment and subsequent academic terms (Bail, Zhang, & Tachiyama, 2008; Tuckman, 2003; Tuckman & Kennedy, 2011; Weinstein, 1994). Moreover, course enrollment appears to improve the likelihood that students are retained between semesters (Forster et al., 1999; Lipsky & Ender, 1990; Tuckman & Kennedy, 2011) and complete their degrees (Bail et al., 2008; Schnell, Louis, & Doetkott, 2003; Tuckman & Kennedy, 2011; Weinstein, Dierking, Husman, Roska, & Powdrill, 1998). Course-takers have reported higher levels of SRL engagement at the end of the semester (Forster et al., 1999; Hofer & Yu, 2003; Petrie & Helmcamp, 1998), a finding that suggests that SRL courses help students become more engaged in managing their own learning processes. Specifically, students have frequently reported higher levels of aspects of achievement motivation, such as self-efficacy, by course's end (Hofer & Yu, 2003).

RECOMMENDATIONS REGARDING COURSE-BASED SRL INTERVENTIONS

Despite the limited research directly evaluating particular components of course-based SRL interventions, it is possible to make recommendations regarding the practices and policies for the design and implementation of these courses. In this section, we consider methods of enhancing college students' awareness, monitoring, and regulation of their motivation and engagement within the context of semester-long SRL courses.

Practices

One consistent message from the research on SRL is that students are more likely to engage in SRL, persist at difficult work, and be effective learners when they activate, hold, or express adaptive motivational beliefs and attitudes (Pintrich, 2000; Weinstein & Palmer, 2002; Zimmerman & Schunk, 2007). These adaptive forms of motivation include competence about doing the task, about themselves, value for the topic, and interest in the learning activities. Of course, one obvious implication of this assumption is that interventions can be designed to directly improve students' motivational beliefs and attitudes. For instance, an intervention can be planned so that students' values for course materials, students' confidence in their academic abilities, or other forms of motivation become stronger and more adaptive for engagement.

A second implication of this assumption is that interventions to improve SRL should promote students' understanding or awareness of the different forms of motivation that may affect their engagement and performance within academic tasks. Many students may understand that material or tasks that are boring or lack value may take more effort and self-restraint to learn. Other nuances of motivation may be understood less pervasively, for instance, the importance of making adaptive attributions about why setbacks have occurred (Weiner, 2012), how a sense of autonomy or relatedness might make some learning more appealing (Jones, 2009), or how breaking down challenging tasks into bite-sized pieces helps increase self-efficacy (Tuckman et al., 2008).

A related implication is that interventions should teach students effective methods for activating adaptive motivational beliefs during the forethought stage of SRL. Students who dwell on past difficulties, perceived shortcomings in their abilities, or the negative implications of potential failures are held down by their own disparaging beliefs. More optimistic or positive thinking may be beneficial, but it may not come naturally for all students. Hence, interventions can help students establish tactics for activating more adaptive beliefs that highlight competencies, interest, value, feelings of autonomy, or other forms of motivation that will encourage the types of engagement, effort, and persistence that more often produce success.

Consistent with the central role of monitoring within SRL, an effective course-based intervention for improving college students' SRL should also include efforts to improve learners' ability and propensity to monitor their motivation. The self-adjusting, self-correcting nature of SRL depends on students' ability to monitor different aspects of their own engagement within a learning task (Butler & Winne, 1995). When considering motivation, for instance, at least two dimensions might be the target of students' monitoring. Students may simply monitor their ongoing level of motivation: Are they feeling motivated and willing to be engaged and work hard at completing a task? Students who fail to take notice of their ongoing level of motivation may find themselves distracted, disengaged, or lacking deep engagement. A second aspect of motivation that can be monitored is the type, source, or form of motivation underlying a student's engagement in learning. For example, some students are motivated to outperform their peers (i.e., performance goals), whereas others are driven by more personal goals, such as being the first in their families to earn a college degree. Research has suggested that some forms of motivation may not be as adaptive as others (Anderman, Gray, & Chang, 2012; Jones, 2009; Schunk & Pajares, 2009). As a result, it may be useful for students to understand the source of their motivation and whether it could be changed. As an example, monitoring might lead students to realize that they are working only to get a good grade or to outperform their peers, rather than to learn the material deeply for more intrinsic reasons.

The usefulness of understanding and monitoring one's own motivation is limited unless students are also able to take steps designed to control, self-correct, adjust, or regulate and improve the situation, when necessary. Students must have and be able to adeptly implement strategies for the regulation of motivation. As with more cognitive strategies (Hadwin & Winne, 1996; Pressley & Harris, 2009), the ability to effectively implement motivational regulation strategies is a function of students' declarative, procedural, and conditional knowledge regarding those strategies. Interventions for improving students' SRL and motivational engagement, therefore, should include efforts to build each of these different forms of strategic knowledge. Declarative knowledge can be improved by exposing students to multiple types of motivational regulation strategies. Interventions should incorporate instruction (e.g., modeling, direct explanation) in how to enact the different types of strategies to build procedural knowledge. Interventions should also include opportunities to engage in varied practice in a way that builds conditional knowledge about when or under what circumstances strategies work best. For learning strategies to become actively implemented outside of the intervention, students need time to practice those strategies in situations similar to ones in which the strategies will actually be used and in diverse settings (Dembo, 2004; Hadwin & Winne, 1996; Weinstein, 1994; Weinstein et al., 1998). Instead of simply teaching students about learning strategies, interventions are most effective when students are able to apply the strategies to real-life problems and learning situations (Hadwin & Winne, 1996; Hattie, Biggs, & Purdie, 1996). For example, an instructor could first teach students how to use positive self-talk to regulate motivation, then allow students time to practice self-talk with a peer for a course in which they are currently enrolled.

The importance of reflection or reaction also has implications for what an effective SRL intervention should include. Unlike monitoring that focuses on more immediate situations and changes in behavior, reflection highlights the need to generate additional metacognitive knowledge about oneself as a learner, about tasks, and about strategies on a broader and more long-term basis. SRL interventions should include efforts to make students aware of these processes and to provide them methods of engaging in these processes in a purposeful and active manner. One well-established type of intervention that illustrates this goal is attribution retraining programs (Haynes et al., 2006; Perry et al., 1993). One shortcoming of this work is that, in many cases, students are trained to make more adaptive attributions but are not provided the insight necessary to be aware of this process to effectively continue to the evaluative process.

Reflection is also an important process for building metacognitive knowledge about the effectiveness of regulatory strategies, including those associated with motivation. Teaching college students effective methods for engaging in reflection about their motivational experiences during learning, what obstacles were most difficult to overcome, which strategies worked best (or worst), and what changes might be necessary in the future should improve their overall SRL. However, simply practicing the strategy does not guarantee that the student will master the SRL process; students must learn to generate and analyze performance data to change their SRL behaviors (Cleary, Platten, & Nelson, 2008; Cleary & Zimmerman, 2004). To truly help students develop effective self-regulation of motivation skills, they need to receive feedback and instruction throughout the semester. It would be beneficial for students to provide data regarding their motivational engagement at multiple times during the course with an opportunity to receive feedback from their instructors or peers. For example, on the first day of the semester, students could be asked to state their reason for being in college (i.e., their goal) as part of an icebreaker exercise. After each student shares his or her goal with the class, the instructor could state that it is important for students to be aware of their goals because, ultimately, these goals will serve as the students' source of motivation throughout their college careers. The definition of *motivation* established by Pintrich and Schunk (2002) could be displayed to the class so that learners see how goals are integral to motivation: "Motivation is the process whereby goal-directed activity is instigated and sustained" (p. 5). This activity could be repeated during the semester by providing students time to reflect on their originally stated goals; the instructor would prompt students to determine if their goals had changed and if the strategies they used to achieve their goals had changed. Moreover, students could be asked to describe any challenges they have faced in reaching their goals or steps they need to take to be successful. This activity could be individualized by having students complete the assignment independently on paper (or through an online course website), so that instructors would be able to provide personalized feedback that students could use to effectively regulate their motivation. This type of instructional activity would give students a chance to become proficient in the full regulation of motivation process, specifically in regard to monitoring.

Policies

Along with these specific considerations of what should be taught (e.g., attribution theory) and how it might get taught (e.g., semester-long courses), it is also possible to make broader recommendations about the structure and policies concerning SRL interventions. First, based on the complexity and breadth of SRL, we suggest that, for many students, longer term and more holistic interventions may be more effective than short-term training with more isolated components. Although shorter term programs, such as workshops, can improve particular aspects of students' SRL (e.g., time management, use of cognitive strategy), SRL is a multifaceted, interdependent, and recursive process. It can be challenging to promote the broad set of beliefs, attitudes, and skills, and to practice the feedback cycles students must master to be effective at SRL without extended attention. Hence, the semester-long duration of for-credit courses may provide a more fitting context to best teach SRL to college students.

The demand for credit-bearing courses is quite robust, even within large, prestigious, and academically rigorous universities (Weinstein et al., 1998). It is reasonable to assume that similar courses would be viable interventions for promoting student success at other institutions. An implication for broader policy, therefore, is that more universities should consider instituting these types of courses. Although student success courses often are offered as part of developmental or remedial education, most students can benefit from instruction that supports greater engagement in SRL (Bembenutty, 2008). Given that many students entering postsecondary education appear underprepared and unable to take responsibility for their own learning, these courses may best be targeted to first- or second-year students.

Another broader principle is that the curriculum and course design should be tailored to the needs of the student population to which the course is aimed. This recommendation has also been made by Hofer et al. (1998), who acknowledged that SRL courses are not one-size-fits-all interventions but must, instead, be created with particular learners in mind. Educators and policymakers should carefully select a textbook, curriculum, assignments, and evaluations based on institutional student need. For example, courses designed to improve the SRL of advanced or honors students might include more theoretical justification and discussion than a course created for struggling at-risk students.

Transfer is another critical issue when it comes to evaluating the effectiveness of SRL interventions (Hofer et al., 1998). When focused on domain-general aspects of SRL, the effectiveness of courses and other interventions depends on students' ability to mindfully transfer what they have learned to the specific contexts where it is needed. This type of high-road or far transfer often proves difficult to achieve in learners of any age. SRL interventions might also include the type of repeated practice that is supposed to promote low-road transfer of particular strategies or skills. Although more easily achieved, this automatic use of strategies can run counter to the more reflective and conscious awareness of one's own learning that is central to SRL.

DIRECTIONS FOR RESEARCH

SRL remains an active and fertile model for conducting research on students' motivation, engagement, and academic achievement. Within this larger area of research are many potentially productive avenues of research examining SRL interventions designed to improve motivation and motivational feedback loops that will reduce disengagement among college students. In this section, we highlight several directions that would add key insights into our understanding of how educators and policymakers can support these interventions.

Perhaps most salient, additional research is needed to establish more firmly that extended for-credit courses positively influence students' academic functioning in ways that promote motivation, engagement, and subsequent achievement. Although some research has shown this connection (e.g., Tuckman & Kennedy, 2011), it is limited and far from conclusive. In particular, additional research is needed that expands the types of academic outcomes linked to SRL. The effectiveness of SRL interventions has most typically been evaluated by the links to individual course grades or to grade point averages for a semester (Bail et al., 2008; Lipsky & Ender, 1990; Tuckman, 2003; Tuckman & Kennedy, 2011; Weinstein et al., 1998). Although important, grades do not provide a complete picture of academic performance and can lack validity with regard to predicting longer term or nonacademic indicators of success. Research linking participation in extended SRL interventions with retention, graduation, choice of major, or other indicators of postsecondary academic success would add substantially to the overall understanding of whether these courses are effective and should be propagated more broadly.

Along with a more diverse set of outcomes, research is needed to better isolate and test the particular components of SRL interventions that are most vital to students' engagement and later success. Courses designed to develop college students' SRL exhibit overlap in their curriculum, yet there is still much diversity in what they teach and how they teach it. Research that evaluates the importance of specific components, content, or activities within these courses would provide instructors and course designers critical guidance. This need may be particularly acute when it comes to evaluating those intervention pieces tied to students' awareness and regulation of their own motivation. In contrast to the work on cognitive and metacognitive strategies (Hattie et al., 1996), research examining these motivational interventions has been more limited.

Another potentially important direction for future research is to evaluate the role that workshops, tutoring, or other short-term interventions can have on college students' SRL and their subsequent motivation, engagement, and academic performance. Not every student must participate in an extended for-credit course to self-regulate their learning more effectively. More limited but targeted interventions may be sufficient, especially for certain students or under some circumstances. For instance, workshops on aspects of SRL that gain increased salience when students enter postsecondary contexts (e.g., time management, help-seeking) may be effective, even for students who are well skilled with regard to other forms of SRL (e.g., cognitive strategies). Especially needed are studies that investigate whether those aspects of SRL tied most closely to motivational regulation can be effectively improved through workshops or similar types of interventions.

Within all these lines of research is a need for more experimental or quasi-experimental work that will produce greater insights into the causal relations between participating in particular interventions and improvements in academic outcomes. The research on SRL has been criticized for an overreliance on cross-sectional designs and self-report data (Winne & Perry, 2000). One reason for this pattern is that experimental designs are not always possible within educational contexts. For instance, college students often cannot be assigned or required to complete particular courses, workshops, or tutoring sessions. Moreover, the diversity of both prior experiences and subsequent course-taking can make it difficult to identify appropriate comparison groups. Preventing or even delaying students from exposure to instructional practices presumed to be useful for their learning and engagement can also be problematic. Still, research that compares groups of students who are or are not exposed to particular SRL interventions is needed to establish the causal connections necessary to more broadly advocate for particular instructional practices.

CONCLUSION

SRL has emerged as an important model for understanding and improving college students' academic functioning (Pintrich & Zusho, 2007). One part of this emergence has been the development of interventions designed to support the growth of students' SRL, including their motivational regulation (Hofer et al., 1998; Tuckman & Kennedy, 2011). A comprehensive articulation of these interventions, including a firm understanding of the elements that are most critical to students' development of SRL and later academic success, however, has not been presented. In particular, the features of these interventions that are necessary for initiating and sustaining a motivational feedback loop, improving motivation, and preventing students' disengagement are still underdeveloped. Additional efforts at designing and testing these interventions are clearly needed.

All signs suggest that, going forward, these efforts will be productive in providing insights that help practitioners create effective SRL interventions. Hopefully, these research-based interventions will shape a future generation of motivated, engaged, self-regulated postsecondary learners confident in their capabilities to learn and, ultimately, positively affect their worlds.

REFERENCES

Abrams, H. G., & Jernigan, L. P. (1984). Academic support services and the success of high-risk college students. *American Educational Research Journal, 21,* 261–274. doi:10.3102/00028312021002261

Anderman, E. M., Gray, D. L., & Chang, Y. (2012). Motivation and classroom learning. In I. B. Weiner, W. M. Reynolds, & G. E. Miller, *Handbook of psychology, Volume 7: Educational psychology* (2nd ed., pp. 99–116). Hoboken, NJ: Wiley.

Azevedo, R. (2005). Computer environments as metacognitive tools to enhance learning. *Educational Psychologist, 40,* 193–197. doi:10.1207/s15326985ep4004_1

Bail, F. T., Zhang, S., & Tachiyama, G. T. (2008). Effects of a self-regulated learning course on the academic performance and graduation rate of college students in an academic support program. *Journal of College Reading and Learning, 39,* 54–73. doi:10.1080/10790195.2008.10850312

Bean, J. P., & Eaton, S. (2000). A psychological model of college student retention. In J. M. Braxton (Ed.), *Rethinking the departure puzzle: New theory and research on college student retention* (pp. 48–61). Nashville, TN: Vanderbilt University Press.

Bembenutty, H. (2008). The teacher of teachers talks about learning to learn: An interview with Wilbert (Bill) J. McKeachie. *Teaching of Psychology, 35,* 363–372. doi:10.1080/00986280802390787

Boekaerts, M. (1996). Self-regulated learning at the junction of cognition and motivation. *European Psychologist, 1,* 100–112. doi:10.1027/1016-9040.1.2.100

Butler, D. L. (2003). Structuring instruction to promote self-regulated learning by adolescents and adults with learning disabilities. *Exceptionality, 11,* 39–60. doi:10.1207/S15327035EX1101_4

Butler, D. L., & Winne, P. H. (1995). Feedback and self-regulated learning: A theoretical synthesis. *Review of Educational Research, 65,* 245–281. doi:10.3102/00346543065003245

Cleary, T. J., Platten, P., & Nelson, A. (2008). Effectiveness of the self-regulation empowerment program with urban high school students. *Journal of Advanced Academics, 20*(1), 70–107.

Cleary, T. J., & Zimmerman, B. J. (2004). Self-regulation empowerment program: A school-based program to enhance self-regulated and self-motivated cycles of student learning. *Psychology in the Schools, 41,* 537–550. doi:10.1002/pits.10177

Cleary, T. J., & Zimmerman, B. J. (2012). A cyclical self-regulatory account of student engagement: Theoretical foundations and applications. In S. L. Christenson, A. Reschly, & C. Wylie (Eds.), *Handbook of research on student engagement* (pp. 237–257). New York, NY: Springer. doi:10.1007/978-1-4614-2018-7_11

Cohen, M. T. (2012). The importance of self-regulation for college student learning. *College Student Journal, 46,* 892–902.

Corno, L. (2001). Volitional aspects of self-regulated learning. In B. J. Zimmerman & D. H. Schunk (Eds.), *Self-regulated learning and academic achievement: Theoretical perspectives* (2nd ed., pp. 191–225). Mahwah, NJ: Erlbaum.

Dembo, M. H. (2004). Students' resistance to change in learning strategies courses. *Journal of Developmental Education, 27,* 2–11.

Dembo, M. H., & Seli, H. (2013). *Motivation and learning strategies for college success: A focus on self-regulated learning.* New York, NY: Routledge.

Downing, S. (2010). *On course: Strategies for creating success in college and in life* (6th ed.). Boston, MA: Wadsworth, Cengage Learning.

Ellis, D. (2013). *Becoming a master student.* Boston, MA: Wadsworth, Cengage Learning.

Forster, B., Swallow, C., Fodor, J. H., & Foulser, J. E. (1999). Effects of a college study skills course on at-risk first-year students. *NASPA Journal, 36,* 120–132.

Greene, J. A., & Azevedo, R. (2007). A theoretical review of Winne and Hadwin's model of self-regulated learning: New perspectives and directions. *Review of Educational Research, 77,* 334–372. doi:10.3102/003465430303953

Hadwin, A. F., & Winne, P. H. (1996). Study strategies have meager support: A review with recommendations for implementation. *Journal of Higher Education, 67,* 692–715. doi:10.2307/2943817

Hadwin, A. F., & Winne, P. H. (2001). CoNoteS2: A software tool for promoting self-regulation. *Educational Research and Evaluation, 7,* 313–334. doi:10.1076/edre.7.2.313.3868

Hattie, J., Biggs, J., & Purdie, N. (1996). Effects of learning skills interventions on student learning: A meta-analysis. *Review of Educational Research, 66,* 99–136. doi:10.3102/00346543066002099

Haynes, T. L., Ruthig, J. C., Perry, R. P., Stupnisky, R. H., & Hall, N. C. (2006). Reducing the academic risks of over-optimism: The longitudinal effects of attributional retraining on cognition and achievement. *Research in Higher Education, 47,* 755–779. doi:10.1007/s11162-006-9014-7

Haynes Stewart, T. L., Clifton, R. A., Daniels, L. M., Perry, R. P., Chipperfield, J. G., & Ruthig, J. C. (2011). Attributional retraining: Reducing the likelihood of failure. *Social Psychology of Education, 14,* 75–92. doi:10.1007/s11218-010-9130-2

Hock, M. F., Deshler, D. D., & Schumaker, J. B. (1999). Tutoring programs for academically underprepared college students: A review of the literature. *Journal of College Reading and Learning, 29,* 101–122. doi:10.1080/10790195.1999.10850073

Hofer, B. K., & Yu, S. L. (2003). Teaching self-regulated learning through a "learning to learn" course. *Teaching of Psychology, 30,* 30–33. doi:10.1207/S15328023TOP3001_05

Hofer, B. K., Yu, S. L., & Pintrich, P. R. (1998). Teaching college students to be self-regulated learners. In D. H. Schunk & B. J. Zimmerman (Eds.), *Self-regulated learning: From teaching to self-reflective practice* (pp. 57–85). New York, NY: Guilford Press.

Jones, B. D. (2009). Motivating students to engage in learning: The MUSIC model of academic motivation. *International Journal of Teaching and Learning in Higher Education, 21,* 272–285.

Kitsantas, A. (2002). Test preparation and performance: A self-regulatory analysis. *Journal of Experimental Education, 70,* 101–113. doi:10.1080/00220970209599501

Lipsky, S. A., & Ender, S. C. (1990). Impact of a study skills course on probationary students' academic performance. *Journal of the First-Year Experience & Students in Transition, 2,* 7–16.

National Center for Education Statistics. (2012). *Digest of education statistics* [Table 376]. Percentage of first-time full-time bachelor's degree seeking students at 4-year institutions who completed a bachelor's degree, by race, ethnicity, time to completion, sex, and control of institution: Selected cohort entry years, 1996 through 2005. Retrieved from http://nces.ed.gov/programs/digest/d12/tables/dt12_376.asp

Norton, L. S., & Crowley, C. M. (1995). Can students be helped to learn how to learn? An evaluation of approaches to learning programme for first year degree students. *Higher Education, 29,* 307–328. doi:10.1007/BF01384496

Park, C. L., Edmondson, D., & Lee, J. (2012). Development of self-regulation abilities as predictors of psychological adjustment across the first year of college. *Journal of Adult Development, 19,* 40–49. doi:10.1007/s10804-011-9133-z

Perry, R. P., Hechter, F. J., Menec, V. H., & Weinberg, L. E. (1993). Enhancing achievement motivation and performance in college students: An attributional retraining perspective. *Research in Higher Education, 34*, 687–723. doi:10.1007/BF00992156

Petrie, T. A., & Helmcamp, A. (1998). Evaluation of an academic study skills course. *Journal of College Student Development, 39*, 112–116.

Pintrich, P. R. (2000). The role of goal orientation in self-regulated learning. In M. Boekaerts, P. R. Pintrich, & M. Zeidner (Eds.), *Handbook of self-regulation: Theory, research, and applications* (pp. 451–502). San Diego, CA: Academic Press. doi:10.1016/B978-012109890-2/50043-3

Pintrich, P. R. (2004). A conceptual framework for assessing motivation and self-regulated learning in college students. *Educational Psychology Review, 16*, 385–407. doi:10.1007/s10648-004-0006-x

Pintrich, P. R., & Schunk, D. H. (2002). *Motivation in education: Theory, research, and applications* (2nd ed.). Upper Saddle River, NJ: Prentice Hall.

Pintrich, P. R., Wolters, C. A., & Baxter, G. P. (2000). Assessing metacognition and self-regulated learning. In G. Schraw & J. C. Impara (Eds.), *Measurement in metacognition* (pp. 43–98) Lincoln, NE: Buros Institute of Mental Measurements.

Pintrich, P. R., & Zusho, A. (2007). Student motivation and self-regulated learning in the college classroom. In R. P. Perry & J. C. Smart (Eds.), *The scholarship of teaching and learning in higher education: An evidence based perspective* (pp. 731–810). New York, NY: Springer. doi:10.1007/1-4020-5742-3_16

Pressley, M., & Harris, K. R. (2009). Cognitive strategies instruction: From basic research to classroom instruction. In P. A. Alexander & P. H. Winne (Eds.), *Handbook of educational psychology* (pp. 265–286). New York, NY: Routledge.

Richardson, M., Abraham, C., & Bond, R. (2012). Psychological correlates of university students' academic performance: A systematic review and meta-analysis. *Psychological Bulletin, 138*, 353–387. doi:10.1037/a0026838

Robbins, S. B., Lauver, K., Le, H., Davis, D., Langley, R., & Carlstrom, A. (2004). Do psychosocial and study skill factors predict college outcomes? A meta-analysis. *Psychological Bulletin, 130*, 261–288. doi:10.1037/0033-2909.130.2.261

Schmidtlein, F. A., & Berdahl, R. O. (2011). Autonomy and accountability: Who controls academe? In P. G. Altbach, P. J. Gumport, & R. O. Berdahl (Eds.), *American higher education in the 21st century: Social, political and economic challenges* (3rd ed., pp. 69–87). Baltimore, MD: Johns Hopkins University Press.

Schnell, C. A., Louis, K. S., & Doetkott, C. (2003). The first-year seminar as a means of improving college graduation rates. *Journal of the First-Year Experience & Students in Transition, 15*, 53–75.

Schunk, D. H., & Pajares, F. (2009). Self-efficacy theory. In K. R. Wentzel & A. Wigfield (Eds.), *Handbook of motivation at school* (pp. 35–53). New York, NY: Routledge.

Schunk, D. H., & Zimmerman, B. J. (1997). Social origins of self-regulatory competence. *Educational Psychologist, 32*, 195–208. doi:10.1207/s15326985ep3204_1

Schunk, D. H., & Zimmerman, B. J. (Eds.). (1998). *Self-regulated learning: From teaching to self-reflective practice*. New York, NY: Guilford Press.

Simpson, M. L., Hynd, C. R., Nist, S. L., & Burrell, L. I. (1997). College assistance programs and practices. *Educational Psychology Review, 9*, 39–87. doi:10.1023/A:1024733706115

Tinto, V. (1993). *Leaving college: Rethinking the causes and cures of student attrition*. Chicago, IL: University of Chicago Press.

Topping, K. J. (1996). The effectiveness of peer tutoring in further and higher education: A typology and review of the literature. *Higher Education, 32*, 321–345. doi:10.1007/BF00138870

Tuckman, B. W. (2003). The effect of learning and motivation strategies training on college students' achievement. *Journal of College Student Development, 44*, 430–437. doi:10.1353/csd.2003.0034

Tuckman, B. W., Abry, D. A., & Smith, D. R. (2008). *Learning and motivation strategies: Your guide to success*. Upper Saddle River, NJ: Prentice Hall.

Tuckman, B. W., & Kennedy, G. J. (2011). Teaching learning strategies to increase success of first-term college students. *Journal of Experimental Education, 79*, 478–504. doi:10.1080/00220973.2010.512318

Van Blerkom, D. L. (2012). *College study skills: Becoming a strategic learner*. Boston, MA: Wadsworth.

Van Overwalle, F. V., & de Metsenaere, M. (1990). The effects of attribution-based interventions and study strategy training on academic achievement in college freshman. *British Journal of Educational Psychology, 60*, 299–311. doi:10.1111/j.2044-8279.1990.tb00946.x

Weiner, B. (2000). Intrapersonal and interpersonal theories of motivation from an attributional perspective. *Educational Psychology Review, 12*, 1–14. doi:10.1023/A:1009017532121

Weiner, B. (2012). An attribution theory of motivation. In P. A. M. Van Lange, A. W. Kruglanski, & E. T. Higgins (Eds.), *Handbook of theories of social psychology*, (Vol. 1, pp. 135–155). London, England: SAGE Publications Ltd.

Weinstein, C. E. (1994). Strategic learning/strategic teaching: Flip sides of a coin. In P. R. Pintrich, D. R. Brown, & C. E. Weinstein (Eds.), *Student motivation, cognition, and learning: Essays in honor of Wilbert J. McKeachie* (pp. 257–273). Hillsdale, NJ: Erlbaum.

Weinstein, C. E., Dierking, D., Husman, J., Roska, L., & Powdrill, L. (1998). The impact of a course in strategic learning on the long-term retention of college students. In J. L. Higbee & P. L. Dwinell (Eds.), *Developmental education: Preparing successful college students* (pp. 85–96). Columbia, SC: National Resource Center for the First-Year Experience & Students in Transition.

Weinstein, C. E., & Palmer, D. R. (2002). *User's manual for those administering the Learning and Study Strategies Inventory* (2nd ed.). Clearwater, FL: H&H.

Winne, P. H. (1997). Experimenting to bootstrap self-regulated learning. *Journal of Educational Psychology, 89,* 397–410. doi:10.1037/0022-0663.89.3.397

Winne, P. H., & Hadwin, A. F. (1998). Studying as self-regulated learning. In D. Hacker, J. Dunlosky, & A. C. Graesser (Eds.), *Metacognition in educational theory and practice* (pp. 277–304). Mahwah, NJ: Erlbaum.

Winne, P. H., & Hadwin, A. F. (2008). The weave of motivation and self-regulated learning. In D. H. Schunk & B. J. Zimmerman (Eds.), *Motivation and self-regulated learning: Theory, research, and applications* (pp. 297–314). Mahwah, NJ: Erlbaum.

Winne, P. H., & Perry, N. E. (2000). Measuring self-regulated learning. In M. Boekaerts, P. R. Pintrich, & M. Zeidner (Eds.), *Handbook of self-regulation: Theory, research, and applications* (pp. 531–566). San Diego, CA: Academic Press. doi:10.1016/B978-012109890-2/50045-7

Wolters, C. A. (1998). Self-regulated learning and college students' regulation of motivation. *Journal of Educational Psychology, 90,* 224–235. doi:10.1037/0022-0663.90.2.224

Wolters, C. A. (2003). Regulation of motivation: Evaluating an underemphasized aspect of self-regulated learning. *Educational Psychologist, 38,* 189–205. doi:10.1207/S15326985EP3804_1

Wolters, C. A. (2011). Regulation of motivation: Contextual and social aspects. *Teachers College Record, 113,* 265–283.

Wolters, C. A., & Taylor, D. J. (2012). A self-regulated learning perspective on student engagement. In S. L. Christenson, A. L. Reschly, & C. Wylie (Eds.), *Handbook of research on student engagement* (pp. 635–651). New York, NY: Springer. doi:10.1007/978-1-4614-2018-7_30

Zimmerman, B. J. (2000). Attaining self-regulation: A social cognitive perspective. In M. Boekaerts, P. R. Pintrich, & M. Zeidner (Eds.), *Handbook of self-regulation: Theory, research, and applications* (pp. 13–29). San Diego, CA: Academic Press.

Zimmerman, B. J., Greenberg, D., & Weinstein, C. (1994). Self-regulating academic study time: A strategy approach. In D. H. Schunk & B. J. Zimmerman (Eds.), *Self-regulation of learning and performance: Issues and educational applications* (pp. 181–199). Hillsdale, NJ: Erlbaum.

Zimmerman, B. J., Moylan, A., Hudesman, J., White, N., & Flugman, B. (2011). Enhancing self-reflection and mathematics achievement of at-risk urban technical college students. *Psychological Test and Assessment Modeling, 53,* 141–160.

Zimmerman, B. J., & Schunk, D. H. (2007). Motivation: An essential dimension of self-regulated learning. In D. H. Schunk & B. J. Zimmerman (Eds.), *Motivation and self-regulated learning: Theory, research, and applications* (pp. 1–30). Mahwah, NJ: Erlbaum.

Zusho, A., & Edwards, K. (2011). Self-regulation and achievement goals in the college classroom [Special issue]. *New Directions for Teaching and Learning, 2011,* 21–31. doi:10.1002/tl.441

4

SUCCESS FOR STUDENTS WITH LEARNING DISABILITIES: WHAT DOES SELF-REGULATION HAVE TO DO WITH IT?

DEBORAH L. BUTLER AND LEYTON SCHNELLERT

Laura is an eighth-grade student with a learning disability. Her assignment today is to read a section from her science textbook and answer the questions at the end of the chapter. Laura has always struggled with reading, so she feels anxious as she faces this task. To make matters worse, most of her past experience is with reading stories, so she's unfamiliar with this kind of "learning through reading" activity. For this kind of assignment, her approach has been to look at the end-of-chapter questions, find bold words in the text related to the topic, and copy definitions verbatim. When she turns in her assignments, she receives 100% every time. But she realizes she must be doing something wrong, because she fails almost every quiz. And, deep down, she knows she doesn't understand the material. So, as she sits staring at her book, she feels lost and demoralized. She sighs, turns to the back of the chapter, and finds what looks like the first key word.

How can we understand Laura's challenges with academic work? What can we do to support her to be and feel more successful? In this chapter, we demonstrate how applying a model of self-regulated learning (SRL) can help in answering these questions. Research has clearly shown that students who engage in effective forms of SRL are more likely to be successful in and out of school. Thus, classroom practices that foster SRL are likely to benefit

---

http://dx.doi.org/10.1037/14641-005
Self-Regulated Learning Interventions With At-Risk Youth: Enhancing Adaptability, Performance, and Well-Being, T. J. Cleary (Editor)
Copyright © 2015 by the American Psychological Association. All rights reserved.

all learners. But research has also consistently documented gaps in effective self-regulation for students with learning disabilities (LD). In many current reviews of research in reading, writing, mathematics, and subject-area learning for students with LD (see Wong & Butler, 2012), authors have emphasized how learners with LD struggle not just with "basic processing" problems but with higher order processes implicated in self-regulation that are essential to successful performance.

In this chapter, we identify why we should and how we can nurture the development of SRL in today's classrooms. To ground our discussion, we start by identifying goals in fostering SRL for all learners. Then we focus specifically on why supporting self-regulation is important for students with LD. Across these opening sections, we underscore the theoretical foundations of SRL and foreground the importance of fostering metacognition, motivation, and strategic action if students are to take greater control over learning. We also elaborate on our description of important goals by defining links between self-regulation and self-determination. In the second half of this chapter, we turn our attention to how educators can support SRL by students with LD and their peers. We describe qualities of learning environments supportive of self-regulation and provide examples of intervention frameworks that educators have used to create SRL-supportive environments. We close with conclusions and important future directions.

THEORETICAL FOUNDATIONS OF SRL

Throughout this chapter, we emphasize how, when built into inclusive educational contexts, supports to SRL have promise to energize and empower a diversity of learners who bring unique strengths and needs to classrooms, including the kinds of processing challenges associated with LD. That said, we also identify how and why more intensive supports to SRL can be particularly beneficial for students with LD. To build this overall case and to anchor our recommendations for practice, we start by defining the key theoretical frameworks and corresponding goals in supporting SRL for both students with LD and their peers.

Definition and Conceptualization of SRL

Self-regulated learning has been defined as the ability to control thoughts and actions to achieve personal goals and respond to environmental demands (Zimmerman, 2008). Consistent with this general concept, researchers have drawn from varying theoretical perspectives, including cognitive–behavioral, social-cognitive, sociocultural, and socioconstructivist theories, to elaborate models of SRL (e.g., Butler & Winne, 1995; Winne & Hadwin, 1998; Zimmerman & Schunk, 2001). In this introductory discussion, we highlight qualities of SRL from across perspectives that are essential to success for all students, including those with LD.

To anchor our description, we draw on a socioconstructivist model of SRL developed by Butler and Cartier (2004a; Cartier & Butler, 2004; see Figure 4.1). They have described *learners' engagement* as being shaped by the interaction between what learners bring to contexts (e.g., learning history, strengths/challenges, metacognition, prior knowledge, motivationally charged beliefs) and features of learning environments (e.g., activities/tasks, resources, assessment, feedback). It follows that understanding how to advance SRL requires attention to the particular strengths and challenges learners bring to tasks and how learning environments can nurture (or undermine) SRL.

Most frameworks for understanding SRL focus on the interplay among metacognition, motivation, and strategic action (e.g., Perry, Nordby, & VandeKamp, 2003). In Butler and Cartier's (2004a) model (see Figure 4.1), these aspects of self-regulated engagement are represented in relation to one another and other factors, with a focus on how they play out and are influenced by the contexts in which students work. These three components represent key goals for supporting SRL for students with LD and their peers. First, Figure 4.1 highlights how, through experience with academic work,

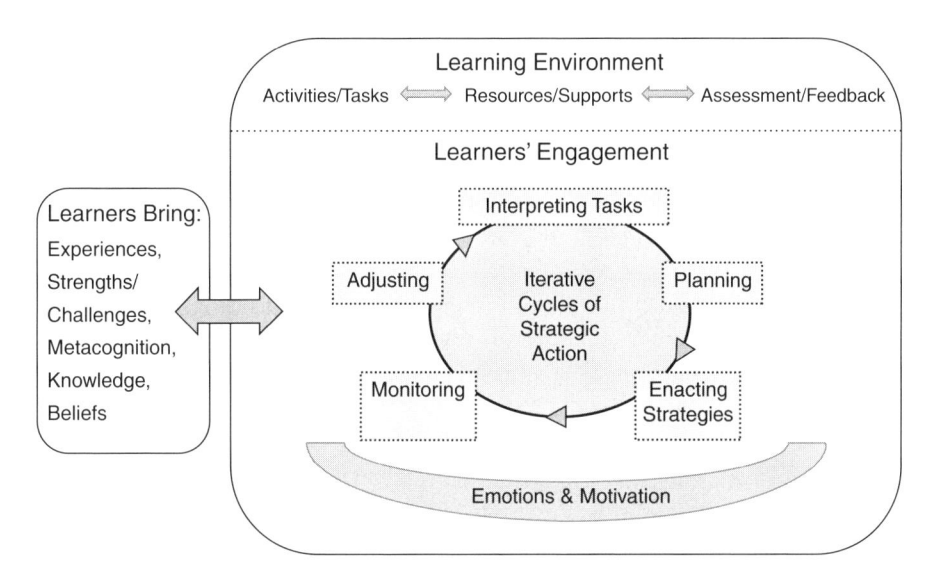

Figure 4.1. A socioconstructivist model of self-regulated learning (see Butler & Cartier, 2004b; Cartier & Butler, 2004). Copyright 2014 by Deborah L. Butler and Leyton Schnellert. Reprinted with permission.

learners construct metacognitive knowledge about themselves as learners, activities/tasks, and strategies. This knowledge shapes the ways in which they then self-regulate learning (e.g., define goals, choose strategies; Butler, 1998a). For instance, in Laura's case, her teacher likely expected her to work actively with ideas in her text to learn about key topics as she grappled with end-of-chapter questions. Instead, Laura interpreted this learning through reading (LTR) activity as requiring her to memorize definitions. Correspondingly, she chose strategies for completing her homework that involved searching for terms and copying text verbatim. Ideally, learning environments will be structured to nurture students' development of more productive forms of metacognitive knowledge (e.g., about LTR tasks as requiring active meaning-making).

Second, learners bring motivationally charged beliefs to contexts, including self-perceptions of competence and control over outcomes (e.g., self-efficacy; Bandura, 1993), mind-sets about intelligence and learning (e.g., "fixed" or "growth" mind-sets; see Dweck, 2010), and attributions for successful and unsuccessful performance (Borkowski, 1992). These beliefs influence learners' perceptions about and reactions (i.e., emotional, motivational) to tasks in a particular setting. For example, students who believe they can build ability through the way they engage in learning (e.g., using strategies effectively) are more likely to view errors as opportunities to learn and persist through challenging situations. In contrast, students like Laura are at risk for feeling anxious and disengaging from learning if they have little sense of control over outcomes. Thus, when building learning environments, a second key goal is to focus on supporting learners' construction of self-perceptions and beliefs that energize and sustain motivation.

At the heart of SRL is learners' engagement in cycles of strategic action. In his highly influential work, Zimmerman (2002) described strategic action as unfolding in three phases: forethought, performance control, and self-reflection, across which learners plan for, guide, and reflect on their engagement in activities. Butler and Winne (1995) and Winne and Hadwin (1998) offered complex descriptions of strategic action as unfolding dynamically. Complementing these other representations, Butler and Cartier (2004a) described cycles of strategic action as unfolding in iterative cycles of goal-directed activity (see Figure 4.1).

Specifically, self-regulating learners recognize the importance of interpreting tasks in self-directing their learning (Butler & Cartier, 2004b). Through task interpretation, learners construct an understanding of performance criteria on the basis of which they plan (e.g., materials, time), choose, adapt, or even invent strategies, monitor the success of their efforts, and make adjustments as needed. Self-regulating learners take time to plan and then flexibly and adaptively enact strategies to achieve task goals. They continuously monitor and adjust all aspects of their performance, focusing on outcomes (e.g., how much they are learning); how learning is unfolding (e.g., how quickly or well they are learning); and how they are managing motivation, emotions, and behavior (e.g., focusing through distractions; Butler & Winne, 1995; Corno, 1994). The key is that self-regulating learners actively interpret resources in their environment, including task descriptions, instruction (i.e., explanations, modeling), and feedback to help them in directing learning, self-assessing, and refining their work.

In Laura's case, problems she was experiencing could be associated with how she was constructing cycles of strategic action. When doing her homework, she was derailed by her faulty interpretation of task requirements (i.e., as about finding bold words and learning definitions), which was not aligned with her teacher's expectations (i.e., that she would actively learn and work with concepts). Her success was further undermined by her choice and use of strategies unlikely to enhance her understanding of the material (e.g., recording definitions verbatim). As she monitored outcomes, she was confused because she initially seemed to be doing well when she achieved 100% on assignments. She interpreted this feedback as evidence that her learning approaches were effective. But when she monitored outcomes associated with quizzes on which she was expected to demonstrate her knowledge of concepts, she recognized a gap between her strategies and her mastery of the material. Yet, with just outcome feedback in hand, she was at a loss for what to do differently (e.g., how to adjust goals, strategies, or both). Ultimately, she felt disempowered and helpless.

Building from this description of SRL, we conclude that if learners are to understand and deliberately take control of their academic engagement, we need to construct learning environments that support their construction of productive metacognitive knowledge about academic tasks, strategies, and themselves as learners; development of positive motivational beliefs; and capacity to engage adaptively and flexibly in iterative cycles of strategic action.

Link Between SRL and Self-Determination Theory

Identifying connections between self-regulation and self-determination theory can enrich understanding of important goals for students with and without LD. For example, in her review, Butler (2004) summarized longitudinal surveys that combined to paint a dismal portrait of life outcomes for adults with LD across social, academic, and vocational domains. However, she also highlighted a more hopeful line of research: one that focused on identifying when and how adults with LD could be successful (e.g., Diaz-Greenberg, Thousand, Cardelle-Elawar, & Nevin, 2000; Gerber, 2001). What these more success-oriented studies showed was that adults with LD could experience positive outcomes when these adults were empowered to take control of their lives. In these studies, researchers argued for personal agency and self-determination to form a "prime directive" for intervention (Brinckerhoff, McGuire, & Shaw, 2002, p. 488).

There are many intersections between self-determination and self-regulation (Diaz-Greenberg et al., 2000; see Chapter 11, this volume). Murray (2003) defined *self-determination* as "an individual's ability to make autonomous decisions, set goals, independently attempt to accomplish goals, independently attain goals, independently evaluate his or her performance, and make adjustments based on goal progress" (p. 23). From this perspective, self-determination requires the kinds of strategic action central to most models of SRL. Across studies on self-determination, authors also have described how, if learners are to adopt personally adaptive approaches for meeting environmental demands, they need to develop self-awareness and self-understanding, positive self-perceptions, and an internal locus of control. These descriptions are well aligned with forms of metacognitive knowledge and positive motivational beliefs that are pivotal in SRL.

An important emphasis added from self-determination theory is the description of how instructional environments need to support students in fulfilling three basic psychological needs: competence, autonomy, and relatedness (Ryan & Deci, 2000). Supports to SRL have great potential to foster students' self-perceptions of competence. For example, if students monitor links between goals they set, strategies they choose and enact, and successful outcomes, they can gain a sense of competence and control over learning (Butler, 1998b; Butler & Winne, 1995). Furthermore, when learners take deliberate control over learning goals and processes, they can achieve their need for autonomy. However, to satisfy a need for relatedness, it is also essential is to consider the quality of environments within which students learn. A sense of relatedness depends on nurturing positive social relationships, a critical aspect of the learning environment depicted in Figure 4.1. A need for relatedness can also be met—or undermined—by how classroom practices are established and implemented (e.g., how assessments are conducted and communicated).

SRL AND STUDENTS WITH LD

Learning disabilities have consistently been conceptualized as specific processing problems intrinsic to an individual that interfere with performance; seem "unexpected" given the person's overall potential; and cannot be explained by "other" factors, such as lack of opportunity to learn or other disabilities. Despite significant critiques leveled at methods used to identify LD, the National Research Center on Learning Disabilities (NRCLD) in the United States has concluded that the concept behind LD remains valid (Reschly, Hosp, & Schmied, 2003). The NRCLD has defined specific LD as disorders of learning and cognition that are intrinsic to the individual and affect a relatively narrow range of academic and performance outcomes. For example, Laura brought to her LTR tasks specific problems with memory and phonological processing that interfered with word-level decoding and reading fluency and, thus, put extra burden on her cognitive resources in ways that impeded her comprehension and learning.

If problems for students with LD emerge from more basic and specific processing problems, why then might support to SRL be particularly useful? One answer is that supports to self-regulation are essential if students with LD are to develop metacognitive knowledge about their unique strengths and needs, and then build from that knowledge to navigate expectations effectively. As students with LD engage in cycles of strategic action, they also need to construct motivational beliefs that support, rather than undermine, persistence and engagement.

Another answer is that among the processing problems that students with LD experience are challenges in the executive functions implicated in resisting distractions, focusing behavior, planning, organizing work, and thinking. These skills are associated with and necessary for effective SRL and learning engagement (see Chapter 1, this volume). Reid, Harris, Graham, and Rock (2012) described challenges for students with LD and attention-deficit/hyperactivity disorder (ADHD):

> Students challenged by either or both LD and ADHD commonly experience difficulties with inhibition of behavior, delay of gratification, persistence while engaged in activities requiring self-regulation, producing the amount and quality of work they are capable of, maintaining on task behaviors, following through when given instructions, and planning and directing goal-directed, future-oriented actions. (pp. 142–143)

Building supports to self-regulation can assist students with LD by enhancing their executive functioning capacities, fostering self-awareness of their strengths and needs, and helping them to develop personalized strategies for navigating academic work in ways that alleviate or compensate for their particular areas of difficulty (Butler, 1998b).

A third answer is that supporting SRL for students with LD is essential because challenges in SRL have been documented in different subject areas and tasks. For example, in reading, students with LD may experience phonological processing problems that affect decoding and fluency. However, comprehension problems also emerge from gaps in metacognitive knowledge (e.g., about text structures) and self-regulating processes (e.g., monitoring understanding; Mason & Hagaman, 2012). In writing, students with LD may struggle with "form and mechanics" (Santangelo, Harris, & Graham, 2007, p. 3), but they also may experience problems in motivation (e.g., self-efficacy, persistence), metacognition (e.g., knowledge about writing tasks or strategies) and strategic action (e.g., planning, generating content, revising). When writing, students with LD focus more on mechanics (e.g., spelling, punctuation, neatness) than on communicating ideas. In math, students with LD may experience basic processing problems in working memory or number sense (Mastropieri, Scruggs, Hauth, & Allen-Bronaugh, 2012), but they also may have trouble "abandoning and replacing ineffective strategies, adapting strategies to other similar tasks, and generalizing strategies to other situations and settings" (Montague, 2008, p. 39).

Why, if challenges for students with LD are specific and narrow (Reschly et al., 2003), do problems in self-regulation arise across so many subject areas and tasks? Wong (1991) argued that problems for students in metacognition may be secondary to initial and more basic processing problems and emerge out of students' accumulated experiences in school. For students with LD, limited access to meaningful, authentic tasks and/or a restrictive focus on remediation can limit opportunities to construct rich metacognitive knowledge about themselves, tasks, and strategies. For example, if students with LD spend most of their time focused on basic skills during literacy instruction, they may come to perceive reading as about decoding words or writing as about spelling and conventions (Butler, 1998b). In Laura's case, her impoverished engagement in LTR tasks seemed to emerge not only from basic processing problems but from her historical struggles with reading, her limited experience with informational text, and the tasks and feedback in her present learning environment.

Similarly, students' development of motivationally charged beliefs can reflect interactions between what an individual brings to tasks (including basic processing problems) and that person's experiences in context. For example, low self-perceptions of competence and control may emerge from learners' experiences of repeated failure and result in disengagement from learning. Conversely, overinflated self-perceptions of efficacy might result if learners with LD are unable to self-monitor performance against expectations. In Laura's case, her ability to assess her progress was undermined when feedback gave mixed messages about her success and failed to provide information about what to do differently. Students' monitoring may also be flawed if they lack opportunities to learn how to interpret or self-generate feedback to judge progress and refine their performance accordingly.

Research has suggested that although SRL is highly related to success in academic work, individuals are not reliably competent at self-regulating learning in classroom contexts. Students with LD may experience significant challenges in SRL. However, if they are to take deliberate control over learning, all students need to build from rich forms of metacognitive knowledge, sustain motivation through challenges, and know how to engage flexibly and adaptively in strategic action, as needed, within a particular environment.

A recent study by Butler, Cartier, Schnellert, Gagnon, and Giammarino (2011) provided evidence for the value of supporting SRL for students with LD and their peers. Participants were 646 high-school students engaged in LTR tasks in subject-area classrooms. The researchers used two coupled assessments—a self-report tool, and a performance-based assessment (PBA)—to create a multidimensional SRL profile for each student, each of which encompassed students' metacognition, motivation, and strategic action in relation to the contexts in which they were working.

Butler et al. (2011) found that, across the entire sample, fewer than half (41%) of the students were confident learners who interpreted LTR tasks in productive ways, chose and used active reading and learning strategies, and scored well on the PBA. In contrast, problematic SRL profiles were evident for 59% of learners. Thirteen percent were "disengaged" and, not surprisingly, performed most poorly on the PBA. Twenty percent appeared to be "actively inefficient" (see also Swanson, 1990). These learners invested effort in learning but were highly stressed, had an impoverished understanding of task demands, and failed to direct their learning activities effectively. Finally, 27% of students seemed "passively efficient" (Butler et al., 2011, p. 88). These learners did reasonably well on the PBA but were not deliberately strategic. The authors speculated that these learners might struggle if faced with challenging or new expectations. The above findings suggest that many students in today's classrooms are likely to benefit from support to SRL. But additional findings also revealed that support for SRL is particularly important for students with LD. As part of the study, SRL profiles were created for the 98 students receiving learning support services, most of whom had been designated as LD. In line with their peers, roughly 20% of these students seemed actively inefficient, fewer fell into the more "successful" profiles (actively engaged and passively efficient), and students receiving learning support services were more likely to have disengaged from learning (27% vs. 10% of peers).

Another contribution of the Butler et al. (2011) study was that it offered an analytic framework for characterizing and studying dynamic interactions among metacognition, motivation, and strategic action as situated within learning environments. In Figure 4.2, we build from this analytic framework, and from other research described earlier, to summarize how SRL might be

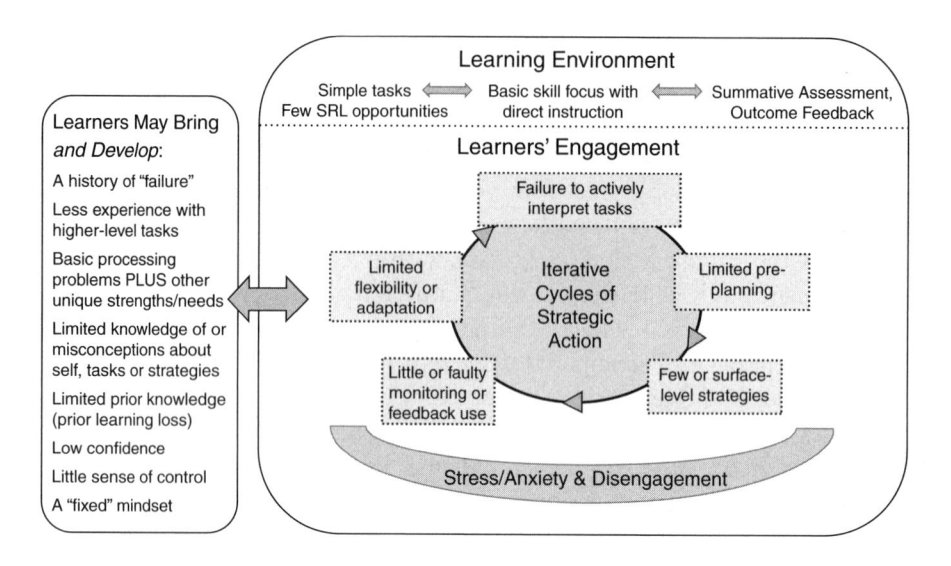

Figure 4.2. Problematic self-regulated learning (SRL) profile for students with learning disabilities in relation to context (see Butler & Cartier, 2004b; Cartier & Butler, 2004). Copyright 2014 by Deborah L. Butler and Leyton Schnellert. Reprinted with permission.

compromised by complex individual–environment interactions. For example, Laura's success in LTR tasks was likely challenged by her basic processing challenges. However, the efficacy of her strategic action also was undermined by interactions between her prior knowledge and experiences, limited metacognitive knowledge (e.g., about learning in science), motivational beliefs in this context (e.g., little sense of control over outcomes), the nature of assignments she was given (i.e., answering chapter questions, quizzes), and the quality of information she had available to inform her strategic action (e.g., feedback).

SRL-SUPPORTIVE INTERVENTIONS AND ENVIRONMENTS

We suggest that the needs of students with LD can be met, in large measure, if supports to SRL are built into classrooms so that all learners can experience success and learn how to take deliberate, strategic control over learning. In some cases, though, students with LD also may need an opportunity to access more support for SRL than might be needed by peers (Lenz, Ehren, & Deshler, 2005). Thus, we need principles and frameworks for structuring support to SRL that can be applied in inclusive classrooms and when providing extra assistance to learners.

Empirically Based Qualities of SRL-Supportive Environments

SRL-supportive environments work to achieve the goals identified in this chapter. In these environments, students are positioned and act as intrinsically motivated, strategic learners who engage positively and productively in activities on their own and with others. Much research has been conducted to identify principles and practices supportive of SRL for students with and without LD. In this section, we look across research traditions to identify the quality of teachers' and students' engagement in environments that support SRL development (see Figure 4.3).

What teachers are doing	What students are doing
Fostering a community of learners by... • positioning all members as learners • celebrating different strengths • accommodating diverse needs • supporting peer colearning *Creating activities that invite SRL that...* • extend over time • involve large chunks of meaning • require multiple processes • allow for a wide range of products • require trying in iterative cycles *Encouraging autonomy by...* • offering choices • supporting learners' control over challenge • requiring decision-making • fostering self-assessment *Structuring activities/tasks to support SRL by...* • creating routines and participation structures • integrating process supports into curricula • sustaining attention to goals over time *Supporting cycles of strategic action by...* • coconstructing criteria with learners • focusing explicitly on learning processes • providing powerful feedback • involving students in self-assessment • supporting students' decision-making through iterative cycles of learning *Fostering metacognitive knowledge and constructive beliefs through activity by...* • using strategic questioning • asking students to articulate ideas • supporting students to see connections between strategic action and outcomes	*Meeting their psychological needs for...* • competence • autonomy • relatedness *Engaging positively in classrooms by...* • navigating learning activities • focusing energies • seeking help when needed • supporting others' learning • interacting positively with others *Making learning-relevant decisions about...* • goals • materials or resources • strategies • environments • products • peers to work with *Approaching activities strategically by...* • interpreting tasks • focusing behavior and learning • choosing strategies • enacting strategies • monitoring outcomes • self-assessing and interpreting feedback • refining and revising • managing emotions/motivation *Building metacognitive knowledge and constructive beliefs about...* • learning • themselves as learners • activities and tasks • strategies for learning • self-regulation and cycles of action

Figure 4.3. Qualities of self-regulated learning–supportive environments.

Figure 4.3 outlines qualities of SRL-supportive classrooms. Highlighted first is the importance of the teacher's role in fostering a community of learners in which all students feel welcome. Safe, caring learning communities can be created by positioning all members of a classroom (adults and children) as colearners, celebrating and building from each learner's unique strengths, accommodating diverse needs, and fostering peer colearning. The SRL-supportive practices identified throughout this section also create conditions in which all members of a classroom community feel comfortable taking risks and advancing learning together (Kessler, 2000).

Generally speaking, SRL is supported when qualities of learning environments both create opportunities for and deliberately support SRL (Perry, 1998). For example, when teachers create activities that invite SRL, they establish contexts in which students have opportunities to develop academically effective forms of metacognition, motivation, and strategic action (Cartier, 2007; Cartier, Butler, & Bouchard, 2010; Perry, 1998). Perry (Perry, Phillips, & Dowler, 2004) has suggested that opportunities for SRL are created in tasks that "address multiple goals, involve large chunks of meaning, extend over long periods of time, engage students in a variety of cognitive and metacognitive processes, and allow for the production of a wide range of products" (p. 1857). Unless activities require planning, time management, or higher order thinking, learners do not have opportunities to build capacity in these important processes (Cartier et al., 2010). Similarly, if children with LD are exposed primarily to remedial instruction in basic skills, at the expense of engagement in deep thinking (e.g., through complex tasks in reading, writing, or math), they are likely to develop second-order deficits in self-regulation.

Opportunities for SRL are also established by encouraging autonomy (Perry, 1998). Supports for autonomy include offering choices (e.g., over materials to use, where to work, what strategy to try, what to write), requiring decision making, and empowering self-assessment. Perry and her colleagues have provided examples of how teachers have embedded complex tasks and autonomy-supportive practices into primary classrooms to afford opportunities for SRL (e.g., Perry & Drummond, 2002). She also has identified how these practices have the potential to accommodate diverse learning needs in classrooms (see Perry, 2004). For example, if given choices (e.g., what text to read for a research project), students with LD can tailor tasks to their learning needs, build metacognitive knowledge about themselves and tasks, experience autonomy, take control over the level of challenge, reduce anxiety, and participate more effectively within whole-class activities.

SRL-supportive environments not only provide rich opportunities for SRL but also include supports for students' development of effective forms of self-regulation (Cartier, 2007; Cartier et al., 2010; Perry, 1998). Important in this respect is to structure activities or tasks to support SRL. Teachers may accomplish this by creating predictable routines within which all students understand their roles and so focus on learning processes, integrating process supports into curricula and sustaining attention to goals over time. Integrating supports for SRL into classrooms is a particularly powerful way to nurture the successful inclusion of students with LD. When opportunities for SRL (e.g., for making choices) are partnered with supports (e.g., to learn how to make good choices), students with LD build important kinds of knowledge and skills essential in successful SRL. Furthermore, for students with LD and their peers, executive function processes are developed when students learn how to deliberately draw on skills and strategies in novel or challenging situations (Butler, Schnellert, & Perry, in press).

Also key is deliberately supporting students' engagement in iterative cycles of strategic action. For example, students learn to actively interpret task requirements when they are involved in interpreting or coconstructing criteria. They learn to use task-appropriate strategies flexibly when instruction integrates attention to content and process. Students learn how to monitor and adjust learning adaptively when they are supported to self-assess and actively interpret feedback from teachers or peers as a basis for judging progress and improving performance.

A critical support to SRL includes deliberately fostering students' construction of metacognitive knowledge and productive motivational beliefs through cycles of self-regulation. For example, teachers can use strategic questioning (e.g., "What is your task here"?) to promote students' metacognitive awareness and construction of metacognitive knowledge (e.g., about tasks). Teachers can support students' perceptions of competence and control if, after students are successful at some aspect of task completion, they support students to monitor connections between strategic action and positive outcomes (e.g., by providing informative feedback).

A good deal of research has undergirded the lists of SRL-supportive practices included in Figure 4.3. For example, Butler, Schnellert, and Cartier (2013) traced the qualities of practices enacted by secondary teachers in subject-area classrooms that were most closely associated with gains in self-regulated LTR by 364 secondary students in 20 humanities classrooms. What they found was that the greatest gains were experienced when teachers sustained attention to process goals over time; integrated process goals into curricula; attended explicitly to reading, thinking, or learning processes; and fostered students' engagement in cycles of strategic action. For example, the greatest gains in SRL were achieved when teachers engaged students in assessing and refining their learning processes. We elaborate on these overall recommendations in Figure 4.3 in the following sections.

A Focus on Assessment and Feedback

Assessment and feedback play a critical role in the development of self-regulating learners. SRL-supportive environments use assessments in two important ways. First, teachers use assessments formatively to define goals for learners, shape instructional practice, and provide feedback that might advance student learning (Cleary & Zimmerman, 2004; Schnellert, Butler, & Higginson, 2008). Second, SRL-supportive environments bring learners deliberately into the assessment process in ways that can support their engagement in iterative cycles of learning.

For example, teachers can support SRL through formative assessment. In a reflection on formative assessment practices, Black and Wiliam (2009) explained that

> practice in a classroom is formative to the extent that evidence about student achievement is elicited, interpreted, and used by teachers, learners, or their peers, to make decisions about the next steps in instruction that are likely to be better, or better founded, than the decisions they would have taken in the absence of the evidence that was elicited. (p. 9)

Black and Wiliam emphasized that through formative assessment practices, information can be gathered to inform next steps for teachers and students.

Hattie and Timperley (2007) made a similar point when discussing what constitutes "powerful" feedback. Based on a comprehensive review of research, they suggested that feedback is only powerful when it supports learners to answer three questions: (a) Where am I going? (i.e., What goals? What criteria?); (b) How am I going? (i.e., progress toward goals); and (c) Where to next? (i.e., What actions are needed now, given the progress I'm making?). Being able to answer these questions is foundational to individuals' taking control over learning through cycles of strategic action, as identified in Figure 4.1.

As potentially powerful as formative assessment and feedback can be, though, to have any effect, learners must deliberately make use of that information. In their theoretical review on feedback, Butler and Winne (1995) emphasized that learners need to actively interpret feedback provided to them if it is to influence knowledge construction or subsequent action. Knowing how to interpret and build from feedback within different forms of classroom work is an important capacity that self-regulating learners need to develop. Furthermore, self-regulating learners also need to know how to generate internal feedback through self-monitoring, which requires that they interpret or generate goals, judge progress, and refine action while working alone or with others. Thus, SRL-supportive environments provide powerful feedback to learners. Such environments can also push students (and teachers) to become progressively more independent at assessing their own and others' learning.

Research Evidence for SRL-Supportive Interventions for Students With LD

The SRL-supportive practices outlined in Figure 4.3 were distilled from a wide range of research focused on supporting SRL for all learners. In this section, we direct readers' attention to some of the empirically validated frameworks researchers have developed to embed SRL-supportive practices in learning environments to support students with LD.

A Focus on Executive Processes

Students with LD often have challenges with the kinds of executive functions needed to organize and focus goal-oriented learning. In a recent book chapter, Reid et al. (2012) provided an excellent review of research on how to support self-regulation in this area for students with LD and ADHD. They described interventions that engage learners in self-monitoring, self-recording, self-evaluation, self-instruction, goal setting, and self-reinforcement. They reported findings from research showing that supporting students' use of these self-regulating capacities fostered improvements in on-task behavior, academic preparedness (e.g., coming to class on time with needed materials), academic productivity (e.g., rates of responding), academic "accuracy" (e.g., in math computation), and disruptive behavior. This research documented how intervention focused on improving executive functioning within classrooms can enhance success by students with LD.

Reading, Writing, and Mathematics

In his work on writing instruction for students with LD, MacArthur (e.g., MacArthur, Philippakos, Graham, & Harris, 2012) has emphasized the importance of providing powerful writing instruction within a complete writing program in inclusive classroom environments. Doing so has the potential to support all learners, including students with LD. He has also emphasized how strategy instruction needs to be part of a writing process-based program. MacArthur et al. (2012) explained how, "within a process approach to writing instruction, strategies instruction provides the explicit instruction and persistent guided practice needed by many students with LD" (p. 256).

One of the most highly researched frameworks for supporting strategy development for students with LD is the Self-Regulated Strategy Development (SRSD) model developed by Harris and Graham (e.g., Graham & Harris, 1989; Harris & Graham, 1996). Considerable research has documented the efficacy of SRSD, particularly in supporting writing (Santangelo et al., 2007). Indeed, this model has been so influential that it has been extended for use across a range of tasks (see Wong & Butler, 2012). The SRSD model interweaves instruction about tasks and strategies with deliberate supports to self-regulation (e.g., to goal setting, self-monitoring, self-evaluation). SRSD has consistently been associated with positive outcomes for learners. For example, in writing instruction, SRSD has fostered improvements for students with LD in writing quality, knowledge of writing, approaches to writing, and self-efficacy.

Montague (2008) developed an influential framework to support SRL in mathematics for students with LD. In her approach to supporting math problem–solving, students are taught seven processes using explicit instruction: (a) read (the problem), (b) paraphrase, (c) visualize, (d) hypothesize, (e) estimate, (f) compute, and (g) check. Simultaneously, as they learn and enact each of these processes, students are supported to self-regulate learning using a "say, ask, check" routine that cues self-instructing, self-questioning, and self-monitoring. Notable in this approach is how say-ask-check cycles are infused in each step during problem solving so that SRL unfolds iteratively as students interpret problems (e.g., reading, paraphrasing), imagine solutions (e.g., visualizing, hypothesizing, estimating), enact tactics (e.g., computing), and check answers.

As another example, Cartier (2007) offered a framework to support SRL in LTR activities. In her framework, she described how educators can establish an LTR "context" within which students have opportunities for SRL and higher order learning (Cartier et al., 2010, p. 387). For example, she explained how to ensure activities are relevant, complex, and sufficiently motivating to foster deep engagement. A notable contribution is that she articulates how supports to SRL can be woven into LTR contexts. Cartier has investigated how teachers can use this framework to advance self-regulated LTR. In line with the four qualities of SRL-supportive practices identified by Butler et al. (2013), Cartier et al. (2010) also found that gains in students' SRL depended on teachers' bridging from guiding learning to fostering independence.

Supporting Iterative Cycles of Strategic Action

In this section, we highlight two approaches for supporting SRL that focus specifically on supporting learners' engagement in iterative cycles of strategic action. The first is the Self-Regulated Empowerment Program (SREP; e.g., Cleary & Platten, 2013). The goals of this program are to empower students "by cultivating positive self-motivational beliefs, increasing their knowledge of learning strategies, and helping them to apply these strategies to academic-related tasks in a self-regulated manner" (Cleary & Zimmerman, 2004, p. 539). In the SREP, SRL coaches use context-specific, diagnostic assessments of students' beliefs and strategies to formatively guide instruction. Then they support learners to turn weaknesses into strengths by empowering learners to feel in control over learning (e.g., by monitoring links between strategy use and outcomes), extending students' strategic repertoire, and supporting their cyclical engagement in self-regulating processes (e.g., goal setting, selecting, monitoring, and adjusting strategies, self-recording, self-evaluating). Particular contributions of the SREP are descriptions of practices that foster learners' engagement in feedback loops central to SRL and of how learners can be supported to construct new knowledge and beliefs (e.g., personal agency; attributions) through cycles of self-regulation.

Another example of a framework for supporting SRL by learners with LD is the Strategic Content Learning (SCL) approach developed by Butler (1995, 1998b). Butler was inspired to develop the SCL model in the early 1990s by her observation that, despite the potential power of direct instruction, modeling, and feedback to foster SRL, many learners with LD receiving strategies instruction were not becoming independent, self-regulating learners. Although they were learning strategies and applying them when cued to do so, they were not independently choosing and using strategies to achieve important task goals. This led Butler to an extended series of studies designed to identify why students with LD were experiencing challenges to SRL, and uncover whether and how to better support them.

Over time, the SCL approach has been applied to support learners in intermediate, secondary, and postsecondary classrooms in a variety of instructional configurations (e.g., one-on-one, small-group, whole class). Indeed, Laura was one of the students in a secondary-level SCL study. Through SCL instruction, Laura was supported to interpret demands for learning in her science classroom, evaluate the efficacy of her current strategies in relation to those demands, and construct new, more powerful strategies for learning in science that built from her unique strengths but also acknowledged her particular learning needs. SCL supports for Laura's self-regulated engagement in LTR led to gains in metacognitive knowledge, self-perceptions of self-efficacy, her ability to take control over her success as a learner, and learning outcomes.

Detailed descriptions of SCL principles and practices are available elsewhere (e.g., see Butler, 2002, 2003), as are examples of how SCL has been applied to promote success for students with LD across a range of tasks (e.g., see Butler, 1995, 1998b; Butler, Beckingham, & Novak Lauscher, 2005; Butler, Elaschuk, & Poole, 2000). Here we note that, like the coaches used in Cleary and Zimmerman's (2004) SREP, SCL coaches build from situated assessments used formatively to personalize instruction; support learners to build knowledge and beliefs through self-monitoring as they associate progress with their deliberate, strategic action; and support learners' deliberate engagement in cycles of SRL. In SCL, students are encouraged to take ownership over learning by positioning them from the outset as decision makers who need to seek out, actively interpret, and critically evaluate information (e.g., from instruction, modeling, resources, feedback) to inform their strategic cycles of goal-directed action. In SCL, learners are supported to become strategic learners who can interpret expectations in different environments, recognize their own strengths and challenges, and choose, adapt, or even invent strategies that work for them to achieve their personal goals.

CONCLUSIONS AND FUTURE DIRECTIONS

Our ultimate goal is for students with LD to become active agents empowered to take control over their learning in and outside of classrooms. To that end, educators need to create environments in which all learners, including students with LD, have opportunities and supports for self-regulation. What happens for learners in environments where SRL-supportive conditions are established? In Figure 4.3, the second column describes the qualities of student activity and learning that teachers aspire to develop in SRL-supportive classrooms. We recommend that all educators conceptualize these as important goals for learners.

What do we see in SRL-supportive environments? In these environments, learners meet their basic psychological needs for competence, autonomy, and relatedness. To achieve these needs, students engage positively in classrooms with teachers and peers. In SRL-supportive contexts, students build capacity to make good decisions, informed by their knowledge of their own strengths and needs. When presented with activities, they approach them strategically. They deliberately interpret tasks and build from task criteria well matched to the demands of classrooms. They select, adapt, or invent strategies and apply them flexibly to achieve their goals. Most essentially, they interpret or self-generate feedback to monitor progress and adjust cycles of strategic engagement recursively based on that information. And, as they reflect on their learning as situated in context, they refine their metacognitive knowledge and beliefs about learning, themselves as learners, activities and tasks, and how to take deliberate control over learning. Furthermore, we argue that it is through cycles of self-regulating activity that learners build content knowledge and skills in classrooms. For example, it is by self-regulating performance in classroom tasks that students construct knowledge about plate tectonics in a science classroom or are successfully able to navigate the demands of a writing assignment.

It seems then, that as an educational community, we know a good deal about the challenges facing students with LD, why supporting SRL by these learners is so important, and about the nature of SRL-supportive learning environments. Educators can now also draw from a plethora of resources and frameworks to inform their work with students with LD. Yet, many students with LD are not thriving. We have a long way to go in ensuring that the needs of students with LD are met within our schools.

Certainly more still needs to be learned about SRL-supportive practices for students with LD. For example, it is important to consider how students with LD can be provided with support to their basic skill development while not undermining their opportunity to engage in higher level learning, and about how to complement instruction in regular classrooms with more intensive supports. However, also critical is research into how educators can be supported to take up and integrate what we know about SRL-supportive practices in their work with students. Promising in this regard are professional development projects that engage educators as self-regulating learners and practitioners. Emerging research has suggested that educators can be supported to bridge research and practice through cycles of self-regulated inquiry through which they access, interpret, critically evaluate, and ultimately mobilize SRL research to inform their learning and teaching (e.g., Butler & Schnellert, 2008, 2012; Cartier et al., 2010; Schnellert et al., 2008). Supporting educators to build from this research has the potential not only to advance practice in classrooms but also to further enrich understanding about how we can support students with LD to take—and feel—in control over learning in and outside of school.

REFERENCES

Bandura, A. (1993). Perceived self-efficacy in cognitive development and functioning. *Educational Psychologist*, 28, 117–148. doi:10.1207/s15326985ep2802_3

Black, P., & Wiliam, D. (2009). Developing the theory of formative assessment. *Educational Assessment, Evaluation and Accountability*, 21, 5–31. doi:10.1007/s11092-008-9068-5

Borkowski, J. G. (1992). Metacognitive theory: A framework for teaching literacy, writing, and math skills. *Journal of Learning Disabilities*, 25, 253–257. doi:10.1177/002221949202500406

Brinckerhoff, L. C., McGuire, J. M., & Shaw, S. F. (2002). *Postsecondary education and transition for students with learning disabilities* (2nd ed.). Austin, TX: PRO-ED.

Butler, D. L. (1995). Promoting strategic learning by postsecondary students with learning disabilities. *Journal of Learning Disabilities*, 28, 170–190. doi:10.1177/002221949502800306

Butler, D. L. (1998a). Metacognition and learning disabilities. In B. Y. L. Wong (Ed.), *Learning about learning disabilities* (2nd ed., pp. 277–307). Toronto, Ontario, Canada: Academic Press.

Butler, D. L. (1998b). The strategic content learning approach to promoting self-regulated learning: A report of three studies. *Journal of Educational Psychology, 90*, 682–697. doi:10.1037/0022-0663.90.4.682

Butler, D. L. (2002). Individualizing instruction in self-regulated learning. *Theory Into Practice, 41*, 81–92. doi:10.1207/s15430421tip4102_4

Butler, D. L. (2003). Structuring instruction to promote self-regulated learning by adolescents and adults with learning disabilities. *Exceptionality, 11*(1), 39–60. doi:10.1207/S15327035EX1101_4

Butler, D. L. (2004). Adults with learning disabilities. In B. Y. L. Wong (Ed.), *Learning about learning disabilities* (3rd ed., pp. 565–598). Toronto, Ontario, Canada: Academic Press. doi:10.1016/B978-012762533-1/50020-2

Butler, D. L., Beckingham, B., & Novak Lauscher, H. J. (2005). Promoting strategic learning by eighth-grade students struggling in mathematics: A report of three case studies. *Learning Disabilities Research & Practice, 20*, 156–174. doi:10.1111/j.1540-5826.2005.00130.x

Butler, D. L., & Cartier, S. C. (2004a, May). *Learning in varying activities: An explanatory framework and a new evaluation tool founded on a model of self-regulated learning.* Paper presented at the annual meeting of the Canadian Society for Studies in Education. Winnipeg, Manitoba, Canada.

Butler, D. L., & Cartier, S. C. (2004b). Promoting effective task interpretation as an important work habit: A key to successful teaching and learning. *Teachers College Record, 106*, 1729–1758. doi:10.1111/j.1467-9620.2004.00403.x

Butler, D. L., Cartier, S. C., Schnellert, L., Gagnon, F., & Giammarino, M. (2011). Secondary students' self-regulated engagement in reading: Researching self-regulation as situated in context. *Psychological Test and Assessment Modeling, 53*(1), 73–105.

Butler, D. L., Elaschuk, C. L., & Poole, S. (2000). Promoting strategic writing by postsecondary students with learning disabilities: A report of three case studies. *Learning Disability Quarterly, 23*, 196–213. doi:10.2307/1511164

Butler, D. L., & Schnellert, L. (2008). Bridging the research-to-practice divide: Improving outcomes for students. *Education Canada, 48*(5), 36–40.

Butler, D. L., & Schnellert, L. (2012). Collaborative inquiry in teacher professional development. *Teaching and Teacher Education, 28*, 1206–1220. doi:10.1016/j.tate.2012.07.009

Butler, D. L., Schnellert, L., & Cartier, S. C. (2013). Layers of self- and co-regulation: Teachers' working collaboratively to support adolescents' self-regulated learning through reading. *Education Research International.* Advance online publication. doi:10.1155/2013/845694

Butler, D. L., Schnellert, L., & Perry, N. E. (in press). *Developing self-regulating learners*. Don Mills, Canada: Pearson.

Butler, D. L., & Winne, P. H. (1995). Feedback and self-regulated learning: A theoretical synthesis. *Review of Educational Research, 65*, 245–281. doi:10.3102/00346543065003245

Cartier, S. C. (2007). *Apprendre en lisant au primaire et au secondaire* [Learning through reading in primary and secondary schools]. Anjou, Canada: Éditions CÉC.

Cartier, S. C., & Butler, D. L. (2004, May). *Elaboration and validation of the questionnaires and plan for analysis*. Paper presented at the annual meeting of the Canadian Society for Studies in Education. Winnipeg, Manitoba, Canada.

Cartier, S. C., Butler, D. L., & Bouchard, N. (2010). Teachers working together to foster self-regulated learning through reading by students in an elementary school located in a disadvantaged area. *Psychological Test and Assessment Modeling, 52*, 382–418.

Cleary, T. J., & Platten, P. (2013). Examining the correspondence between self-regulated learning and academic achievement: A case study analysis. *Education Research International*. Advance online publication. doi:10.1155/2013/272560

Cleary, T. J., & Zimmerman, B. J. (2004). Self-regulation empowerment program; A school-based program to enhance self-regulated and self-motivated cycles of student learning. *Psychology in the Schools, 41*, 537–550. doi:10.1002/pits.10177

Corno, L. (1994). Student volition and education: Outcomes, influences, and practices. In D. H. Schunk & B. J. Zimmerman (Eds.), *Self-regulation of learning and performance: Issues and educational applications* (pp. 229–251). Hillsdale, NJ: Erlbaum.

Diaz-Greenberg, R., Thousand, J., Cardelle-Elawar, M., & Nevin, A. (2000). What teachers need to know about the struggle for self-determination (conscientization) and self-regulation: Adults with disabilities speak about their education experiences. *Teaching and Teacher Education, 16*, 873–887. doi:10.1016/S0742-051X(00)00032-9

Dweck, C. S. (2010). Even geniuses work hard. *Educational Leadership, 68*(1), 16–20.

Gerber, P. J. (2001). Learning disabilities: A life span approach. In D. P. Hallahan & B. K. Keogh (Eds.), *Research and global perspectives in learning disabilities* (pp. 167–180). Mahwah, NJ: Erlbaum.

Graham, S., & Harris, K. R. (1989). Components analysis of cognitive strategy instruction: Effects on learning disabled students' compositions and self-efficacy. *Journal of Educational Psychology, 81*, 353–361. doi:10.1037/0022-0663.81.3.353

Harris, K. R., & Graham, S. (1996). *Making the writing process work: Strategies for composition and self-regulation*. Cambridge, MA: Brookline Books.

Hattie, J., & Timperley, H. (2007). The power of feedback. *Review of Educational Research, 77*(1), 81–112. doi:10.3102/003465430298487

Kessler, R. (2000). *The soul of education: Helping students find connection, compassion, and character at school*. Alexandria, VA: ASCD.

Lenz, B. K., Ehren, B., & Deshler, D. D. (2005). The content literacy continuum: A school reform framework for improving adolescent literacy for all students. *Teaching Exceptional Children, 37*(6), 60–63.

MacArthur, C. A., Philippakos, Z., Graham, S., & Harris, K. R. (2012). Writing instruction. In B. Wong & D. L. Butler (Eds.), *Learning about learning disabilities* (4th ed., pp. 243–270). Amsterdam, The Netherlands: Elsevier Academic Press.

Mason, L. H., & Hagaman, J. L. (2012). Highlights in reading comprehension intervention research for students with learning disabilities. In B. Wong & D. L. Butler (Eds.), *Learning about learning disabilities* (4th ed., pp. 191–215). Amsterdam, The Netherlands: Elsevier Academic Press. doi:10.1016/B978-0-12-388409-1.00007-2

Mastropieri, M. A., Scruggs, T. E., Hauth, C., & Allen-Bronaugh, D. (2012). Instructional interventions for students with mathematics learning disabilities. In B. Wong & D. L. Butler (Eds.), *Learning about learning disabilities* (4th ed., pp. 217–241). Amsterdam, The Netherlands: Elsevier Academic Press. doi:10.1016/B978-0-12-388409-1.00008-4

Montague, M. (2008). Self-regulation strategies to improve mathematical problem-solving for students with learning disabilities. *Learning Disability Quarterly, 31*, 37–44.

Murray, C. (2003). Risk factors, protective factors, vulnerability, and resilience: A framework for understanding and supporting the adult transitions of youth with high-incidence disabilities. *Remedial and Special Education, 24*(1), 16–26. doi:10.1177/074193250302400102

Perry, N. E. (1998). Young children's self-regulated learning and contexts that support it. *Journal of Educational Psychology, 90*, 715–729. doi:10.1037/0022-0663.90.4.715

Perry, N. E. (2004). Using self-regulated learning to accommodate differences amongst students in classrooms. *Exceptionality Education Canada, 14*(2&3), 65–87.

Perry, N. E., & Drummond, L. (2002). Helping young students become self-regulated researchers and writers. *Reading Teacher, 56*, 298–310.

Perry, N. E., Nordby, C. J., & VandeKamp, K. O. (2003). Promoting self-regulated reading and writing at home and school. *Elementary School Journal, 103*, 317–338. doi:10.1086/499729

Perry, N. E., Phillips, L., & Dowler, J. (2004). Examining features of tasks and their potential to promote self-regulated learning. *Teachers College Record, 106*, 1854–1878. doi:10.1111/j.1467-9620.2004.00408.x

Reid, R. R., Harris, K. R., Graham, S., & Rock, M. (2012). Self-regulation among students with LD and ADHD. In B. Wong & D. L. Butler (Eds.), *Learning about learning disabilities* (4th ed., pp. 141–173). Amsterdam, The Netherlands: Elsevier Academic Press. doi:10.1016/B978-0-12-388409-1.00005-9

Reschly, D. J., Hosp, J. L., & Schmied, C. M. (2003, August). *And miles to go. . . . State SLD requirements and authoritative recommendations*. Nashville, TN: National Research Center on Learning Disabilities.

Ryan, R. M., & Deci, E. L. (2000). Self-determination theory and the facilitation of intrinsic motivation, social development, and well-being. *American Psychologist, 55,* 68–78. doi:10.1037/0003-066X.55.1.68

Santangelo, T., Harris, K. R., & Graham, S. (2007). Self-regulated strategy development: A validated model to support students who struggle with writing. *Learning Disabilities: A Contemporary Journal, 5*(1), 1–20.

Schnellert, L., Butler, D. L., & Higginson, S. (2008). Co-constructors of data, co-constructors of meaning: Teacher professional development in an age of accountability. *Teaching and Teacher Education, 24,* 725–750. doi:10.1016/j.tate.2007.04.001

Swanson, H. L. (1990). Instruction derived from the strategy deficit model: Overview of principles and procedures. In T. Scruggs & B. Y. L. Wong (Eds.), *Intervention research in learning disabilities* (pp. 34–65). New York, NY: Springer-Verlag. doi:10.1007/978-1-4612-3414-2_2

Winne, P. H., & Hadwin, A. (1998). Studying as self-regulated learning. In D. Hacker, J. Dunlosky, & A. Graesser (Eds.), *Metacognition in educational theory and practice* (pp. 279–306). Hillsdale, NJ: Erlbaum.

Wong, B., & Butler, D. L. (Eds.). (2012). *Learning about learning disabilities* (4th ed.). Amsterdam, The Netherlands: Elsevier Academic Press.

Wong, B. Y. L. (1991). The relevance of metacognition to learning disabilities. In B. Y. L. Wong (Ed.), *Learning about learning disabilities* (pp. 231–258). New York, NY: Academic Press. doi:10.1016/B978-0-12-762530-0.50014-X

Zimmerman, B. J. (2002). Becoming a self-regulated learner: An overview. *Theory Into Practice, 41*(2), 64–70. doi:10.1207/s15430421tip4102_2

Zimmerman, B. J. (2008). Investigating self-regulation and motivation: Historical background, methodological developments, and future prospects. *American Educational Research Journal, 45,* 166–183. doi:10.3102/0002831207312909

Zimmerman, B. J., & Schunk, D. H. (Eds.). (2001). *Self-regulated learning and academic achievement: Theoretical perspectives* (2nd ed.). Hillsdale, NJ: Erlbaum.

5

SUPPORTING SELF-REGULATED READING FOR ENGLISH LANGUAGE LEARNERS IN MIDDLE SCHOOLS

ANA TABOADA BARBER AND MELISSA A. GALLAGHER

The number of children and adolescents in the U.S. educational system who need to learn English represents an emerging and complex educational issue. According to the 2010 United States Census, children who come from homes where English is not the primary language represent 21.8% of the total public school population (National Center for Education Statistics, 2012). Furthermore, population projections in the United States indicate that by 2050, 34% of children either will be immigrants or children of immigrants, compared with 23% in 2005. Furthermore, and specifically in reference to the Hispanic population, a relatively large increase is expected: from 20% in 2005 to 35% in 2050 (Passel & Cohn, 2008). Of particular interest is that, although approximately two thirds of English language learners (ELLs) speak Spanish as their native language (National Center for Education Statistics, 2012), the estimated 60.6 million ELLs in the United States speak more than 381 languages (Ryan, 2013). When ELLs progress through the U.S. educational system, they

---

http://dx.doi.org/10.1037/14641-006
Self-Regulated Learning Interventions With At-Risk Youth: Enhancing Adaptability, Performance, and Well-Being, T. J. Cleary (Editor)
Copyright © 2015 by the American Psychological Association. All rights reserved.

not only have to cope with the same challenges that all students face, such as a greater volume and complexity of assigned coursework and increasing demands for self-sufficiency (see Chapter 11, this volume), they also must overcome important motivation and self-regulation vulnerabilities that can limit their success in schools, particularly on tasks that involve literacy skills (LeClair, Doll, Osborn, & Jones, 2009; Szpara & Ahmad, 2007; Taboada & Rutherford, 2011).

Given that a relatively large percentage of ELLs struggle in school with academic language and comprehending content-area texts (Lesaux, Kieffer, Faller, & Kelley, 2010; Taboada Barber et al., 2014; Taboada & Rutherford, 2011), their efficacy beliefs, or perceptions of confidence to perform specific tasks, tend to be frail and lower than those of English monolinguals (EMs; LeClair et al., 2009; Taboada Barber et al., 2014). When students' self-efficacy declines because of persistent academic difficulties, they are at increased risk of disengaging from learning or providing minimal effort (Bandura, 1997). To complicate matters, ELLs are often unaware of their learning strengths and the areas in which they need help or assistance (Taboada Barber & Buehl, 2013)—a problem for ELLs, given that they often exhibit academic difficulties, particularly on literacy activities. Along the same lines, ELLs tend to lack the metacognitive skills needed to effectively plan, monitor, and self-reflect during reading. Thus, ELLs struggle not only with the academics per se but also with the motivational and regulatory skills that most successful learners exhibit.

In this chapter, through the lens of reading instruction in the content domain of social studies, we discuss the importance of targeting ELLs' motivation and self-regulated learning (SRL) processes. We first provide a detailed overview of the challenges faced by ELLs in schools and then discuss how SRL theoretical principles are intertwined with reading instruction. The key part of our chapter involves using a research-based case scenario to illustrate how a social studies teacher infused SRL instruction into a reading lesson with ELLs. We emphasize how this instruction enhanced students' self-efficacy and enabled them to generate data or feedback about their progress on reading tasks. We also present the instructional challenges that occurred during teacher–student interactions and conclude with suggestions for future research and practice.

ENGLISH LANGUAGE LEARNERS: READING COMPREHENSION ACROSS DISCIPLINES

ELLs are a diverse group of individuals who often vary in their literacy experiences, including their level of exposure to English and their native language, the rate of oral and written English language development, the number of years they have received English instruction, and how much they code-switch or alternate between the two languages in everyday speech. However, as a whole, linguistically diverse students tend to struggle with academics, especially with content-area reading. For instance, on the Nation's Report Card fourth-grade reading assessment, only 31% of ELLs scored at or above the basic level compared with 72% of EMs (U.S. Department of Education, Institute of Education Sciences, National Center for Education Statistics, National Assessment of Educational Progress [NAEP], 2011). In addition, schools and teachers often struggle to identify the best instructional practices for students who face the challenge of learning to read and speak in English while also learning content presented in a language for which they are not always fully proficient. Furthermore, many linguistically diverse students are born in the United States but do not receive English as a Second Language services despite speaking another language at home and not being fully proficient in either their native language or English. Even when ELLs receive language supports, such instruction is not always integrated with the content material needed to succeed academically in middle and high school (August & Hakuta, 1997).

Research has found that by the time they reach early adolescence, U.S.-born children of Spanish-speaking immigrants who were enrolled in U.S. schools since preschool or the primary grades exhibit age-appropriate word reading skills (e.g., decoding, phonics) but significantly weaker vocabulary levels, as based on national norms (e.g., Mancilla-Martinez & Lesaux, 2011). When students' vocabulary is underdeveloped, they often struggle with reading comprehension and writing, which, in turn, can exert a negative effect on their overall academic performance (Lesaux & Marietta, 2012).

As teachers may understand, the language and cognitive difficulties that ELLs face are closely intertwined with their level of motivation to read and learn. Within the general school population, research has shown that as students move from the elementary grades to middle school, their motivation to read (and learn, in general) tends to decrease (Anderman, Maehr, & Midgley, 1999; Jacobs, Lanza, Osgood, Eccles, & Wigfield, 2002; Wigfield, Eccles, Schiefele, Roeser, & Davis-Kean, 2006; see also Chapter 11, this volume). Results from NAEP (2011) revealed that only 18% of eighth-grade students in the United States reported reading for fun on a daily basis; an alarming 33% of eighth graders reported never or hardly ever reading for fun on their own time. Furthermore, with the emergence of the Common Core state standards (National Governors Association Center for Best Practices, Council of Chief State School Officers, 2010), the call for students to engage with a range of complex texts across the disciplines is increasingly pronounced—with a requirement that content teachers support the integration of students' language and literacy skills with content knowledge. Given the challenges of the transitions to middle school and high school, rigorous Common Core state standards expectations, and the enhanced expectations for self-sufficiency that secondary school students encounter, it is clear that ELLs frequently will need to be provided with a multipronged instructional approach that nurtures the academic, motivational, and regulatory skills required for successful literacy development.

THEORETICAL FOUNDATIONS OF SELF-REGULATED LEARNING IN CONTENT LITERACY CLASSES

From a social-cognitive perspective, SRL is typically conceptualized as a multifaceted process in which three interrelated phases—forethought, performance control, and self-reflection—act in a feedback loop (Schmitz & Wiese, 2006; Zimmerman, 2000). In general, forethought phase processes, those that precede efforts to learn, include goal setting, strategic planning, and motivation beliefs. These processes set the stage for learning and affect students' strategic and regulatory processes during learning, such as using a learning or self-control strategy to optimize learning or using self-monitoring tactics to track learning progress or areas of challenge or improvement. Following performance or completion of academic tasks, self-regulated students will use this self-monitored data—and externally provided data, when available—to evaluate their learning progress and make judgments about the causes underlying their growth (or lack thereof). These reflective adjustments are critical because they serve as the basis for how students react to or draw conclusions about how best to approach and strategically engage during future learning. In this chapter, we ground our discussion in Zimmerman's (2000) three-phase cyclical feedback loop and focus on how a series of reading instructional practices support SRL processes in ELLs during a class lesson. Although many instructional practices could be used to support ELLs' self-regulation in reading, we highlight those that we implemented as a part of our intervention research (described later). We discuss these practices in depth and also outline them in Figure 5.1 as a quick reference.

To promote adaptive forethought phase processes in ELLs, teachers should encourage goal-setting activities for learning how to use reading strategies and for content learning. To facilitate students' actual use of reading strategies during the performance phase, teachers can model and guide students' use of these strategies, such as comprehension monitoring, and teach students to self-observe and self-record their thought processes related to reading. Teachers can promote effective self-reflective thinking by providing students with opportunities to evaluate whether their reading skills are improving and by assessing the causes of their successes or failures during reading (i.e., attributions). In this way, the three phases of SRL are naturally

1. Forethought Phase
- Establish a purpose for content and comprehension strategies to create a goal orientation.
- Post and refer to essential questions to set goals for long-term learning.
- Use engaging materials (i.e., trade books) to promote intrinsic interest.
- Provide specific feedback to foster students' self-efficacy.
- Allow students to select a comprehension strategy according to reading goals.

3. Self-Reflection Phase
- Tie the lesson back to the essential questions so students can self-evaluate their learning.
- Reinforce students' success with specific feedback so students are aware of areas of strength and weakness.
- Allow students to share comprehension strategies they used and reflect on their success.

Teacher Practices to Support Self-Regulated Learning in Literacy

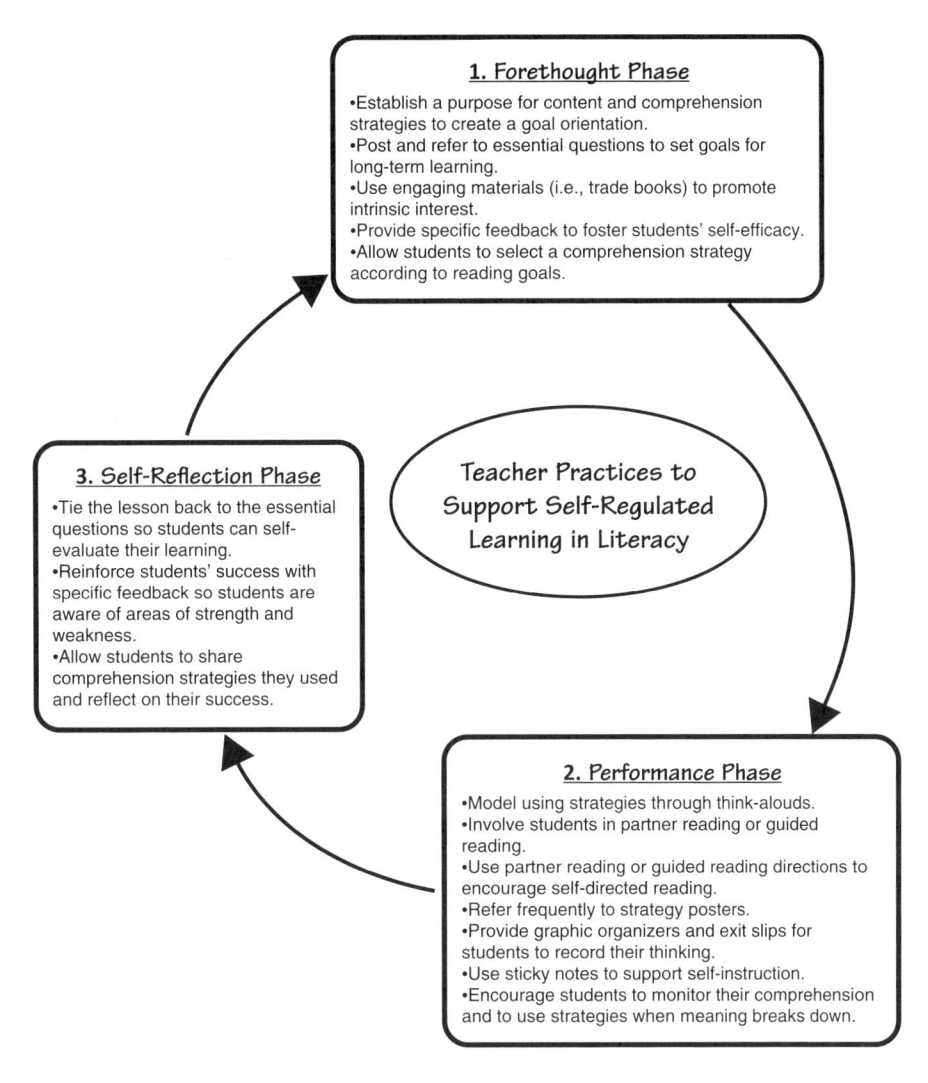

2. Performance Phase
- Model using strategies through think-alouds.
- Involve students in partner reading or guided reading.
- Use partner reading or guided reading directions to encourage self-directed reading.
- Refer frequently to strategy posters.
- Provide graphic organizers and exit slips for students to record their thinking.
- Use sticky notes to support self-instruction.
- Encourage students to monitor their comprehension and to use strategies when meaning breaks down.

Figure 5.1. Teacher practices to support self-regulated learning in literacy.

integrated with the specific components of the reading comprehension process, whereby students set goals for reading, use strategies and read to understand, and assess their understanding.

Although research on SRL with ELLs currently is limited, given that relational and self-regulatory aspects of classroom environments have been shown to affect the achievement of non-ELL students (Doll, LeClair, & Kurien, 2009), it is likely that these instructional characteristics will also have an effect on ELLs' success. For example, empirical evidence exists that supportive learning environments can "close the gap" between low- and high-socioeconomic status students (Hamre & Pianta, 2005). Given that a large number of ELLs come from low-socioeconomic status backgrounds, we postulate that social and motivational variables within classroom contexts will affect not only these students' academic achievement but also their self-regulatory processes (e.g., Taboada Barber & Buehl, 2013). Furthermore, our own research (e.g., Taboada Barber et al., 2014) has consistently shown that ELLs have lower self-efficacy for literacy tasks than their EM counterparts, and when practices to increase ELLs' self-efficacy for reading are instilled as part of classroom routines, their reading self-efficacy shows marked improvements (e.g., Taboada Barber & Buehl, 2013; Taboada Barber et al., 2014). Therefore, it can be expected that the ineffective strategic approaches that many ELLs exhibit during reading can be remediated if we, as teachers, are aware of the importance of SRL in students' learning and can create classroom contexts that foster these processes.

Research has shown that as students leave the elementary grades, they encounter a more rigorous academic context in middle and high school, a context that includes being taught by several teachers and having to read in a comprehensive manner (i.e., thoroughly and deeply) large amounts of information across subjects. As self-regulation researchers have pointed out, these contextual changes, along with the cognitive and emotional changes brought by adolescence, require that students use several self-regulatory skills, such as self-monitoring and strategic planning, to successfully navigate these challenging transitions (Butler, 2005; Chavous et al., 2003; Eccles & Wigfield, 2002; Zito, Adkins, Gavins, Harris, & Graham, 2007; see also Chapter 11, this volume).

Furthermore, as described in many chapters in this book, self-efficacy is a key component of SRL. *Self-efficacy* refers to individuals' judgments of their capabilities to perform specific tasks in specific situations (Bandura, 1986; Pajares, 1996). Students are more likely to persist during activities when they believe they will be able to succeed at them. Self-efficacy beliefs are a powerful predictor of achievement and of measures of cognitive ability (Pajares & Kranzler, 1995). Because self-efficacy beliefs require some consideration of the skills one possesses, ability and efficacy judgments are usually highly correlated. Teachers can influence students' self-efficacy by attending to how they shape students' beliefs and the experiences those teachers provide in the classroom. Even students who doubt their capabilities within a given academic area or domain can improve their confidence when taught the requisite skills to succeed and ultimately improve their performance. Schunk and Miller (2002) listed several practices that teachers might use to enhance students' self-efficacy beliefs: helping students set proximal goals, rather than long-term goals; teaching students when and how to use specific cognitive strategies; giving opportunities to witness models completing the same or similar tasks (i.e., similar models); and offering students feedback about their performance that focuses on their use of specific strategies. We illustrate some of these practices in our review of a case scenario in the next section.

RESEARCH-BASED APPLICATIONS OF SRL INTERVENTIONS IN CONTENT CLASSROOMS

In this section, we present a research-based case scenario of how SRL principles can be infused during content-area class activities and can target specific academic skills, such as reading comprehension. Given that few studies have examined SRL in content-area classes with ELLs, this case scenario can serve as a framework for exploring additional SRL research with ELLs in the domains of history and literacy. This case scenario was derived from a multiyear intervention project called United States History for Engaged Reading (USHER) that was designed to increase the reading comprehension skills and motivation for reading history among ELLs and EM students. Broadly speaking, the study included sixth- and seventh-grade social studies and language arts teachers and their students of whom 65% were ELLs; 90% of the ELLs were of Hispanic origin. USHER focused on building middle-school students' nonfiction reading comprehension by explicitly teaching reading strategies,[1] such as using text features to activate background knowledge, monitoring comprehension, identifying main ideas, and asking text-based questions. Comprehension strategies were taught using the gradual release of the responsibility model widely used in comprehension instruction (e.g., Pearson & Gallagher, 1983), whereby teachers first model a strategy, then guide students in using it, and then provide supports for students' independent use of the strategy. USHER lessons were designed so that students learned to use reading strategies as they read about U.S. history. In this way, students came to see that comprehension strategies were tools for learning about history through reading. Students became increasingly engaged in reading American history because teachers fostered their self-efficacy for several strategies, helped students make connections between specific content and their lives, promoted the relevance and value of history topics, and supported collaboration among students for literacy activities. Previous investigations have shown that these practices were successful in increasing ELLs' and EMs' reading comprehension, strategy use, and self-efficacy for reading from pre- to post-USHER intervention (Taboada Barber et al., 2014; Taboada Barber, Richey, & Buehl, 2013).

---

[1] For the purposes of reading instruction, we have used *reading strategies* or *cognitive strategies* instead of *task strategies*, which is prevalent in much of the literature on SRL, because these strategies are cognitive tools that enable readers to become self-regulated. In addition, we have used the terms *cognitive strategies*, *reading strategies*, and *comprehension strategies* interchangeably because they are equally present in the literacy literature.

We chose to focus on one Grade 6 teacher in this project, Ms. Greene, because she had consistently supported her students' self-efficacy and other aspects of SRL for reading throughout USHER. This case scenario represents a snapshot of her teaching by portraying SRL practices within one lesson. As part of Ms. Greene's participation during the final 2 years of the USHER project, she attended five professional development sessions in which she learned how to infuse cognitive strategies and motivation practices with American history content. We discuss how Ms. Greene used various instructional practices (see Figure 5.1) to enhance students' comprehension and to support the three phases of SRL within one 60-minute lesson.

Forethought: Supporting Students Through Structured Teaching

In years preceding the USHER project, Ms. Greene taught language arts and history in two separate blocks daily. However, during the project year, she integrated both content areas as part of USHER. Ms. Greene started a unit on colonization by posting a few open-ended content questions for the unit: Why did Europeans establish colonies in North America? How did people use the natural resources of their region to earn a living? and, What were the interactions between the natives and the explorers like? Given that teaching students reading comprehension strategies was a key goal of this project, specialized posters that focused on comprehension strategies, such as "Using Text Features to Support My Reading," "Monitoring My Comprehension," and "Identifying Main Idea & Supporting Details," were hung around the room. The lesson we portray here took place midway through the 10-day unit, and, thus, students had previously learned how to use text features to activate their prior knowledge on a new topic. During this lesson, Ms. Greene placed primary emphasis on teaching students to use and apply comprehension monitoring strategies during reading—a key data-based aspect of the SRL cyclical feedback model.

Throughout the lesson, Ms. Greene paid particular attention to the needs, motivation, and regulatory processes of Juan, Andrea, and Ahmad, three ELLs who had joined her class during the month before the lesson. These students came from a different district, where they had received services for English for speakers of other languages (ESOL) until fourth grade. They received these services in a self-contained ESOL class that did not integrate content knowledge and language as a daily practice. Although Ms. Greene had not yet had a chance to formally assess these three students, she noticed that they exhibited below-average reading skills based on standardized reading assessments from Grade 5, but all three communicated fluently in English. Juan and Andrea appeared eager to learn, and although history seemed not to be their favorite subject, they enjoyed the trade books offered as part of USHER. Ahmad, on the other hand, seemed reluctant to read and participate unless Ms. Greene prompted him and engaged him one-on-one. She had also noticed that although he could decode most words, he struggled with answering follow-up questions about the text.

Before beginning the lesson, Ms. Greene set up her classroom to facilitate the students' capacity to effectively regulate their reading-related behaviors. She hung the essential questions and strategy posters around the room as visual reminders of students' goals and strategic plans. She wrote the essential questions, that is, those that students aimed to answer throughout the unit, on the board. These questions served as specific learning goals set by the teacher. The strategy posters were designed to provide a visual reminder to students regarding the different strategies they had been previously taught and had practiced. From a regulatory perspective, students who possess strong knowledge and a repertoire of strategies often find it easier to engage in forethought or planning because they have several strategic options from which to choose when deciding how best to approach a task. Ms. Greene also placed on the students' desks baskets of books they would need; this represented her attempt to structure the physical environment and to facilitate students' self-control of their own learning. If students have direct access to the resources they need, and, when possible, have some choices among those resources, their sense of control over their learning is increased. In addition, using trade books that present information in more detail and with more graphical and pictorial information than textbooks can foster students' intrinsic motivation to read history texts. By having the essential questions, strategy posters, and trade books at the ready, Ms. Greene created an environment that would enhance student motivation, strategic learning, and success.

Once students were seated in their small groups, they pulled from their baskets the class set of trade books titled *Jamestown and the Virginia Colony* by Daniel Rosen (Rosen, 2004). Ms. Greene introduced the comprehension monitoring strategy as she began the lesson:

> Sometimes when we read, we don't understand everything or we get distracted. Sometimes when I'm reading, I get to the bottom of the page and realize that I spent so much time sounding out the words that I didn't pay attention to what they meant. This is something that happens to many readers, but good readers monitor, or watch, their thinking to be sure they understand what they read. The purpose of reading, especially in history, is to learn new things, and we need to monitor our reading to make sure we are doing just that.

In this way Ms. Greene set the goal for reading expository texts (i.e., to learn from text and gain information) and indicated that to meet the goal, students need a tool or a strategy to help them build knowledge from text.

One important component of the forethought phase is goal-setting (Cleary & Zimmerman, 2012; Zimmerman & Campillo, 2003). In content-area literacy classrooms, the reading and content goals that the teacher sets for the students or that students themselves choose become the purposes of the lesson. Ms. Greene started her lesson by sharing with her students the purpose for comprehension monitoring and for learning content on American Indian tribes. All students were told from the onset of the lesson that they were reading to learn about a specific topic (i.e., goal) and that they were going to be using a concrete strategy to help them dig deeply into the text (i.e., strategic plan). The inclusion of forethought-phase instructional elements was designed to be useful for all students, and ELLs in particular. Because ELL students frequently struggle with understanding content texts and comprehending the academic language in these texts, they can benefit from the explicitness in regulatory language that they can then practice using during the learning activities. Broadly speaking, we believe that teachers can help ELLs become more goal directed in reading, as Ms. Greene did, by explicitly stating content and reading goals at the beginning of the lesson, posting the essential questions, and reflecting on these goals when concluding.

Establishing goals and a strategic plan, however, is not enough to engage students during the reading process; they need to be motivated to accomplish those goals and enact the plans. Self-efficacy and intrinsic interest are two self-motivational beliefs that affect students' desire to learn (e.g., Zimmerman & Campillo, 2003). One way to foster self-efficacy is to provide examples of role models who persevere through tasks (Schunk & Zimmerman, 2007). In this vein, Ms. Greene contributed to building students' self-efficacy by letting them know that even proficient readers like her get distracted when reading, but they often are able to refocus on the text by using specific strategies or tools, such as comprehension monitoring. When all students, particularly ELLs, come to realize that even teachers or mastery learners struggle at times to understand the meaning of a text passage, the stress and pressure involved in comprehending on their first reading attempt are often lessened. Simultaneously, this type of modeling helps to foster the idea that comprehension struggles are a natural part of the reading process but can be improved by using specific strategies. Another way that teachers can build students' self-efficacy is to provide specific feedback that describes or identifies what the child did successfully or not. Ms. Greene provided feedback that informed students about how their specific actions helped or hindered their progress. This information helped students become more aware of desirable and effective actions versus those they should discontinue. Again, this teaching practice is especially important for ELLs, who are less likely to know what they need to do to be successful in reading.

In her lesson, Ms. Greene used many of the instructional practices that are identified for helping students to become successful self-regulators during the forethought phase. She helped them identify the goals and the strategies they would use to accomplish those goals, and she helped them develop self-efficacy by modeling perseverance (e.g., showing how she struggled with decoding multi-syllabic words and using fix-up strategies to decode them effectively). Ms. Greene also facilitated her students' transformation of forethought processes into strategic actions as students shifted into the performance, or learning, phase of self-regulation.

Performance: Enhancing Strategic Practice and Self-Awareness

During the same lesson, Ms. Greene proceeded to read aloud and model her thinking while reading. *Think-alouds* are an effective strategy to demonstrate to students one's use of strategies such as comprehension monitoring, and how such strategies facilitate understanding (Bereiter & Bird, 1985; Collins & Smith, 1982; Kucan & Beck, 1997). Ms. Greene asked her students to place sticky notes in their books to indicate when they noticed her struggling and what she did to help her own understanding. During the think-aloud demonstration, Ms. Greene stopped to ask one of her ELL reluctant readers, Ahmad, why the Native Americans did not think the English settlers were friendly. He was silent for a few moments, and then reread the text and said, "It says things were not easy—they were uneasy between the settlers and Indians . . . so the English and the Indians did not seem to get along." Ms. Greene probed by asking what evidence in the text supported the tense relations between the English settlers and the Indians. In this way, she ensured that Ahmad was using text information to generate his answer, rather than his own opinion on the subject—a way to reinforce the importance of distinguishing text-supported information versus one's opinions on a topic. Ms. Greene also responded to Ahmad's response: "I like that thinking. Are you saying that the English were the settlers, then?" Ahmad nodded. Ms. Greene emphasized, "I like how you are making that connection when you read. Please write down on your sticky note what you did to make that connection." Ms. Greene continued to model reading strategies (for this and subsequent lessons) through a think-aloud technique using these steps:

- Ask yourself: Does this make sense?
- Go back and reread sentences or short paragraphs.
- Use context clues (e.g., pictures) and the glossary to help understand difficult words.
- Visualize in your mind a picture of what you read.
- Connect new information to what you already know.

- Connect new information to previous text sections.
- Replace words within a sentence with others that you think fit.
- When stuck on a sentence, refer to content in previous sentences.

After discussing the content of the pages that she read with her students, Ms. Greene often reminded them about the importance of using such strategies to enhance their understanding. During this particular lesson, she said, "So, I used different tools to make sure I was monitoring what I was reading. What tools did you see me using?"

"I saw you reread," Juan volunteered from the back.

"I went back and I reread," Ms. Greene agreed.

"You asked questions to make sure you knew what you were reading," volunteered Juan.

"That's right," Ms. Greene encouraged, as she wrote these strategies on the board.

"You thought hard," Andrea offered.

Ms. Greene responded, "How do you know that? Think of exactly what you saw me doing."

Andrea continued, "You stopped between sentences and made connections between them."

"Good thinking. Let me write that down," Ms. Greene replied.

"You used the glossary or reread the sentence; you used context clues," Andrea continued.

"That's right," answered Ms. Greene. "I used some of the other words around the word I did not know if I was stuck with a sentence. If I had not been monitoring, then I would not have been paying attention that closely and I would have read faster." Ms. Greene continued to explain, "Sometimes, when the topic is new, or when the text is difficult, and I am reading it for the first time, I want to make sure I am closely checking my understanding. This is what we call *comprehension monitoring*. And these are some of the strategies that we use when we monitor our comprehension."

Following this exchange with the students, Ms. Greene pointed to the list of strategies on the board and gave her students a strategy checklist (see Figure 5.2) so they could check off strategies as they monitored their understanding of the next page of *Jamestown and the Virginia Colony* (Rosen, 2004) during partner reading. Using a strategy checklist promotes SRL because it provides information that students can use to make judgments about their learning specifically in terms of the effectiveness of the strategies that they are being taught to use. This self-recording tactic provides data or information that immerses students in the reflective regulatory process.

Ms. Greene helped engage students in the performance phase of SRL by using a host of effective intervention tactics and techniques, such as teaching

> **Comprehension Monitoring Checklist**
>
> As you read, place a check by the strategy you used. You can check off a strategy more than once. Remember, you don't have to use all the strategies every time you read!
>
> ____I used text features to activate my background knowledge.
>
> ____I stopped and asked, "Does this make sense?"
>
> ____I asked, "Where did I lose track?"
>
> ____I reread.
>
> ____I visualized (made a picture in my mind).
>
> ____I connected what I read to what I have previously read.
>
> ____I connected what I read to my own life.
>
> ____I asked myself questions about what I read.
>
> ____I asked questions or wondered about the ideas in the book.
>
> ____I used context clues or the glossary to help figure out a word that I didn't understand.
>
> ____I explained what I read to myself or to someone else.

Figure 5.2. A representation of a checklist of comprehension strategies students can use during independent or guided reading to track their strategy use.

cognitive strategies and giving feedback about their use, creating an environment that minimized distractions and focused students' attention on the relevant task features, and helping students to become more mindful of strategies that are linked to successful learning. Ms. Greene helped build her students' repertoire of cognitive strategies by modeling comprehension monitoring during reading. By breaking comprehension monitoring down into its component parts—rereading, asking questions, making connections—Ms. Greene helped her students understand step-by-step what they needed to do to track their understanding when reading text. In addition to explicitly modeling comprehension monitoring, she helped students focus on the task by asking them to use sticky notes to track the strategies she was using. Modeling is important to building both self-efficacy and self-regulation skills, and students who are observing the model need to attend to the sequence of events being modeled (Schunk & Zimmerman, 2007). At the close of the think-aloud, Ms. Greene reviewed the strategies students had recorded on their sticky notes. Because

Ms. Greene acted as a coping model (i.e., displayed some mistakes which she fixed by using strategies), the students were exposed to key regulatory principles, such as the importance of being flexible when using different types of strategies to guide their own comprehension during independent reading.

Another way to help students maintain self-control of their reading is by creating an environment that helps them focus their attention (e.g., Zimmerman & Campillo, 2003). One approach content literacy teachers can take is to have students read in partners or small groups, the activity Ms. Greene transitioned into at the end of her lesson. Working in small groups can help students regulate each other's reading to focus on their goal. In addition, the checklist of comprehension monitoring strategies provides increased feedback to students and can foster their ability to focus on specific components or aspects of the reading tasks. Self-observation involves tracking one's own performance and its effects (Zimmerman & Campillo, 2003). Students' observations of their own performance are directly influenced by the specific feedback they receive.

In addition to having students self-generate their own process or strategic data, Ms. Greene provided data that further fostered their engagement in a data-based cyclical process of thinking and action. For example, she provided process feedback to Ahmad by pointing out how he had appropriately connected information from the text to support his statements: "I can see that you made a connection when you read and that helped you support what you said." Specific feedback, particularly when it focuses on processes or strategy use, provides students with explicit information about what they are doing successfully or what they need to change. These data are of value for sustaining cyclical regulatory ways of thinking and acting because they assist students in evaluating their learning progress and in making decisions about how best to improve their strategic approach to learning (see the section Self-Reflection: Encouraging Students to Evaluate Their Performance in this chapter). ELLs, such as Ahmad, benefit when teachers scaffold their strategy use (e.g., suggest that a student go back to the text when prompted to justify an answer with text information) and provide frequent, consistent feedback (e.g., specifically naming how a student came to the correct answer), in part because students often are often unaware of their strengths, weaknesses, and what they need to do differently to improve. Furthermore, praise for a specific behavior supports students in accurately remembering which strategies help them to be successful. Timely constructive feedback helps students take corrective action. It is important that teachers provide specific feedback so students will understand what they are doing correctly or incorrectly and recognize when to repeat or modify their use of that strategy in the future.

During the performance phase of instruction, Ms. Greene set up her students to be successful in reading and history by modeling and breaking down cognitive strategies, helping students to improve their concentration, creating opportunities for them to self-record their thinking and strategy use, and providing timely and specific feedback to help students track and observe their own performance. By implementing these SRL-infused instructional practices, she helped students have a successful experience and attribute that success, or any failure, to the strategies they were using and not to their own abilities as they self-reflected in the third phase of self-regulation.

Self-Reflection: Encouraging Students to Evaluate Their Performance

Engaging in accurate and adaptive self-reflection phase processes is a core aspect of SRL and is directly influenced by one's strategic engagement and monitoring during the performance phase. The latter components of Ms. Greene's lesson comprised *partner reading*, a procedure in which students independently read a section of the text, reread it aloud to each other, and used the monitoring checklist to track their use of a strategy, and discussed that use with their partners. Following partner reading, the lesson concluded with a whole-class activity in which students shared the strategies they used and Ms. Greene tied those strategies to the essential questions. Throughout these activities, Ms. Greene supported students' self-judgment and self-reactions by providing specific feedback and encouraging students to share and reflect on their success with the strategies they used.

Specific feedback is an important practice for informing students' self-regulation during all three phases. Feedback influences students' initial motivation to engage in the learning activity during the forethought phase, the way they self-observe during the performance phase, and the way they make judgments about the causes of their success or failure and how they need to adapt during the self-reflection phase. In terms of self-reflective phase attribution judgments, when students attribute errors to their own ability, something they often believe that they cannot change, they typically display negative affective and behavioral reactions, such as frustration or anxiety, and perhaps may choose to not put forth effort in the future. However, when students attribute errors to ineffective strategy use, they often are more willing to persevere and try a new strategy because they believe that learning is under their control (e.g., Schunk & Zimmerman, 2007; Zimmerman & Campillo, 2003). During partner reading, Ms. Greene circulated among her students and provided feedback that helped to guide their reflective thinking toward emphasizing strategy use rather than their own abilities. For instance, at one point, she approached Andrea and Juan as Andrea was reading. Andrea said, "It says, 'to the Powhatan they were invaders.' But I don't know what 'invaders' means!" Ms. Greene asked Andrea which strategy she had used to determine the meaning of the word. Andrea replied that she had tried using context clues but had been unable to determine the meaning. Ms. Greene further facilitated Andrea's adaptive thinking by prompting:

> Good for you for trying that strategy. That's a good place to start when you don't know a word, but often there aren't enough clues in the context to figure out a word's meaning. What's another strategy you can use to figure it out?

Her response was particularly effective because it not only helped Andrea assess the quality of the strategy she had used during reading but facilitated her to make strategic attributions and to consider how to potentially use alternative reading strategies in the future. Helping students with their attributions is an important dimension of providing useful feedback and the overall self-regulatory process (Zimmerman & Campillo, 2003).

Ms. Greene also helped students engage in adaptive self-reflection by having them share the different ways they monitored their comprehension as they read and the answers they found to the essential questions. Having students share their use of strategies helped them compare their strategy use with the goals set at the beginning of the lesson: the essential questions and purpose for reading. This reflection-oriented activity helped students come full circle in that they came to understand that the reasons for comprehension monitoring discussed early in the lesson made sense; the use of comprehension monitoring helped them answer the essential questions, thereby meeting the goals set forth at the beginning of the lesson by Ms. Greene. After students shared their successes and difficulties, Ms. Greene reiterated that using comprehension monitoring strategies had helped them better understand the historical content and find answers to the essential questions. Tying success with the history content questions (one of the purposes of the lesson) to the use of strategy is advisable because it can also help students positively self-evaluate their performance. Not only do these reflection activities feed back into the forethought phase by increasing students' self-efficacy for strategy use, they also can help students make more adaptive inferences in the future (i.e., choose a more effective strategy), rather than become discouraged and react with task avoidance or other defensive self-reactions.

FUTURE DIRECTIONS AND CONCLUSIONS

Abundant empirical research has documented the struggles that ELLs have with academic language; literacy, in general; and reading comprehension, in particular. However, the motivational processes that affect these children often do not receive the same attention or are somewhat neglected in the empirical literature. SRL is a cyclical process in which personal, behavioral, and environmental factors typically change during learning and must be monitored (Schunk, Meece, & Pintrich, 2014). Several self-regulatory processes come into play in the three phases (Cleary & Zimmerman, 2012; Zimmerman, 2000) and, therefore, learners go into learning situations with different goals and varying levels of self-efficacy for attaining those goals (Schunk et al., 2014). Struggling readers, particularly ELLs, who frequently are failing academically, approach literacy with fluctuating but generally low levels of self-efficacy, impoverished learning strategy repertoires, and vocabulary knowledge below grade level; such factors directly affect their reading development and achievement. The challenges encountered by ELLs are compounded by their likely negative self-evaluations of performance (e.g., perception that one is not reaching goals or making progress) and corresponding maladaptive attributions to ability rather than to effort following failure experiences. When students become immersed in these negative cycles of regulatory thinking, their subsequent goal setting and the motivation to attain their goals are also adversely affected.

Given ELLs' suspected SRL deficits, their self-regulating skills need to be fostered through environmental affordances. That is, these students need to be helped not only in their cognitive and language development, as espoused in the broader literature, but also in regulating their achievement-related beliefs, behaviors, and affect—including self-evaluations of their capabilities and progress in strategy acquisition. In this chapter, we aimed to present a few instructional strategies and affordances that can help strengthen these children's regulatory processes within each of the three cyclical phases: forethought, performance, and self-reflection. We did so from the angle of literacy instruction in the content area of history, one that presents particular linguistic and contextual challenges for ELLs.

Future research should consider ways in which the SRL of ELLs can be most effectively studied. For instance, each of the SRL phases could be the focus of instructional interventions. Examining in greater depth each of these subprocesses and the components that we delved into in our case scenario can be useful in determining which aspects of the regulatory feedback loop are most problematic for ELLs. Alternatively, one can approach the study of SRL in ELLs by examining different reading strategies in relation to SRL components, such as looking at how the SRL process plays out in relation to comprehension strategies, including student-led questioning and graphic organizing and summarizing. Such an approach could provide teachers and students with a clear rationale for the use of each strategy and an understanding of the steps involved in their use that expands the cognitive benefits of comprehension strategies to their motivational ones. We believe that if teachers become increasingly aware of how classroom factors and modes of instruction affect the self-regulation cycle, they can more effectively influence children's achievement-related cognitions, behaviors, and motivation to read and learn.

REFERENCES

Anderman, E. M., Maehr, M. L., & Midgley, C. (1999). Declining motivation after the transition to middle school: Schools can make a difference. *Journal of Research & Development in Education, 32,* 131–147.

August, D., & Hakuta, K. (Eds.). (1997). *Improving schooling for language-minority children: A research agenda.* Washington, DC: National Academy Press.

Bandura, A. (1986). *Social foundations of thought and action: Social cognitive theory.* Upper Saddle River, NJ: Prentice Hall.

Bandura, A. (1997). *Self-efficacy: The exercise of control.* New York, NY: Freeman.

Bereiter, C., & Bird, M. (1985). Use of thinking aloud in identification and teaching of reading comprehension strategies. *Cognition and Instruction, 2,* 131–156. doi:10.1207/s1532690xci0202_2

Butler, R. (2005). Competence assessment, competence, and motivation between early and middle childhood. In A. J. Elliot & C. S. Dweck (Eds.), *Handbook of competence and motivation* (pp. 202–221). New York, NY: Guilford.

Chavous, T. M., Bernat, D. H., Schmeelk-Cone, K., Caldwell, C. H., Kohn-Wood, L., & Zimmerman, M. A. (2003). Racial identity and academic attainment among African American adolescents. *Child Development, 74,* 1076–1090. doi:10.1111/1467-8624.00593

Cleary, T. J., & Zimmerman, B. J. (2012). A cyclical self-regulatory account of student engagement: Theoretical foundations and applications. In S. L. Christenson & A. L. Reschley (Eds.), *Handbook of research on student engagement* (pp. 237–257). New York, NY: Sprinter Science + Business Media. doi:10.1007/978-1-4614-2018-7_11

Collins, A., & Smith, E. E. (1982). Teaching the process of reading comprehension. In D. K. Detterman & R. J. Sternberg (Eds.), *How and how much can intelligence be increased* (pp. 173–185). Norwood, NJ: Ablex.

Doll, B., LeClair, C., & Kurien, S. (2009). Effective classrooms: Classroom learning environments that foster school success. In T. B. Gutkin & C. R. Reynolds (Eds.), *The handbook of school psychology* (pp. 791–807). Hoboken, NJ: Wiley.

Eccles, J. S., & Wigfield, A. (2002). Motivational beliefs, values, and goals. *Annual Review of Psychology, 53,* 109–132. doi:10.1146/annurev.psych.53.100901.135153

Hamre, B. K., & Pianta, R. C. (2005). Can instructional and emotional support in the first-grade classroom make a difference for children at risk of school failure? *Child Development, 76,* 949–967. doi:10.1111/j.1467-8624.2005.00889.x

Jacobs, J. E., Lanza, S., Osgood, D. W., Eccles, J. S., & Wigfield, A. (2002). Changes in children's self-competence and values: Gender and domain differences across grades one through twelve. *Child Development, 73,* 509–527. doi:10.1111/1467-8624.00421

Kucan, L., & Beck, I. L. (1997). Thinking aloud and reading comprehension research: Inquiry, instruction, and social interaction. *Review of Educational Research, 67,* 271–299. doi:10.3102/00346543067003271

LeClair, C., Doll, B., Osborn, A., & Jones, K. (2009). English language learners' and non-English language learners' perceptions of the classroom environment. *Psychology in the Schools, 46,* 568–577. doi:10.1002/pits.20398

Lesaux, N. K., Kieffer, M. J., Faller, S. E., & Kelley, J. G. (2010). The effectiveness and ease of implementation of an academic vocabulary intervention for linguistically diverse students in urban middle schools. *Reading Research Quarterly, 45*(2), 196–228. doi:10.1598/RRQ.45.2.3

Lesaux, N. K., & Marietta, S. H. (2012). *Making assessments matter: Using test results to differentiate reading instruction.* New York, NY: Guilford Press.

Mancilla-Martinez, J., & Lesaux, N. K. (2011). The gap between Spanish speakers' word reading and word knowledge: A longitudinal study. *Child Development, 82,* 1544–1560. doi:10.1111/j.1467-8624.2011.01633.x

National Center for Education Statistics. (2012, August). Number and percentage of children ages 5–17 who spoke a language other than English at home and who spoke English with difficulty, by sex, race/ethnicity, and nativity: 2010 [Table E-4-1]. Retrieved from http://nces.ed.gov/pubs2012/2012046/tables/e-4-1.asp

National Governors Association Center for Best Practices, Council of Chief State School Officers. (2010). *Common Core state standards for English language arts and literacy in history/social studies, science, and technical subjects.* Washington, DC: National Governors Association Center for Best Practices and the Council of Chief State School Officers. Retrieved from http://www.corestandards.org/

Pajares, F. (1996). Self-efficacy beliefs in academic settings. *Review of Educational Research, 66,* 543–578. doi:10.3102/00346543066004543

Pajares, F., & Kranzler, J. (1995). Self-efficacy beliefs and general mental ability in mathematical problem-solving. *Contemporary Educational Psychology, 20,* 426–443. doi:10.1006/ceps.1995.1029

Passel, J. S., & Cohn, D. (2008). *Population projections: 2005–2050.* Washington, DC: Pew Hispanic Center. Retrieved from http://pewhispanic.org/files/reports/85.pdf

Pearson, P. D., & Gallagher, M. C. (1983). The instruction of reading comprehension. *Contemporary Educational Psychology, 8,* 317–344. doi:10.1016/0361-476X(83)90019-X

Rosen, D. (2004). *Jamestown and the Virginia colony.* Washington, DC: National Geographic Society.

Ryan, C. (2013). *Language use in the United States: 2011*. Washington, DC: U.S. Census Bureau. Retrieved from http://www.census.gov/prod/2013pubs/acs-22.pdf

Schmitz, B., & Wiese, B. S. (2006). New perspectives for the evaluation of training sessions in self-regulated learning: Time-series analyses of diary data. *Contemporary Educational Psychology, 31*(1), 64–96. doi:10.1016/j.cedpsych.2005.02.002

Schunk, D. H., Meece, J. L., & Pintrich, P. R. (2014). *Motivation in education: Theory, research, and applications* (4th ed.). Upper Saddle River, NJ: Pearson Education.

Schunk, D. H., & Miller, S. D. (2002). Self-efficacy and adolescents' motivation. In F. Pajares & T. Urdan (Eds.), *Academic motivation of adolescents* (pp. 1–28). Greenwich, CT: Information Age.

Schunk, D. H., & Zimmerman, B. J. (2007). Influencing children's self-efficacy and self-regulation of reading and writing through modeling. *Reading & Writing Quarterly: Overcoming Learning Difficulties, 23*(1), 7–25. doi:10.1080/10573560600837578

Szpara, M. Y., & Ahmad, I. (2007). Supporting English-language learners in a social studies class: Results from a study of high school teachers. *Social Studies, 98*, 189–196. doi:10.3200/TSSS.98.5.189-196

Taboada, A., & Rutherford, V. (2011). Developing reading comprehension and academic vocabulary for English language learners through science content: A formative experiment. *Reading Psychology, 32*, 113–157. doi:10.1080/02702711003604468

Taboada Barber, A., & Buehl, M. M. (2013). Relations among Grade 4 students' perceptions of autonomy, engagement in science, and reading motivation. *Journal of Experimental Education, 81*(1), 22–43. doi:10.1080/00220973.2011.630045

Taboada Barber, A., Buehl, M. M., Kidd, J. K., Sturtevant, E., Richey, L. N., & Beck, J. (2014). Reading engagement in social studies: Exploring the role of a social studies literacy intervention on reading comprehension, reading self-efficacy, and engagement in middle school students with different language backgrounds. *Reading Psychology, 36*(1), 31–85. doi:10.1080/02702711.2013.815140

Taboada Barber, A., Richey, L. N., & Buehl, M. M. (2013). Promoting comprehension and motivation to read in the middle school social studies classroom: Examples from a research-based curriculum. In R. T. Boon & V. Spencer (Eds.), *Adolescent literacy: Strategies for content comprehension in inclusive classrooms* (pp. 13–28). Baltimore, MD: Brookes.

U.S. Department of Education, Institute of Education Sciences, National Center for Education Statistics, National Assessment of Educational Progress. (2011). *National data explorer*. [Data file]. Retrieved from http://www.nationsreportcard.gov/reading_math_2013/#/

Wigfield, A., Eccles, J. S., Schiefele, U., Roeser, R. W., & Davis-Kean, P. (2006). Development of achievement motivation. In N. Eisenberg, W. Damon, & R. M. Lerner (Eds.), *Handbook of child psychology: Vol. 3, Social, emotional, and personality development* (6th ed., pp. 933–1002). New York, NY: Wiley.

Zimmerman, B. J. (2000). Attaining self-regulation: A social cognitive perspective. In M. Boekaerts, P. R. Pintrich, & M. Zeidner (Eds.), *Handbook of self-regulation* (pp. 13–39). San Diego, CA: Academic Press. doi:10.1016/B978-012109890-2/50031-7

Zimmerman, B. J., & Campillo, M. (2003). Motivating self-regulated problem solvers. In J. E. Davidson & R. J. Sternberg (Eds.), *The psychology of problem-solving* (pp. 233–262). New York, NY: Cambridge University Press. doi:10.1017/CBO9780511615771.009

Zito, J. R., Adkins, M., Gavins, M., Harris, K. R., & Graham, S. (2007). Self-regulated strategy development: Relationship to the social-cognitive perspective and the development of self-regulation. *Reading & Writing Quarterly: Overcoming Learning Difficulties, 23*, 77–95. doi:10.1080/10573560600837693

II

SELF-REGULATED LEARNING INTERVENTIONS TARGETING MENTAL AND PHYSICAL HEALTH

6

EMOTION REGULATION INTERVENTIONS FOR YOUTH WITH ANXIETY DISORDERS

CYNTHIA SUVEG, MOLLY DAVIS, AND ANNA JONES

Self-regulation, the ability to modulate behavior according to contextual demands (Calkins & Fox, 2002), has been linked to a variety of important developmental outcomes, including academic success, social competence, and psychological adaptation (Blair & Razza, 2007; Garner & Waajid, 2012; McClelland, Cameron, Wanless, & Murray, 2007; Rydell, Berlin, & Bohlin, 2003). Because development is hierarchical, early difficulties in self-regulation interfere with the attainment of the increasingly complex regulation skills required for successful adaptation later in development, such as when academic demands increase or in the context of initiating and maintaining peer relationships (Calkins, 2009; Keane & Calkins, 2004). Given the importance of self-regulation for adaptive development, interventions have been developed that can enhance such skills in youth either at-risk for poor self-regulation or who are already experiencing difficulties in self-regulation. Empirically supported treatments for youth with anxiety

http://dx.doi.org/10.1037/14641-007
Self-Regulated Learning Interventions With At-Risk Youth: Enhancing Adaptability, Performance, and Well-Being, T. J. Cleary (Editor)
Copyright © 2015 by the American Psychological Association. All rights reserved.

disorders, for example, encourage youth to identify their feelings and behaviors in anxiety-provoking situations, learn a variety of anxiety management skills, and then practice skills in real-life situations—all while self-reflecting on their efforts toward managing their anxious feelings. Collectively, the processes of identification, practice, and self-observation compose a *feedback loop* (Zimmerman, 2000) that fosters future adaptation, in part, by increasing self-efficacy.

This chapter highlights the feedback loop that is embedded within empirically supported treatments for anxious youth. It begins with a review of the literature that links emotion regulation difficulties to anxiety in youth. Simply, *emotion regulation* involves modifying any aspect of one's emotional experience in a manner that is consistent with one's goals. It is a component of the broader self-regulatory system (Calkins & Fox, 2002; Karreman, van Tuijl, van Aken, & Dekovic, 2009), and it is within this specific domain of self-regulation that anxiety disorders in youth have received the most attention (Hannesdottir & Ollendick, 2007; Southam-Gerow & Kendall, 2000; Suveg & Zeman, 2004). In particular, self-regulation refers to a set of distinct yet related processes that include attention, effortful control, and emotion regulation. Emotion regulation is viewed as one component of the broader self-regulatory system and interventions designed to specifically enhance emotion regulation skills and thus facilitate self-regulated learning (SRL) more broadly (see Chapter 7, this volume, for a discussion of emotion regulation and SRL relative to depression). A review of the empirical data documenting emotion regulation difficulties among youth with anxiety disorders sets the stage for a subsequent discussion on the principles and applicability of SRL interventions for anxious youth. An example of an emotion-focused cognitive–behavioral treatment program is presented to highlight the ways in which such a program encourages SRL.

THEORETICAL AND RESEARCH FOUNDATIONS

Emotion Regulation and Youth Anxiety

Adaptive emotion regulation is composed of a variety of specific emotion-related skills that are collectively necessary for adaptive management of emotional experiences, such as the ability to identify emotions, understand emotional experiences, and be aware of fluctuations in emotion intensity. For instance, emotion understanding with regard to oneself and others is crucial for adaptive regulation; without an accurate awareness of an emotional experience, regulation efforts are likely to be unsuccessful (Bradley & Lang, 2000). In addition, the ability to identify subtle increases in emotion intensity assists individuals in regulating their emotional experiences through awareness of physiological cues, such as a racing heart in an anxiety-provoking situation or clenched teeth and a furrowed brow when beginning to feel angry. Emotion regulation is crucial for adaptive functioning and has been linked to a variety of important developmental outcomes, including social skills (Eisenberg, Fabes, Guthrie, & Reiser, 2000), cognitive functioning (Lemerise & Arsenio, 2000), and academic success (Graziano, Reavis, Keane, & Calkins, 2007).

Youth with anxiety disorders show deficits in emotion regulation skills (e.g., cognitive reappraisal; Carthy, Horesh, Apter, & Gross, 2010) and in abilities that underlie adaptive emotion regulation (e.g., emotion identification and emotion understanding). For instance, Simonian, Beidel, Turner, Berkes, and Long (2001) found that socially phobic children made significantly more errors in identifying positive, negative, and ambiguous facial expressions, which suggests deficits in emotion understanding. Southam-Gerow and Kendall (2000) found that 7- to 14-year-old youth with anxiety disorders demonstrated significantly less understanding of how to hide and change emotions. These findings suggested that some anxious youth may have difficulties in emotion regulation due to knowledge deficits related to how to effectively manage emotional experiences.

With respect to emotion regulation, Zeman, Shipman, and Suveg (2002) used self-report questionnaires and peer ratings of emotional functioning to examine the predictive relationship between anger and sadness regulation, and internalizing and externalizing symptoms, in a community sample of elementary school-age children. Results of regression analyses indicated that the inability to identify emotional states predicted internalizing symptoms. Furthermore, the inhibition of anger, the dysregulated expression of anger and sadness, and maladaptive anger coping significantly predicted internalizing symptoms. Suveg and Zeman (2004) found that youth with anxiety disorders experienced their emotions more intensely and perceived themselves as less able to successfully manage emotionally provocative situations than children without a psychological disorder. When particular patterns of emotion management were examined, children with anxiety disorders exhibited more dysregulated management (i.e., culturally inappropriate emotional expression) and less adaptive coping across anger, sadness, and worry experiences than did nonclinical youth. Mothers of anxious children also perceived their children as significantly more inflexible, labile, and emotionally negative than did mothers of children without anxiety disorders. In combination with prior work (Blumberg & Izard, 1986), the collective results make a strong case for the notion that anxious children have emotion regulation difficulties that extend beyond the experience of anxiety.

Whether emotion regulation deficits precede or follow the development of anxiety disorders in youth is unknown, and the order of effects may vary across individuals. Preliminary research has supported the notion, however, that emotion dysregulation serves as a mechanism by which variables known to confer risk for anxiety disorders (e.g., temperamental behavioral inhibition, negative emotion parenting) exert their effects. In a retrospective path analysis, Suveg, Morelen, Brewer, and Thomassin (2010) found that emotion dysregulation fully mediated the link between behavioral inhibition and anxiety symptoms, and partially mediated links between emotion parenting (negative family emotional expressivity) and anxiety.

Self-Regulated Learning Principles and Anxiety Treatment

Given the emotion dysregulation that children with anxiety disorders experience, teaching skills to enhance the emotion regulation component of self-regulation is a key feature of many anxiety treatments for children. Major principles of SRL (Zimmerman, 2000) are consistent themes across child anxiety treatment modalities. This section reviews several SRL principles implicated in childhood anxiety treatments and focuses substantially on how these principles relate to cognitive–behavioral therapy (CBT) for children with anxiety.

In general, SRL is based on the notion that individuals are "metacognitively, motivationally, and behaviorally active participants in their own learning process" (Zimmerman, 1986, p. 308). As active participants, self-regulated learners must be aware of their abilities and progress, and consistently monitor their performance to adjust their goals and motivation, as needed (Butler & Winne, 1995). Moreover, self-regulated learners must be self-directed and cannot wholly depend on others to gain knowledge and skills (Zimmerman, 1989). Thus, from the time strategies are initiated to the point at which specified goals are achieved, self-regulated learners must remain engaged and active participants in their own learning process.

Zimmerman (2000) provides a cyclical self-regulation model that is pertinent to anxiety treatment for children broadly and, specifically, to several components of CBT. The model depicts a process whereby forethought contributes to performance or volitional control, which then leads to self-reflection. In turn, self-reflection influences forethought, thus creating a feedback loop. Figure 6.1 and the remainder of this section detail how this SRL feedback loop can be applied to better understand treatment for childhood anxiety disorders.

The forethought phase of Zimmerman's (2000) feedback loop has two major components: task analysis (e.g., goal setting and strategic planning) and self-motivation beliefs (e.g., self-efficacy, outcome expectations, intrinsic interest/value, goal orientation). In CBT, children engage in task analysis largely through the creation of a fear hierarchy. At this time, the child has the

```
                    ┌─────────────────────────┐
                    │ Performance or Volitional│
                    │        Control          │
                    │                         │
                    │ • Coping strategies (e.g.,│
                    │   relaxation, cognitive │
                    │   restructuring)        │
                    │ • Awareness of thoughts and│
                    │   feelings              │
                    │ • Subjective Units of Distress│
                    └─────────────────────────┘
```

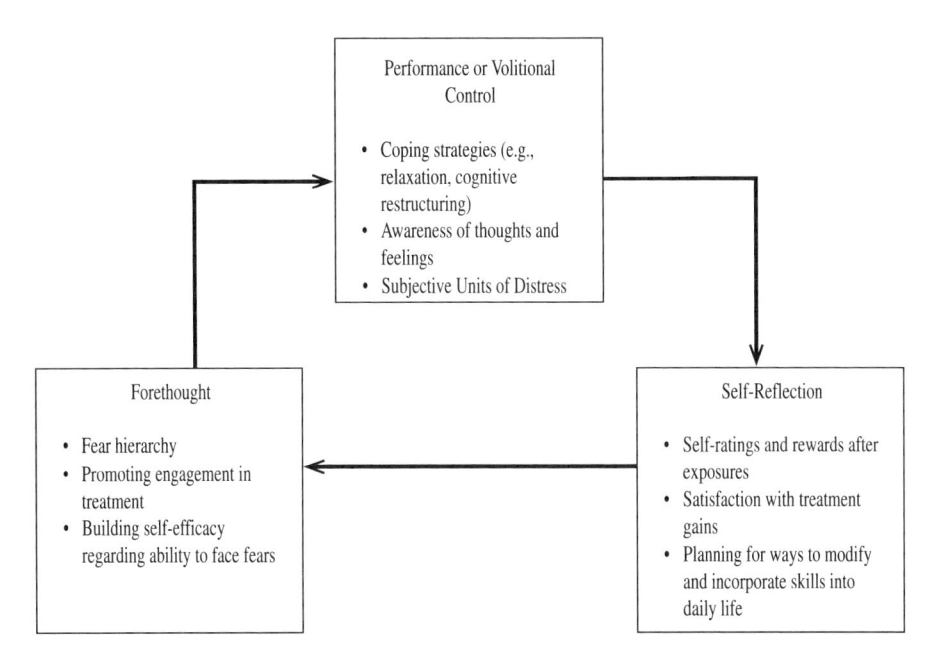

Figure 6.1. Components of empirically supported treatments for treating anxiety disorders in youth are consistent with the SRL feedback loop (Zimmerman, 2000).

Forethought
- Fear hierarchy
- Promoting engagement in treatment
- Building self-efficacy regarding ability to face fears

Self-Reflection
- Self-ratings and rewards after exposures
- Satisfaction with treatment gains
- Planning for ways to modify and incorporate skills into daily life

opportunity to identify fears he or she wishes to tackle. Through this process, the child not only helps to select situations to include in the hierarchy but also assists in determining the relative order in which to face each fear based on the amount of anxiety each situation is likely to evoke. Although often a collaborative process with the therapist (Kendall et al., 2005), the creation of a fear hierarchy certainly provides children with the opportunity to play an instrumental role in setting treatment goals and thus planning the course of therapy.

Promoting children's self-motivation and, thus, overall engagement, in CBT for anxiety is a critical part of treatment, particularly at the outset, given that children are often enrolled in anxiety treatment by their parents rather than on their own volition (Kingery et al., 2006). Thus, it is important for the therapist to present material in creative, fun ways that are tailored to the child or adolescent's interests and are developmentally appropriate (Kingery et al., 2006). Furthermore, the use of rewards can serve to increase motivation toward treatment compliance (Kingery et al., 2006). In a feedback loop fashion, children's development of self-motivation is not only pertinent to the initial treatment phase but is also augmented through the process of engaging in and reflecting on exposures. Exposures are based on learning principles, such as counterconditioning and extinction, and require the child to face increasingly anxiety-provoking situations (Gosch, Flannery-Schroeder, Mauro, & Compton, 2006; Kendall et al., 2005). Generally, youth are expected to stay in the anxiety-provoking situation until their anxiety is reduced by at least 50% (Kendall et al., 2005). Thus, exposure tasks provide youth with an opportunity to further develop and successfully use coping skills. In turn, the development of coping skills and accompanying decrease in anxiety symptoms may enhance children's positive self-judgment and, following the feedback loop, contribute to further increases in their sense of self-efficacy. Such theoretical reasoning suggests that developing self-efficacy is crucial for helping children to improve their ability to regulate their anxiety and builds on seminal work that implicated changes in self-efficacy as a mediator of positive behavior change (Bandura, 1977; Bandura, Reese, & Adams, 1982).

Empirical investigations have supported the role of self-efficacy in treatment outcomes for anxious youth, in particular. For instance, Tiwari, Kendall, Hoff, Harrison, and Fizur (2013) found that youth ranging from about age 7 to 13 years who were treatment responders were more likely to be given homework assignments to complete between sessions than nonresponders. The authors concluded that out-of-session exposures likely contributed to positive treatment outcomes by reinforcing children's self-efficacy for coping in anxiety-provoking situations. Furthermore, children's responses on a coping questionnaire following treatment suggested that participation in a CBT program increases self-efficacy, particularly with regard to youths' ability to manage anxiety. For instance, 9- to 13-year-old children who participated in a CBT program rated their ability to cope with anxiety-provoking situations higher at posttreatment and at 7.4 years posttreatment (Kendall, Safford, Flannery-Schroeder, & Webb, 2004; Kendall & Treadwell, 2007). Such findings collectively have provided support for the role of self-efficacy in treatment outcomes.

In the CBT feedback loop, the self-control (e.g., self-instruction, imagery, attention focusing, task strategies) component of the performance or volitional control phase corresponds to the A step ("Attitudes and Actions that can help") of the FEAR plan, which is introduced in the Coping Cat CBT program for anxious youth (Kendall & Hedtke, 2006). The Coping Cat encompasses traditional CBT techniques within a package that is developmentally appropriate for youth. Youth are taught CBT skills using the FEAR acronym: to recognize their feelings during the F step, identify anxious thoughts/bad things they are expecting to happen during the E step, generate attitudes and actions that can help during the A step, and reward themselves for putting forth effort to face their fears during the R step. Regarding self-control techniques, during the A step, the child generates problem-solving strategies to cope with his or her anxiety, such as relaxation (e.g., progressive muscle relaxation, deep breathing, imagery) and cognitive restructuring (i.e., replacing negative thoughts with positive self-talk), that allow the child to be able to endure an exposure. Each of these coping strategies reflects multiple aspects of the self-control portion of this phase. For instance, when using positive self-talk, the child is engaging in attention focusing by turning his or her attention away from negative cognitions and toward more positive thoughts. Moreover, through positive self-talk, children are using self-instruction by guiding themselves through ways to successfully complete the task. Collectively, by building their coping strategies, children are able to promote their emotion regulation abilities and thus contribute to decreases in their anxiety.

Self-observation is another key component of the performance or volitional control step of the SRL feedback loop; this component requires a person to monitor his or her performance (Zimmerman, 2000) and is used across treatments for children with anxiety. One treatment modality that exemplifies the importance of self-observation is mindfulness-based cognitive therapy for children (MBCT-C; Lee, Semple, Rosa, & Miller, 2008; Semple, Lee, Rosa, & Miller, 2010). In MBCT-C, children are taught to mindfully attend to their thoughts and emotions to improve their emotion regulation (Semple et al., 2010). Such mindful attention requires the child to observe, without judgment, his or her thoughts and feelings. In addition, the Coping Cat program (Kendall & Hedtke, 2006) relies on self-observation of not only somatic signs of anxiety but also of negative cognitions. Developing an understanding of physiological cues is important for helping the child to recognize his or her anxiety and is therefore key to aiding the child in ultimately being able to cope with this distress (Gosch et al., 2006). This emphasis on self-observation of emotions is particularly evident in emotion-focused CBT (ECBT) for anxious youth (Suveg, Kendall, Comer, & Robin, 2006). In this treatment, which is described in greater detail later in the chapter, children practice identifying their emotions each session; the goal is to promote skills important to adaptive emotion regulation (Suveg et al., 2006). In ECBT and CBT, children are also taught to recognize their negative expectations about a feared stimuli or situation, and through this recognition, to modify these thoughts into adaptive ways of coping (Kendall, 1994; Suveg et al., 2006).

Children in anxiety treatment also engage in a mode of self-observation known as subjective units of distress (SUDS) that, in many ways, combines self-observation of anxious thoughts and body cues. Children provide SUDS throughout the exposure, as well as before and after, thus indicating their levels of anxiety based on a specified scale. This process allows children to combine the knowledge they have gained from observing their physiological and cognitive signs of anxiety to inform the therapist and themselves of the extent to which they are experiencing anxiety. SUDS provide data about children's anxiety responses in a situation (Gosch et al., 2006; Kendall et al., 2005). Overall, it is clear that treatments for children with anxiety incorporate a focus on self-observation that fosters increased emotion regulation abilities.

In both the CBT and SRL feedback loops, self-observation contributes to self-reflection (i.e., self-judgment and self-reaction). Within the context of CBT for anxiety, children who observe their own successful performance during exposure are likely to evaluate themselves positively and experience an overall sense of self-satisfaction. In contrast, children who do not experience success during the performance or volitional control phase may develop maladaptive self-reflections that, as a result, hinder their self-regulation development.

The self-judgment portion of the self-reflection phase "involves self-evaluating one's performance and attributing causal significance to the results" (Zimmerman, 2000, p. 21). Individuals can provide themselves with internal feedback, a process pertinent to SRL (Butler & Winne, 1995) and to anxiety treatment for children. Following exposures in anxiety treatment for youth, children rate their effort in facing their fears (Albano & Kendall, 2002), which allows the opportunity for self-evaluation. With regard to self-ratings, children are encouraged to rate their efforts in attempting to manage their anxiety. For the rewards component of the Coping Cat program, children are encouraged to reward themselves through self-praise (Gosch et al., 2006). The therapist praises the child for his or her efforts throughout treatment, ultimately teaching the child to praise him- or herself by modeling this skill for the child (Gosch et al., 2006). Through the process of self-judgment and, therefore, by generating internal feedback, children continue to reinforce the skills they have learned for managing anxiety on their own—without a need for consistent material rewards or praise from others. Overall, this process of self-ratings and rewards emphasizes the importance of recognizing children's efforts instead of focusing on their performance, because children with anxiety often have very high standards of achievement and are unforgiving if they do not reach those standards (Podell, Mychailyszyn, Edmunds, Puleo, & Kendall, 2010). Thus, children's self-ratings and rewards serve as a way for them to acknowledge their progress without being overly concerned with perfection. By rating their effort following exposures and providing themselves with rewards for those efforts, children have important opportunities to monitor, and therefore further promote, their progress in managing their anxiety.

Another critical process involved in the self-reflection phase, self-reaction, represents in a sense the culmination of benefits yielded from the previously described processes. Self-reaction encompasses self-satisfaction and adaptive–defensive inferences. In the context of anxiety treatment, self-satisfaction often results from treatment gains, which can include reductions in a child's anxiety and more general improvements in their ability to cope with their emotions. Self-satisfaction can then lead to increased self-efficacy, thus perpetuating the self-regulatory feedback loop.

Other important aspects of self-reflection include *adaptive* or *defensive inferences*, which are thoughts about how a person should change his or her self-regulation strategies for future tasks (Zimmerman, 2000). On the one hand, adaptive inferences can lead people to adopt even better self-regulatory strategies. On the other hand, defensive responses, such as helplessness and procrastination, can preclude further adaptive development with regard to self-regulatory processes. Self-reflection is implicated throughout CBT for child anxiety. Continuously throughout the therapeutic process, children are able to update the fear hierarchy and refine their coping skills. Therefore, children have the opportunity to reflect on their progress and to share their thoughts with the therapist regarding future treatment targets and ways to achieve those goals. Also, during treatment, the child and therapist discuss how to implement the skills learned in therapy into the child's everyday life, thus maximizing their opportunities for adaptive inferences. This approach allows children to plan for the future and to identify ways to continue to meet their goals following treatment.

It is clear that SRL principles play a key role in anxiety treatment for children. The following section focuses on ECBT and highlights the role of feedback in this treatment.

SELF-REGULATED LEARNING INTERVENTIONS FOR YOUTH WITH ANXIETY DISORDERS

Cognitive–behavioral therapies for youth with anxiety disorders (e.g., Kendall & Hedtke, 2006) exemplify SRL interventions. Furthermore, CBT approaches for treating youth with anxiety disorders have garnered much empirical support from independent research teams and when administered in a variety of formats (Khanna & Kendall, 2010; Silverman et al., 1999; Wuthrich et al., 2012). Despite the relative efficacy of CBT approaches, however, up to one third of youth who receive such treatments do not benefit to a clinically meaningful degree (Legerstee et al., 2010). The reasons for nonresponse are unknown and may involve different factors across youth. For instance, for some youth, simply providing more of the same treatment may be effective for improving symptoms. For other youth, comorbid psychopathology may interfere with treatment progress, although research generally has not found support for this notion (Flannery-Schroeder, Suveg, Safford, Kendall, & Webb, 2004; Rapee et al., 2013). Still, for other nonresponders, it could be that another treatment approach, or a variant of CBT, might be more effective. Regardless of the reasons for nonresponse, however, it is evident that treatment nonresponders have not learned adequate self-regulatory skills throughout the course of treatment to effectively manage emotional experiences. Even for treatment responders, preliminary research has suggested that they only evidence improvements in anxiety regulation, not anger or sadness regulation (Suveg, Sood, Comer, & Kendall, 2009), despite their broad-based difficulties with emotion regulation.

ECBT (Suveg et al., 2006) was developed as a variant of CBT in response to the previously reviewed basic research that found that youth with anxiety disorders exhibit difficulties managing emotional experiences broadly. Theoretically, it could be that youth who demonstrate greater deficits in emotion regulation at pretreatment may benefit more from a treatment that has emotion-focused components infused throughout than from one that does not. Although preliminary research has supported its efficacy in treating anxiety in youth (Suveg et al., 2006), results from rigorous comparisons are not yet available. ECBT, like CBT, also exemplifies the use of SRL principles in anxiety treatment. Furthermore, the focus on emotions throughout treatment encourages a relatively intense reflection on one's engagement and progress in treatment, a hallmark of SRL interventions. The following is a description of the ECBT program; the ways in which SRL principles are integrated throughout the treatment are highlighted. The discussion that follows includes a particular focus on the emotional processing component of ECBT, given its uniqueness from traditional CBT and relevance to SRL interventions. The feedback loop that is embedded within the treatment is highlighted using a case scenario of a 9-year-old girl with separation anxiety disorder.

The first phase of ECBT focuses on providing the youth with skills to identify and manage emotional experiences. Building on typical CBT approaches that focus on identifying anxious feelings, ECBT assists youth in recognizing a variety of emotional experiences, some of which are considered "basic" emotions (i.e., fear, sadness, anger, happiness, guilt, pride, jealousy; Ekman & Cordaro, 2011). Each week, the session is devoted to learning about one specific emotion through a variety of techniques. For instance, at the start of each session, youth are first asked to identify how they are feeling, how they know they are feeling that way, and why they are feeling that way. Several therapy materials assist with the process and encourage youth participation, such as a poster board that lists several different emotions, along with pictures of corresponding facial expressions. Youth who provide minimal answers are encouraged to elaborate. For instance, in the case of Sarah, a 9-year-old with separation anxiety disorder, she indicates one week that she is feeling angry, that she knows she is angry because she feels like yelling, and that she is angry because she cannot have a friend over that weekend. In that case, the therapist probes further, asking Sarah to identify additional ways that she knows she is angry (i.e., "And how does your body feel?" or "What does your face look like?"). The therapist also engages Sarah in a more in-depth discussion about the reasons for feeling angry. For example, through a discussion, Sarah acknowledges that she feels angry at her parents for making her take the bus to school that morning, and also is angry at herself for still feeling scared to take the bus to school. When necessary, therapists model the task for children or otherwise assist in helping them identify the particular emotion components. The overall purpose of the task is to assist youth with developing the skills necessary to identify emotions in themselves and others, and to gain a greater understanding of the contexts of emotional experience. During the therapy session, youth sometimes journal about these experiences and are encouraged to go back and reference these documents at a later point.

A portion of each session during the first half of therapy also includes the presentation of a vignette that describes a scenario designed to elicit an intended emotion in the protagonist. For instance, in one vignette, a child practices hard to make the soccer team. The day after tryouts, she notices on the bulletin board the list of children who made the team and sees that she did not make the team, but her friends did. Youth are invited to engage in a discussion regarding the emotional aspects of the scenario. First, youth are asked to identify how the child is likely to feel and how they might know the child is feeling a particular emotion (i.e., using facial, bodily, vocal cues). Youth are also asked whether it is possible that someone else might feel a different emotion and whether they believe it is possible to feel some other way than the intended emotion. Next, children are encouraged to discuss the context of the intended emotion (in this case, sadness). At times, youth become visibly distressed while discussing the particular scenario, which provides opportunities for experiential learning. Similar to the emotion identification task identified previously, the vignette activity is intended to be a discussion and to actively engage the youth to reflect on and carefully consider emotional experiences. Thus, therapists attempt to engage youth by using Socratic questioning, role-plays, and other strategies to encourage active participation in the therapy process.

Overall, much time is spent on emotion identification and its contextual basis because adaptive emotion regulation depends on accurate identification of the emotional experience. However, emotion awareness and attention to emotion processes themselves may actually serve to effect change in anxiety symptoms. In one study, school-age youth were given electronic diaries to record their emotional experiences for 1 week (i.e., what emotion they were feeling and the intensity of the emotion; Thomassin & Suveg, 2012). Girls who reported poor emotion coping or who were reluctant to express their emotions based on parent report showed a reduction in anxiety symptoms 1 week after tracking their emotional experiences via the electronic diaries. The reflection on emotional states that enhances future adaptation represents the feedback loop of SRL interventions. It could be that tracking emotional experiences provided opportunities for the girls to reflect on and become more confident in identifying their emotions. This explanation is consistent with the self-regulation theory of expressive writing, which contends that attention to emotions builds emotional self-efficacy (Frattaroli, 2006), and with empirical work that has shown that anxious youth have low levels of emotional self-efficacy (Suveg & Zeman, 2004). Greater confidence and mastery in identifying emotional experiences may have then resulted in the use of more adaptive regulation strategies.

As key components underlying the initial phase of the feedback loop of SRL interventions, self-efficacy and outcome expectations motivate youth to use the skills they have learned. For instance, in the case of Sarah, tracking emotional experiences may have given her greater confidence in regulating her emotions. In turn, Sarah may have believed that learning to better regulate her emotions would lead to enhanced peer friendships (i.e., outcome expectations) because peers would no longer view her as a "baby" for crying each time her mother dropped her off at school. Tracking emotional experiences also may have given girls who were reluctant to express their emotions via other mechanisms a nonthreatening outlet, thus bypassing the negative effects associated with chronically inhibiting emotional experiences (Gross & Levenson, 1997). Either way, such an intense focus on emotion identification and the contexts in which emotions occur during ECBT undoubtedly encourages a variety of processes involved in the feedback loop of SRL interventions, including forethought (e.g., promoting engagement) and performance or volitional control (e.g., awareness of feelings).

The first half of the ECBT treatment program also includes other traditional CBT tasks, such as the identification of thoughts that may contribute to anxiety. In addition to anxiety, the identification of thoughts in ECBT is applied to other negative emotions. Youth are taught to identify the ways that their thoughts can contribute to negative feelings and interfere with adaptive emotion regulation. They are encouraged to track their thoughts via a variety of ways, including journals or "thought bubbles." Through the identification of thoughts, youth continue to gain mastery in coping, and self-efficacy broadly, by observing their own thoughts and by identifying the links between thoughts, emotions, and behaviors. Youth are also taught ways to replace their unhelpful thoughts with more helpful ones. For instance, Sarah identified that she feared her mother would get into a car accident dropping Sarah off at school. Sarah was encouraged to generate thoughts to decrease her anxiety, such as the thought that it was very unlikely her mother would get into a car accident. Sarah also thought about her mother's safe driving record and how, even if her mother did get into a car accident, she had a cell phone to quickly call for help. Active strategies to manage anxiety are key components of the feedback loop and, in particular, the performance or volitional control phase that increases the chances that youth will successfully reach their goals.

The second half of the ECBT treatment program also models traditional CBT and primarily involves imaginal and in vivo exposure tasks that provide youth with an opportunity to gain mastery over anxiety-provoking situations. The main difference in ECBT is the inclusion of exposure tasks designed to help youth gain mastery over any emotional experience that they typically have difficulty regulating. For instance, if a youth typically has difficulty adaptively managing anger scenarios, then exposure tasks designed to give youth opportunities to experience anger and then engage in a variety of regulatory efforts are implemented. Throughout the exposures portion of treatment in ECBT, youth may confront a variety of emotional experiences. By generating the fear hierarchy, oftentimes through collaboration between the therapist, child, and parent, youth begin to reflect on the nature of their emotional difficulties. They learn to differentiate among levels of emotional discomfort and to identify triggers for emotional dysregulation. Actual engagement in the exposure tasks that are listed on the hierarchy also provides youth with feedback on the nature of the emotional experience. For instance, Sarah initially indicated that she would be more nervous separating from her mother if she had to ride the bus to school than if her mother dropped her off at school. However, when exposure tasks started, Sarah quickly learned that separating from her mother at the school was much harder than separating at her home when she got on the bus in the morning. Through the feedback loop of identifying, observing, and practicing, Sarah learned about the nuances of her own emotional experience that she could then apply in a meaningful way to her life.

Collectively, CBT and ECBT contain several strategies consistent with SRL paradigms. Strategies such as self-monitoring and observation provide youth with feedback regarding their emotional experiences, the contexts in which they occur, and the effectiveness of the strategies used to regulate emotions. Youth are active participants throughout the therapy process, and engagement is key for success.

IMPLICATIONS AND FUTURE DIRECTIONS

Traditional CBT offers approximately two thirds of youth much relief from impairing levels of anxiety at posttreatment. CBT contains several feedback loop mechanisms involved in SRL that collectively may contribute to its success. A contemporary variant of CBT, ECBT, also offers great promise in addressing the global emotion deficits that anxious youth experience and that basic research has identified. Future research must examine what it is within the treatments that is responsible for change, that is, what are the "active ingredients" of the treatment program?

Many of the components involved in SRL interventions have theoretical support for their inclusion, and some have empirical support, but only when part of a treatment package and not when administered on their own. Dismantling studies in which essential strategies for therapeutic success are identified may be helpful in this regard. Alternatively, monitoring improvement based on the timing of when strategies are introduced also may be helpful. For instance, self-monitoring is a key ingredient of SRL interventions, and when they studied it within the context of a CBT program for youth anxiety, Nakamura, Pestle, and Chorpita (2009) found that youth benefited from self-monitoring and psychoeducation when these components were introduced before exposure tasks. In contrast, Kendall et al. (1997) conducted exploratory analyses to examine the relative benefits of the first portion of treatment (i.e., psychoeducation and skills training) and the second part of treatment (i.e., exposure training) and found positive effects only for exposures. Such studies are necessary to identify key ingredients of treatment programs for anxious youth. It could be that various factors are involved in success, and they may vary across individuals. However, several of the key processes involved in SRL, such as self-monitoring and observation, have been identified via a distillation approach as common elements among empirically supported treatments for childhood disorders (Chorpita, Becker, Daleiden, & Hamilton, 2007; Chorpita & Daleiden, 2009).

Whether it be through dismantling and distillation studies or even via randomized control trials, further research on the application of SRL-based emotion regulation skills to treatment for youth is critical, given that emotion regulation difficulties are implicated in many forms of childhood psychopathology (for a review, see Keenan, 2000), including anxiety disorders (Suveg & Zeman, 2004). Specifically, it is important for researchers to continue to investigate the mechanisms through which previously identified SRL strategies serve to promote adaptive emotion regulation functioning as these researchers also identify additional SRL strategies that can be incorporated into the treatment of anxious youth. Such research efforts, once applied, can help children undergoing anxiety treatment to become increasingly self-directed, active participants in their own treatment progress, therefore potentially enhancing treatment outcomes.

SRL and emotion-based approaches to treating child anxiety have implications not only for clinical contexts but also for school settings. Traditional cognitive–behavioral methods used to treat child anxiety disorders have been shown to be efficacious in reducing child anxiety in outpatient clinics and within the schools (Bernstein, Layne, Egan, & Tennison, 2005; Ginsburg &

Drake, 2002; Kendall et al., 1997). Although ECBT is effective for the treatment of child anxiety (Suveg et al., 2006), the basic underlying principles (e.g., emotion regulation skills, self-monitoring) are applicable to a range of disorders (e.g., oppositional defiant disorder, major depressive disorder; Casey, 1996; Casey & Schlosser, 1994). In addition, emotion regulation skills and SRL strategies, such as self-monitoring, self-evaluation, and goal setting, have implications for prevention efforts in school settings (e.g., increasing self-efficacy and independent learning); however, the inclusion of the abovementioned strategies in the schools to prevent anxiety symptoms needs to be tested empirically. Specifically, processes associated with the SRL feedback loop, such as goal setting in a hierarchical fashion (i.e., forethought), may work in the classroom to increase motivation through the direction provided by goal setting. For example, teachers may ask students to write down their goals for that particular day. Teachers can guide children in writing action-oriented goals (e.g., "Write topic sentence of essay on dinosaurs" rather than "essay on dinosaurs") to increase the specificity of the goal. In the classroom, teachers may also discuss the creation of realistic goals (e.g., coming up with a plan for a class project, rather than completing the project that same day).

In addition, the use of imagery and self-instruction (i.e., performance) not only increases creative and imaginative thinking but also improves mastery of concepts by reinforcing them in multiple ways (e.g., visual, oral, written). One way to apply this principle in the classroom is through problem-solving strategies when a child becomes stuck during an assignment. For example, a child may have difficulty coming up with a topic for creative writing. Rather than providing the child with a list of possible topics, the teacher encourages the child to think about different things he or she enjoys, and to generate a list of possible topics for the report. After generating the list, the child could decide which topic may be the most suitable for the assignment and begin writing. This strategy allows children to develop problem-solving skills that are applicable in the classroom and in daily life.

Finally, self-evaluation and self-satisfaction (i.e., self-reflection) serve as ways to reward effort when working toward the achievement of a goal. Adaptive (e.g., "I tried really hard," "I did a great job") inferences lead to increased self-efficacy and reinforce the previous steps in the feedback loop (Zimmerman, 2000). For instance, in the classroom, a teacher may ask the children to write a short sentence at the end of each assignment about their perceived self-satisfaction with their work. To increase child motivation, children could be encouraged to think positively when writing their statement (e.g., "That is the first time I have tried this type of math problem. It will get easier with practice" rather than "I did a terrible job and will never be able to do this type of math problem"). The steps of the SRL feedback loop tie nicely into those steps associated with traditional cognitive–behavioral practice. Taken together, the integration of SRL and CBT/ECBT principles has far-reaching implications for not only intervention in clinical populations but also widespread prevention and intervention within school settings. Researchers could discern whether, for instance, children exhibit changes in their abilities to set goals, use problem-solving strategies, and engage in constructive self-evaluation following teacher instruction. Teachers could be trained in such methods, and researchers could examine the effectiveness of the strategies using pre–post designs.

REFERENCES

Albano, A. M., & Kendall, P. C. (2002). Cognitive behavioural therapy for children and adolescents with anxiety disorders: Clinical research advances. *International Review of Psychiatry, 14*, 129–134. doi:10.1080/09540260220132644

Bandura, A. (1977). Self-efficacy: Toward a unifying theory of behavioral change. *Psychological Review, 84*, 191–215. doi:10.1037/0033-295X.84.2.191

Bandura, A., Reese, L., & Adams, N. E. (1982). Microanalysis of action and fear arousal as a function of differential levels of perceived self-efficacy. *Journal of Personality and Social Psychology, 43*, 5–21. doi:10.1037/0022-3514.43.1.5

Bernstein, G. A., Layne, A. E., Egan, E. A., & Tennison, D. M. (2005). School-based interventions for anxious children. *Journal of the American Academy of Child & Adolescent Psychiatry, 44*, 1118–1127. doi:10.1097/01.chi.0000177323.40005.a1

Blair, C., & Razza, R. P. (2007). Relating effortful control, executive function, and false belief understanding to emerging math and literacy ability in kindergarten. *Child Development, 78*, 647–663. doi:10.1111/j.1467-8624.2007.01019.x

Blumberg, S. H., & Izard, C. E. (1986). Discriminating patterns of emotions in 10- and 11-year-old children's anxiety and depression. *Journal of Personality and Social Psychology, 51*, 852–857. doi:10.1037/0022-3514.51.4.852

Bradley, M. M., & Lang, P. J. (2000). Measuring emotion: Behavior, feeling, and physiology. In R. D. Lane & L. Nadel (Eds.), *Cognitive neuroscience of emotion* (pp. 242–276). New York, NY: Oxford University Press.

Butler, D. L., & Winne, P. H. (1995). Feedback and self-regulated learning: A theoretical synthesis. *Review of Educational Research, 65*, 245–281. doi:10.3102/00346543065003245

Calkins, S. D. (2009). Regulatory competence and early disruptive behavior problems: The role of physiological regulation. In S. L. Olson & A. J. Sameroff (Eds.), *Biopsychosocial regulatory processes in the development of childhood behavioral problems* (pp. 86–115). New York, NY: Cambridge University Press. doi:10.1017/CBO9780511575877.006

Calkins, S. D., & Fox, N. A. (2002). Self-regulatory processes in early personality development: A multilevel approach to the study of childhood social withdrawal and aggression. *Development and Psychopathology, 14,* 477–498. doi:10.1017/S095457940200305X

Carthy, T., Horesh, N., Apter, A., & Gross, J. J. (2010). Patterns of emotional reactivity and regulation in children with anxiety disorders. *Journal of Psychopathology and Behavioral Assessment, 32,* 23–36. doi:10.1007/s10862-009-9167-8

Casey, R. J. (1996). Emotional competence in children with externalizing and internalizing disorders. In M. Lewis & M. W. Sullivan (Eds.), *Emotional development in atypical children* (pp. 161–183). Mahwah, NJ: Erlbaum.

Casey, R. J., & Schlosser, S. (1994). Emotional responses to peer praise in children with and without a diagnosed externalizing disorder. *Merrill-Palmer Quarterly, 40,* 60–81.

Chorpita, B. F., Becker, K. D., Daleiden, E. L., & Hamilton, J. D. (2007). Understanding the common elements of evidence-based practice: Misconceptions and clinical examples. *Journal of the American Academy of Child and Adolescent Psychiatry, 46,* 647–652. doi:10.1097/chi.0b013e318033ff71

Chorpita, B. F., & Daleiden, E. L. (2009). Mapping evidence-based treatments for children and adolescents: Application of the distillation and matching model to 615 treatments from 322 randomized trials. *Journal of Consulting and Clinical Psychology, 77,* 566–579. doi:10.1037/a0014565

Eisenberg, N., Fabes, R. A., Guthrie, I. K., & Reiser, M. (2000). Dispositional emotionality and regulation: Their role in predicting quality of social functioning. *Journal of Personality and Social Psychology, 78,* 136–157. doi:10.1037/0022-3514.78.1.136

Ekman, P., & Cordaro, D. (2011). What is meant by calling emotions basic. *Emotion Review, 3,* 364–370. doi:10.1177/1754073911410740

Flannery-Schroeder, E., Suveg, C., Safford, S., Kendall, P. C., & Webb, A. (2004). Comorbid externalising disorders and child anxiety treatment outcomes. *Behaviour Change, 21,* 14–25. doi:10.1375/bech.21.1.14.35972

Frattaroli, J. (2006). Experimental disclosure and its moderators: A meta-analysis. *Psychological Bulletin, 132,* 823–865. doi:10.1037/0033-2909.132.6.823

Garner, P. W., & Waajid, B. (2012). Emotion knowledge and self-regulation as predictors of preschoolers' cognitive ability, classroom behavior, and social competence. *Journal of Psychoeducational Assessment, 30,* 330–343. doi:10.1177/0734282912449441

Ginsburg, G. S., & Drake, K. L. (2002). School-based treatment for anxious African-American adolescents: A controlled pilot study. *Journal of the American Academy of Child & Adolescent Psychiatry, 41,* 768–775. doi:10.1097/00004583-200207000-00007

Gosch, E. A., Flannery-Schroeder, E., Mauro, C. F., & Compton, S. N. (2006). Principles of cognitive–behavioral therapy for anxiety disorders in children. *Journal of Cognitive Psychotherapy, 20,* 247–262. doi:10.1891/jcop.20.3.247

Graziano, P. A., Reavis, R. D., Keane, S. P., & Calkins, S. D. (2007). The role of emotion regulation and children's early academic success. *Journal of School Psychology, 45*, 3–19. doi:10.1016/j.jsp.2006.09.002

Gross, J. J., & Levenson, R. W. (1997). Hiding feelings: The acute effects of inhibiting negative and positive emotion. *Journal of Abnormal Psychology, 106*, 95–103. doi:10.1037/0021-843X.106.1.95

Hannesdottir, D. K., & Ollendick, T. H. (2007). The role of emotion regulation in the treatment of child anxiety disorders. *Clinical Child and Family Psychology Review, 10*, 275–293. doi:10.1007/s10567-007-0024-6

Karreman, A., van Tuijl, C., van Aken, M. A., & Dekovic, M. (2009). Young children's self-regulation and the development of moral conduct. In W. Koops, D. Brugman, T. J. Ferguson, & A. F. Sanders (Eds.), *The development and structure of conscience* (pp. 271–285). New York, NY: Psychology Press.

Keane, S. P., & Calkins, S. D. (2004). Predicting kindergarten peer social status from toddler and preschool problem behavior. *Journal of Abnormal Child Psychology, 32*, 409–423. doi:10.1023/B:JACP.0000030294.11443.41

Keenan, K. (2000). Emotion dysregulation as a risk factor for child psychopathology. *Clinical Psychology: Science and Practice, 7*, 418–434. doi:10.1093/clipsy.7.4.418

Kendall, P. C. (1994). Treating anxiety disorders in children: Results of a randomized clinical trial. *Journal of Consulting and Clinical Psychology, 62*, 100–110. doi:10.1037/0022-006X.62.1.100

Kendall, P. C., Flannery-Schroeder, E., Panichelli-Mindel, S. M., Southam-Gerow, M., Henin, A., & Warman, M. (1997). Therapy for youths with anxiety disorders: A second randomized clinical trial. *Journal of Consulting and Clinical Psychology, 65*, 366–380. doi:10.1037/0022-006X.65.3.366

Kendall, P. C., & Hedtke, K. A. (2006). *Cognitive–behavioral therapy for anxious children: Therapist manual* (3rd ed.). Ardmore, PA: Workbook.

Kendall, P. C., Robin, J. A., Hedtke, K. A., Suveg, C., Flannery-Schroeder, E., & Gosch, E. (2005). Considering CBT with anxious youth? Think exposures. *Cognitive and Behavioral Practice, 12*, 136–148. doi:10.1016/S1077-7229(05)80048-3

Kendall, P. C., Safford, S., Flannery-Schroeder, E., & Webb, A. (2004). Child anxiety treatment: Outcomes in adolescence and impact on substance use and depression at 7.4-year follow-up. *Journal of Consulting and Clinical Psychology, 72*, 276–287. doi:10.1037/0022-006X.72.2.276

Kendall, P. C., & Treadwell, K. R. (2007). The role of self-statements as a mediator in treatment for youth with anxiety disorders. *Journal of Consulting and Clinical Psychology, 75*, 380–389. doi:10.1037/0022-006X.75.3.380

Khanna, M. S., & Kendall, P. C. (2010). Computer-assisted cognitive behavioral therapy for child anxiety: Results of a randomized clinical trial. *Journal of Consulting and Clinical Psychology, 78*, 737–745. doi:10.1037/a0019739

Kingery, J. N., Roblek, T. L., Suveg, C., Grover, R. L., Sherrill, J. T., & Bergman, R. L. (2006). They're not just "little adults": Developmental considerations for implementing cognitive–behavioral therapy with anxious youth. *Journal of Cognitive Psychotherapy, 20*, 263–273. doi:10.1891/jcop.20.3.263

Lee, J., Semple, R. J., Rosa, D., & Miller, L. (2008). Mindfulness-based cognitive therapy for children: Results of a pilot study. *Journal of Cognitive Psychotherapy, 22*, 15–28. doi:10.1891/0889.8391.22.1.15

Legerstee, J. S., Tulen, J. H., Dierckx, B., Treffers, P. D., Verhulst, F. C., & Utens, E. M. (2010). CBT for childhood anxiety disorders: Differential changes in selective attention between treatment responders and non-responders. *Journal of Child Psychology and Psychiatry, 51*, 162–172. doi:10.1111/j.1469-7610.2009.02143.x

Lemerise, E. A., & Arsenio, W. F. (2000). An integrated model of emotion processes and cognition in social information processing. *Child Development, 71*, 107–118. doi:10.1111/1467-8624.00124

McClelland, M. M., Cameron, C. E., Wanless, S. B., & Murray, A. (2007). Executive function, behavioral self-regulation, and social–emotional competence. In O. N. Saracho & B. Spodek (Eds.), *Contemporary perspectives on social learning in early childhood education* (pp. 113–137). Charlotte, NC: Information Age.

Nakamura, B. J., Pestle, S. L., & Chorpita, B. F. (2009). Differential sequencing of cognitive–behavioral techniques for reducing child and adolescent anxiety. *Journal of Cognitive Psychotherapy, 23*, 114–135. doi:10.1891/0889-8391.23.2.114

Podell, J. L., Mychailyszyn, M., Edmunds, J., Puleo, C. M., & Kendall, P. C. (2010). The Coping Cat program for anxious youth: The FEAR plan comes to life. *Cognitive and Behavioral Practice, 17*, 132–141. doi:10.1016/j.cbpra.2009.11.001

Rapee, R. M., Lyneham, H. J., Hudson, J. L., Kangas, M., Wuthrich, V. M., & Schniering, C. A. (2013). Effect of comorbidity on treatment of anxious children and adolescents: Results from a large, combined sample. *Journal of the American Academy of Child & Adolescent Psychiatry, 52*, 47–56. doi:10.1016/j.jaac.2012.10.002

Rydell, A. M., Berlin, L., & Bohlin, G. (2003). Emotionality, emotion regulation, and adaptation among 5- to 8-year-old children. *Emotion, 3*, 30–47. doi:10.1037/1528-3542.3.1.30

Semple, R. J., Lee, J., Rosa, D., & Miller, L. F. (2010). A randomized trial of mindfulness-based cognitive therapy for children: Promoting mindful attention to enhance social–emotional resiliency in children. *Journal of Child and Family Studies, 19*, 218–229. doi:10.1007/s10826-009-9301-y

Silverman, W. K., Kurtines, W. M., Ginsburg, G. S., Weems, C. F., Lumpkin, P. W., & Carmichael, D. H. (1999). Treating anxiety disorders in children with group cognitive–behavioral therapy: A randomized clinical trial. *Journal of Consulting and Clinical Psychology, 67*, 995–1003. doi:10.1037/0022-006X.67.6.995

Simonian, S. J., Beidel, D. C., Turner, S. M., Berkes, J. L., & Long, J. H. (2001). Recognition of facial affect by children and adolescents diagnosed with social phobia. *Child Psychiatry and Human Development, 32,* 137–145. doi:10.1023/A:1012298707253

Southam-Gerow, M. A., & Kendall, P. C. (2000). A preliminary study of the emotion understanding of youths referred for treatment of anxiety disorders. *Journal of Clinical Child Psychology, 29,* 319–327. doi:10.1207/S15374424JCCP2903_3

Suveg, C., Kendall, P. C., Comer, J. S., & Robin, J. (2006). Emotion-focused cognitive–behavioral therapy for anxious youth: A multiple-baseline evaluation. *Journal of Contemporary Psychotherapy, 36,* 77–85. doi:10.1007/s10879-006-9010-4

Suveg, C., Morelen, D., Brewer, G. A., & Thomassin, K. (2010). The emotion dysregulation model of anxiety: A preliminary path analytic examination. *Journal of Anxiety Disorders, 24,* 924–930. doi:10.1016/j.janxdis.2010.06.018

Suveg, C., Sood, E., Comer, J. S., & Kendall, P. C. (2009). Changes in emotion regulation following cognitive–behavioral therapy for anxious youth. *Journal of Clinical Child and Adolescent Psychology, 38,* 390–401. doi:10.1080/15374410902851721

Suveg, C., & Zeman, J. (2004). Emotion regulation in children with anxiety disorders. *Journal of Clinical Child and Adolescent Psychology, 33,* 750–759. doi:10.1207/s15374424jccp3304_10

Thomassin, K., & Suveg, C. (2012). Parental autonomy support moderates the link between ADHD symptomatology and task perseverance. *Child Psychiatry and Human Development, 43,* 958–967. doi:10.1007/s10578-012-0306-1

Tiwari, S., Kendall, P. C., Hoff, A. L., Harrison, J. P., & Fizur, P. (2013). Characteristics of exposure sessions as predictors of treatment response in anxious youth. *Journal of Clinical Child and Adolescent Psychology, 42,* 34–43. doi:10.1080/15374416.2012.738454

Wuthrich, V. M., Rapee, R. M., Cunningham, M. J., Lyneham, H. J., Hudson, J. L., & Schniering, C. A. (2012). A randomized controlled trial of the Cool Teens CD-ROM computerized program for adolescent anxiety. *Journal of the American Academy of Child & Adolescent Psychiatry, 51,* 261–270. doi:10.1016/j.jaac.2011.12.002

Zeman, J., Shipman, K., & Suveg, C. (2002). Anger and sadness regulation: Predictions to internalizing and externalizing symptoms in children. *Journal of Clinical Child and Adolescent Psychology, 31,* 393–398. doi:10.1207/S15374424JCCP3103_11

Zimmerman, B. J. (1986). Becoming a self-regulated learner: Which are the key subprocesses? *Contemporary Educational Psychology, 11,* 307–313. doi:10.1016/0361-476X(86)90027-5

Zimmerman, B. J. (1989). A social cognitive view of self-regulated academic learning. *Journal of Educational Psychology, 81,* 329–339. doi:10.1037/0022-0663.81.3.329

Zimmerman, B. J. (2000). Attaining self-regulation: A social cognitive perspective. In M. Boekaerts, P. R. Pintrich, & M. Zeidner (Eds.), *Handbook of self-regulation* (pp. 13–39). San Diego, CA: Academic Press. doi:10.1016/B978-012109890-2/50031-7

7

EMOTION REGULATION INTERVENTIONS AND CHILDHOOD DEPRESSION

JILL EHRENREICH-MAY, SARAH M. KENNEDY, AND CARA S. REMMES

Depressive disorders are common psychological disorders of childhood and adolescence that affect between 4% and 7% of youth (Costello, Mustillo, Erkanli, Keeler, & Angold, 2003; Merikangas et al., 2010). Depressed mood is even more common: Between 25% and 40% of girls and 20% and 35% of boys experience depressed mood during adolescence (Petersen et al., 1993). Many studies have suggested that, in perhaps the majority of cases, depression does not occur alone: Between 28% and 75% of youth diagnosed with a depressive disorder also experience at least one comorbid anxiety disorder (Angold, Costello, & Erkanli, 1999; Lewinsohn, Zinbarg, Seeley, Lewinsohn, & Sack, 1997). Youth anxiety and depression are associated with social impairment, academic difficulties, and low self-esteem (Essau, Conradt, & Franz Petermann, 2000; Messer & Beidel, 1994;

http://dx.doi.org/10.1037/14641-008
Self-Regulated Learning Interventions With At-Risk Youth: Enhancing Adaptability, Performance, and Well-Being, T. J. Cleary (Editor)
Copyright © 2015 by the American Psychological Association. All rights reserved.

Strauss, Frame, & Forehand, 1987). In addition, youth with comorbid anxiety and depressive disorders have more severe symptomatology and impairment than youth with anxiety disorders without comorbid depression (O'Neil, Podell, Benjamin, & Kendall, 2010; Queen & Ehrenreich-May, 2014). The high prevalence and impact of comorbid internalizing disorders in youth has motivated the development of transdiagnostic models of psychopathology that identify shared processes underlying multiple disorders (e.g., Aldao & Nolen-Hoeksema, 2010; Harvey, Watkins, Mansell, & Shafran, 2004).

Emotion dysregulation may be one shared process that both contributes to and maintains symptoms of depression and anxiety, as well as other psychological disorders (Kring & Sloan, 2009). Although consensus on the definition of *emotion regulation* has not been forthcoming, this construct likely comprises a number of processes that "serve to decrease, maintain, or increase one or more aspects of emotion" (Werner & Gross, 2010, p.12). Emotion regulation may be adaptive or maladaptive, and the extent to which emotion regulation strategies are adaptive may depend on whether they help or hinder self-regulation. The term *self-regulation* is defined in this context as methods by which individuals control internal or external processes to better optimize or achieve goals, standards, or values (Baumeister, Heatherton, & Tice, 1994; Carver & Scheier, 1998, 2011). We define emotion regulation in this chapter as an internal process that is distinct from self-regulation, because it does not need to occur in the context of explicitly goal-directed behavior; however, it is also a process that must be deployed for effective self-regulation to occur. Emotion regulation may either facilitate or inhibit goal-directed self-regulation, depending on the type of emotion regulation strategies used and the individual's effectiveness in using those strategies.

In this chapter, we address the ways in which ineffective emotion regulation may contribute to depression and comorbid emotional disorders in youth by interfering with effective self-regulation, and how new transdiagnostic treatments, such as the Unified Protocol for the Treatment of Emotional Disorders in Adolescence (UP-A; Ehrenreich et al., 2008), target these failures of self-regulation directly and indirectly via the UP-A's focus on increasing adaptive emotion regulation. Deficits in emotion regulation and self-regulation in emotional disorders, and both observed and hypothesized changes in these processes over the course of treatment, are illustrated through a case scenario. We also discuss preliminary evidence for the efficacy of the UP-A and future directions for applying theories of emotion regulation and self-regulation to treatment development and refinement of the Unified Protocol models.

EMOTION REGULATION, SELF-REGULATION, AND PSYCHOPATHOLOGY: THEORETICAL AND RESEARCH FOUNDATIONS

According to Gross's modal model of emotion, the experience of emotion comprises a three-component system: attention to an emotional experience, appraisal of that experience, and the activation of a multisystem set of action tendencies (Gross & Thompson, 2007). Compared with individuals without depression, those with depression show apparent deficits across all levels of the model, such that they are more attentive to negative environmental cues (e.g., Gotlib, Krasnoperova, Yue, & Joormann, 2004; Joormann & Gotlib, 2007), interpret ambiguous events more negatively (Cowden Hindash & Amir, 2012; Mathews & MacLeod, 2005; Mogg, Bradbury, & Bradley, 2006), and engage in social withdrawal (Strauss, Forehand, Smith, & Frame, 1986) and rumination processes (Nolen-Hoeksema, 1991) more frequently in response to negative events. Emotion regulation may affect any part of the emotional experience, including its physiological, experiential, and/or behavioral aspects. Emotion regulation processes may be used before the full onset of an emotional experience (antecedent-focused processes), such as in situation selection, attentional deployment, or cognitive change. They also may be used after the onset of an emotion to change its course or intensity (response-focused strategies), as in situation modification or response modulation (Gross & Thompson, 2007). Emotion regulation involves modulating one, some, or all of these processes in the service of goal attainment, and the extent to which individual processes are adaptive or maladaptive depends on the extent to which they serve these goals. Emotion regulation thus may involve up-regulating emotions, maintaining emotions, or down-regulating emotions, depending on the desired goal.

Youth with elevated symptoms of depression and anxiety have been shown to have difficulty with regulating their emotions, tending to overuse strategies that prolong or exacerbate negative emotions and underuse strategies that aid in mood repair (e.g., Aldao, Nolen-Hoeksema, & Schweizer, 2010; Carthy, Horesh, Apter, & Gross, 2010). Research has shown that certain emotion regulation strategies may be more effective at decreasing the experience of negative emotion than other strategies, and children and adolescents who primarily use these less effective strategies may be at greater risk for psychopathology. For example, evidence has suggested that *suppression*, which involves inhibiting the behavioral expression of emotion, may be associated with greater sympathetic activation among adults (Gross, 1998; Hofmann, Heering, Sawyer, & Asnaani, 2009), greater experience of negative emotion (Gross & John, 2003), and heightened anxiety and depression symptoms in children and adolescents (Aldao et al., 2010; Gullone & Taffe, 2012). Conversely, youth with emotional disorders may be ineffective at using protective strategies, such as *reappraisal*, which involves changing one's appraisal of the meaning of a situation to alter the situation's emotional impact (Gross & Thompson, 2007). Anxious children have been shown to use lower levels of spontaneous and cued reappraisal (Carthy et al., 2010), and youth who have reported using reappraisal more frequently have been found to exhibit lower levels of psychopathology (Aldao et al., 2010). It is also possible that some youth may use strategies (e.g., reappraisal) that are thought to be protective against psychopathology, but they may do so ineffectively or incompletely. Individuals may inaccurately perceive themselves as having emotion regulation deficits or overestimate the extent of their deficits (Carthy et al., 2010), a hypothesis supported by studies that have found that perceived effectiveness in regulating anxiety is an important predictor of anxiety severity (e.g., Weems, Costa, Watts, Taylor, & Cannon, 2007; Weems, Silverman, Rapee, & Pina, 2003).

How do difficulties with emotion regulation influence the abilities of children and adolescents to self-regulate their behavior? According to Tice and Bratslavsky (2000), self-regulation has three components: *standards*, or abstract concepts of how things should be; *self-monitoring*, or continuous evaluation of current circumstances against invoked standards; and *strengths*, or exerting self-control to override impulses so that one can achieve higher order goals. Goal-oriented action occurs within a feedback loop, whereby present circumstances are compared with standards through a process of self-monitoring, and discrepancies are reduced through the exertion of strength (Carver & Scheier, 1990, 1998). As illustrated in Figure 7.1, negative emotion occurs when rate of progress toward a goal is perceived as inadequate, whereas positive emotion occurs when rate of progress is perceived as being in excess of some criterion (Carver & Scheier, 1990, 1998). Negative emotion, however, is not inherently undesirable; rather, as long as it is not excessive or poorly regulated, negative emotion may serve an adaptive function by allowing individuals to increase effort toward goal attainment, reprioritize goals currently out of awareness (Simon, 1967), or abandon goals that may be unrealistic in favor of new, more realistic ones (Carver & Scheier, 2011). When this feedback system is functioning properly, emotion regulation and self-regulation are two interrelated processes that operate in concert to promote goal attainment (Johnson, Carver, & Fulford, 2010). Insufficient progress toward goals, identified in the self-regulation feedback loop, triggers negative emotion, and negative emotion is regulated or eliminated as a result of successful goal pursuit or goal reprioritization. However, a "black box" exists at the center of this theory: What are the factors that determine whether negative affect promotes or hinders goal-directed behavior? Carver

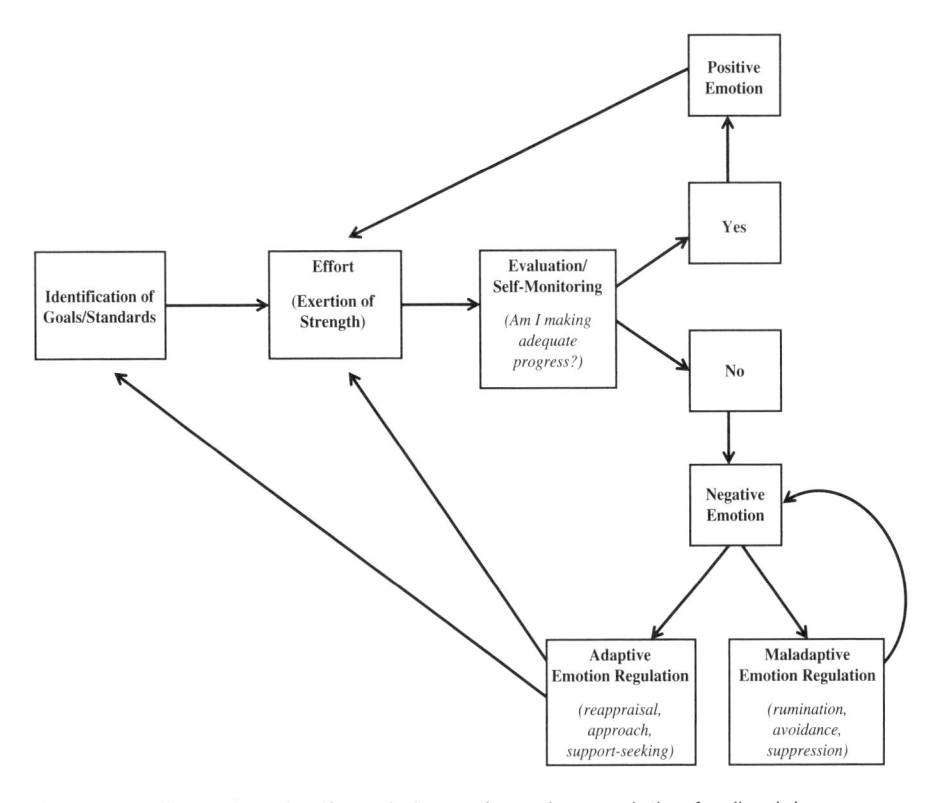

Figure 7.1. Illustration of self-regulation and emotion regulation feedback loops.

and Scheier (2011) contended that the attainability of a particular goal is one such factor, but we argue that an individual's emotion regulation repertoire also determines whether an individual is motivated or stymied by the experience of negative emotions.

Although negative emotions can aid in self-regulation by motivating individuals to pursue or change goals, emotions also may hinder self-regulation. When experiencing aversive emotional states, individuals often shift from goal pursuit to mood repair and abandon long-term goals in favor of immediate gratification (Koole, 2009; Tice, 2009). In doing so, they enter a separate feedback loop, which we term the *emotion regulation feedback loop*, that functions to help repair negative mood states so that individuals can reenter the self-regulation feedback loop (see Figure 7.1). Repairing negative mood states, although necessary for effective self-regulation, may at least temporarily detract from self-regulated goal attainment. Under a limited resources model of self-control (Baumeister et al., 1994; Baumeister, Bratslavsky, Muraven, & Tice, 1998), emotion regulation and self-regulation may compete for the same pool of limited psychological resources, and energy invested in emotion regulation depletes energy that otherwise could be used in the service of goal attainment (Koole, 2009). This may not present much of a problem for individuals who are skilled at using emotion regulation strategies that are thought to be adaptive (e.g., reappraisal), because they are able to accurately identify their emotional states, reframe negative cognitions, and listen to what their emotional experience is telling them about their goals and behaviors. They move out of the emotion regulation feedback loop relatively quickly and return to goal pursuit. However, individuals who are less skilled at using adaptive strategies, or who rely on maladaptive emotion regulation strategies, may get stuck in the emotion regulation feedback loop.

Certain emotion regulation strategies (e.g., expressive suppression, rumination, avoidance) have been shown to be ineffective at repairing negative moods states or effective only in the short term and result in a later rebound of negative emotion. The use of suppression in adults, for example, has been associated with increased sympathetic arousal (Gross, 1998; Hofmann et al., 2009) and increased amygdala activity (McRae, Ochsner, & Gross, 2011). Similarly, a ruminative response style (Nolen-Hoeksema, 1991) confers risk for and maintains negative affect by enhancing negative thinking (Lyubomirsky & Nolen-Hoeksema, 1995; Moulds, Kandris, & Williams, 2007), impairing problem solving (Lyubomirsky & Nolen-Hoeksema, 1995), and reducing motivation to engage in goal-directed behavior (Lyubomirsky & Nolen-Hoeksema, 1993). Behavioral or emotional avoidance, although immediately reinforcing, also may maintain or even increase negative affect in the long term by preventing habituation and disconfirmation of distorted beliefs while limiting access to positively reinforcing activities (Campbell-Sills & Barlow, 2007; Harvey et al., 2004). The maintenance of negative affective states through the use of ineffective emotion regulation strategies effectively short-circuits discrepancy-reducing feedback loops and makes it difficult for individuals to pursue goal-directed behaviors that would reduce those discrepancies.

UNIFIED PROTOCOL FOR THE TREATMENT OF EMOTIONAL DISORDERS IN ADOLESCENCE

Targeting Regulatory Processes With a Transdiagnostic Treatment Model

Burgeoning interest in the role of emotion dysregulation in child and adolescent psychopathology has initiated the development of new treatments that specifically target deficits in emotion regulation. These treatments include Emotion-Focused Cognitive Behavioral Therapy for anxiety (ECBT; Suveg, Kendall, Comer, & Robin, 2006), Contextual Emotion-Regulation

Therapy for Childhood Depression (CERT; Kovacs et al., 2006), and the UP-A (Ehrenreich et al., 2008) and Unified Protocol for the Treatment of Emotional Disorders in Children (UP-C; Ehrenreich-May & Bilek, 2012). In part, the development of such treatments has been motivated by the recognition that high comorbidity rates among emotional disorders in children and adolescents (Angold et al., 1999; Seligman, Goza, & Ollendick, 2004) require shifting the focus of treatment from disorder-specific processes to common processes shared among emotional disorders. This shift in focus is particularly important because some evidence has suggested that comorbidity may predict poorer treatment outcomes when single-disorder or single-domain treatments are used. For example, some studies have found that comorbid depression symptoms predict poorer treatment outcome for youth who are receiving treatment for a primary anxiety disorder (e.g., Berman, Weems, Silverman, & Kurtines, 2000; O'Neil & Kendall, 2012), and comorbid anxiety in depressed children and adolescents has been shown to result in poorer outcomes in the treatment of primary depression (see Ollendick, Jarrett, Grills-Taquechel, Hovey, & Wolff, 2008). In addition, some evidence has indicated that anxiety- and depression-specific treatments may not affect the regulation of emotions that are not directly targeted by the treatment. For example, in a pilot study of an emotion-focused cognitive–behavioral treatment for youth with anxiety, youth evidenced positive treatment gains in anxiety symptoms and regulation of worry, but there were no pre- or posttreatment gains in the regulation of sadness or anger (Suveg, Sood, Comer, & Kendall, 2009).

Such findings have motivated the development of treatments for children and adolescents that address emotion regulation deficits that cut across disorder classes. In this chapter, we discuss one such treatment package: the UP-A (Ehrenreich et al., 2008). The UP-A is an emotion-focused, transdiagnostic treatment for adolescents (ages 12–17) with a primary anxiety, primary depression, or coprincipal anxiety and depression diagnosis. Like the Unified Protocol for the Transdiagnostic Treatment of Emotional Disorders in adults (UP; Barlow et al., 2010), of which it is a downward extension, the UP-A draws on recent findings in the field of emotion science to deliver traditional evidence-based treatment skills within a broad emotion-focused context.

The theoretical basis of the UP-A is Gross and Thompson's (2007) modal model of emotions reviewed earlier, in which emotion occurs through a situation-attention-appraisal-response sequence. Gross and Thompson distinguished emotion regulation strategies on the basis of whether they occur early or late along the trajectory of an emotional experience. Antecedent emotion regulation processes (i.e., situation selection, situation modification, attentional deployment, cognitive change) occur early in the trajectory of an emotional experience, whereas response-focused emotion regulation processes occur after emotional responses have been generated (Gross & Thompson, 2007). The UP-A focuses on altering maladaptive antecedent-focused processes, such as avoidance (a type of situation selection), parental accommodation or safety behavior use (a type of situation modification), distraction and rumination (types of attentional deployment), and negative cognitive styles. As adolescents learn more adaptive emotion regulation strategies, they become better able to self-regulate their behavior in the service of goal attainment.

Flexibility is a cornerstone of the UP-A. In addition to its five required sections, the UP-A also contains three optional sections that incorporate techniques from motivational interviewing, additional parent training, and safety planning to address the variety of issues with which adolescents may present. Each module also contains a flexible number of sessions so that clinicians can choose to spend additional time on those skills that may be most applicable to a particular adolescent's presentation or that an adolescent may have particular difficulty acquiring. Typical treatment length varies from 8 to 21 sessions, which enables effective adaptation for the adolescent with a single simple phobia diagnosis and for the adolescent with multiple comorbid emotional disorders. In the following section, we discuss the specific content of each UP-A section and focus on how the specific emotion regulation processes targeted in each module can help correct failures of self-regulation (see Table 7.1).

Core Components of UP-A

Section 1: Emotion Education

The primary content delivered in Section 1 includes psychoeducation about the purpose and function of emotions; the goal is to promote adolescents' awareness of their own emotional experiences. To facilitate emotional awareness, the three parts of an emotional experience are introduced (i.e., physical sensations, thoughts, emotion-driven behaviors), and adolescents are encouraged to apply this tripartite model of emotions to their own experiences through in-session practice exercises and homework. Adolescents also learn to conduct their own functional assessment of emotions by identifying antecedents, behaviors, and consequences associated with their emotional experiences. Clinicians also work with adolescents throughout this module to normalize emotional experiences as natural and necessary. In addition to these core skills, time is devoted in the initial sessions to explaining treatment structure, building rapport, and helping adolescents identify treatment goals.

This first section of treatment lays the groundwork for later sections, which focus on correcting maladaptive emotion regulation processes, by providing data about which emotions adolescents experience most often,

TABLE 7.1
Intervention Techniques Used in the UP-A and the Mechanism Through Which These Techniques Address Deficits in Self-Regulation

Section number	Intervention strategies used	Application of strategies to self-regulation feedback loop
1	Emotion education	Introduce the function of emotion in motivating behavior
2	Nonjudgmental awareness Generalized emotion exposures	Teach youth to accept negative affect in order to use it appropriately to motivate goal-directed behavior
3	Cognitive reappraisal	Reduce intensity of negative emotional states to allow for greater energy toward promotion goals
	Problem solving	Teach youth to identify appropriate goals and concretize steps toward goal pursuit
4	Emotion exposures Behavioral activation	Encourage adolescent to pursue goals despite negative affect
5	Relapse prevention	Teach youth to recognize indicators of times when they are stuck and unable to pursue goals appropriately

which processes adolescents use most frequently to regulate these emotions, and how the use of such processes impacts adaptive functioning and progress toward goals. Adolescents begin to learn how to self-monitor their own emotional processes (Shapiro & Cole, 1999) and to identify how potentially maladaptive emotion regulation strategies, such as avoidance or suppression, may maintain negative emotions and prevent progress toward goals. Overuse of these strategies may prolong time spent in the emotion regulation feedback loop and prevent individuals from engaging in goal-directed behavior. Although many adolescents focus on their experiences with anxiety and sadness during this module, the broad emotion-focused approach of the UP-A allows clinicians to address the function of positive emotions, anger, shame, guilt, and others.

Section 2: Emotion Awareness and Experiencing

Section 2 focuses on teaching adolescents to fully feel emotions through the use of generalized emotion exposures and mindfulness-based exercises. Generalized emotion exposures in the UP-A are based on traditional mood induction paradigms and involve eliciting emotional experiences (e.g., by watching a sad movie clip or thinking about an upsetting memory) while preventing emotional avoidance. Mindfulness-based strategies also are used to teach adolescents nonjudgmental awareness of emotions in which they are encouraged to notice subjective emotional experiences while refraining from judgment (Hayes, Follette, & Linehan, 2004; Orsillo, Roemer, & Holowka, 2005).

This section of treatment targets attentional processes involved in emotion regulation and encourages adolescents to fully experience their emotions without using suppression, distraction, or avoidance. Studies have found that adolescents with high levels of worry use more avoidant strategies, such as thought suppression, thought substitution, and distraction, than do adolescents with moderate levels of worry (Gosselin et al., 2007). In addition to maintaining or even worsening negative affect through a rebound effect, these strategies make effective problem solving difficult (Campbell-Sills & Barlow, 2007), perhaps because the use of emotionally avoidant strategies consumes resources that could otherwise be devoted to goal-directed behavior. In addition, because negative affect functions as a discrepancy signal in feedback loops, failure to attend to this signal prevents adolescents from engaging in strategies, such as problem solving, that might help correct this discrepancy. As adolescents begin to fully experience their emotions, they reenter goal-directed self-regulation feedback loops and gain the ability to use goal-promoting strategies.

Section 3: Cognitive Flexibility and Reappraisal

The third section of treatment focuses on increasing cognitive flexibility by teaching adolescents to identify and restructure maladaptive cognitions about emotions and emotional situations. These skills are taught as *detective thinking*, in which adolescents learn to identify cognitive errors (i.e., "thinking traps"), such as overestimating the likelihood that a negative event will occur, catastrophizing the consequences of a negative event, mind reading, and ignoring the positive. Adolescents then learn to challenge these cognitions through *detective questioning*, which involves assessing the accuracy and true probability of these cognitions to reframe them. This section also promotes flexible thinking by teaching adolescents problem-solving skills to use in situations where they may feel stuck.

Section 3 focuses on cognitive errors that are typical of adolescents with emotional disorders and teaches them to replace these cognitions with more accurate or realistic ways of thinking. Although some support exists for Beck's (1976) cognitive content-specificity hypothesis that psychological disorders have distinct cognitive profiles, research has suggested that some cognitive errors may be common to emotional disorders more generally. For example, maladaptive cognitive styles, such as catastrophizing and overgeneralizing, may be transdiagnostic cognitive processes (e.g., Weems et al., 2007) that cut across emotional disorders. Engaging in these negative cognitive styles (or thinking traps) may interfere with effective self-regulation by leading to avoidance behaviors and failure to make progress toward goals. These cognitive styles may solidify as adolescents fail to make progress toward promotion goals, thus leading to or worsening depressive symptoms (Strauman, 1996). The goal of reframing maladaptive cognitions is to reduce the intensity and duration of negative emotional states, thereby allowing adolescents to devote increased energy and attention to promotion goals.

This section's focus on problem solving also corrects maladaptive attentional processes, such as self-focused rumination, an emotion regulation strategy that has been associated with symptoms of depression and anxiety (Aldao & Nolen-Hoeksema, 2010). Compared with individuals who use other emotion regulation strategies, those high in rumination exhibit less confidence in their ability to solve problems and are less willing to implement problem-solving strategies (Lyubomirsky, Tucker, Caldwell, & Berg, 1999). By teaching adolescents to replace ruminative tendencies with more proactive and action-oriented problem-solving strategies, Section 3 encourages adolescents to reengage in the pursuit of both lower and higher order goals.

Section 4: Emotion Exposure

In the fourth section of treatment, adolescents learn the concept of opposite action in the face of high negative emotionality (Linehan, 1993); they also complete in-session and out-of-session exposures to emotion-provoking stimuli and situations, based on their own individualized emotion and avoidance hierarchies. This section focuses on altering emotion-drive action tendencies (i.e., by encouraging approach behaviors rather than avoidance behaviors) and preventing emotional avoidance (i.e., by preventing adolescents from using safety behaviors or cognitive avoidance strategies during exposures). Clinicians begin this section by explaining the rationale behind emotion exposures, which includes explaining the process of habituation and the negative consequences of avoidance. Adolescents then begin to complete emotion exposures across a variety of potential categories (e.g., exposures to physiological sensations of distress, situational exposures to fear-evoking stimuli or situations—particularly those highly avoided—and activating experiences to counter dysregulation of sadness and behavioral withdrawal), which can be adapted to address any emotion-related avoidance behavior. The use of subjective units of distress allows clinicians to monitor adolescent affect and patients to self-monitor their subjective levels of emotion during exposures. For adolescents with difficulty regulating sadness and exhibiting concomitant withdrawal, Section 4 also incorporates components of behavioral activation, such as pleasant activity scheduling, under the umbrella of "positive emotion exposures." Because depressed individuals have a tendency to avoid or suppress positive emotions (Campbell-Sills, Barlow, Brown, & Hofmann, 2006) or withdraw from situations or activities, positive emotion exposures are conceptualized as opposite action tendencies.

Section 4 targets maladaptive situation selection and situation modification strategies, such as avoidance and use of safety behaviors, which help to maintain negative emotional experiences and prevent contact with positive emotional experiences. Avoidance is an attractive emotion regulation strategy for adolescents because it is immediately reinforcing, but it unfortunately maintains emotional distress in the long term by preventing disconfirmation of distorted beliefs and limiting access to positively reinforcing activities (Campbell-Sills & Barlow, 2007; Werner & Gross, 2010). Avoidance also interferes with effective self-regulation because it allocates resources to avoiding negative affect in the short term at the expense of goal pursuit, and it constricts activities and social interactions in such a way as to make goal pursuit more difficult. The consequence is that actual–ideal discrepancies are enlarged, and adolescents are more likely to continue to engage in avoidance behaviors or abandon goals altogether. As adolescents begin to approach previously avoided situations, and negative affect experiences in these situations decreases, they can reallocate energy previously allotted to mood repair to self-regulation goals. Emotion exposures also build self-efficacy as adolescents learn to approach situations and sit with negative emotions, and these feelings of self-efficacy may spill over into their beliefs about their ability to attain nonemotional goals, too.

Section 5: Relapse Prevention

Section 5 is devoted to skill review and consolidation, relapse prevention, and planning. The clinician and adolescent again rate items on the adolescent's emotion and avoidance hierarchy, discuss the progress that has been made in problem areas, and identify areas that still require work. The adolescent is encouraged to reflect on which skills he or she found most helpful, and the adolescent is encouraged to continue to use these skills to effectively regulate emotions and behavior in the future. The clinician and adolescent develop a relapse prevention plan and discuss how the latter can use skills learned in treatment if symptoms return. Section 5 thus encourages adolescents to reflect on improvements—not just in symptoms but also in regulating emotions and overall functioning. In addition, by encouraging adolescents to identify warning signs of relapse (e.g., not completing schoolwork, staying away from friends, avoiding feared situations), clinicians encourage adolescents to identify how self-regulation failures may be indicators of increased negative mood or difficulty regulating emotions.

The Case of Jane

Jane is a 15-year-old girl who presents for treatment at a specialty research clinic. Her intake assessment consists of adolescent and parent diagnostic interviews using the *Anxiety Disorders Interview Schedule for DSM–IV: Child and Parent Versions* (ADIS–IV–CP; Silverman & Albano, 1996). In addition, Jane and her mother complete self-report and parent-report questionnaires about Jane's anxiety and depressive symptoms, and emotion regulation strategies. Jane reports depressive symptoms such as anhedonia, low energy, social withdrawal, and difficulty sleeping. She also reports generalized anxiety symptoms and endorses worry about a number of different areas, including her schoolwork and interpersonal relationships. Based on information obtained during the ADIS–IV–CP, a principal diagnosis of major depressive disorder–recurrent, moderate and a secondary diagnosis of generalized anxiety disorder are assigned.

Interview and questionnaire data regarding Jane's emotion regulation strategies indicate high degrees of emotional suppression. Jane's use of emotional suppression in managing her negative affect is having negative effects on her academic performance and interpersonal relationships. For example, Jane and her mother report that Jane is performing poorly in her mathematics class and that her mother commonly provides her with homework suggestions, which Jane reports interpreting as criticism. She reports trying to ignore these comments, because they are distressing to her; however, she continued to think about this perceived criticism while attempting homework, and subsequently had difficulty completing assignments. In this case, Jane's attempts to suppress negative emotions that arose in response to her mother's comments interfered with self-regulation because her use of this maladaptive emotion regulation strategy resulted in a rebound of negative emotions. She became stuck in the emotion regulation feedback loop when her efforts at suppression were unsuccessful, thus leading to rumination and preventing her from completing the assignment. Jane also states that she has frequently "lashed out" at others when they have provided her with homework advice, because of her frustration about her poor performance. Therefore, Jane's attempts at suppressing her emotions also have led to dysregulated emotional expression, resulting in further academic and interpersonal difficulties.

In addition, Jane also endorses frequently engaging in social withdrawal when she experiences a depressed mood. She reports that she had recently planned on going to the beach with friends; however, she decided to stay home instead, because of low energy and worry about her appearance. Although it may have alleviated worry in the short term, Jane's engagement in avoidance prevented her from engaging in goal-directed activity (i.e., socializing with friends) and from using a potentially more adaptive emotion regulation strategy (i.e., seeking social support). In that way, Jane's attempts at emotion regulation contributed to further difficulties in interpersonal relationships and prevented her from using positive social interactions to more effectively regulate her mood.

Treatment for Jane consists of 18 weekly, 50-minute sessions. Treatment begins with psychoeducation about emotions and focuses on a discussion about the function of emotions in directing behavior. During the second section of treatment, Jane is taught nonjudgmental awareness of her emotions and is encouraged to fully engage in her negative emotional experiences instead of attempting to suppress these emotions. These sessions also include a direct discussion about her attempts to suppress her emotions regarding interactions with her mother about her academic performance. She is able to identify the effect that this suppression has on her continued rumination while attempting to complete academic work, and on her later dysregulated emotional expression and interpersonal relationships. During treatment, her use of these nonjudgmental awareness exercises allows her to engage fully in these uncomfortable emotions and then focus her energy on academic goal-directed behavior (e.g., homework), instead of becoming stuck in the cycle of suppression and rumination (i.e., the emotion regulation feedback loop).

In Section 3, Jane is taught to identify cognitive biases regarding her academic difficulties and challenge her automatic thoughts through use of detective thinking strategies. Through identifying and challenging her cognitive biases before entering emotionally charged situations, Jane is able to identify the possibility that the homework advice provided to her was not criticism. By adapting this new interpretation, she is able to experience less negative emotional reactions when others provide her with academic advice and is able to seek out help more frequently. By using this more adaptive strategy to help regulate her emotions before entering emotionally charged situations, Jane becomes better able to use homework advice to monitor and adjust her progress toward goals (i.e., the self-regulation feedback loop), while not getting too distracted by negative emotional states. Treatment with Jane also includes an emphasis on problem solving; she learns to replace her previously used suppression strategies with alternate modes of interacting with her mother and friends regarding difficult topics.

Section 4 focuses on the use of behavioral activation as a strategy to target negative mood states, as Jane was previously avoiding social interaction and other enjoyable activities because of low motivation and anhedonia. She monitors her mood and pleasurable activities over the course of a week and then graphs these activities to identify how they were related. In addition, she creates a fun activity list and is assigned weekly homework to gradually increase her activity. Jane is able to use these behavioral activation exercises to pursue fun activities and goal-directed activities, despite a negative mood state. Section 4 also includes interoceptive exposure exercises that induce physical symptoms of anxiety to teach Jane that these physiological feelings are benign. Situational exposure exercises are then introduced to target Jane's anxiety regarding perfectionism. Before beginning situational exposures, Jane learns about avoidance as an emotion-driven behavior, and she completes a fear and avoidance hierarchy regarding situations that she is currently avoiding because of anxiety. Exposure exercises begin by facing fears lower on her hierarchy, and then she gradually faces fears of increasing difficulty both in session and during homework. Through these exercises, Jane learns to work toward goals despite feelings of anxiety.

Section 5 consists of a discussion about ways that Jane can continue to practice skills taught in therapy, such as nonjudgmental awareness, problem solving, and behavioral activation to manage her symptoms of depression and remain focused on goal-directed activity. Jane is also able to identify the difference between normative sadness and depression, and to identify signs of clinical deterioration and strategies that she can use should this occur.

Research Support and Current Studies

Current research support for the UP-A includes an initial multiple-baseline trial (Ehrenreich, Goldstein, Wright, & Barlow, 2009), an open trial (Ellard, Fairholme, Boisseau, Farchione, & Barlow, 2010), and a recently completed waitlist-controlled trial. Results from the multiple-baseline trial and the open trial have been published previously and are summarized here; results from the waitlist-controlled trial, which included 51 adolescents with a primary diagnosis of an emotional disorder, will be discussed in future publications.

The initial multiple-baseline trial of the UP-A, which included three adolescents, provided preliminary support for the use of a transdiagnostic, emotion-focused treatment model in targeting symptoms of anxiety and depression in adolescents. All participants experienced a reduction in anxiety and/or depressive symptoms at posttreatment, as measured by clinician severity ratings (CSRs) using the ADIS–IV–CP (Silverman & Albano, 1996), and by the 6-month follow-up point, none of the participants still met criteria for a clinical emotional disorder diagnosis (Ehrenreich et al., 2009). Subsequently, an open trial investigation of the UP-A, including 12 adolescents who met criteria for principal anxiety and/or depressive disorder, was conducted to examine treatment feasibility and preliminary efficacy (see Trosper, Buzzella, Bennett, & Ehrenreich, 2009). Comorbidity was substantial in that sample: 58% of adolescents met criteria for both an anxiety and a depressive disorder. Results indicated significant reductions in clinician-rated CSRs from pre-posttreatment, and gains were maintained at 3- and 6-month follow-up points. Parents' ratings of adolescents' emotion regulation also improved: Parents reported improvements in general emotion dysregulation, worry and sadness-related emotion dysregulation, and coping with anger

(Trosper et al., 2009). Preliminary results from a waitlist-controlled trial demonstrate greater improvements in principal disorder CSRs and symptoms of anxiety and depression in our immediate treatment group, as compared with a waitlist-control, as well as improvements in various measures of emotion regulation (Ehrenreich-May et al., 2013).

DISCUSSION AND FUTURE DIRECTIONS

Maladaptive emotion regulation processes (e.g., rumination, suppression, avoidance) contribute to depression and other emotional disorders by interfering with effective self-regulation. Transdiagnostic treatments that target these maladaptive strategies may improve both emotion regulation and self-regulation. For example, Jane's reliance on suppression and avoidance as emotion regulation strategies caused her to become stuck in the pursuit of her academic and interpersonal goals by preventing her from focusing on her schoolwork and from experiencing rewarding social interactions with her mother and peers. After she learned to address these maladaptive strategies using more adaptive emotion regulation skills, she experienced improvements in self-regulation in academic and interpersonal contexts and in depressive symptoms. Research is needed, though, to determine the timing of and relationship between changes in emotion regulation and self-regulation over the course of treatment, as well as how these changes relate to symptom improvement. Understanding these change processes will help researchers develop more effective treatments for emotional disorders in youth, particularly for depression.

Depression and anxiety in children and adolescents traditionally have been treated with separate protocols in the evidence-based treatment literature, and several meta-analyses have suggested that current psychotherapeutic treatments for depression may be less effective than those for anxiety. For example, a meta-analysis conducted by Weisz, McCarty, and Valeri (2006) found a small mean effect size averaging across 35 treatment studies for depression (Cohen's $d = .34$), whereas a recent meta-analysis of 55 randomized trials for anxiety found a mean effect size in the medium range (Cohen's $d = .65$; Reynolds, Wilson, Austin, & Hooper, 2012). In addition, comorbidity (particularly with anxiety disorders) has generally been found to negatively affect treatment outcomes for depressed youth (see Ollendick et al., 2008, for a review). Given that up to 75% of youth with a depressive disorder may have comorbid clinical anxiety (Angold et al., 1999), the continued development and further refinement of transdiagnostic treatments for children and adolescents, such as the UP-A, is an important step in improving treatment outcomes for anxious youth and depressed youth.

Deficits in emotion regulation are hypothesized to both confer risk for emotional disorders and help maintain symptoms; therefore, future studies should examine changes in emotion regulation as both treatment outcomes and potential treatment mechanisms. Although changes in disorder symptoms and diagnostic remission status traditionally have been favored as primary outcome variables, several studies have begun to examine changes in emotion regulation as secondary outcomes. Indeed, preliminary evidence suggests that cognitive–behavioral treatments for anxiety (e.g., Suveg et al., 2009), emotion-focused treatments for anxiety (Suveg et al., 2006), and transdiagnostic treatments for emotional disorders (Ehrenreich et al., 2009) positively affect the ability of children and adolescents to regulate a variety of emotions. However, the field of emotion regulation, especially in children and adolescents, is still in its nascency, and barriers must be overcome with respect to the measurement of emotion regulation processes. For example, many existing measures of emotion regulation for children and adolescents are downward extensions of measures developed for adults that may lack developmental specificity (Sloan & Kring, 2007). In addition, the development of multimodal measures of emotion regulation processes is important given that children and adolescents may have difficulty self-reporting on regulation processes because they may be highly automatic or just outside awareness. Advances in the measurement of emotion regulation will give researchers the tools to more reliably examine how emotion regulation processes change over the course of treatment.

The focus on symptom change and diagnostic remission has also meant that many treatment studies have failed to report on changes in functional impairment related to diagnoses. Research has suggested that improvements in symptoms may not always correspond to improvements in general functioning (Winters, Collett, & Myers, 2005), so it is important to examine not only how much symptoms have improved but also how much youths' ability to self-regulate their behavior and function effectively across a variety of domains also has improved. This effort could include, for example, an assessment of academic improvement, changes in participation and engagement in activities, or increases in the number of social contacts over the course of treatment. These types of outcomes are rarely assessed in a systematic way, but they would provide good indications of improvements in the ability to self-regulate behavior across a variety of domains.

Emotion dysregulation may be an important risk factor for the development of depression and other emotional disorders, and changes in emotion regulation and, consequently, self-regulation may be a key mechanism through which treatments for emotional disorders in youth work. Continued refinements to methods of assessing emotion regulation and self-regulation, and the incorporation of these measures in a more systematic way in treatment studies, will enable a better understanding of these relationships.

REFERENCES

Aldao, A., & Nolen-Hoeksema, S. (2010). Specificity of cognitive emotion regulation strategies: A transdiagnostic examination. *Behaviour Research and Therapy*, 48, 974–983. doi:10.1016/j.brat.2010.06.002

Aldao, A., Nolen-Hoeksema, S., & Schweizer, S. (2010). Emotion-regulation strategies across psychopathology: A meta-analytic review. *Clinical Psychology Review*, 30, 217–237. doi:10.1016/j.cpr.2009.11.004

Angold, A., Costello, E. J., & Erkanli, A. (1999). Comorbidity. *Journal of Child Psychology and Psychiatry*, 40, 57–87. doi:10.1111/1469-7610.00424

Barlow, D. H., Farchione, T. J., Fairholme, C. P., Ellard, K. K., Boisseau, C. L., Allen, L. B., & Ehrenreich-May, J. T. (2010). *Unified Protocol for transdiagnostic treatment of emotional disorders: Therapist guide*. New York, NY: Oxford University Press.

Baumeister, R. F., Bratslavsky, E., Muraven, M., & Tice, D. M. (1998). Ego depletion: Is the active self a limited resource? *Journal of Personality and Social Psychology*, 74, 1252–1265. doi:10.1037/0022-3514.74.5.1252

Baumeister, R. F., Heatherton, T. F., & Tice, D. M. (1994). *Losing control: How and why people fail at self-regulation*. San Diego, CA: Academic Press.

Beck, A. T. (1976). *Cognitive therapy and the emotional disorders*. Madison, CT: International Universities Press.

Berman, S. L., Weems, C. F., Silverman, W. K., & Kurtines, W. M. (2000). Predictors of outcome in exposure-based cognitive and behavioral treatments for phobic and anxiety disorders in children. *Behavior Therapy*, 31, 713–731. doi:10.1016/S0005-7894(00)80040-4

Campbell-Sills, L., & Barlow, D. H. (2007). Incorporating emotion regulation into conceptualizations and treatments of anxiety and mood disorders. In J. J. Gross (Ed.), *Handbook of emotion regulation* (pp. 542–559). New York, NY: Guilford Press.

Campbell-Sills, L., Barlow, D. H., Brown, T. A., & Hofmann, S. G. (2006). Effects of suppression and acceptance on emotional responses of individuals with anxiety and mood disorders. *Behaviour Research and Therapy*, 44, 1251–1263. doi:10.1016/j.brat.2005.10.001

Carthy, T., Horesh, N., Apter, A., & Gross, J. J. (2010). Patterns of emotional reactivity and regulation in children with anxiety disorders. *Journal of Psychopathology and Behavioral Assessment*, 32, 23–36. doi:10.1007/s10862-009-9167-8

Carver, C. S., & Scheier, M. F. (1990). Origins and functions of positive and negative affect: A control-process view. *Psychological Review*, 97, 19–35. doi:10.1037/0033-295X.97.1.19

Carver, C. S., & Scheier, M. F. (1998). *On the self regulation of behavior*. New York, NY: Cambridge University Press. doi:10.1017/CBO9781139174794

Carver, C. S., & Scheier, M. F. (2011). Self-regulation of action and affect. In K. D. Vohs & R. F. Baumeister (Eds.), *Handbook of self-regulation: Research, theory, and applications* (2nd ed., pp. 3–21). New York, NY: Guilford Press.

Costello, E. J., Mustillo, S., Erkanli, A., Keeler, G., & Angold, A. (2003). Prevalence and development of psychiatric disorders in childhood and adolescence. *Archives of General Psychiatry, 60*, 837.

Cowden Hindash, A. H., & Amir, N. (2012). Negative interpretation bias in individuals with depressive symptoms. *Cognitive Therapy and Research, 36*, 502–511.

Ehrenreich, J. T., Buzzella, B. A., Trosper, S. E., Bennett, S. M., Wright, L. R., & Barlow, D. H. (2008). *The Unified Protocol for treatment of emotional disorders in adolescents*. Unpublished manuscript, Department of Psychological and Brain Sciences, Boston University.

Ehrenreich, J. T., Goldstein, C. M., Wright, L. R., & Barlow, D. H. (2009). Development of a Unified Protocol for the treatment of emotional disorders in youth. *Child & Family Behavior Therapy, 31*, 20–37. doi:10.1080/07317100802701228

Ehrenreich-May, J. T., & Bilek, E. L. (2012). The development of a transdiagnostic, cognitive behavioral group intervention for childhood anxiety disorders and co-occurring depression symptoms. *Cognitive and Behavioral Practice, 19*, 41–55. doi:10.1016/j.cbpra.2011.02.003

Ehrenreich-May, J. T., Queen, A. H., Bilek, E. L., Girio-Herrera, E., Kennedy, S., Remmes, C., . . . Barlow, D. H. (2013, July). *Transdiagnostic treatment for anxiety and depression in adolescence: Results from a waitlist-controlled trial*. Paper presented at the 7th World Congress of Behavioral and Cognitive Therapies, Lima, Peru.

Ellard, K. K., Fairholme, C. P., Boisseau, C. L., Farchione, T. J., & Barlow, D. H. (2010). Unified Protocol for the transdiagnostic treatment of emotional disorders: Protocol development and initial outcome data. *Cognitive and Behavioral Practice, 17*, 88–101. doi:10.1016/j.cbpra.2009.06.002

Essau, C. A., Conradt, J., & Franz Petermann, P. (2000). Frequency, comorbidity, and psychosocial impairment of anxiety disorders in German adolescents. *Journal of Anxiety Disorders, 14*, 263–279. doi:10.1016/S0887-6185(99)00039-0

Gosselin, P., Langlois, F., Freeston, M. H., Ladouceur, R., Laberge, M., & Lemay, D. (2007). Cognitive variables related to worry among adolescents: Avoidance strategies and faulty beliefs about worry. *Behaviour Research and Therapy, 45*, 225–233. doi:10.1016/j.brat.2006.03.001

Gotlib, I. H., Krasnoperova, E., Yue, D. N., & Joormann, J. (2004). Attentional biases for negative interpersonal stimuli in clinical depression. *Journal of Abnormal Psychology, 113*, 127–135. doi:10.1037/0021-843X.113.1.121

Gross, J. J. (1998). Antecedent- and response-focused emotion regulation: Divergent consequences for experience, expression, and physiology. *Journal of Personality and Social Psychology, 74*, 224–237. doi:10.1037/0022-3514.74.1.224

Gross, J. J., & John, O. P. (2003). Individual differences in two emotion regulation processes: Implications for affect, relationships, and well-being. *Journal of Personality and Social Psychology, 85*, 348–362. doi:10.1037/0022-3514.85.2.348

Gross, J. J., & Thompson, R. A. (2007). Emotion regulation: Conceptual foundations. In J. J. Gross (Ed.), *Handbook of emotion regulation* (Vol. 3, pp. 3–26). New York, NY: Guilford Press.

Gullone, E., & Taffe, J. (2012). The Emotion Regulation Questionnaire for Children and Adolescents (ERQ-CA): A psychometric evaluation. *Psychological Assessment, 24*, 409–417. doi:10.1037/a0025777

Harvey, A. G., Watkins, E., Mansell, W., & Shafran, R. (2004). *Cognitive behavioural processes across psychological disorders: A transdiagnostic approach to research and treatment.* New York, NY: Oxford University Press.

Hayes, S. C., Follette, V. M., & Linehan, M. M. (2004). *Mindfulness and acceptance: Expanding the cognitive–behavioral tradition.* New York, NY: Guilford Press.

Hofmann, S. G., Heering, S., Sawyer, A. T., & Asnaani, A. (2009). How to handle anxiety: The effects of reappraisal, acceptance, and suppression strategies on anxious arousal. *Behaviour Research and Therapy, 47*, 389–394. doi:10.1016/j.brat.2009.02.010

Johnson, S. L., Carver, C. S., & Fulford, D. (2010). Goal dysregulation in the affective disorders. In A. M. Kring & D. M. Sloan (Eds.), *Emotion regulation and psychopathology: A transdiagnostic approach to etiology and treatment* (pp. 204–228). New York, NY: Guilford Press.

Joormann, J., & Gotlib, I. H. (2007). Selective attention to emotional faces following recovery from depression. *Journal of Abnormal Psychology, 116*, 80–85. doi:10.1037/0021-843X.116.1.80

Koole, S. L. (2009). Does emotion regulation help or hurt self-regulation? In J. P. Forgas, R. F. Baumeister, & D. M. Tice (Eds.), *Psychology of self-regulation: Cognitive, affective, and motivational processes* (pp. 217–232). New York, NY: Psychology Press.

Kovacs, M., Sherrill, J., George, C. J., Pollock, M., Tumuluru, R. V., & Ho, V. (2006). Contextual emotion-regulation therapy for childhood depression: Description and pilot testing of a new intervention. *Journal of the American Academy of Child & Adolescent Psychiatry, 45*, 892–903. doi:10.1097/01.chi.0000222878.74162.5a

Kring, A. M., & Sloan, D. M. (2009). *Emotion regulation and psychopathology: A transdiagnostic approach to etiology and treatment.* New York, NY: Guilford Press.

Lewinsohn, P. M., Zinbarg, R., Seeley, J. R., Lewinsohn, M., & Sack, W. H. (1997). Lifetime comorbidity among anxiety disorders and between anxiety disorders and other mental disorders in adolescents. *Journal of Anxiety Disorders, 11*, 377–394. doi:10.1016/S0887-6185(97)00017-0

Linehan, M. M. (1993). *Cognitive behavioral treatment of borderline personality disorder.* New York, NY: Guilford Press.

Lyubomirsky, S., & Nolen-Hoeksema, S. (1993). Self-perpetuating properties of dysphoric rumination. *Journal of Personality and Social Psychology, 65*, 339–349. doi:10.1037/0022-3514.65.2.339

Lyubomirsky, S., & Nolen-Hoeksema, S. (1995). Effects of self-focused rumination on negative thinking and interpersonal problem solving. *Journal of Personality and Social Psychology, 69*, 176–190. doi:10.1037/0022-3514.69.1.176

Lyubomirsky, S., Tucker, K. L., Caldwell, N. D., & Berg, K. (1999). Why ruminators are poor problem solvers: Clues from the phenomenology of dysphoric rumination. *Journal of Personality and Social Psychology, 77*, 1041–1060. doi:10.1037/0022-3514.77.5.1041

Mathews, A., & MacLeod, C. (2005). Cognitive vulnerability to emotional disorders. *Annual Review of Clinical Psychology, 1*, 167–195. doi:10.1146/annurev.clinpsy.1.102803.143916

McRae, K., Ochsner, K. N., & Gross, J. J. (2011). The reason in passion: A social cognitive neuroscience approach to emotion regulation. In K. D. Vohs & R. F. Baumeister (Eds.), *Handbook of self-regulation* (2nd ed., pp. 186–203). New York, NY: Guilford Press.

Merikangas, K. R., He, J. P., Brody, D., Fisher, P. W., Bourdon, K., & Koretz, D. S. (2010). Prevalence and treatment of mental disorders among U.S. children in the 2001–2004 NHANES. *Pediatrics, 125*, 75–81. doi:10.1542/peds.2008-2598

Messer, S. C., & Beidel, D. C. (1994). Psychosocial correlates of childhood anxiety disorders. *Journal of the American Academy of Child & Adolescent Psychiatry, 33*, 975–983. doi:10.1097/00004583-199409000-00007

Mogg, K., Bradbury, K. E., & Bradley, B. P. (2006). Interpretation of ambiguous information in clinical depression. *Behaviour Research and Therapy, 44*, 1411–1419. doi:10.1016/j.brat.2005.10.008

Moulds, M. L., Kandris, E., & Williams, A. D. (2007). The impact of rumination on memory for self-referent material. *Memory, 15*, 814–821. doi:10.1080/09658210701725831

Nolen-Hoeksema, S. (1991). Responses to depression and their effects on the duration of depressive episodes. *Journal of Abnormal Psychology, 100*, 569–582. doi:10.1037/0021-843X.100.4.569

Ollendick, T. H., Jarrett, M. A., Grills-Taquechel, A. E., Hovey, L. D., & Wolff, J. C. (2008). Comorbidity as a predictor and moderator of treatment outcome in youth with anxiety, affective, attention deficit/hyperactivity disorder, and oppositional/conduct disorders. *Clinical Psychology Review, 28*, 1447–1471. doi:10.1016/j.cpr.2008.09.003

O'Neil, K. A., & Kendall, P. C. (2012). Role of comorbid depression and co-occurring depressive symptoms in outcomes for anxiety-disordered youth treated with cognitive–behavioral therapy. *Child & Family Behavior Therapy, 34*, 197–209. doi:10.1080/07317107.2012.707086

O'Neil, K. A., Podell, J. L., Benjamin, C. L., & Kendall, P. C. (2010). Comorbid depressive disorders in anxiety-disordered youth: Demographic, clinical, and family characteristics. *Child Psychiatry and Human Development, 41*, 330–341. doi:10.1007/s10578-009-0170-9

Orsillo, S. M., Roemer, L., & Holowka, D. W. (2005). Acceptance-based behavioral therapies for anxiety. In S. M. Orsillo & L. Roemer (Eds.), *Acceptance and mindfulness-based approaches to anxiety* (pp. 3–35). New York, NY: Springer. doi:10.1007/0-387-25989-9_1

Petersen, A. C., Compas, B. E., Brooks-Gunn, J., Stemmler, M., Ey, S., & Grant, K. E. (1993). Depression in adolescence. *American Psychologist, 48*, 155–168. doi:10.1037/0003-066X.48.2.155

Queen, A. H., & Ehrenreich-May, J. T. (2014). Anxiety-disordered adolescents with and without a comorbid depressive disorder: Variations in clinical presentation and emotion regulation. *Journal of Emotional and Behavioral Disorders, 22*, 160–170.

Reynolds, S., Wilson, C., Austin, J., & Hooper, L. (2012). Effects of psychotherapy for anxiety in children and adolescents: A meta-analytic review. *Clinical Psychology Review, 32*, 251–262. doi:10.1016/j.cpr.2012.01.005

Seligman, L. D., Goza, A. B., & Ollendick, T. H. (2004). Treatment of depression in children and adolescents. In P. M. Barrett & T. H. Ollendick (Eds.), *Handbook of interventions that work with children and adolescents: From prevention to treatment* (pp. 301–328). New York, NY: Wiley. doi:10.1002/9780470753385.ch13

Shapiro, E. S., & Cole, C. L. (1999). Self-monitoring in assessing children's problems. *Psychological Assessment, 11*, 448–457. doi:10.1037/1040-3590.11.4.448

Silverman, W. K., & Albano, A. M. (1996). *Anxiety Disorders Interview Schedule for DSM–IV: Child and Parent Versions*. San Antonio, TX: Psychological Corporation.

Simon, H. A. (1967). Motivational and emotional controls of cognition. *Psychological Review, 74*, 29–39. doi:10.1037/h0024127

Sloan, D. M., & Kring, A. M. (2007). Measuring changes in emotion during psychotherapy: Conceptual and methodological issues. *Clinical Psychology: Science and Practice, 14*, 307–322. doi:10.1111/j.1468-2850.2007.00092.x

Strauman, T. J. (1996). Self-beliefs, self-evaluation, and depression: A perspective on emotional vulnerability. In L. L. Martin & A. Tesser (Eds.), *Striving and feeling: Interactions among goals, affect, and self-regulation* (pp. 175–201). Mahwah, NJ: Erlbaum.

Strauss, C. C., Forehand, R., Smith, K., & Frame, C. L. (1986). The association between social withdrawal and internalizing problems of children. *Journal of Abnormal Child Psychology, 14*, 525–535. doi:10.1007/BF01260521

Strauss, C. C., Frame, C. L., & Forehand, R. (1987). Psychosocial impairment associated with anxiety in children. *Journal of Clinical Child Psychology, 16*, 235–239. doi:10.1207/s15374424jccp1603_8

Suveg, C., Kendall, P. C., Comer, J. S., & Robin, J. (2006). Emotion-focused cognitive–behavioral therapy for anxious youth: A multiple-baseline evaluation. *Journal of Contemporary Psychotherapy, 36*, 77–85. doi:10.1007/s10879-006-9010-4

Suveg, C., Sood, E., Comer, J. S., & Kendall, P. C. (2009). Changes in emotion regulation following cognitive–behavioral therapy for anxious youth. *Journal of Clinical Child and Adolescent Psychology, 38*, 390–401. doi:10.1080/15374410902851721

Tice, D. M. (2009). How emotions affect self-regulation. In J. P. Forgas, R. F. Baumeister, & D. M. Tice (Eds.), *Psychology of self-regulation: Cognitive, affective, and motivational processes* (pp. 201–216). New York, NY: Psychology Press.

Tice, D. M., & Bratslavsky, E. (2000). Giving in to feel good: The place of emotion regulation in the context of general self-control. *Psychological Inquiry, 11*, 149–159. doi:10.1207/S15327965PLI1103_03

Trosper, S. E., Buzzella, B. A., Bennett, S. M., & Ehrenreich, J. T. (2009). Emotion regulation in youth with emotional disorders: Implications for a unified treatment approach. *Clinical Child and Family Psychology Review, 12*, 234–254. doi:10.1007/s10567-009-0043-6

Weems, C. F., Costa, N. M., Watts, S. E., Taylor, L. K., & Cannon, M. F. (2007). Cognitive errors, anxiety sensitivity, and anxiety control beliefs: Their unique and specific associations with childhood anxiety symptoms. *Behavior Modification, 31*, 174–201. doi:10.1177/0145445506297016

Weems, C. F., Silverman, W. K., Rapee, R. M., & Pina, A. A. (2003). The role of control in childhood anxiety disorders. *Cognitive Therapy and Research, 27*, 557–568. doi:10.1023/A:1026307121386

Weisz, J. R., McCarty, C. A., & Valeri, S. M. (2006). Effects of psychotherapy for depression in children and adolescents: A meta-analysis. *Psychological Bulletin, 132*, 132–149. doi:10.1037/0033-2909.132.1.132

Werner, K., & Gross, J. J. (2010). Emotion regulation and psychopathology: A conceptual framework. In A. M. Kring & D. M. Sloan (Eds.), *Emotion regulation and psychopathology* (pp. 13–37). New York, NY: Guilford Press.

Winters, N. C., Collett, B. R., & Myers, K. M. (2005). Ten-year review of rating scales, VII: Scales assessing functional impairment. *Journal of the American Academy of Child & Adolescent Psychiatry, 44*, 309–338. doi:10.1097/01.chi.0000153230.57344.cd

8

SELF-REGULATION–BASED INTERVENTIONS FOR CHILDREN AND ADOLESCENTS WITH ASTHMA

NOREEN M. CLARK AND MINAL R. PATEL

This work is dedicated to the loving memory of Noreen M. Clark. Dr. Clark devoted her career to developing interventions based in self-regulation to improve the management of chronic disease. She has touched millions of lives with her innovative programs, exemplary leadership, genuine kindness, and thoughtful mentorship and friendship.

Chronic disease exerts a significant burden on Americans and the health care system. About half of adults in the United States have one or more chronic conditions. Two thirds of older adults also are afflicted, as are about 15% of children and adolescents—a group with rising prevalence, especially since the reclassification of obesity as a chronic disease (Torpy, Campbell, & Glass, 2010).

Some diseases of childhood continue through the life span (e.g., asthma), whereas others can develop into different but related conditions in adulthood (e.g., obesity). A few are no longer evident as a child matures, but underlying tendencies may remain (e.g., mental illnesses, developmental disabilities; Torpy et al., 2010). For most chronic diseases, lifetime management is required to keep the condition under control, which, in turn, helps to prevent acute complications and allows for more stable daily and developmental functioning. Disease management may entail a range of tasks, including acquiring and taking medicines, using medical devices, monitoring symptoms and symptom triggers, and maintaining a health-promoting lifestyle related to physical activity, diet, and stress.

Children and adolescents with asthma compose a unique population that is at particularly high risk for poor self-management and adverse outcomes. Asthma is the most common chronic condition of childhood and accounts for the greatest number of missed schools days and use of urgent health care services. Managing asthma through adolescence presents significant challenges. For example, youth face several transitions to increasingly advanced cognitive abilities as they age, and, over time, must negotiate more responsibility for managing their condition with parental figures as they gain the cognitive resources to manage on their own (e.g., taking medicines, monitoring symptoms and exacerbations). Transitions between early childhood, middle childhood, adolescence, and young adulthood also relate to socialization with peer groups. Chronic illness has been shown to be a potential disrupter of these important socialization processes and of school attendance and academic performance (Gullotta, 2000). Developmental changes related to physical, psychological, and emotional functioning inevitably coincide with continuous changes in treatment and management recommendations from clinicians and other health care providers. The evolving and complicated context in which young people manage asthma requires them to become self-regulating to adapt to changes and continuously learn how to maintain control of their condition over the long term.

In this chapter, we discuss a model for self-regulation in managing chronic disease that explains a process for helping to improve a child or adolescent's capacity to regulate and manage asthma that will lead to enhanced health outcomes. We also provide an overview of the theoretically based feedback loop that facilitates self-regulated chronic disease management in children and adolescents, and two case scenarios outlining how the model for management of chronic disease (MMCD) was used in interventions for economically disadvantaged children with asthma.

SELF-REGULATION THEORY AND PRINCIPLES

Principles and explanations for self-regulation evolved from a large body of work on self-control in social-cognitive theory, in which the cyclical nature of learning is described as a function of personal cognitive and affective factors, current behavior (e.g., actions and responses of the individual), and environmental and social influences (Bandura, 1986). From the theoretical articulations of social-cognitive theory, *self-regulation* is the process by which an individual attempts to control these three factors to reach a goal

(Clark & Zimmerman, 1990). A triadic (cognition, behavior, environment) self-regulation loop is initiated through the use of strategies and sustained or modified on the basis of enactive feedback (Bandura, 1977). We describe this feedback loop as observation, judgment, and reaction to achieve desired endpoints (e.g., goals), which serve as a source of motivation in enacting behavior change. Self-regulation in children and adolescents has been most commonly studied by psychologists with regard to academic learning and the modification of psychological influences on behavior (Schunk & Usher, 2012; Schunk & Zimmerman, 2013; Zimmerman, 2008). This work has examined the major components of learning as they are explicated in social-cognitive theory. Components include vicarious learning and role models; self-regulation, including development of self-efficacy; modification of physical and social environments; and verbal persuasion.

A sequence of training conditions that integrate these concepts has been espoused to enable children to develop self-regulated behavior (Bandura, 1986). First, desired behavior can be modeled by agents, such as parents or teachers. Second, an explicit set of performance requirements can be set and linked to a system of incentives. Third, as the role model reduces support, children can be taught self-regulatory functions: standard and goal setting, evaluation and self-reinforcement. Children initially learn self-regulation through external social means, such as observation of similar others (e.g., peers) or parental modeling and assistance, and gradually assume personal control of these functions (Bandura, 1986; Schunk, 1989). This sequential training process has been shown to be highly effective by Bandura, Jeffery, and Gajdos (1975); Rosenthal and Bandura (1978); and Zimmerman (1977); thus, it is adaptable to self-regulation in the management of chronic disease that facilitates observation, judgment, and reaction when engaging in self-management tasks.

Self-Regulation Asthma Interventions in Children and Adolescents

Over the past 25 years, interventions addressing some aspect of self-regulation have been developed and evaluated in children and adolescents with chronic disease. These interventions have focused on conditions such as obesity and asthma. A number of self-regulation interventions have been developed to optimize asthma management. Most have used techniques to enhance the capacity of children and caregiving adults to observe the trajectory of the disease. For example, they have included monitoring and observations via written asthma diaries kept by both the parent and child (Bonner et al., 2002; Guendelman, Meade, Benson, Chen, & Samuels, 2002), use of peak flow meters for monitoring air flow that also included electronic recording versions (Bonner et al., 2002; Shames et al., 2004), and electronic metered-dose inhalers for families to track adherence to medicines (Bartlett, Lukk, Butz, Lampros-Klein, & Rand, 2002). These means of monitoring symptoms and treatment adherence can provide data for children, families, and care providers to adjust strategies, including vicarious learning and simulations in meeting asthma management and treatment goals. Some interventions have introduced problem-solving strategies to enhance determinants of self-regulation, such as mobilizing social resources, developing goals, and increasing information about the disease. Goal setting often has been implemented with the help of influential others (e.g., caregivers, nurses, health educators, clinicians, peers; Bartholomew et al., 2000; Bartlett et al., 2002; Bonner et al., 2002; Bruzzese, Unikel, Gallagher, Evans, & Colland, 2008; Bruzzese et al., 2011; Evans et al., 1987; Guendelman et al., 2002; Shegog et al., 2001).

Computer games with simulations and role models have been used to build children's self-regulation capacity in information-seeking and application to asthma management (Bartholomew et al., 2000; McPherson, Glazebrook, Forster, James, & Smyth, 2006; Shegog et al., 2001). Electronic feedback as part of these technologies has taken the form of the child's entering data on his or her asthma symptoms and navigating the program as a character in scenarios in which the child can adjust strategies based on outcomes the child has observed from the actions he or she has taken to control asthma in the simulations. For example, Bartholomew et al. (2000) integrated a computer game in primary care offices to develop specific asthma management skills. The program included basic asthma information. Inputs into the program, such as the child's triggers, symptoms, and medication use, allowed children to navigate through problem-solving scenarios in which they could observe results of actions they took in an asthma monitoring mode and adjust actions to successfully reach goals. Outcomes revealed that overall, engagement of children and acceptance of the interactive computer program was high. Developmental differences were evident in the improved outcomes observed: Younger children had fewer hospitalizations, and asthma management information increased for older children.

Several of the aforementioned self-regulation interventions for children and adolescents with asthma have been associated with a number of improved outcomes. Evaluations of interventions using a randomized controlled design with less than a 6-month follow-up period have demonstrated reductions in activity limitation (Guendelman et al., 2002), increases in asthma information (Bonner et al., 2002), increases in self-efficacy (Bonner et al., 2002), and improved compliance with treatment plans (Bonner et al., 2002). Trials also have shown increases in family problem-solving ability, increases in children's use of asthma management steps, and reductions in nighttime symptoms (Bruzzese et al., 2008). Randomized controlled trials of self-regulation interventions also have demonstrated improved outcomes of children and adolescents up to a year postintervention, including improvements in asthma management behavior and self-efficacy (Bruzzese et al., 2011; Evans et al., 1987); increased asthma information for older children (Bartholomew et al., 2000); fewer asthma symptom episodes, including reductions in nighttime awakenings and activity limitation (Bruzzese et al., 2011; Evans et al., 1987); better grades in school (Evans et al., 1987); reductions in self-reported school absences (Bruzzese et al., 2011); and reductions in acute-care office visits, emergency department visits, and hospitalizations (Bruzzese et al., 2011), particularly for younger children (Bartholomew et al., 2000).

Model for Management of Chronic Disease

Over many years, our research team has evolved a model of self-regulation specific to chronic conditions that has informed the development of self-regulation interventions for children and adolescents with asthma. The MMCD (see Figure 8.1) recognizes the importance of describing the subprocesses and phases of self-regulation (Clark, Gong, & Kaciroti, 2001). The model initially was formed to explore the specific capacities that adults, whether directed at themselves or when acting on behalf of their children, need to possess to manage conditions that have no cure but can be controlled with day-to-day actions. It evolved from the understanding that most individuals with a long-term illness will display great variations in what they do to reduce the effects of the condition. Furthermore, they often will show differences in how they perceive clinicians' recommendations; perceptions range from potentially ideal, to mundane, to ineffective, or excessively difficult. These perceptions often will affect whether children will follow the recommendations. Some individuals with chronic disease may exhibit great efforts to apply recommended therapeutics but either will continue or discontinue those efforts depending on their experiences (e.g., becoming bored with the routine, lacking self-regulation skills, encountering competing priorities). Some may decide to apply clinically provided regimens and explore additional, optimal ways to control the condition. This range of responses accompanies the fact that people with chronic illness may possess varying levels of self-regulatory skill, have different degrees of interest and ability to develop the skills needed to change their behavior, and live in differing social and environmental conditions that shape it.

Figure 8.1 presents the MMCD and illustrates the reciprocal and continuous nature of self-regulation processes in chronic disease prevention and management (Clark et al., 2001). It draws on Bandura's (1986) explication of processes of self-regulation and on Zimmerman's (1994) model, particularly related to the inclusion of personal goals as motivational factors. In this

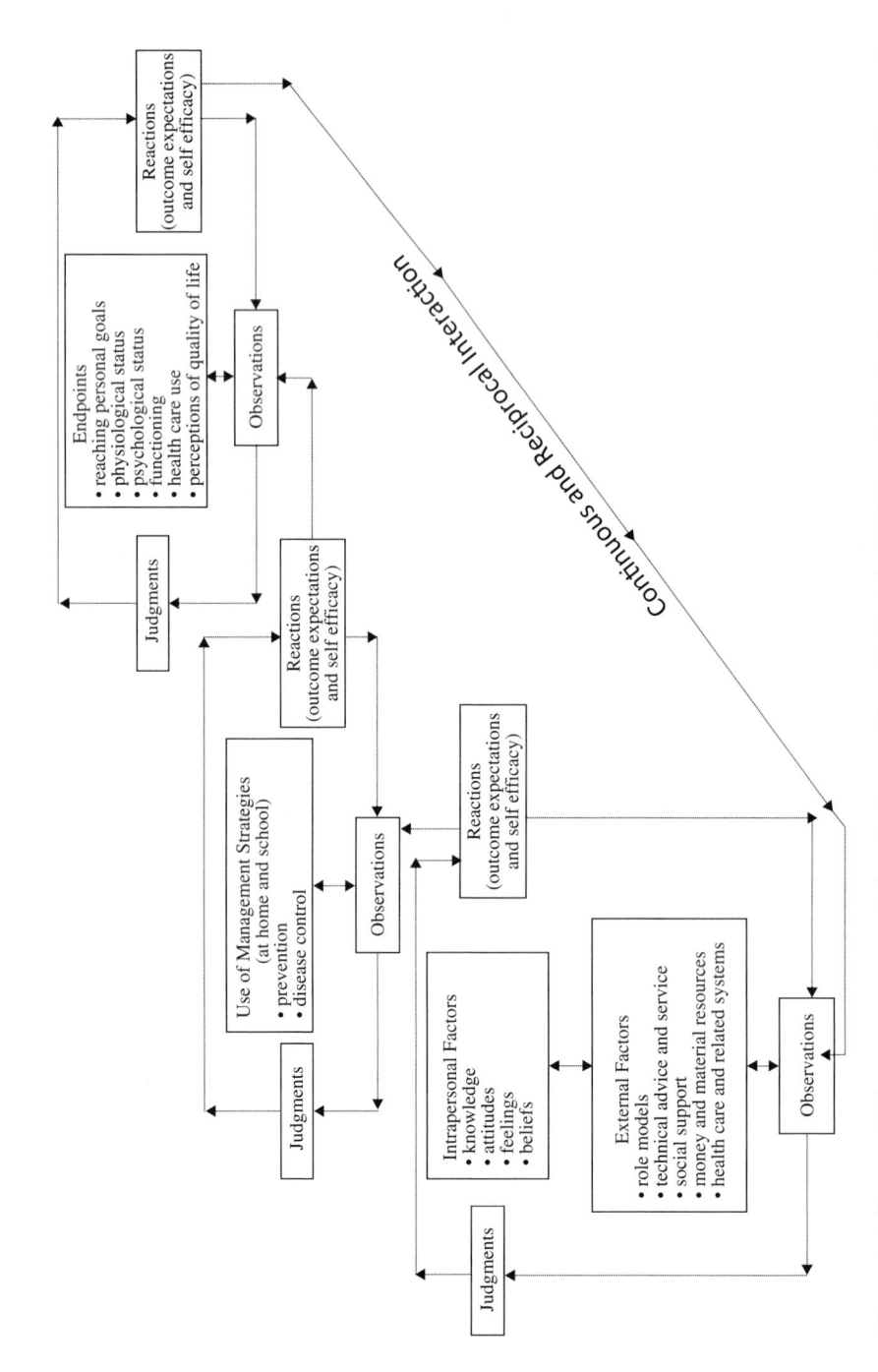

Figure 8.1. The model for management of chronic disease. From "A Model of Self-Regulation for Control of Chronic Disease," by N. M. Clark, M. Gong, and N. Kaciroti, 2001, *Health Education and Behavior, 28*, p. 771. Copyright 2001 by Sage Publications. Adapted with permission.

model, the ability of the person to be self-regulating is viewed as central to achieving desired endpoints (Clark & Starr-Schneidkraut, 1994).

Three aspects of self-regulation are central to the MMCD: observation, judgment, and reactions. The content and skills of disease management are derived and refined through the process of being self-regulating. A person is motivated to be self-regulating by a desired goal or endpoint. The more salient the goal, the more self-regulating the person will try to be. The power of the goal is associated with its value and personal meaningfulness to the individual. Being self-regulating in this model means being observant about one's own behavior and the social and physical environments that compose the context for behavior, and making judgments based on observation (vs. habit, fear, or tradition). It entails reacting appropriately in efforts to achieve one's personal goal. The model is also predicated on the idea that the processes composing self-regulation are continuous and reciprocal. Information, behavior, feelings, and conclusions generated from any one element of self-regulation as defined in the model (i.e., observing, judging, reacting) continually influence other elements.

The MMCD suggests that intrapersonal and external factors give rise to and are modified by the individual's observations, judgments, and reactions, which lead him or her to undertake disease management strategies (including modification of the physical and social environments) to achieve the desired endpoint or goal. Self-observation efforts may be, for example, a person with asthma using a peak flow meter to assess air flow through the airways when exposed to changes in the environment, or a person with heart disease using a pedometer to measure the achievable level of physical activity without symptoms. It may involve tracking symptoms in a log or diary to determine what might trigger them, or it may simply be recognition of a situation in which signs of a serious episode of breathlessness or chest tightness appear. Noting influences on behavior generates information to guide the learner to options for modifications of contextual factors or new practices. These examples represent observation in the self-regulation feedback loop. Judging what to try and how to implement a change strategy entails analysis of the information generated through observation and selection of potential solutions based on personal determinations, such as potential for success, manageability, affordability, personal relevance, and other salient criteria. Trial behavior can target small changes, such as alteration of the time scheduled for taking medicine, or larger ones—for example, enrolling in nutritional counseling to make significant changes in one's diet. Through these processes, an individual makes judgments regarding what to do and how to do it (e.g., judgment in the self-regulation feedback loop). One reaction is to determine whether the action taken produced the expected outcome (*outcome expectancy* is the belief that the behavior will produce the goal). Another reaction is whether one feels confident to continue the action (e.g., self-efficacy; Bandura, 1986). Observation leads to judgments that lead to action and, subsequently, reactions following trial of a change strategy. Over time, continuous observation, judgment, and appropriate reaction lead to modification of management strategies and sometimes modification of the goal itself.

In the MMCD, additional elements of self-regulation are considered central to achieving desired change. In one sense, these elements compose the "content" of change and have been labeled *internal* and *external factors* and *management strategies*, which, to some extent, also reflect Zimmerman's concept of self-regulation phases (Zimmerman & Campillo, 2003). The MMCD posits that when taking a disease management action, an individual is influenced by *intrapersonal factors*—that is, information and beliefs he or she has concerning the specific health problem. For example, when attempting to manage asthma, people will use (or not use) inhaled corticosteroids (anti-inflammatory drugs) based, in part, on what they know about the role and importance of inflammation in asthma control and about using a metered-dose inhaler (Clark & Partridge, 2002). The extent to which the person holds the requisite knowledge and beliefs to support an action also depends, in part, on a range of external factors, including role models who can be observed making efforts in asthma situations, or interpersonal relationships through which emotional and instrumental social support is given and received. Almost certainly involved is technical advice from a clinician who provides therapeutic recommendations. Availability of money and other material resources (e.g., the price of medicine and a way to get to the pharmacy) also will influence the person's behavior. Management strategies compose the individual's means to keep the disease and its effects under control (Clark et al., 1998; Karoly & Kanfer, 1982). These strategies may be effective or ineffective and may or may not be consistent with clinicians' recommendations. A management strategy evolves from the person's observations, judgments, and reactions, given the aforementioned internal and external factors. Others (e.g., role models, technical experts, family and friends) can influence the strategy chosen, but, in the end, the individual's personal goals, combined internal and external resources, and the degree of self-regulation will dictate which management strategy will be derived and used further.

The predominant motivating factor in taking a disease management action is a personal goal. Goals are highly idiosyncratic. When an educator or clinician (or any other person attempting to assist with disease management) has a different goal than the individual, the opportunity for successful goal attainment is attenuated. Usually, the clinician has a goal (e.g., a better peak expiratory flow rate in a patient with asthma) that, although considered a gold standard in medical practice, is not likely to be perceived by the patient as being as important as the patient's personal goal (e.g., spending time with a loved one whose cat precipitates asthma symptoms). When the clinician or educator focuses on achieving the patient's personal goal, the chances are greater that the therapeutic regimen will appeal to patient's interests and be implemented by the patient. Evidence that clinical and personal goals are not always compatible is found, for example, in the work of Juniper et al. (1996), whose data showed little relationship between clinical measures, such as scores on pulmonary function tests, and patients' own ratings of the asthma-related quality of their lives, or being able to do what they wished to do.

INTERVENTION APPLICATIONS OF MMCD FOR CHILDREN WITH ASTHMA IN URBAN CONTEXTS

The MMCD has been applied to self-regulation interventions for economically disadvantaged children with asthma in elementary and middle-school settings in Detroit, Michigan (see Chapter 5, this volume, for academic self-regulated learning applications with minority populations). Asthma prevalence, morbidity, and mortality are particularly high in these populations. For children and adolescents, enhancing self-regulation requires moving through a process in which the young person can identify goals and use strategies to manipulate behavior and the environment to attain the desired outcome. The process entails observation, judgment, and reaction. The case scenarios examined here use guided problem-solving with role models, vicarious learning, and direct experience to help children and adolescents manage their asthma by enhancing self-regulation. Specifically, these interventions aimed to increase their self-confidence and help them acquire skills to manage asthma and interact with those in their social environment to facilitate control over asthma symptoms and minimize disruptions to daily life.

Both interventions used a tailored version of the Open Airways for Schools program (OAS; Clark et al., 1986) designed for children with asthma that was developed by researchers at the Center for Managing Chronic Disease and is a national program of the American Lung Association. OAS was created as the result of a growing recognition that providing asthma education in schools may be a way to reach the majority of children with asthma in an environment that is already oriented toward learning and is concerned about outcomes the program could ameliorate, such as absenteeism. Educational sessions were focused on children in Grades 3 through 5 and emphasized helping the child take medicine, learning steps to take in an asthma attack, communicating with the doctor and school personnel, and keeping the child generally healthy. Sessions were organized into 40-minute group lessons, held during the school day, for children with asthma. OAS classes were led by trained facilitators, who could be the school nurse or other school personnel, parents, or community volunteers (Kaplan et al., 1986). The OAS program has demonstrated positive outcomes: Children who completed the program have taken more steps to manage their asthma, improved their school performance, and have had fewer and less severe asthma episodes (Evans et al., 1987). Parents of children participating in OAS have reported taking more steps to help manage their children's asthma. The school environment also has become more supportive: Children without asthma were more willing to help children with asthma, and children with asthma were able to give support to each other (Evans et al., 1987).

Environmental Detectives: A Case for Study

To illustrate self-regulatory dimensions of OAS, we use a component of the intervention for elementary school children called Environmental Detectives. The intervention was provided to children in Grades 2 through 5 in 14 elementary schools in Detroit, Michigan. Table 8.1 outlines activities in the program organized by MMCD self-regulation subprocesses. Environmental Detectives comprises three sessions for children with asthma and their classmates to increase their understanding of factors that influence respiratory health, their understanding of challenges children with asthma face, and to develop empathy for their peers with asthma and develop their ability to give effective help and support (Clark et al., 2004). Environmental Detectives takes children and their classmates through a series of activities based on observation, judgment, and reaction concerning what environmental factors can cause problems in their own homes and in the classroom, what best options are for ameliorating those factors, which option is most effective for their situation, and which options they believe they can actually undertake. Home assignments for child and parent take them through these steps, and subsequent class discussions help children to share observations, defend their decisions, and express both their level of faith in the behavior producing the outcome and their own confidence to take action. Information is integrated regarding the sources and health effects of outdoor air pollutants and indoor asthma triggers, such as insects and air problems. Exercises are based on vicarious learning and making judgments. For example, children are shown in demonstration models how lungs work and how clean air is essential to healthy lungs. They are asked to use a pinched straw to demonstrate what happens in an asthma attack and brainstorm ways in which to help a friend in the event of an asthma episode. Breathing exercises are practiced to encourage feelings of calmness when symptoms threaten.

TABLE 8.1
Activities of the Environmental Detectives Component
of the Open Airways for Schools Program Designed
to Address Self-Regulation in Elementary School

Model for managing chronic disease self-regulation principles	Program activity addressing self-regulation principle
	Environmental Detective outdoors
Vicarious learning, observation, and making judgments	Discussion: Sources and health effects of outdoor air pollutants • Introduce Environmental Detectives to students. • Explain how breathing is an essential function of the body and clean air is essential for healthy lungs. • Get children to stand and demonstrate the prevalence of asthma among their peers, and ask children to define asthma. • Ask children what an asthma attack sounds like, and have them demonstrate. • Ask children what they think a friend should do when a child is having an asthma attack.
Vicarious learning and role models for observation and judgment; confidence building	Demonstration: How it feels to breathe during an asthma attack • Have children individually breathe with an unobstructed and a partially obstructed straw, and ask them how it feels. • Introduce athletes who have asthma; for each one, emphasize a different management step.
Observation	Discussion: Where does air pollution come from? How does it affect human health? • Using open-ended questions to generate discussion, conduct an interactive conversation about air pollution (e.g., smog, ozone, chemicals, smoke), its sources, and its health effects. Exercise: Air pollution—can you see it? Can you measure it? • Show the group a pollution device, explain how to make the device and how it works; groups make devices and choose areas inside the classroom and outside the building to hang them.
Reaction: Confidence building	Exercise: Belly breathing and homework assignment • Teach children how to do belly breathing and explain that they are learning it to help a friend who feels an attack is coming on to stay calm. • Practice belly breathing with the children. • Reinforce empathy for children with asthma; ask children what they should do if a friend is having an asthma attack; ask them when a person ought to use belly breathing. • Instruct children to teach belly breathing to someone in their family.

(continues)

TABLE 8.1
Activities of the Environmental Detectives Component
of the Open Airways for Schools Program Designed
to Address Self-Regulation in Elementary School *(Continued)*

Model for managing chronic disease self-regulation principles	Program activity addressing self-regulation principle
	Environmental Detective indoors: Bug busters at school and at home
Observation	Discussion of results collected from air pollution devices • Children draw and write what they saw.
	Discussion/overview: Indoor environmental problems and their sources • Go over handout that identifies specific asthma triggers and ask how they could start a person's asthma; introduce cockroaches and dust mites.
Judgment	Insect investigators • Teach children about cockroaches and dust mites through activity and games. • Children split into two groups: one half, cockroaches; one half, dust mites. • Read factsheet about bugs out loud and explain how they can cause an asthma reaction.
	Game/exercise: Bug busters in the classroom • Give each group of three students the bug buster board and container of bug pieces; take turns drawing a bug card and put the card on the activity that works to get rid of that bug; reassemble the group and ask for volunteers to share their matching answers. Correct any wrong matches. • Discuss ways in which children can takes action in their own classrooms; first affirm any steps they are already taking, then try to think of one or two things the class could do to be bug busters.
	Role-play: Remind a classmate to move away from a problem if symptoms start • Role-play activity: Do role-play with four volunteers who play four different asthma characters. Educator presents scenario to the class and have students act out the role-play. Students come up with possible solutions for the character.
Observation and judgment	Homework: Bug busters at home • Assign students homework—How To Be a Bug Buster at Home—which they must complete at home with family.

TABLE 8.1
Activities of the Environmental Detectives Component
of the Open Airways for Schools Program Designed
to Address Self-Regulation in Elementary School *(Continued)*

Model for managing chronic disease self-regulation principles	Program activity addressing self-regulation principle
	Environmental Detective indoors: Air problems
Judgment	Review: Reporting back on bug busters
	Discussion: Indoor air problems • Discuss indoor air problems that can be inhaled and, as a group, come up with a list of things that can be inhaled and cause breathing problems; provide an example. • Explain what is actually inhaled when a person has a reaction to animals; discuss how chemicals are found in many home products. • Ask children where to find information about a product that may bother them (how to read labels), or call a manufacturer.
Observation	Exercise: Find the indoor air problems in the classroom • Instruct students to find and circle the indoor air problems that can be breathed on "Indoor Air Problems" handout.
Judgment	Exercise • Conduct interactive class discussion about solutions to exposure to indoor air problems. • Demonstrate the presence of animal dander in the classroom. Ask students to find evidence of dander; discuss ways to lessen someone's reaction to animal dander.
Observation	Homework assignment: Find the indoor air problems at home • Children need to act as the teacher at home and explain to their parents material they just learned regarding indoor air problems.
Reaction and confidence	Scenarios and role-plays: Talking to people who smoke around you • Review smoking information/dangers for children. • Brainstorm with the class ways to lessen the effects of secondhand smoke. • Role-play the situation of a child talking to a parent/adult who smokes.
	Exercise: A plan to help a friend with asthma • Review the steps children can take to help a classmate prevent and/or manage an asthma episode; reinforce specific material. • Ask for volunteers to perform a role-play of the steps they can take to help a classmate with asthma manage an asthma episode in class.

Children also are introduced in person or through stories to athletes who have asthma and are successful in their sports. The role model athletes discuss a different asthma self-management step. Interactive discussions also focus on sources and health consequences of air pollution. Children are given air pollution devices to place around the classroom and areas around the school to observe air-quality problems in their environments. Games, interactive discussion, and role-plays provide opportunities for children to reflect on their observations and judgments, and their commitments to being active in reducing problems and helping their friends with asthma.

Environmental Detectives, as part of an overall effort to educate children, school personnel, and parents, proved successful in engaging classmates and modifying the social and physical environment of a child with asthma, and in contributing to children's capacity to effectively observe, judge, and react to asthma-related challenges and management.

A randomized trial assessing outcomes in the overall OAS program was conducted in 14 elementary schools in Area D of the Detroit school system. The composition of the communities where these schools were located was 94% African American, and greater than 40% met federal guidelines for poverty, according to the 1990 census (Clark et al., 2004). Evaluation involved 835 parents and children in Grades 2 through 5 with active symptoms of asthma and a physician's diagnosis or a history of exacerbations. Improved asthma outcomes were evident up to 2 years after intervention. Children with persistent disease who participated in the OAS program had significant declines in both daytime (14% fewer, $p < .0001$) and nighttime (14% fewer, $p < .0001$) symptoms. Among children with both mild intermittent and persistent disease, program participants had 17% fewer daytime symptoms ($p < .0001$). Program children had higher grades for science ($p < .05$). No differences in school absences for all causes between groups were noted in school records. However, parents of program group children reported fewer absences attributable to asthma in the previous 3 months (34% fewer, $p < .01$) and 12 months (8% fewer, $p < .05$). Parents of program children had higher scores ($p = .02$) on an asthma management index. Among the subset of children 11 to 12 years in age ($n = 21$), those who participated in the expanded OAS program had a decrease by 33% in asthma severity for both daytime and nighttime symptoms. At 2 years followup, there was a 24% increase improvement in intervention children's school grades compared with controls.

Detroit Middle School Asthma Project

A second example of an MMCD-based self-regulation intervention for low-income students with asthma is a program for middle-school–aged children. The Detroit Middle School asthma project grew from an evident need to address significant problems with asthma in preteens in low-income, minority communities (Crain et al., 1994). The overarching aim of the project was to strengthen the school social environment for students with asthma and their peers by creating peer-level empathy and support, including peer tracking. The project specifically aimed to evaluate whether a peer component to the overall OAS intervention could increase positive influences that aided young people in their management efforts and enhance asthma outcomes. The peer component emphasized creating a positive social environment for younger students managing asthma (seventh graders) by engendering support for them among their classmates and older peers (eighth graders). Table 8.2 outlines activities in the peer component of the program that are organized by self-regulation MMCD subprocesses. First, role models were sought from the general population of eighth-grade students who applied to be part of the peer leader group. Among peer leaders, 18% had asthma. Two to three peer leaders were trained as a team by members of the study team to provide three asthma lessons to seventh-grade students. Peer leaders developed skits and game shows delivered in the classroom for seventh-grade students. Similar to Environmental Detectives, the lesson activities focused on increasing students' ability to observe the extent and consequences of asthma on themselves and their classmates, explore consequences of failure to support their friends with the condition, select supportive action steps, and examine potential effects of action steps and their own confidence to carry out their selected supportive actions. Participants discussed a video depicting an asthma attack at school, played games demonstrating and testing their understanding of asthma, and used problem-posing methodology in which older students assisted younger students in making judgments. The seventh-grade students then voted on key messages to communicate to their sixth-grade schoolmates. Subsequently, with help from the role model peer leaders and a teacher, seventh-grade students translated asthma messages into skits, songs, creative dramas, or music that encompassed their selected messages. They then performed them for an assembly of sixth-grade students.

The role model peer component was evaluated as part of the larger OAS program in a randomized trial in 19 Detroit middle schools. Over a 2-year period, 1,292 students were enrolled in the study. Two years after the program, no changes were seen in students' asthma symptoms or quality of life. The intervention showed an evident decline in self-regulation behavior in undiagnosed preteens at 12 months and increased their self-regulation at 24 months ($p = .04$; $p = .003$). Feedback from students who participated in the OAS program indicated that the program was engaging, and students both with and without asthma gave intervention activities positive marks.

TABLE 8.2
Peer Component Activities of the Open Airways for
Schools Program Designed to Address Self-Regulation
in Middle School Children

Model for managing chronic disease self-regulation principles	Program activity: All activities are led by peer leaders (eighth grade) who engage seventh graders.
	Basic information: Learning about asthma
Observation and judgment	Discussion: What is asthma? • Show "Relieve the Squeeze, Part 2" video. • Explain the need to learn about asthma by using the "Three Essential Needs" strategy. • Read asthma facts.
Reaction: Outcome expectancy and confidence	Asthma Medications • Briefly describe asthma management medications with an emphasis on the difference between controllers and quick relief. • Demonstrate the correct use of devices and practice using inhalers with spacers.
	Recognizing and managing asthma symptoms
Observation and judgment	Discussion: Early warning signs of asthma • Demonstrate how it feels to have asthma by using the straw activity, and ask the students how it may relate to someone with asthma. • Discuss with the group the symptoms and signs of asthma.
Reaction: Outcome expectancy and confidence	Trigger factors • Define *asthma triggers*. • Divide the class into two to three groups. • Have groups use the trigger diagram to identify different types of triggers and fill in blanks with ways to avoid triggers. • Play charades for the exercise-induced asthma activity.
	Issues faced by students with asthma
Observation and judgment	• Show "Lookin' Good, Feelin' Good" video.
Reaction: Outcome expectancy	• Divide students into two to three groups and have them work through the video questions. Have students present their answers to the group in pairs.
	Smoking and asthma
Observation and judgment	Facts about asthma • Have students complete the smoking statement and then read the questions; ask the group to call out the correct answers.
Reaction: Outcome expectancy	Saying "no" to smoking • Have students form a circle and think of how they would say "no" to someone offering them a cigarette. Practice "no" responses with dummy cigarette exercise. Saying "no" to other people's smoke • Ask students for suggestions on how to ask people to stop smoking around them.

TABLE 8.2
Peer Component Activities of the Open Airways for
Schools Program Designed to Address Self-Regulation
in Middle School Children   *(Continued)*

Model for managing chronic disease self-regulation principles	Program activity: All activities are led by peer leaders (eighth grade) who engage seventh graders.
	Asthma messages
Observation and judgment	Ask the group for important asthma messages that could be presented as skits in an assembly.
	Management of an asthma episode
Reaction: Outcome expectancy and confidence	• Act out the three steps to manage an asthma episode. • Role-play an asthma episode using information in the *Asthma Peer Leader's Manual*. • Remind students to get assistance from a staff member if an asthma episode occurs at school.
	Communicating with your doctor
Observation and judgment	• Have students share their doctor visit experiences and come up with ways to improve communication with their doctor. • Discuss why it is important for a person with asthma to visit a doctor and develop an asthma action plan.
	Asthma quiz show
Reaction: Outcome expectancy and confidence	• Divide the students into two teams and play the quiz show activity.
	Development of student asthma performances

Observation and judgment	• Assign each group an asthma message:
	  1. Know your triggers
	  2. Don't smoke
	  3. How to manage an episode
	  4. Take your medicine
	• Have students work in small groups to develop skits based on assigned messages.

Reaction: Outcome expectancy and confidence	• Have students perform skits at a school assembly based on assigned messages.

IMPLICATIONS AND FUTURE RESEARCH DIRECTIONS

Interventions aimed at children and adolescents managing asthma can improve health outcomes and have positive spillover effects on school performance. Effective programs based on the MMCD and focused on its self-regulation premises have proven effective in reaching and helping low-income children. The MMCD draws from social-cognitive theory and reflects basic human capacities that are appropriate for any age group. Learning activities can be adjusted to the group's cognitive abilities and tailored to varying levels of socioeconomic status. In the two case scenarios, it was evident that children and adolescents who participated in the program were in the mastery-and-beyond stage of development. Learning activities enabled active engagement in interventions and were considered appropriate and acceptable by children and school personnel. As evidenced in evaluation data, interventions that build self-regulatory capacity in children with asthma had an effect on outcomes.

In self-regulation interventions for children and adolescents with asthma, consider that although self-regulation components of asthma interventions (i.e., observation, judgment, reaction) are typically well accepted by children, building asthma-management capacity in children and adolescents can vary, depending on their stage of development and the severity of their condition. For example, the cognitive ability level of elementary school children may preclude some activities related to goal setting or vicarious learning. Active learning strategies appear to be most effective in initiating the processes of observation, judgment, and reaction in disease management situations for these children. Variation in building asthma-management capacity also may be a function of the severity of the individual's disease, a factor that can greatly affect the extent and nature of management strategies required to keep the condition under control. However, the very general disease self-management tasks that patients are expected to perform from their point of view, as evidenced in evaluation data, align well with the model. To control asthma, effective asthma managers need to attain a certain level of observation capacity, choose among complicated recommendations and treatments, and make decisions in a variety of situations and changing contexts.

In addition, external resources, such as finances, in the MMCD are an important aspect to recognize in interventions for younger children and adolescents, especially those in families with limited income that reside in urban contexts. Important self-regulation skills often depend on parents and ancillary caregivers. External resources, such as family income, resources in the school system, and costs of asthma care, may substantially influence students' successful initiation of self-regulatory processes and outcomes. Nonetheless, the triadic (cognition, behavior, environment) self-regulation loop can provide a powerful means for monitoring symptoms and treatment adherence while providing data for children, families, and care providers to adjust strategies in meeting asthma management and treatment goals over the long term.

Enhancing self-regulation in children and adolescents with asthma can build on a model for managing chronic disease that emphasizes developing skills of observation, judgment, and reaction. Self-regulation in children and adolescents requires personal development in which children can identify personal health goals and can use cognitive–behavioral strategies to manipulate their physical and social environments to attain the desired goal. An objective in chronic disease management is for the child to, over time, assume management responsibility and acquire the various social and physical supports needed to achieve disease control.

Self-regulation has gained considerable attention in chronic disease management. Yet, a historical tendency in medicine and public health has been to emphasize information and content rather than emphasize and build the capacity of young people to be more self-regulating in disease management efforts. Future research might focus on capacity building, especially in conditions similar to asthma in which monitoring and judgment is so important to disease control. Children and adolescents with advanced cognitive abilities are capable of goal setting, which is a powerful motivating factor in building management capacity and, as reflected in the MMCD, central to principles of self-regulation and in facilitating the feedback loop of observation, judgment, and reaction with chronic disease management strategies. The most valued personal goals tend to be covert. Research is needed to examine how children's personal goals can be addressed in self-regulation programs designed to increase disease management capacity. Also worthy of investigation is how to align children's developmental levels, disease severity, and self-regulation activities to achieve the most powerful enhancements in self-regulation and in disease outcomes.

Self-regulation enhancement can build the capacity of economically disadvantaged children, their families, and peers to control asthma and create social and environmental conditions in which disease management has the best chance to succeed. Using elements of self-regulation that align with the developmental capacities of children and adolescents may prove most salient in improving their ability to manage their asthma and, subsequently, in improving the quality of their lives.

REFERENCES

Bandura, A. (1977). *Social learning theory*. Englewood Cliffs, NJ: Prentice Hall.

Bandura, A. (1986). *Social foundations of thought and action: A social cognitive theory*. Englewood Cliffs, NJ: Prentice Hall.

Bandura, A., Jeffery, R. W., & Gajdos, E. (1975). Generalizing change through participant modeling with self-directed mastery. *Behaviour Research and Therapy*, *13*(2–3), 141–152. doi:10.1016/0005-7967(75)90008-X

Bartholomew, L. K., Gold, R. S., Parcel, G. S., Czyzewski, D. I., Sockrider, M. M., Fernandez, M., . . . Swank, P. (2000). Watch, discover, think, and act: Evaluation of computer-assisted instruction to improve asthma self-management in inner-city children. *Patient Education and Counseling*, *39*(2–3), 269–280. doi:10.1016/S0738-3991(99)00046-4

Bartlett, S. J., Lukk, P., Butz, A., Lampros-Klein, F., & Rand, C. S. (2002). Enhancing medication adherence among inner-city children with asthma: Results from pilot studies. *Journal of Asthma, 39*, 47–54. doi:10.1081/JAS-120000806

Bonner, S., Zimmerman, B. J., Evans, D., Irigoyen, M., Resnick, D., & Mellins, R. B. (2002). An individualized intervention to improve asthma management among urban Latino and African-American families. *Journal of Asthma, 39*, 167–179. doi:10.1081/JAS-120002198

Bruzzese, J. M., Sheares, B. J., Vincent, E. J., Du, Y., Sadeghi, H., Levison, M. J., . . . Evans, D. (2011). Effects of a school-based intervention for urban adolescents with asthma: A controlled trial. *American Journal of Respiratory and Critical Care Medicine, 183*, 998–1006. doi:10.1164/rccm.201003-0429OC

Bruzzese, J. M., Unikel, L., Gallagher, R., Evans, D., & Colland, V. (2008). Feasibility and impact of a school-based intervention for families of urban adolescents with asthma: Results from a randomized pilot trial. *Family Process, 47*(1), 95–113. doi:10.1111/j.1545-5300.2008.00241.x

Clark, N. M., Brown, R., Joseph, C. L., Anderson, E. W., Liu, M., & Valerio, M. A. (2004). Effects of a comprehensive school-based asthma program on symptoms, parent management, grades, and absenteeism. *Chest, 125*, 1674–1679. doi:10.1378/chest.125.5.1674

Clark, N. M., Feldman, C. H., Evans, D., Duzey, O., Levison, M. J., Wasilewski, Y., . . . Mellins, R. B. (1986). Managing better: Children, parents, and asthma. *Patient Education and Counseling, 8*(1), 27–38. doi:10.1016/0738-3991(86)90024-8

Clark, N. M., Gong, M., & Kaciroti, N. (2001). A model of self-regulation for control of chronic disease. *Health Education & Behavior, 28*, 769–782. doi:10.1177/109019810102800608

Clark, N. M., Gong, M., Schork, M. A., Evans, D., Roloff, D., Hurwitz, M., . . . Mellins, R. B. (1998). Impact of education for physicians on patient outcomes. *Pediatrics, 101*, 831–836. doi:10.1542/peds.101.5.831

Clark, N. M., & Partridge, M. R. (2002). Strengthening asthma education to enhance disease control. *Chest, 121*, 1661–1669. doi:10.1378/chest.121.5.1661

Clark, N. M., & Starr-Schneidkraut, N. J. (1994). Management of asthma by patients and families. *American Journal of Respiratory and Critical Care Medicine, 149*, S54–S66. doi:10.1164/ajrccm/149.2_Pt_2.S54

Clark, N. M., & Zimmerman, B. J. (1990). A social cognitive view of self-regulated learning about health. *Health Education Research, 5*, 371–379. doi:10.1093/her/5.3.371

Crain, E. F., Weiss, K. B., Bijur, P. E., Hersh, M., Westbrook, L., & Stein, R. E. K. (1994). An estimate of the prevalence of asthma and wheezing among inner-city children. *Pediatrics, 94*, 356–362.

Evans, D., Clark, N. M., Feldman, C. H., Rips, J., Kaplan, D., Levison, M. J., . . . Mellins, R. B. (1987). A school health education program for children with asthma aged 8–11 years. *Health Education & Behavior, 14*, 267–279. doi:10.1177/109019818701400302

Guendelman, S., Meade, K., Benson, M., Chen, Y. Q., & Samuels, S. (2002). Improving asthma outcomes and self-management behaviors of inner-city children: A randomized trial of the Health Buddy interactive device and an asthma diary. *Archives of Pediatrics & Adolescent Medicine, 156,* 114–120. doi:10.1001/archpedi.156.2.114

Gullotta, T. P. (2000). *The adolescent experience.* San Diego, CA: Academic Press.

Juniper, E. F., Guyatt, G. H., Feeny, D. H., Ferrie, P. J., Griffith, L. E., & Townsend, M. (1996). Measuring quality of life in children with asthma. *Quality of Life Research: An International Journal of Quality of Life Aspects of Treatment, Care & Rehabilitation, 5*(1), 35–46. doi:10.1007/BF00435967

Kaplan, D. L., Rips, J. L., Clark, N. M., Evans, D., Wasilewski, Y., & Feldman, C. H. (1986). Transferring a clinic-based health education program for children with asthma to a school setting. *Journal of School Health, 56,* 267–271. doi:10.1111/j.1746-1561.1986.tb05748.x

Karoly, P., & Kanfer, F. H. (1982). *Self-management and behavior change: From theory to practice.* New York, NY: Pergamon Press.

McPherson, A. C., Glazebrook, C., Forster, D., James, C., & Smyth, A. (2006). A randomized, controlled trial of an interactive educational computer package for children with asthma. *Pediatrics, 117,* 1046–1054. doi:10.1542/peds.2005-0666

Rosenthal, T. L., & Bandura, A. (1978). Psychological modeling: Theory and practice. In S. L. Garfield & A. E. Bergin (Eds.), *Handbook of psychotherapy and behavior change: An empirical analysis* (2nd ed., pp. 621–658). New York, NY: Wiley.

Schunk, D. H. (1989). Social cognitive theory and self-regulated learning. In B. J. Zimmerman & D. H. Schunk (Eds.), *Self-regulated learning and academic achievement: Theory, research, and practice* (pp. 83–110). New York, NY: Springer-Verlag. doi:10.1007/978-1-4612-3618-4_4

Schunk, D. H., & Usher, E. L. (2012). Social cognitive theory and motivation. In R. M. Ryan (Ed.), *The Oxford handbook of human motivation* (pp. 13–27). New York, NY: Oxford University Press.

Schunk, D. H., & Zimmerman, B. J. (2013). Self-regulation and learning. In W. M. Reynolds, G. E. Miller, & I. B. Weiner (Eds.), *Handbook of psychology: Volume 7—Educational psychology* (2nd ed., pp. 45–68). Hoboken, NJ: Wiley.

Shames, R. S., Sharek, P., Mayer, M., Robinson, T. N., Hoyte, E. G., Gonzalez-Hensley, F., . . . Umetsu, D. T. (2004). Effectiveness of a multicomponent self-management program in at-risk, school-aged children with asthma. *Annals of Allergy, Asthma & Immunology, 92,* 611–618. doi:10.1016/S1081-1206(10)61426-3

Shegog, R., Bartholomew, L. K., Parcel, G. S., Sockrider, M. M., Mâsse, L., & Abramson, S. L. (2001). Impact of a computer-assisted education program on factors related to asthma self-management behavior. *Journal of the American Medical Informatics Association, 8*(1), 49–61. doi:10.1136/jamia.2001.0080049

Torpy, J. M., Campbell, A., & Glass, R. M. (2010). Chronic diseases of children. *JAMA, 303,* 682. doi:10.1001/jama.303.7.682

Zimmerman, B. J. (1977). Modeling. In H. Hom & P. Robinson (Eds.), *Psychological processes in early education* (pp. 37–70). New York, NY: Academic Press.

Zimmerman, B. J. (1994). Dimensions of academic self-regulation: A conceptual framework for education. In B. J. Zimmerman & D. H. Schunk (Eds.), *Self-regulation of learning and performance: Issues and educational applications* (pp. 3–21). Hillsdale, NJ: Erlbaum.

Zimmerman, B. J. (2008). Investigating self-regulation and motivation: Historical background, methodological developments, and future prospects. *American Educational Research Journal, 45*(1), 166–183.

Zimmerman, B. J., & Campillo, M. (2003). Motivating self-regulated problem solvers. In J. E. Davidson & R. J. Sternberg (Eds.), *The psychology of problem solving* (pp. 233–262). New York, NY: Cambridge University Press.

III

SELF-REGULATED LEARNING INTERVENTIONS ACROSS DIVERSE CONTEXTS

9

PROFESSIONAL DEVELOPMENT CONTEXTS THAT PROMOTE SELF-REGULATED LEARNING AND CONTENT LEARNING IN TRAINEES

ERIN E. PETERS-BURTON, TIMOTHY J. CLEARY, AND SUSAN G. FORMAN

Professional development (PD) training and coaching are important avenues for enhancing the instructional skills and knowledge of educators (Hill, 2007; Yoon, Duncan, Lee, Scarloss, & Shapley, 2007). Although the nature of PD can vary in intensity, scope, and methodology, for the purposes of this chapter *PD* is defined as organized plans of programs offered beyond an initial certification whereby professionals progressively acquire a set of knowledge and skills that they assimilate into practice (Loucks-Horsley, Love, Stiles, Mundry, & Hewson, 2003). Whether at the local level or through federal initiatives, such as No Child Left Behind, considerable attention and resources have been devoted over the past decade to examining the nature of PD activities in school contexts and exploring how these programs need to be structured to optimize trainees' learning and skill development (Han & Weiss, 2005; Yoon et al., 2007).

---

http://dx.doi.org/10.1037/14641-010
Self-Regulated Learning Interventions With At-Risk Youth: Enhancing Adaptability, Performance, and Well-Being, T. J. Cleary (Editor)
Copyright © 2015 by the American Psychological Association. All rights reserved.

This increased focus on improving the quality of PD training was due, in part, to a 1998 National Research Council Synthesis report on research on human learning (Donovan, Bransford, & Pelligrino, 1999). The report criticized PD programs for school staff; it indicated that the programs were not learner centered but were arranged without consideration of teacher needs; were not knowledge centered but, rather, were focused on procedures without information about why, when, and where, and how they might be useful; were not assessment centered in that they lacked opportunity for learners to try out new practices, receive feedback, and evaluate their success; and were not community centered because they lacked opportunities for future contact with and support from trainers. Over the past decade or so, substantial progress has been made in creating PD programs that are more meaningful and relevant to teacher educators and that can be implemented to optimize teacher learning and transfer of PD-taught skills to the classroom setting. For example, PD trainers have given teacher trainees choices in planning and implementation to best fit their new skills with state-mandated objectives (Tallerico, 2005), and they have tapped into local expertise to take into account the contextual factors in teaching and learning (Loucks-Horsley et al., 2003). Best practices also recognizes the importance of acknowledging time limitations for learning during PD activities, translating trainee knowledge into teaching practice (Bennett, 1987), and making learning more applied in nature by making clear linkages from theory to practice (Brundage & Mackeracher, 1980). An additional best practice in PD programs focuses on having teachers use and reflect on student learning artifacts as a way to evaluate whether their skills and instructional behaviors have improved (e.g., Gerard, Spitulnik, & Linn, 2010; Trautmann & MaKinster, 2010).

Although these improvements have been impressive, such progress in practice has not been widespread, and several important aspects of teacher-focused PD training programs need to be refined and improved. There is concern that many PD programs often do not consider teacher experiences and needs (Gerard, Varma, Corliss, & Linn, 2011) and may be implemented with a greater focus on the objectives and goals of administrators rather than those of teachers (Opfer & Pedder, 2011). Furthermore, many teacher PD programs do not focus teachers' attention on student learning processes (Loucks-Horsley et al., 2003), particularly self-regulation. *Self-regulated learning* (SRL) has been defined as a process of thinking and action whereby individuals strategically implement and modify strategies during their pursuit of personal goals (Zimmerman, 2000). An emerging literature base has shown that although teachers and other school-based personnel desire PD training in SRL-related processes and believe such processes are a critical determinant of student success, they often do not receive this form of training (Cleary & Zimmerman, 2006; Wehmeyer, Agran, & Hughes, 2000). Moreover, even fewer PD programs are designed to target the motivation and SRL processes of teacher trainees as they learn and acquire specific skills during the PD training.

In this chapter, we propose a theoretically grounded model of PD training that underscores the need to provide teachers with knowledge of SRL and extensive practice and feedback when applying content area skills taught during the training. It also focuses on the importance of nurturing teacher motivation and SRL processes as teachers apply their newly acquired skills and knowledge. Given the paucity of effective PD programs, specifically for science teachers of school-age populations (Yoon et al., 2007), this chapter focuses on SRL-promoting PD activities as applied to science education contexts. Science education-based PD contexts are important to consider because the goals of these PD experiences are to provide science teachers with the ability to integrate developmentally appropriate content knowledge (outcomes), scientific practices (processes), and the nature of scientific knowledge (epistemologies) when designing learning environments—quite a complex task. After providing a comprehensive rationale for this PD model and an overview of its theoretical foundation and structural components, we discuss in depth how a contextualized assessment approach called *SRL microanalysis* can be used to help PD trainers provide process or SRL feedback to teacher trainees. Underlying our model is the premise that creating PD contexts that incorporate multiple feedback loop mechanisms will enhance the capacity of PD trainers to guide, structure, and enhance the knowledge and skills of teacher trainees. We also discuss implications and areas of future research.

CHALLENGES FOR TEACHER PROFESSIONAL DEVELOPMENT PROGRAMS IN SCHOOL CONTEXTS

Teachers, like most other professionals, are expected to engage in lifelong learning activities that nurture and optimize their knowledge and teaching skills. PD training represents one of the key mechanisms through which teachers can refine their skills (see Chapter 10, this volume). The reality, however, is that teachers possess a unique set of needs that arise, in part, from the characteristics of the systems within which they work. One of the primary challenges in implementing effective PD in school contexts involves the often conflicting interests of the school as an organization and teachers' needs or desires. When implementing a new initiative, school administrators typically offer PD activities so that teachers can successfully carry out the initiative. However, administrators will often assume that teachers will implement the initiative with high levels of fidelity; that is, all teachers should be doing exactly what the training intends (Brazer & Peters, 2007). Because learning is not a linear and exacting process, and because classroom contexts are fluid and dynamic, teachers often will need to be provided with guided practice opportunities to help customize the instructional program or initiative to their specific classroom contexts.

Frequently, PD programs do not consider differences in teachers' proficiency levels. The teaching profession typically does not use identifying labels that characterize teacher proficiency, with the exception of the National Board for Professional Teaching Standards (Bond, Smith, Baker, & Hattie, 2000), a nationally recognized certification of master teacher. Thus, without prior evaluation of teacher skills, it is difficult for a PD trainer to gauge the level of instruction appropriate for a group of teachers. Although the length of time it takes teachers to master their work has been debated, some consensus exists that teachers with between 1 and 5 years of experience are considered novice and tend to focus their attention on managing the classroom rather than enhancing methods for deeper student learning (e.g., Harris & Sass, 2011). Lack of information regarding teacher proficiencies makes training difficult because of the uncertainty surrounding when to offer training on novice topics, such as classroom management, or expert topics, such as teaching with inquiry.

Given that school districts often play a key role in arranging the PD program and/or determining the logistics (i.e., number of hours, location of training), another challenge is the limited opportunities for teachers to adequately process and apply new knowledge and skills or to receive the necessary feedback to refine those skills over time. Along a similar vein, teacher PD training rarely provides information in a form that is ready for teachers to implement immediately. For example, if teachers attend a PD workshop regarding how to teach students about scientific investigations, the training they receive may include an overview of the theoretical foundation of the approach and perhaps a discussion of a lesson plan that teachers are supposed to emulate. However, because teachers will play the role of "student" during the PD sessions, they typically will not have sufficient practice in using the new skills in their role as teacher. That is, teachers must take the knowledge learned in PD sessions and transform and apply that knowledge in real-word contexts—often without being provided sufficient opportunities for practice, feedback, and refinement.

SELF-REGULATED LEARNING MODEL OF PROFESSIONAL DEVELOPMENT TRAINING

Background and Rationale

One of the most important limitations of many PD training programs is the insufficient amount of time devoted to structured practice and feedback sessions for teacher trainees. It is unreasonable to expect teachers to quickly learn about a particular instructional approach or intervention tactics and then to independently and proficiently apply such techniques without continuous feedback about the quality of their skills. Recent research focusing on PD training for teachers to implement classroom management/mental health interventions has demonstrated the importance of a consultant or coach who creates opportunities for guided practice and feedback in an on-the-job context for teachers (Webster-Stratton, Reid, & Beauchaine, 2011). That research found that a coach provided job-embedded support for teachers and worked with them to ensure their understanding of core intervention components and how to adapt the intervention to address specific student and context problems and needs. In addition, the coaches conducted regularly scheduled observations of fidelity and held follow-up meetings that focused on feedback regarding implementation, development of goals for improved implementation of the intervention, and goals for positive student outcomes.

Han and Weiss (2005) also emphasized the importance of coaching in the successful implementation of evidence-based interventions in schools. In their model, a consultant provides ongoing support to teachers by observing their implementation efforts and student responses to those efforts, providing feedback and working collaboratively with the teacher to solve problems, modeling new techniques and strategies, focusing the teacher's efforts on student improvement, and expressing connections between use of the new intervention and improved student functioning.

Another potential avenue to pursue in supporting student learning through teacher PD is to systematically and purposefully enhance teacher knowledge of SRL principles along with their regulatory capacities for independently practicing and refining skills during and following PD training activities. For example, the survey literature has shown that teachers and other school-based personnel rarely receive PD training in SRL-related processes, despite desiring such training and perceiving it to be useful (Cleary & Zimmerman, 2006; Wehmeyer et al., 2000). Along the same lines, teachers often are not provided with information about how students approach and perform authentic learning tasks, and they tend to lack sufficient knowledge and skills to provide quality SRL-related instruction and feedback. Wehmeyer et al. (2000) found that 41% of teachers reported that they had not received the necessary training and skills to teach SRL to students. Cleary and Zimmerman (2006) showed that although teachers wanted to receive more information about student SRL processes, because such information would be helpful in improving their roles as teachers, they reported rarely ever receiving such information.

The lack of attention to SRL processes in PD training is unfortunate given the increased interest in melding SRL practice and content-area instruction. A joint focus on cyclical inquiry learning cycles and content learning within a PD context has been found to affect teacher fidelity with PD tasks (Borman, Gamoran, & Bowdon, 2008) and has promise to enhance positive learning features in PD experiences. Examining trainees' SRL processes and content knowledge also gives the PD trainer information about trainee learning processes and learning outcomes. When these processes and outcomes are analyzed together, the trainer can better understand how and why the trainee arrived at a particular outcome. Without directly examining trainees' SRL processes, the PD trainer would only be able to make inferences based on the product and, thus, would have to retrospectively reflect on and hypothesize about deficient regulatory or task processes that led to the given product. By simultaneously gathering information about how the learning is proceeding and what it has produced, a trainer can be fully informed about a trainee's needs and thus better positioned to provide timely feedback.

Theoretical and Empirical Foundation

Our PD training program is largely grounded in social-cognitive theory and research, and pulls from the SRL, PD, and feedback literature. From a social-cognitive perspective, human functioning is best explained by, "a model of triadic reciprocality in which behavior, cognition and other personal factors, and environmental events all operate as interacting determinants of each other" (Bandura, 1986, p. 18). Central to this theoretical framework is the premise that humans often learn vicariously (i.e., observing others) and that learning environments can be structured to provide students with optimal learning opportunities. Furthermore, individuals are not merely passive players in the learning process; rather, through the development of personal perceptions of efficacy, they have the potential to exert personal agency and control over their learning goals along with their behaviors, emotions, and environments that lead to these goals (Bandura, 2001). Our proposed PD model is aligned with these general features due to its focus on building teacher self-efficacy, use of modeling and highly structured PD practice sessions, and reliance on context-specific forms of measurement. However, the primary theoretical influences on our PD model are derived from a three-phase cyclical feedback model of SRL (Zimmerman, 2000) and an instructional framework delineating the progressive levels that individuals move through during the development of strategic and regulatory skills (Schunk, 2001); both models have social-cognitive origins and foundations.

Cyclical Model of Self-Regulated Learning Thinking and Action

Expanding on Bandura's (1986) original postulations about human regulation, Zimmerman (2000) defined *SRL* as self-generated thoughts, feelings, and behaviors that are planned and cyclically adapted based on performance feedback in order to attain self-set goals. From this perspective, SRL is conceptualized as a three-phase cyclical feedback loop consisting of *forethought* (i.e., processes that precede efforts to learn), *performance control* (i.e., processes occurring during learning efforts), and *self-reflection phase processes* (i.e., processes occurring after learning or performance; see Chapters 1, 5, 6, and 12, this volume, for additional applications of this cyclical model). The three phases are hypothesized to be interdependent so that changes in forethought processes will induce changes during the performance phase. This, in turn, will influence self-reflection phase processes that subsequently affect forethought beliefs and behaviors exhibited during future learning. In a simplistic sense, sophisticated self-regulated learners are those who purposefully and strategically approach tasks (e.g., high self-efficacy, set goals, make strategic plans), actively use various learning and self-control strategies during the learning process (e.g., monitor quality of learning, create optimal learning environments), and consistently evaluate and reflect on the quality of one's strategic efforts after learning or performance (e.g., self-evaluate goal progress, attributions; Dweck & Master, 2008; Weiner, 1986; Weinstein, Husman, & Dierking, 2000).

Self-regulated learners are self-aware of what they know and what they do not know, are strategic in their approach to learning, and attribute their successes and failures in learning to modifiable self-processes, rather than to uncontrollable factors, such as innate talent. Improvement using SRL strategies have been found in diverse areas related to academic learning: intrinsic motivation (Ryan, Connell, & Deci, 1984), academic studying (Thomas & Rohwer, 1986), classroom interaction (Rohrkemper, 1989; Wang & Peverly, 1986), use of instructional media (Henderson, 1986), metacognitive engagement (Corno & Mandinach, 1983), self-monitoring learning (Ghatala, 1986; Paris, Cross, & Lipson, 1984), dart throwing (Kitsantas, Zimmerman, & Cleary, 2000), and writing revision (Zimmerman & Kitsantas, 2002), and has the potential to illuminate successes and challenges that teachers face when learning about innovative teaching techniques during PD.

Developmental Levels of Self-Regulated Learning

The instructional components of our proposed PD training program model are grounded in a research-based social-cognitive model that delineates four developmental levels of strategic and regulatory skill: observation, emulation, self-control, and self-regulation (Schunk, Pintrich, & Meece, 2008; Zimmerman, 2000). The adopted components of this instructional framework have been studied in several contexts and shown to promote strategic and regulatory thinking and action (Pape, Bell, & Yetkin-Özdemir, 2013; Peters & Kitsantas, 2010; Zimmerman & Kitsantas, 1997).

Observation, the initial level of the instructional model, entails the use of models to demonstrate effective behaviors and ways of thinking via think-alouds, demonstrations, and explanations. During this level, PD facilitators will provide behavioral and cognitive forms of modeling to demonstrate the target behavior and underscore the thought processes and reasoning behind the actions. At emulation, the second developmental level, the PD facilitators will organize highly structured practice activities during which teachers emulate the modeled behaviors and receive prompts, suggestions, and feedback from the facilitators, as needed. The practice sessions are also known as *guided practice* or *scaffolding* activities, and are recognized by PD researchers as a core component of effective PD (Han & Weiss, 2005, Joyce & Showers, 2002). At the self-control level of the developmental model, emphasis shifts from trainer-directed to trainee-led activities. At this level, trainees practice applying skills on their own but can access and seek out assistance and feedback, as needed. At the final level, self-regulation, the trainees should be capable of engaging in sophisticated forms of SRL thought and action characterized by independently adapting their behaviors in response to changing contexts and demands. Although each of these levels is important, our PD training model places the greatest emphasis on the observation and emulation levels because of the strong focus on the initial learning of novel skills and the provision of extensive guided practice opportunities during PD activities.

Instructional Characteristics

Our SRL PD training program is designed to impart conceptual knowledge in SRL theory and principles to teachers and to develop their competency levels by providing them with highly structured feedback and intensive guided practice sessions (Donovan et al., 1999; McHugh & Barlow, 2010). We draw from the three-phase cyclical model to illustrate the process of SRL that we hope trainees will exhibit, whereas the four-level developmental model serves as an instructional guide for trainers to develop SRL skills in teachers. Furthermore, this PD program integrates SRL PD training with training in content-specific principles, such as how to teach students to conduct scientific investigations or how to use inquiry-based lesson plans during class activities.

Although didactic training provides foundational knowledge that is important to the process, the key component of the PD is the use of guided practice sessions that enable teacher participants to transform new facts and principles into usable knowledge and skills. To this end, our PD training program places primary importance on application, extensive practice, and provision of immediate and process-oriented feedback to trainees. A focus on building competency is important, given the research showing that didactic training alone is ineffective in changing practitioner behavior (Grimshaw, Ward, Rubery, & Beynon, 2001; King et al., 2002; Sholomskas et al., 2005).

Because teachers rarely obtain consistent and comprehensive feedback about their teaching skills from other adults and thus must rely on self-generated systems of feedback, we envision effective PD training contexts as those that are capable of providing continuous, multilayered feedback to help trainees enhance their content or task skills and are capable of gathering information about trainees' SRL skills that PD trainers can use to modify PD training activities and experiences to meet trainees' needs.

SRL Training Institute

The SRL Training Institute consists of module-based workshops that provide essential information regarding SRL theory and principles, and the nature of the instructional or intervention skills targeted in the PD training. Sessions typically occur before teachers attempt to apply the target skills in their classrooms. In addition to didactic training, the institute workshops use a highly systematic process of skill development or competency training via modeling and guided practice activities. Thus, it is during the institute level of the model when the observation phase of SRL development first begins. Trainers are exposed to behavioral (i.e., showing how) and cognitive forms of modeling (i.e., revealing underlying thoughts processes) to clearly illustrate the overt actions and the covert behaviors or thought processes that experts would exhibit when applying the target skill in a PD program. For example, suppose the institute workshop involved enhancing science teachers' skills in providing feedback regarding the quality of students' scientific investigations (i.e., lab reports). To model the skill of generating effective feedback, a trainer would talk aloud while reviewing an authentic scientific investigation report and would purposefully and overtly convey his or her underlying thoughts, reasoning, and rationale behind the types of feedback that are most relevant, and how such feedback optimally should be delivered. Table 9.1 illustrates the connections among the four developmental levels of SRL and the PD activities discussed in this section.

Following these modeling experiences, the PD facilitators would provide teachers with highly structured and frequent opportunities to practice and refine the target skills taught during PD activities. Guided practice sessions, which involve having trainees perform skills while being observed by PD facilitators, is an essential part of becoming proficient in using strategies, because trainees, during their attempts to apply the target skills, receive immediate feedback from trainers in the form of prompts, hints, and suggestions. Guided practice and scaffolding support has been used extensively in academic contexts and is a critical component of most effective PD training programs (Forman et al., 2013; Han & Weiss, 2005; Yoon et al., 2007). For example,

TABLE 9.1
Relation Between Developmental Model of Self-Regulated Learning
Instruction and Components of Professional Development Training Activities

Level of development	Component of PD training	Instructional tactics
Observation	SRL Training Institute	PD facilitators provide behavioral and cognitive modeling to trainees to illustrate effective forms of feedback behaviors and thought processes governing that feedback; for this level of instruction, the following activities can occur: • think-alouds, • explanation of reasoning behind actions, and • demonstrations of behaviors.
Emulation	SRL Training Institute, ongoing coaching	PD facilitators organize highly structured practice opportunities for trainees; core characteristics of these practice sessions include • student emulation of modeled actions; • immediate and continuous feedback, as needed; and • additional feedback generated with SRL microanalytic protocols.
Self-control	Ongoing coaching, feedback hotline	Emphasis on shift to trainee-directed activities with available feedback from PD facilitators; the PD facilitators may observe trainee actions, provide additional feedback during coaching sessions, and respond to questions initiated proactively by the trainees.
Self-regulated	Feedback hotline	The trainees are capable of engaging in sophisticated forms of SRL thought and action characterized by independently adapting their behaviors and strategies to varying conditions; the PD facilitator continues to provide assistance and redirects behaviors, as required, but places greater emphasis on nurturing and enabling trainees to adapt their SRL behaviors for varying conditions.

Note. PD = professional development; SRL = self-regulated learning.

if the content focus of the PD training involves enhancing teacher skills in providing feedback to students following scientific investigations, teachers would receive direct instruction on practices in the science discipline and on the strategies for providing feedback to students. They would then be given opportunities to practice providing feedback about student work products while being guided by the PD instructors.

Ongoing Coaching Sessions

Although the institute training incorporates knowledge and application training opportunities, and provides great latitude to trainers in addressing teacher trainees' needs, the next level of support in the SRL PD model involves the provision of ongoing, intensive feedback supports or coaching outside of these workshop experiences. Providing continuous feedback to trainees as they attempt to independently practice and use the content skills learned during the institute training is critical to long-term learning and is something that teachers rarely receive as part of their job (Fixsen, Naoom, Blasé, Friedman, & Wallace, 2005). Trainees often lack confidence in applying skills taught in workshop contexts and may have misconceptions about how to apply the new information and, perhaps, adapt it in authentic and dynamic situations. Thus, the PD training model also develops and refines teachers' skills via in-the-field coaching and feedback sessions following a specified attempt to apply the skills. In the case of the example PD on scientific investigations, the ongoing coaching sessions could occur after each investigation is completed, or perhaps a couple of times per semester, depending on the frequency with which the teachers required students to complete scientific investigations. Although modeling and guided practice activities can still occur during these sessions, the emphasis is on providing feedback to teachers after they attempt to apply and practice their newly acquired skills and behaviors. These activities most closely resemble the self-control level of the development model (see Table 9.1) because the teachers are attempting to use the target skills without explicit guidelines and prompting from an expert.

Feedback Hotline

To further nurture and support teachers' independent use of skills taught during the PD training, a third level of feedback is recommended: a feedback hotline system. Although this PD activity is similar to the ongoing coaching component in that it seeks to enhance the fidelity with which teachers independently apply their skills, the hotline is distinctive, because it provides teachers with continuous and immediate forms of feedback needed to problem solve or troubleshoot minor logistical or conceptual issues not requiring intensive supports. The hotline uses technology to support teacher activities: phone, email, and online discussion forums. The use of multiple formats is ideal because it can account for differences in the amount of privacy teachers want in addressing their personal concerns and the level of community and elaborated conversations to which they are exposed. For example, whereas one teacher may elect to use the hotline on a weekly basis to ensure that he or she is applying skills in an efficient way, another teacher may appreciate reading the public discussion forum exchanges between his or her colleagues and the PD trainers.

Self-Regulated Learning Microanalysis as a Feedback Mechanism

The key purpose of the three-level SRL PD model is to create a feedback-rich environment that enables teachers to, over time, learn, practice, and adapt skills taught in a PD program. Although we have not formally tested the viability or efficacy of the aforementioned three PD components, we have begun to examine the application of a formative assessment tool, called SRL microanalysis, to generate information about the quality with which trainees strategically apply the skills taught during PD (Cleary & Platten, 2013; Peters-Burton, 2013). SRL microanalysis is a context-specific structured interview protocol that directly examines individuals' cyclical-phase SRL processes as they engage in authentic learning or performance activities (Cleary, 2011). These protocols are customized to specific tasks and are designed to capture individuals' phase-specific SRL processes (i.e., forethought, performance, self-reflection) during task engagement. Figure 9.1 illustrates sample questions in each phase of SRL. Researchers have developed and applied SRL microanalytic protocols across a myriad of tasks, including athletic skills (Cleary, Zimmerman, & Keating, 2006), clinical-related activities (Artino, Cleary, Dong, Hemmer, & Durning, 2014), and academic tasks (DiBenedetto & Zimmerman, 2010). Regardless of the specific task, the most essential principle is to customize the SRL microanalytic protocol to tasks that have a clear beginning, middle, and end. Microanalytic questions are purposefully administered to link the temporal dimension of a task (i.e., before task is started, during completion of task, and following task) with the phase dimensions of the three-phase cyclical feedback loop (Cleary, 2011; Zimmerman, 2000). Thus, an SRL microanalytic protocol would be used to assess individual responses to forethought phase questions (e.g., goal setting) before beginning a given activity, performance phase questions (e.g., metacognitive monitoring) during that activity, and self-reflection items (e.g., attributions) after completion of the activity. By linking the temporal dimensions of a given task or activity to the cyclical SRL phases, one is better able to draw conclusions about individuals' task-specific regulatory processes.

There is ample support for the interrater reliability and validity of SRL microanalytic protocols across academic and nonacademic contexts (Cleary, 2011). A couple of case study investigations have illustrated how coaches or PD trainers incorporated microanalytic assessment protocols during instruction and subsequently formatively used trainee/student responses to either modify instruction or PD training activities (Cleary & Platten, 2013; Peters-Burton, 2013). In the following section, we illustrate the application and use of SRL microanalysis during PD training activities as a tool that enabled PD trainers to provide individualized, process forms of feedback to PD participants.

Performance Questions
(administered **during** task or immediately after the task is completed)

MONITORING: "Did you monitor yourself during your time spent planning your inquiry lesson? What did you do to monitor yourself?"

STRATEGY USE: "Can you explain to me how you are going about collecting data? What exactly are you doing?"

Forethought Questions
(administered **before** task is started)

GOAL: "Do you have a goal in mind as you prepare to perform this activity? If so, what is it?"

PLAN: "What will you do to perform well on this activity?"

SELF-EFFICACY: "How sure are you that you can develop an exemplary _____?"

Academic Task

Self-Reflection Questions
(administered **after** task is completed)

SELF-EVALUATION: (a) "How well do you think you did on this activity?" (b) "What criteria did you use to judge how well you performed?"

ATTRIBUTION: "What is the main reason why you received a _____ on this activity? Tell me all the reasons."

ADAPTIVE INFERENCES: "What do you need to do to perform well if you were given another chance to do this activity?"

Figure 9.1. Selected examples of SRL microanalytic questions administered before, during, and after PD participants complete a PD task.

Although most evaluations of PD effectiveness are measured after training has concluded, we postulate that SRL microanalysis can be used as a formative assessment tool to help PD instructors identify gaps in trainees' strategic thinking and regulatory processes as the trainees attempt to apply the skills they were taught during PD. SRL microanalysis also can be used to help PD instructors make changes in PD instruction and activities to optimize trainees' strategic skills and regulatory behaviors.

Peters-Burton (2013) conducted a qualitative study to examine the utility of a modified version of an SRL microanalytic protocol with 14 in-service elementary school teachers during a 15-week PD face-to-face intensive training.

The objective of the PD training was to increase teachers' skills in developing and implementing inquiry lessons in earth science, an area that is notoriously difficult because the large scale and long time frames of the topics are hard for young children to understand. Peters-Burton (2013) used the microanalytic protocol as a way to gather diagnostic information about teachers' strategic regulatory processes relative to developing inquiry lesson plans and to use such information to subsequently inform modifications to the PD instruction.

The SRL microanalytic protocol targeted various teacher subprocesses within forethought, performance, and self-reflection. Although microanalytic protocols traditionally are embedded within a time-limited task (e.g., 12-minute basketball practice session, 30-minute study session), Peters-Burton's (2013) pilot study used an SRL microanalytic protocol across the 15-week PD training program. The forethought phase questions, which focused on self-efficacy, goal setting, strategic planning, and task value, were administered at the beginning of the PD program. The purpose of these questions was to gather data about the participants' regulatory and strategic approaches when first developing the inquiry lesson. The performance questions, which focused on self-monitoring and self-instruction, were administered twice during the program: once at 5 weeks into the PD training, when the teachers developed their first lesson; and another at 10 weeks, when the teachers developed their second lesson. Consistent with linking the phase-specific SRL processes to the microanalytic questions, the self-monitoring and self-instruction questions were administered during teachers' attempts to design a particular inquiry lesson plan. The self-reflection phase questions, which focused on self-satisfaction, self-evaluation, and attributions, were administered at the conclusion of the course. Figure 9.2 details the PD feedback loops and modifications that occurred with each administration of the SRL microanalysis protocol during the PD. The basic premise of using SRL microanalytic protocols was that if trainers can identify SRL processes that are prominent and those that are underused by the trainees, then trainers can provide additional scaffolding and/or modify the PD training activities to enhance teacher learning and their skills in preparing lesson plans or other activities related to teaching (Cleary & Platten, 2013).

Reviewing the Peters-Burton (2013) study, we focus primarily on how the PD trainers used the teachers' microanalytic responses during forethought and performance phases to enact changes to the PD instruction and activities. Before the PD activities began, the author asked teachers to answer a series of forethought phase questions: self-efficacy to plan inquiry lessons on the topic of earth science, perceived value of the PD training, goal setting, and strategic planning. To interpret the goal-setting and planning questions, the author compared teacher-stated goals to characteristics of effective goal setting described in the literature (e.g., specificity, proximity of goals, process

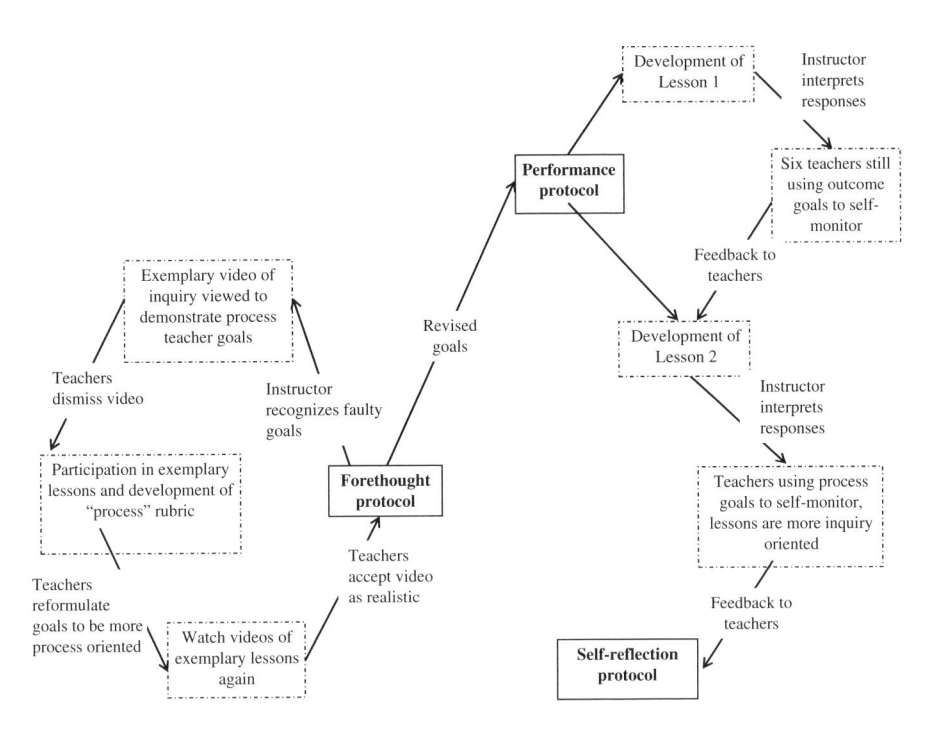

Figure 9.2. Feedback loops supported by forethought protocol and performance protocol.

or outcomes) and then examined how teachers planned on achieving those goals. The descriptive results revealed that all 16 teachers provided general, distal, and outcome-oriented goals relative to the task of lesson plan development. Given that those goals are not effective in motivating and guiding behavior, particularly for those learning novel skills, the teachers were at-risk of not fully engaging or learning during the PD. Thus, Peters-Burton used the microanalytic data as an empirical platform from which to help the teachers recognize their faulty goals and, more important, to help them to establish more effective goals, such as those that emphasize specific, measurable, and process-oriented dimensions.

Evidence of teachers' disengagement from the PD activities was observed in all 16 teachers' reactions to the first activity in the PD: viewing a video of exemplary inquiry lessons that focused on earth science. The purpose of viewing the videos was to assist teachers in understanding that their initial goals, such as "I will be sure my lesson meets the state standards for learning," were too general, distal, and outcome oriented. This is a faulty goal for the PD because the state standards are based on subject matter and not on inquiry processes, and there is no indication of the steps toward creating an environment in which students can begin engaging in open-ended inquiry. To the surprise of Peters-Burton (2013), the teachers dismissed the videos of the students engaging in inquiry as too unrealistic; they reported that their students were unable to have scientific discussions on the high cognitive level of the students in the video. It was clear that another strategy was needed to scaffold teacher goal setting to be more specific and process oriented.

In this attempt to have teachers reformulate their goals, Peters-Burton (2013) provided teachers with three exemplary lesson plans that they carried out in the role of students. After implementing each lesson, the teachers collectively analyzed the lesson. Peters-Burton acted as a facilitator and gathered the prominent elements that characterized the lessons as inquiry based. These characteristics were compiled on a rubric that teachers then used as a process checklist when writing their lesson plans. The creation of the rubric served as a model for developing process-oriented goals for planning inquiry lessons. The author and teachers discussed how goals for developing inquiry lessons hinged on accurately portraying each model characteristic in their own lesson, and set new goals based on those processes of designing a lesson plan.

Using the rubric, the teachers were able to reestablish their goals to be more short term, specific, and process oriented. For example, instead of "I will make sure the lesson meets the state standards," a teacher reformulated her goal as "I will direct students' attention to answering two key questions based on empirical evidence." After the teachers read the rubric and reestablished their goals for planning lessons, they were asked to view the exemplary videos of inquiry classroom interactions a second time. During this viewing, teachers were taught to visualize actions in inquiry that would form proximal and measurable goals for implementation, similar to the process of setting goals for lesson planning via the model characteristics from the rubric. Although, after the first viewing, the teachers dismissed the videos and explained that the lessons in the videos were unrealistic given their students' backgrounds in their classrooms, the teachers reported during the second viewing that they could achieve the classroom interactions demonstrated in the video. After the scaffolding process using the exemplary lessons to create the rubric and visualizing the enactment of the elements on the rubric, the author was confident that the teachers set process goals for the PD.

After the modification to teachers' forethought phase processes, Peters-Burton (2013) shifted the focus to having the teachers write the inquiry lesson. Given that this phase represented behaviors exhibited during the target task of interest, the teachers were asked to periodically answer performance phase microanalytic questions (e.g., "Did you monitor your progress during the time you spent planning your inquiry lesson? If so, what did you use to monitor yourself?") During the development of Lesson 1, six of the

16 teachers reported that they self-monitored their progress using their original outcome goals, such as "I made sure the lesson met the state standards," rather than using their revised goals. Given that the performance phase questions of the SRL microanalytic interview were administered during the target task, Peters-Burton was able to provide immediate feedback regarding the need and importance of self-monitoring using the teachers' revised, more process-oriented goals. The teachers were asked to develop a second lesson plan, and a second SRL microanalysis interview for the performance phase occurred during that time. All 16 teachers reported that they self-monitored their progress using their revised, process-oriented goals, which provided evidence that the administration of the SRL microanalysis during the learning task was beneficial in redirecting maladaptive behaviors.

It appeared that the feedback provided to the trainees before an attempt to develop the inquiry lesson and during their initial attempts on this task was helpful in redirecting them to focus on more adaptive task-related learning processes. During their second attempt at creating the inquiry lessons, the teachers noted that they focused primarily on the steps articulated in the process-oriented rubric instead of just focusing on the final product. Along with their shift to process goals, the teachers also began to increase the frequency with which they sought help and assistance to fine-tune their lesson plans (Borman et al., 2008), in part because they could better explain the help they needed, rather than try to accomplish an outcome without knowing what steps they needed to take to be successful (Hanuscin, Lee, & Akerson, 2011).

IMPLICATIONS AND FUTURE DIRECTIONS

PD training represents a core mechanism through which teachers can enhance their knowledge and skills, and/or refine skills that initially were developed during their teacher training education. Our PD model places feedback loops as the central underlying characteristic to ensure that teachers can proficiently apply skills introduced during PD training activities. Given that we recognize the importance of SRL processes in enabling teachers to apply, practice, and refine their skills, our model not only focuses on providing teachers with didactic instruction in key SRL principles but also emphasizes the importance of structured coaching sessions and contextualized forms of assessment to systematically evaluate and monitor the quality of trainees' SRL processes as they practice and apply these skills.

Future research is needed to evaluate the components of the model, such as examining gaps and inconsistencies within each component and the interactions between each component. Additional work is needed to examine how SRL microanalytic protocols can be used most effectively as part of PD activities and whether this type of protocol is used most effectively in PD contexts, in particular. Although the Peters-Burton (2013) study was an example of how to use SRL microanalytic protocols as part of a workshop context (i.e., institute training), we believe that applying this assessment approach to other components of the model, such as ongoing coaching, can also be valuable, because it is during these sessions when PD facilitators meet with trainees to review and reflect on trainees' experiences in applying their skills in real time during authentic classroom experiences. Thus, unlike institute sessions, SRL microanalytic protocols used during the ongoing coaching component can help PD facilitators to better understand and evaluate the quality of the teachers' regulatory processes in real-world contexts.

Although there is much empirical support for SRL microanalysis as an assessment approach (Cleary, 2011; Cleary, Callan, & Zimmerman, 2012), researchers have acknowledged that the administration and interpretation of microanalytic measures can be labor intensive, particularly as the number of students or trainees increases. Emerging technologies are changing learning spaces, interactions with students, and teaching and learning perspectives (Kitsantas & Dabbagh, 2011). Technology-enriched learning can enhance student SRL and motivation, which, in turn, can facilitate academic performance and increase positive attitudes toward learning (López-Morteo & López, 2007). Although research surrounding SRL and use of learning technology is in its initial stages (Azevedo, Greene, & Moos, 2007; Kitsantas & Dabbagh, 2011), we believe that future research should consider using different types of learning technologies (e.g., tablets on which students record work and receive immediate feedback on their processes) to increase the ease with which microanalytic assessment information can be tracked and organized. It is also important to recognize that teachers often face competing objectives in their roles as teachers. For example, they must strive to not only meet their students' diverse learning needs, particularly as they relate to high-stakes testing outcomes, but to also be cognizant of implementing interventions or PD-related skills with fidelity, or as is specified in an intervention manual or program. To meet these often contrasting objectives, teachers need to continue to strive to become career-long learners and engage in multiple PD efforts. Of greater importance is their need to get timely and informative feedback about the quality of their skills and progress toward their objectives. From our perspective, the promise of the PD model presented in this chapter needs to be examined in relation to both teacher and student outcomes, including teacher satisfaction, the fidelity with which teachers implement interventions, teacher SRL and self-efficacy, and student achievement outcomes.

REFERENCES

Artino, A. R., Jr., Cleary, T. J., Dong, T., Hemmer, P. A., & Durning, S. J. (2014). Exploring clinical reasoning in novices: A self-regulated learning microanalytic assessment approach. *Medical Education, 48,* 280–291. doi:10.1111/medu.12303

Azevedo, R., Greene, J. A., & Moos, D. C. (2007). The effect of a human agent's external regulation upon college students' hypermedia learning. *Metacognition and Learning, 2*(2–3), 67–87. doi:10.1007/s11409-007-9014-9

Bandura, A. (1986). *Social foundations of thought and action: A social cognitive theory.* Englewood Cliffs, NJ: Prentice Hall.

Bandura, A. (2001). Social cognitive theory: An agentic perspective. *Annual Review of Psychology, 52,* 1–26. doi:10.1146/annurev.psych.52.1.1

Bennett, B. B. (1987). *The effectiveness of staff development training practices: A meta-analysis.* Unpublished doctoral dissertation, University of Oregon, Eugene.

Bond, L., Smith, R., Baker, W. K., & Hattie, J. A. (2000). *Certification system of the National Board for Professional Teaching Standards: A construct and consequential validity study.* Washington, DC: National Board for Professional Teaching Standards.

Borman, G. D., Gamoran, A., & Bowdon, J. (2008). A randomized trial of teacher development in elementary science: First-year achievement effects. *Journal of Research on Educational Effectiveness, 1,* 237–264. doi:10.1080/19345740802328273

Brazer, S. D., & Peters, E. E. (2007). Deciding to change: One district's quest to improve overall student performance. *International Journal of Education Policy & Leadership, 2*(5), 1–14.

Brundage, D. H., & Mackeracher, D. (1980). *Adult learning principles and their application to program planning.* Toronto, Ontario, Canada: Ministry of Education.

Cleary, T. J. (2011). Emergence of self-regulated learning microanalysis: Historical overview, essential features, and implications for research and practice. In B. J. Zimmerman & D. H. Schunk (Eds.), *Handbook of self-regulation of learning and performance* (pp. 329–345). New York, NY: Routledge.

Cleary, T. J., Callan, G. L., & Zimmerman, B. J. (2012). Assessing self-regulation as a cyclical, context-specific phenomenon: Overview and analysis of SRL microanalytic protocols. *Education Research International, 2012,* 1–19.

Cleary, T. J., & Platten, P. (2013). Examining the correspondence between self-regulated learning and academic achievement: A case study analysis [Special Issue; advance online publication]. *Education Research International, 2013,* 1–18. doi:10.1155/2013/272560

Cleary, T. J., & Zimmerman, B. J. (2006). Teachers' perceived usefulness of strategy microanalytic assessment information. *Psychology in the Schools, 43,* 149–155. doi:10.1002/pits.20141

Cleary, T. J., Zimmerman, B. J., & Keating, T. (2006). Training physical education students to self-regulate during basketball free throw practice. *Research Quarterly for Exercise and Sport, 77,* 251–262. doi:10.1080/02701367.2006.10599358

Corno, L., & Mandinach, E. (1983). The role of cognitive engagement in classroom learning and motivation. *Educational Psychologist, 18*, 88–108. doi:10.1080/00461528309529266

DiBenedetto, M. K., & Zimmerman, B. J. (2010). Differences in self-regulatory processes among students studying science: A microanalytic investigation. *International Journal of Educational & Psychological Assessment, 5*, 2–24.

Donovan, S., Bransford, J. D., & Pelligrino, J. (1999). *How students learn: History, mathematics, and science in the classroom.* Washington, DC: National Academies Press.

Dweck, C. S., & Master, A. (2008). Self-theories motivate self-regulated learning. In D. H. Schunk & B. J. Zimmerman (Eds.), *Motivation and self-regulated learning: Theory, research, and applications* (pp. 31–51). Mahwah, NJ: Erlbaum.

Fixsen, D. L., Naoom, S. F., Blasé, K. A., Friedman, R. M., & Wallace, F. (2005). *Implementation research: A synthesis of the literature.* Tampa: University of South Florida.

Forman, S. G., Shapiro, E. S., Codding, R. S., Gonzales, F. E., Reddy, L. A., Rosenfield, S. A., . . . Stoiber, K. C. (2013). Implementation science and school psychology. *School Psychology Quarterly, 28*, 77–100.

Gerard, L. F., Spitulnik, M. W., & Linn, M. C. (2010). Teacher use of evidence to customize inquiry science instruction. *Journal of Research in Science Teaching, 47*, 1037–1063. doi:10.1002/tea.20367

Gerard, L. F., Varma, K., Corliss, S. B., & Linn, M. C. (2011). Professional development for technology-enhanced inquiry science. *Review of Educational Research, 81*, 408–448. doi:10.3102/0034654311415121

Ghatala, E. S. (1986). Strategy monitoring training enables young learners to select effective strategies. *Educational Psychologist, 21*, 43–54. doi:10.1080/00461520.1986.9653023

Grimshaw, D., Ward, K. G., Rubery, J., & Beynon, H. (2001). Organisations and the transformation of the internal labour market in the UK. *Work, Employment and Society, 15*(1), 25–54. doi:10.1177/09500170122118760

Han, S. S., & Weiss, B. (2005). Sustainability of teacher implementation of school-based mental health programs. *Journal of Abnormal Child Psychology, 33*, 665–679. doi:10.1007/s10802-005-7646-2

Hanuscin, D. L., Lee, M. H., & Akerson, V. L. (2011). Elementary teachers' pedagogical content knowledge for teaching the nature of science. *Science Education, 95*, 145–167. doi:10.1002/sce.20404

Harris, D. N., & Sass, T. R. (2011). Teacher training, teacher quality, and student achievement. *Journal of Public Economics, 95*, 798–812. doi:10.1016/j.jpubeco.2010.11.009

Henderson, R. W. (1986). Self-regulated learning: Implications for the design of instructional media. *Contemporary Educational Psychology, 11*, 405–427. doi:10.1016/0361-476X(86)90032-9

Hill, H. C. (2007). Learning in the teaching workforce. *The Future of Children, 17*(1), 111–127. doi:10.1353/foc.2007.0004

Joyce, B. R., & Showers, B. (2002). *Student achievement through staff development* (3rd ed.). Alexandria, VA: Association for Supervision and Curriculum Development.

King, M., Davidson, O., Taylor, F., Haines, A., Sharp, D., & Turner, R. (2002). Effectiveness of teaching general practitioners skills in brief cognitive behaviour theory to treat patients with depression: Randomised controlled trial. *British Medical Journal, 324,* 947–953.

Kitsantas, A., & Dabbagh, N. (2011, Summer). The role of Web 2.0 technologies in self-regulated learning. *New Directions for Teaching and Learning, 126,* 99–106. doi:10.1002/tl.448

Kitsantas, A., Zimmerman, B. J., & Cleary, T. (2000). The role of observation and emulation in The development of athletic self-regulation. *Journal of Educational Psychology, 92,* 811–817. doi:10.1037/0022-0663.92.4.811

López-Morteo, G., & López, G. (2007). Computer support for learning mathematics: A learning environment based on recreational learning objects. *Computers & Education, 48,* 618–641.

Loucks-Horsley, S., Love, N., Stiles, K. E., Mundry, S., & Hewson, P. W. (2003). *Designing professional development for teachers of science and mathematics* (2nd ed.). Thousand Oaks, CA: Corwin Press.

McHugh, R. K., & Barlow, D. H. (2010). Dissemination and implementation of evidence-based psychological interventions: A review of current efforts. *American Psychologist, 65,* 73–84.

Opfer, V. D., & Pedder, D. (2011). Conceptualizing teacher professional learning. *Review of Educational Research, 81,* 376–407. doi:10.3102/0034654311413609

Pape, S. J., Bell, C. V., & Yetkin-Özdemir, I. E. (2013). Sequencing components of mathematics lessons to maximize development of self-regulation: Theory, practice, and intervention. In H. Bembenutty, T. J. Cleary, and A. Kitsantas (Eds.), *Applications of self-regulated learning across diverse disciplines: A tribute to Barry J. Zimmerman* (pp. 29–58). Charlotte, NC: Information Age.

Paris, S. G., Cross, D. R., & Lipson, M. Y. (1984). Informed strategies for learning: A program to improve children's reading awareness and comprehension. *Journal of Educational Psychology, 76,* 1239–1252. doi:10.1037/0022-0663.76.6.1239

Peters, E. E., & Kitsantas, A. (2010). The effect of nature of science metacognitive prompts on science students' content and nature of science knowledge, metacognition, and self-regulatory efficacy. *School Science and Mathematics, 110,* 382–396. doi:10.1111/j.1949-8594.2010.00050.x

Peters-Burton, E. E. (2013). Student work products as a teaching tool for nature of science pedagogical knowledge: A professional development project with inservice secondary science teachers. *Teaching and Teacher Education, 29,* 156–166. doi:10.1016/j.tate.2012.09.005

Rohrkemper, M. M. (1989). Self-regulated learning and academic achievement: A Vygotskian view. In B. J. Zimmerman & D. H. Schunk (Eds.), *Self-regulated learning and academic achievement: Theory, research, and practice* (pp. 143–168). New York, NY: Springer-Verlag.

Ryan, R. M., Connell, J. P., & Deci, E. L. (1984). A motivational analysis of self-determination and self-regulation in education. In C. Ames & R. Ames (Eds.), *Research on motivation in education* (Vol. 2, pp. 13–52). New York, NY: Academic Press.

Schunk, D. H. (2001). Social cognitive theory and self-regulated learning. In B. J. Zimmerman & D. H. Schunk (Eds.), *Self-regulated learning and academic achievement* (2nd ed., pp. 125–151). Mahwah, NJ: Erlbaum.

Schunk, D. H., Pintrich, P. R., & Meece, J. L. (2008). *Motivation in education: Theory, research, and applications* (3rd ed.). Upper Saddle River, NJ: Pearson/Merrill Prentice Hall.

Sholomskas, D. E., Syracuse-Siewert, G., Rounsaville, B. J., Ball, S. A., Nuro, K. F., & Carroll, K. M. (2005). We don't train in vain: A dissemination trial of three strategies of training clinicians in cognitive–behavioral therapy. *Journal of Consulting and Clinical Psychology, 73*, 106–115. doi:10.1037/0022-006X.73.1.106

Tallerico, M. (2005). *Supporting and sustaining teachers' professional development: A principal's guide*. Thousand Oaks, CA: Corwin Press.

Thomas, J. W., & Rohwer, W. D., Jr. (1986). Academic studying: The role of learning strategies. *Educational Psychologist, 21*, 19–41. doi:10.1080/00461520.1986.9653022

Trautmann, N. M., & MaKinster, J. G. (2010). Flexibly adaptive professional development in support of teaching science with geospatial technology. *Journal of Science Teacher Education, 21*, 351–370. doi:10.1007/s10972-009-9181-4

Wang, M. C., & Peverly, S. T. (1986). The self-instructive process in classroom learning contexts. *Contemporary Educational Psychology, 11*, 370–404. doi:10.1016/0361-476X(86)90031-7

Webster-Stratton, C., Reid, M. J., & Beauchaine, T. P. (2011). Combining parent and child training for young children with ADHD. *Journal of Clinical Child and Adolescent Psychology, 40*(2), 1–13.

Wehmeyer, M. L., Agran, M., & Hughes, C. A. (2000). National survey of teachers' promotion of self-determination and student-directed learning. *Journal of Special Education, 34*, 58–68. doi:10.1177/002246690003400201

Weiner, B. (1986). *An attributional theory of motivation and emotion*. New York, NY: Springer-Verlag. doi:10.1007/978-1-4612-4948-1

Weinstein, C. E., Husman, J., & Dierking, D. R. (2000). Self-regulation interventions with a focus on learning strategies. In M. Boekaerts, P. R. Pintrich, & M. Zeidner (Eds.), *Handbook of self-regulation* (pp. 727–747). Orlando, FL: Academic Press. doi:10.1016/B978-012109890-2/50051-2

Yoon, K. S., Duncan, T., Lee, S. W.-Y., Scarloss, B., & Shapley, K. L. (2007). *Reviewing the evidence on how teacher professional development affects student achievement.* Washington, DC: National Center for Educational Evaluation and Regional Assistance, Institute of Education Sciences. doi:10.1037/e607942011-001

Zimmerman, B. J. (2000). Attaining self-regulation: A social-cognitive perspective. In M. Boekaerts, P. R. Pintrich, & M. Zeidner (Eds.), *Handbook of self-regulation* (pp. 13–39). San Diego, CA: Academic Press. doi:10.1016/B978-012109890-2/50031-7

Zimmerman, B. J., & Kitsantas, A. (1997). Developmental phases in self-regulation: Shifting from process goals to outcome goals. *Journal of Educational Psychology, 89,* 29–36. doi:10.1037/0022-0663.89.1.29

Zimmerman, B. J., & Kitsantas, A. (2002). Acquiring writing revision and self-regulatory skill through observation and emulation. *Journal of Educational Psychology, 94,* 660–668. doi:10.1037/0022-0663.94.4.660

10

USING TEACHER LEARNING TEAMS AS A FRAMEWORK FOR BRIDGING THEORY AND PRACTICE IN SELF-REGULATED LEARNING

NANCY E. PERRY, CHARLOTTE A. BRENNER,
AND NICOLE MacPHERSON

Lucy began kindergarten as a bright and enthusiastic 5-year-old, having had a terrifically advantaged preschool experience. As a result, she arrived at school having a rich and expansive lexicon, reading primers, listening to chapter books, and having good number sense. Each skill is important and will serve her well as she settles into school. But even better predictors of Lucy's likely success in school are her abilities to pay attention, follow directions, resist distractions, work well with others, cope with challenges, and adapt to complex environments. These qualities are associated with self-regulation, which recent research has indicated predicts early success in school better than children's numeracy skills and ability to read when they enter school, or than traditional measures of cognitive ability/IQ (Diamond, Barnett, Thomas, & Munro, 2007). Kindergarten teachers have rated skills associated with self-regulation as essential for school success and have reported that children who struggle with self-regulation have difficulty adjusting to

---

http://dx.doi.org/10.1037/14641-011
Self-Regulated Learning Interventions With At-Risk Youth: Enhancing Adaptability, Performance, and Well-Being, T. J. Cleary (Editor)
Copyright © 2015 by the American Psychological Association. All rights reserved.

school: They have difficulty completing academic tasks, meeting behavioral expectations, and relating to peers and teachers (McClelland, Morrison, & Holmes, 2000; Rimm-Kaufman & Chiu, 2007; Rimm-Kaufman, Curby, Grimm, Nathanson, & Brock, 2009).

Across grade levels and academic settings, self-regulation is recognized as a significant source of achievement differences among students (Zimmerman & Schunk, 2011). General and special education teachers have cited students' abilities to self-regulate as a major influence on their adaptive functioning and attainment of academic success (Cleary & Zimmerman, 2006; Wehmeyer, Yeager, Bolding, Agran, & Hughes, 2003). Fortunately, self-regulation can be developed and supported in learning contexts. Practices that promote self-regulated learning (SRL) have been successful in improving social and academic outcomes for students who struggle in school—even students with exceptional learning needs (Graham & Harris, 2003; Wong, Harris, Graham, & Butler, 2003).

In this chapter, we advance a framework for how researchers and teachers can work together to support self-regulation in schools. In particular, we develop a rationale for involving teachers in designing and implementing opportunities for SRL to occur in their classrooms, which will enable them to adapt research principles to suit the unique needs of their teaching and learning contexts. We agree with Randi and Corno (2000) that, for teaching toward SRL to become widespread in school systems, it needs to be "developed harmoniously within existing curriculum" (p. 652), and researchers need to collaborate with teachers in the development and implementation of SRL innovations (p. 681). We begin by defining self-regulation and SRL. Then we provide a retrospective review and constructive critique of researcher-derived interventions in the field of SRL to date. This sets the stage for our promotion of participatory models of professional development (PD) that use teacher inquiry, action research, and communities of practice frameworks to support effective and sustainable innovations in classrooms and schools. We review research in this regard and provide detailed examples from our work with teacher learning teams (TLTs). We conclude with a discussion of implications for teaching and learning, research, and policy.

THEORETICAL FOUNDATIONS OF SELF-REGULATION AND SELF-REGULATED LEARNING

The term *self-regulation* is used to describe individuals' ability to control thoughts and actions to achieve personal goals and respond to environmental demands (Zimmerman, 2008). Individuals who are productively self-regulating recognize and attend to key features in the environment (e.g., instructions for carrying out tasks or norms for social interactions) and can inhibit automatic responses (e.g., expressions of dislike or frustration) that will not serve them well in particular situations (Blair & Razza, 2007; Ponitz, McClelland, Matthews, & Morrison, 2009). They use self-regulation to control cognition, motivation, emotion, and action (Eisenberg & Spinrad, 2004; Tice, Baumeister, & Zhang, 2004). It supports them to persist when faced with challenges and to respond appropriately and flexibly in a range of contexts.

Successful self-regulation relies on metacognition, motivation, and strategic action (Winne & Perry, 2000; Zimmerman, 1990, 2008). Students who engage in SRL exercise metacognition by considering their strengths and weaknesses in relation to an assignment or activity and, where challenges exist, considering strategies they can use to be successful. These learners are motivated for learning; they value personal progress and deep understanding, and they view errors as opportunities for learning. So they are willing to try challenging tasks that prompt self-regulation (Hadwin, Järvelä, & Miller, 2011). *Strategic action* describes how these learners approach challenging tasks and problems: They strategically choose from a developing repertoire of strategies those best suited to a situation and then apply them effectively (Perry, 2013).

Well-known models of SRL are cyclical: They describe processes learners use to guide their thoughts and actions before, during, and after they engage in learning and other types of tasks (Winne & Hadwin, 1998; Zimmerman & Campillo, 2003). These models commonly describe how successfully self-regulating learners actively interpret tasks, make plans, enact strategies, monitor progress, and make adjustments as they grapple with the demands and challenges learning can present. In particular, monitoring and self-reflection are powerful processes in the cycle of self-regulation (Winne & Perry, 2000) because they produce a feedback loop learners can use to judge whether they are succeeding. When a mismatch between a learner's goal and the current state of task completion is noted, self-regulating learners use this feedback to make adjustments or enact strategies (e.g., help-seeking) to get back on track. Similarly, learners' motivations (e.g., their beliefs about their likelihood of success and the value they place on success in particular situations) predict their willingness to enact self-regulatory processes cyclically and recursively to facilitate learning (Zimmerman, 2008).

CONSIDERING AND RECONSIDERING INTERVENTION RESEARCH ON SELF-REGULATED LEARNING

Efforts to understand and support the development of SRL can be traced back to the 1950s and 1960s, and have evolved through a number of different theoretical orientations and research methodologies. Initially, operant theorists sought to identify measurable (i.e., observable) events to explain people's self-control of behavior (Skinner, 1967). Interested in how desired actions were shaped and maintained through rewards, self-reinforcements, and punishments, those researchers highlighted the role of self-monitoring in the production/execution of goal-orientated behaviors (Zimmerman, 1989). In the 1970s and 1980s, cognitive and social-cognitive theories (see e.g., Bandura, 1986; Zimmerman, 2002) expanded behavioral views of self-control by examining how internal processes, such as metacognition and motivation, are implicated in strategic/self-regulated behavior. Next, researchers began to examine factors associated with successful SRL and methods for enhancing students' SRL, particularly for students who appeared to struggle with learning (Pressley, 1986; Zimmerman, 2002).

The 1980s and early 1990s could be considered the heyday of strategy intervention research. During that period, researchers designed instructional methods that emphasized direct teaching of specific, researcher-prescribed strategies, such as goal setting, self-monitoring, self-instructions, and selection of strategies to meet the demands of specific tasks (Pressley, 1986; Schumaker, Deshler, & Ellis, 1986). Often, those strategy interventions targeted specific groups of students (e.g., students with learning disabilities) thought to lack self-regulatory capacities, such as metacognition and strategic action. The goal was to develop and enhance the learners' acquisition, implementation, and maintenance of SRL skills (Pressley, 1986). Typically, those students were taught task-specific strategies (e.g., summarization, outlining) in one-on-one or small group settings and, generally, they demonstrated improved performance on assessments at the end of the interventions (Zimmerman, 2008). However, students seldom maintained and generalized the strategies across time and in nonexperimental contexts (Brown, Campione, & Day, 1981; Wong, 1994; Zimmerman, 2008).

In response to concerns about maintenance and generalization, SRL interventions became increasingly elaborate, and a pedagogical shift occurred in methods used to study and promote students' development of SRL. Researchers began encouraging students to be active agents in their development of SRL (see, e.g., strategic content learning, Butler, 1995; Self-Regulated Strategy Development, Harris & Graham, 1999; and the Self-Regulation Empowerment Program, Cleary & Zimmerman, 2004). Although still focused primarily on students with identified learning difficulties, those models of SRL intervention were embedded in the curriculum, included students in the process of SRL strategy development, addressed individual strengths and weaknesses, allowed students to set their own learning goals and adapt strategies to suit their learning needs, and provided multiple opportunities for scaffolded support and online (real-time) feedback. Including those features in SRL intervention models resulted in an increase in students' autonomous and effective application of SRL strategies, and generalization and maintenance of those strategies over time and across contexts (Wong et al., 2003).

Up until the 1990s, and even today, few programs of research about SRL have focused on whether and how practicing teachers in general educational settings promote SRL in regularly occurring activities in classrooms. Exceptions include Perry and colleagues (Perry, 1998; Perry, VandeKamp, Mercer, & Nordby, 2002) and Wharton-McDonald and colleagues (Wharton-McDonald, Pressley, & Hampston, 1998; Wharton-McDonald, Pressley, Rankin, Mistretta, Yokoi, & Ettenberger, 1997), who studied teachers' promotion of SRL within whole class settings. Perry's in-depth, qualitative observations identified how task features, instructional practices, and interpersonal relationships supported students' SRL in classrooms. Specifically, she observed SRL in classrooms in which teachers gave students opportunities to experience choice, engage in complex tasks, control their level of challenge, access teacher and peer support, and receive ongoing informative feedback. More generally, Wharton-McDonald et al. (1997) characterized highly effective primary teachers as those who designed single lessons to address multiple goals (i.e., content, process, social) and used some explicit teaching, but also engaged in extensive scaffolding, encouraged SRL, and had high but realistic expectations for all students.

Perry's (1998) research revealed a range of teaching practices, even in classrooms in which teachers were implementing innovations, such as process writing and portfolio assessments, believed to incorporate SRL supportive practices. The differences Perry observed in this regard likely reflect the complexities of creating contexts that promote thoughtful and strategic approaches to learning. Brown and Campione (1994) argued that, to do this, teachers need to understand the first principles—not just the surface procedures—that have originated particular tools and techniques. Formative assessment, project-based learning, and approaches to differentiating instruction (e.g., universal designs for learning) are contemporary examples of curricular/classroom innovations with principles that align well with promoting SRL. We agree with Randi and Corno (2007) and others (e.g., Butler & Schnellert, 2012; Gersten, Dimino, Jayanthi, Kim, & Santoro, 2010; Putnam & Borko, 2000) that teachers, viewed as learners, must have opportunities to understand the relevance of, and theory behind, the strategies they are being asked to apply in their classrooms; have guided and sustained opportunities to apply theory to practice; and be given the freedom to tailor their instruction about SRL to the unique teaching and learning needs in their classrooms. In the following sections, we describe participatory approaches to research and teacher development, and how they create forums for teachers and researchers to share knowledge and, together, meaningfully translate SRL theory into sustainable practice.

PARTICIPATORY FRAMEWORKS FOR DESIGNING SELF-REGULATED LEARNING SUPPORTING CONTEXTS

Participatory approaches to research revealed themselves in a variety of fields as early as the 1940s (Lewin, 1948). In educational contexts, Lewin emphasized that teachers' practices benefit greatly when they act as primary researchers in teacher study groups. The term *action research* derived from this work to capture the idea of disciplined inquiry, or research, in the context of dedicated efforts to improve teaching quality and learning outcomes (Lewin, 1948). Specifically, action research served as a platform for groups of teachers to work together to identify and research a compelling question and to discover new information and actions as a consequence of answering it (Lambert, 2002).

Decades later, in the 1980s, the buzz of *learning teams* surfaced. Similar to action research groups, learning teams offered opportunities for educators to come together as communities of professionals to set and share goals, monitor and measure progress, receive and use assistance, as needed, and engage in continuous instructional improvement (Butler, Lauscher, Jarvis-Selinger, & Beckingham, 2004; Palincsar, Magnusson, Marano, Ford, & Brown, 1998; Perry, Walton, & Calder, 1999). Typically, learning teams engage in cyclical processes, often referred to as *cycles of inquiry*, which have much in common with cycles of self-regulation. They involve teachers, as learners, in identifying a problem/focus, planning action, implementing strategies, collecting and analyzing data, and using feedback generated through these processes to plan for future action (Butler & Schnellert, 2012; Hilliard, 1991). The overarching goal of these collaborative learning teams is to help teachers generate knowledge about teaching and learning they then can use to develop and implement more effective practices in their classrooms (Lambert, 2002; Timperley, Parr, & Bertanees, 2009).

Variously conceived as communities of practice, collaborative inquiry groups, action research groups, teacher study groups, and learning teams, participatory approaches to research and PD distinguish themselves from more typical top-down, transmission models of teachers' PD in a number of ways. Primarily, they emphasize the social and situated nature of teacher learning—the need for teachers to actively participate in the PD experience, locate their PD activities in their own classrooms, and support one another (Koellner et al., 2007; Putnam & Borko, 2000). Also, they recognize the need for skilled facilitation to guide teachers' examination and implementation of research-based practices, a contribution researchers and teacher educators can make. However, characteristically, learning teams or collaborative inquiry groups "position teachers centrally in change efforts . . . [assuming] meaningful, sustained changes in classrooms are fostered by engaging teachers jointly [with researchers] in locally situated, inquiry-based, longitudinal, and critical examinations of practice" (Butler & Schnellert, 2012, p. 1206).

Proponents have argued that participatory approaches to research and PD hold promise for addressing the gap between theory/research and practice, a long-standing discussion in the educational literature (Butler et al., 2004; Duffy, 2005; Palincsar, 1999). Spencer and Logan (2003) suggested that this discrepancy may exist because teachers are unfamiliar with, or lack access to, effective research strategies, receive inadequate training and support during implementation, and fear that adaptations for some learners may interfere in the learning of students who do not require modifications. Furthermore, according to Nuthall (2004), teachers often feel that research is too theoretical or idealistic to relate to their lives in classrooms, and they have difficulty implementing rigid or prescribed practices from theory and research, because of the shifting circumstances of classrooms and student learning.

Proponents of participatory approaches to research and PD have advocated for educational innovations that are sensitive to local contexts and take advantage of local knowledge generated within teacher and school communities (Butler & Schnellert, 2012). They have recognized teaching as a complex intellectual activity that requires contextualized decision making (Butler et al., 2004; Duffy, 2005; Palincsar, 1999). A one-size approach will not fit all classrooms and all learners. Also, they have argued that initiatives that make false distinctions between formal and practical knowledge and locate expertise in outsiders only perpetuate the research to practice gap (Butler et al., 2004; Duffy, 2005; Palincsar, 1999). Supporting meaningful, continuous, and sustainable shifts in practice likely requires critical and collaborative conversations between researchers and teachers that enable the generation and exchange of data and of feedback that leads to the coconstruction of knowledge about teaching and learning.

Randi and Corno (2007) recommended that researchers revisit the way they transfer theory and instructional interventions to teachers. Instead of, or in addition to, applying theory to practice, teachers might adapt practice to theory, which personalizes the whole process. Randi and Corno (2005) found that when teachers were involved in the design of innovations within their own classrooms, they developed a higher capacity to adapt, be flexible, and tailor instruction to their students' unique needs. Similarly, Gersten et al. (2010) observed positive effects on teachers' uptake of research-based instructional practices when teachers were involved in teacher study groups compared with more typical forms of PD. From a motivational point of view, educators who engaged in self-directed learning within their own classrooms found the process intellectually satisfying (McIntyre, 2005). They reported gains in understanding research and how to modify instructional strategies to suit their teaching and learning contexts. Those gains in knowledge made them more motivated to adapt instruction, as needed. It appears that teachers experience a sense of empowerment when they develop and perform their own research (Cochran-Smith & Lytle, 1990; McIntyre, 2005). Often, teachers' voices are absent in educational research, and their questions, which are among the most important to improve their practices, are not addressed. Participatory approaches to research and PD address this absence and, as a result, benefit both teachers and researchers.

Since 1997, Perry has used participatory approaches to researching SRL. Specifically, she has worked with teachers to design tasks and develop practices to support SRL in their classrooms (see Perry, Phillips, & Hutchinson, 2006; Perry et al., 1999). Building on action research and community of practice frameworks, her work brings teachers together as communities of professionals and provides them with opportunities to identify goals for themselves and their students, design and implement activities in their classrooms that address their goals, monitor and evaluate outcomes, and make adjustments based on the feedback they generate as they regulate their teaching and learning.

RESEARCH-BASED SELF-REGULATED LEARNING APPLICATIONS OF TEACHER-DESIGNED PROJECTS

The following are two examples of projects teachers carried out while participating in two TLTs that Perry facilitated.[1] One team grew out of elementary school teachers' expressed interest in developing SRL-promoting practices. This team was a district-level initiative. The second team was part of a provincewide initiative to improve results for students who struggled with reading: the Changing Results for Young Readers (CR4YRs; http://youngreaders.ca) initiative in British Columbia, Canada. Perry is a member of the Provincial Resource Team (PRT) that guides this initiative and, in that role, has opportunities to facilitate teachers' SRL processes as they engage in inquiry-oriented professional learning activities.

"What's My Job?" Finding Kid-Friendly Language to Support Elementary-Age Children's Self-Regulated Learning

Kelsey teaches Grades 1, 2, and 3 in a Montessori program in a large publicly funded school district in British Columbia. She participated in the

---

[1] Excerpts from each project and quotes came from face-to-face communications and documents shared with the first author; each is cited as a personal communication or by document name, and includes the date.

district TLT that focused on SRL. The team included 14 elementary teachers and met six times during the school year. Perry facilitated this team as part of a research and PD collaboration she has with the school district (the district has a long history of supporting TLTs—in most years, approximately one third of the teachers in the district are involved in this form of PD). The team followed a cycle of inquiry that maps onto the self-regulation cycles referenced earlier in this chapter (i.e., teachers were encouraged to find a focus related to SRL, develop a question to guide their inquiry project, make a plan, take action, monitor progress, and make adjustments, as needed). Teachers designed their projects at the group meetings with guided and sustained support from their colleagues and Perry. Each group meeting began with a time for reflection and sharing; teachers first wrote about and then shared what they had been thinking and doing in their classrooms between meetings. Then they participated in a more focused discussion (often Perry made a short presentation) about some facet of SRL. Teachers were given time to work independently or collaboratively on their projects. Each meeting ended with teachers reporting to colleagues about what they would do between meetings to advance their projects. At the end of the year, this TLT participated in a districtwide learning exchange in which all the TLTs in the district came together to share their projects as posters or at roundtable discussions.

The question that guided Kelsey's project was: How can we define self-regulation in "kid-friendly" terms? How could she help her Grade 1, 2, and 3 students to understand it? Kelsey and her students defined self-regulation as "being able to do your job without being asked, shown, told." Then, at one of the group meetings, the focused discussion emphasized the role of task understanding for successful self-regulation (Butler & Cartier, 2004; Hadwin & Winne, 2012). This struck a chord for Kelsey: How can children find a focus/set a meaningful goal, develop a plan, apply strategies, monitor progress, and make adjustments if they do not have a clear understanding of the task ("What their job is!")? So she used this new insight to adjust her SRL project in her classroom. Again, Kelsey enlisted the support of her students to identify things they needed to know to be able to do their job. They agreed they needed to attend to the following three questions: What is the job? How can we do the job? And why do we need to do the job? These questions became headings on posters, or prompts that were displayed in the classroom (see Figure 10.1). Kelsey and her students consulted the posters regularly when they were beginning a job and when they lost their way during the completion of a job. This process, called *checking in*, is a clear example of how Kelsey and her students engaged in cycles of self-regulation, continuously and iteratively planning, enacting, monitoring, and adjusting until they managed to successfully complete their jobs. Kelsey described how she observed students "standing in front of the posters and systematically self-assessing . . . asking what's my job . . . how

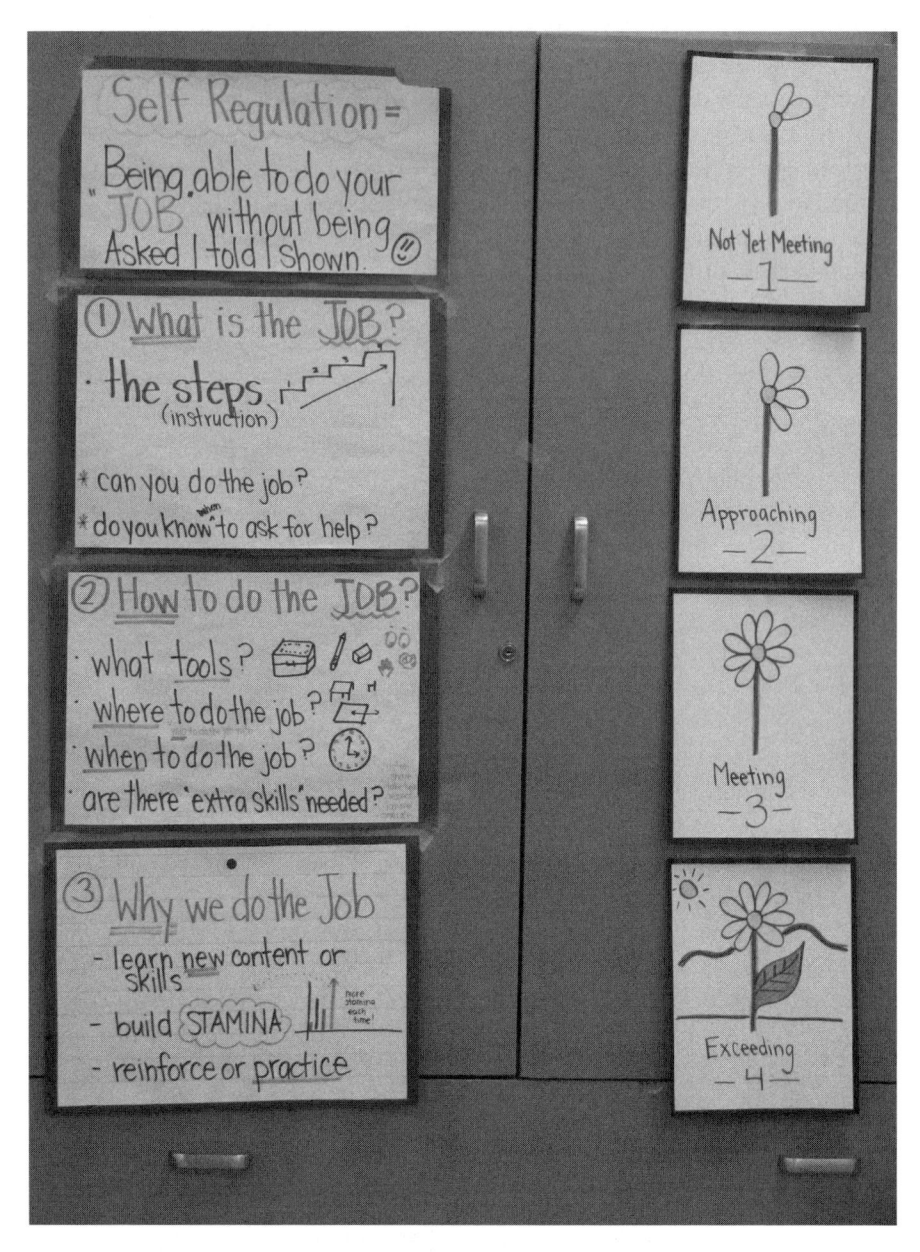

Figure 10.1. Kid-friendly language used in Kelsey's classroom to describe self-regulation. Copyright 2014 by Kelsey B. Keller. Reprinted with permission.

am I doing at my job," and using the feedback generated by answers to these questions to consider when and what adjustments they might need to make (personal communication, November 12, 2013).

Over the course of the year, Kelsey and her students developed a system for monitoring their self-regulation and progress toward job completion. Their four-point rating scheme (shown in Figure 10.1) was posted beside their self-regulation posters in the classroom. Using the language of the British Columbia performance standards (British Columbia Ministry of Education, 2013), they would stop work periodically to judge whether they were not yet meeting, approaching, meeting, or exceeding expectations in terms of their self-regulation and task performance. On one occasion, Kelsey was working with her Grade 1 and 2 students and noticed her Grade 3 students were not meeting her expectations in terms of self- and coregulating for successful task completion. She interrupted the group to comment that their behavior was not typical (she could usually count on these students to work productively whether they were working independently or collaboratively) and asked them to think about what the problem was: What was not working? Once she set her Grade 1 and 2 students to work, she went to check on the Grade 3 students—thinking she would need to guide their self-assessment and coregulate them back on task. However, when she arrived, the group told her that she could leave them to their work—they had discussed the problem and "they just needed to make a new plan."

Reflecting on students' developing SRL over the course of her project, Kelsey said, "I have to admit I'm pretty thrilled to see my students taking ownership . . . taking pride in their self-regulation . . . being so honest and self-aware" (personal communication, ca. January 18, 2013). She also reported to the TLT during one meeting that she and her students had decided that they could apply their definition of self-regulation to "everything they do in their classroom" and that they stopped to consider "what is my job" and "how am I doing at my job" often throughout the school day (TLT meeting, January 28, 2013). Reflecting on her own learning in the project, Kelsey commented that one thing had become clear to her from working with her students to address her original question (How can I talk with Grade 1, 2, and 3 students about SRL?):

> Having that common, kid-friendly [self-regulation] language has a positive impact on coregulation, self-reflection, and work stamina. Being a Montessori teacher . . . SRL has always been part of how my classroom operates. . . . What this project gave me the opportunity to explore is the *language* [Kelsey's emphasis] of [self-regulation]. What I came to realize is my students needed a common language to help them reflect on their [self-regulation] and to create an additional coregulation support system. (personal communication, November 12, 2013)

Practice Makes Perfect: Revisiting and Reevaluating Reading Strategies Across Text Genres

The second project occurred in the context of the CR4YRs initiative in British Columbia. Starting in September 2012, this government-sponsored initiative focused on supporting young children's reading and learning through teachers' development of effective, evidence-based approaches to instruction. Since then, the scope has expanded to include adolescents and teachers across a range of school levels and subject domains (e.g., teachers wanting to support reading in science and social studies, and English/language arts, particularly for students who struggle because of an identified or unidentified learning disability or because they are English language learners). TLTs and teacher inquiry provide the PD frameworks for the CR4YRs initiative.

In 2012 and 2013, sixty TLTs across the province participated in CR4YRs, each involving three to four schools and approximately 12 to 16 teachers. A requirement for participating in the initiative is that representatives from each school include classroom teachers (one to two); at least one special education/resource teacher; and to the extent possible, a building administrator/principal. A goal is to foster collaboration and team-teaching among classroom and special education teachers, and to build capacity in schools to support learners who struggle with reading. The PRT that includes learning, curriculum, and staff-development specialists, and university researchers supports the TLTs. Members of the PRT cofacilitate TLTs with district staff development and reading advocates. The CR4YRs initiative focuses on three themes in relation to reading: SRL, social–emotional learning, and aboriginal ways of knowing.

TLT participants are asked to identify a focus and a project that addresses a need in their classroom. Their focus guides their movement through a *spiral of inquiry* (Halbert & Kaser, 2013), which maps onto the cycles of inquiry and self-regulation referenced throughout this chapter (i.e., teachers find a focus, make a plan, engage in professional learning and take action, monitor progress, and make adjustments). TLTs meet seven times over the course of the school year, and four activities provide a framework for those meetings. Check-in provides teachers with time when they arrive for the meeting to reflect on what has happened for them and their students since the last TLT meeting. Typically, they write their thoughts and then have an opportunity to share them with their colleagues. Focus group is the time for more focused conversation. Typically, the facilitators or district advocates lead this activity, which often targets some aspect of the spiral of inquiry (e.g., What's a good question/focus? Are we making a difference? How do we know? What could/should we do differently?) or a broader theme of the initiative, such as SRL. During work time, teachers work in their school-based teams or connect with teachers from other schools to plan their projects. They also complete case study records that document their questions and actions in relation to their projects across the year. These records provide data for the PRT to use in reporting results from the initiative to the ministry and broader community, but they are intentionally designed to scaffold teachers to monitor and adjust their projects/activities in response to the data they are generating and feedback they are receiving (from students and colleagues). The case record form is divided into four quadrants that ask teachers to respond to four questions: What did you do [between our last meeting and this meeting]? What happened? What have you learned? What will you do next? Teachers report to their colleagues what they are planning to do next before they leave the TLT meeting. This activity is referred to as *making a commitment*. The PRT, facilitators, and district advocates also meet several times throughout the year. Their meetings focus on the broad themes of the initiative and supporting teachers' inquiry.

Derek and Liz participated in the first Changing Results for Adolescent Readers (CR4ARs) TLT, facilitated by Perry, who is also a member of the PRT. Eight teachers who represented three secondary schools (Grades 9–12) were on this learning team. These teachers taught diverse groups of students across a range of subject domains, including English/language arts, history, and science (i.e., biology, chemistry). As a group, these teachers had a particular interest in SRL and a commitment to improving their teaching of reading across content areas, especially for students who were struggling with reading. Derek and Liz taught at the same school, and Derek initiated their participation in the TLT. Teaching strategies to students was already a well-established practice in Liz's classroom; however, she had never evaluated—or involved her students in evaluating—which of the various reading strategies she used on a regular basis were most favored by the Grade 9 students in her English class. Which strategies did they perceive worked best for them, for which reading tasks, and why? So, her goal for this project was to be more explicit with students about the strategies she used and why she chose them. In her words:

> The tendency . . . is to get students to do certain exercises in class, but they don't necessarily "get" why they are doing them. . . . I want for students to remember the strategies, develop a large repertoire of them, and select from said repertoire when presented with a reading task. Making the purpose of the strategy overt, along with the idea that it can be used and reused in English, or even other subject areas where reading takes place, is critical for students' acquisition of a reading strategy repertoire. . . . A reflective exercise that promotes metacognition is critical for this understanding/development. (Written in a message to her British Columbia teacher colleagues during the June 26, 2013, meeting of her CR4ARs TLT)

As a special education/resource teacher, Derek shared Liz's interest in helping students to become more self-regulating in their strategy use.

For their project, Liz and Derek introduced students to a range of reading strategies, which are described in Table 10.1, and revisited the strategies as they cycled through several reading assignments and reading genres (e.g., narrative texts, poetry, short stories). Strategies were taught, and students then had an opportunity to apply them. Also, as part of their project, Liz and Derek asked students to provide individual reflections and engage in group discussions about what they perceived to be the pros and cons of a particular strategy, whether they believed it improved their reading, and whether they thought they would use it again. Liz and Derek used the data generated from students' reflections to assess the progress individual students were making in reading and to identify patterns for groups of students with similar attitudes or approaches to learning. They also considered students' data to produce the case records for the CR4YRs initiative.

Reflecting on the outcomes of their project, Liz wrote that "revisiting the strategies" with several different genres helped students to "fine-tune" them (i.e., make adjustments), and "also develop the idea that some strategies are better for some genres [or subjects] than others." In terms of her own learning, she realized, "Doing a strategy once isn't enough if you are interested in students incorporating the strategy into a repertoire for lifetime use" (message to British Columbia teacher colleagues, June 26, 2013). Also, as a consequence of observing students' use of strategies more closely than she had in previous years, she recognized that introducing the strategies all at once was overwhelming for students. "Next time," she indicated, her plan would be to introduce the strategies one at a time and to provide more explicit instruction about some of the strategies.

From her case records, she identified patterns for individuals and groups of learners. For example, she observed that one student with significant reading difficulties made "major progress" over the course of this project (Case Study 6 Summary, June 26, 2013). She witnessed increases in his confidence and noted that the "apparently foggy and mysterious process of reading was made less foggy and less mysterious" over the course of the project. This student learned that there are concrete things he can do as a reader that will aid comprehension. Liz and Derek recognized that, once this student had a set of effective strategies to use, his "formidable work ethic took over, and he started doing them—again, and again, and again."

Similarly, students who previously seemed to lack motivation for reading "were surprised . . . there was more to reading than they thought, and [a little] pleased to discover there were things they could do to avoid the blank mind that comes at the end of some reading when active attention has not been paid. . . . They seemed more willing to give reading strategies a try before letting the disengagement set in" (Case Study 2 Summary, June 10, 2013). Overall, Derek and Liz noticed students' "heightened awareness that there are things you can do while you are reading" (Case Study 4 Summary, June 25, 2013).

TABLE 10.1
Reading Strategies Liz and Derek Introduced to Grade 9 Students

Strategy	Description
Bloom's taxonomy	Students were taught the levels in Bloom's taxonomy and then given sample questions about a literary text that illustrated each level. Their task was to generate their own questions as they read. Student-generated questions were used to guide student-led discussion groups.
Sticky notes	Students chose a point in the text at which they had something to say about one of five topics: character, author language, setting, theme, or plot. They wrote their point on a sticky note and placed it in the text. They shared the contents of their sticky notes with their discussion groups.
Think-Trix	Similar to the Bloom's taxonomy strategy, students generated questions using the Cooperative Learning Think-Trix question categories: recall/remember, similarity, difference, cause and effect, from idea to example, from example to idea, evaluation (Lyman, 1987).
Setting map detail	Students created maps of settings based on the description provided in the novel.
Pause & think	Students paused to think at key points in the text. They recorded their thoughts. At first, the teacher chose the pause points and provided specific thinking questions. Over time, these supports were faded, and students took responsibility for when to pause and what to think.
Highlight showing vs. telling	Students were taught to distinguish places in text at which authors showed vs. told something to the reader. Students highlighted showing and telling in two different colors. They made a note to indicate what was shown beside the showing portions of the text.
Symbol and prior knowledge	Students discussed how concrete objects are used to represent abstract concepts/symbols. Students identified symbols and discussed their meaning in particular texts.
Using inference to figure out ending	Students were given stories with ambiguous endings. First, the teacher explained the ending and highlighted the clues the writer provided that allowed her to correctly infer the ending. Students practiced inferring endings with other stories.
Rereading	Students were divided into two groups: One group read the story once and answered questions; the other read the story twice and answered the same questions.

Reflecting on their practice of revisiting the strategies across genres and assignments, they observed:

> By the time the third unit rolled around, [students] were actively asking which strategy would be used and asking if they could use a different one if they didn't like [our] choice. They were interested in inventing variations on the theme of a strategy or just doing their own thing, but they were aware that reading strategies existed and that active reading was something that can be achieved and improved upon, like writing. (Case Study 4 Summary, June 25, 2013)

Liz, in particular, observed how the adjustments she made to her previous approach to teaching strategies (i.e., being more explicit with students about why she chose the strategies she did and involving them in evaluating the efficacy of the strategies) benefited students from a learning and motivational point of view. Moreover, the feedback she received from students through her project was helping her to plan future adjustments to her promotion of SRL.

Both of the aforementioned projects show how teachers participating in TLTs engage in cycles of inquiry, which correspond to the cycles of self-regulation described in this chapter. For both projects, teachers identified and addressed an aspect of SRL that was important to them and their students (i.e., developing a kid-friendly language to talk about SRL, developing and personalizing a repertoire of effective reading strategies), made a plan, took action, reflected on the action, and made adjustments, as necessary. In both cases, teachers made use of SRL theory and principles, but tailored their actions to suit their unique teaching and learning contexts. Two things particularly impressed us about both projects. First, the SRL focus became an integral aspect of teaching and learning in these classrooms—it was not a separate curriculum. Second, teachers' reports indicated that the focus on SRL benefited the teachers and the students. Teachers' reports provided evidence concerning students' metacognition in the form of person, task, and strategy awareness; motivation evidenced in efficacy and engagement; and strategic action. Moreover, it appeared that teachers' involvement in the processes advocated by the TLTs supported their SRL, which supported their development of SRL-promoting practices in a safe and supportive context much like the one we wanted them to create for their students. From a sustainability perspective, these teachers appeared to recognize the importance of an SRL framework for supporting effective teaching and learning in their classrooms. Reflecting on the experience (June 26, 2013), Liz said, "It made me remember the value of giving time to heavy exercises, such as metacognitive exercises," and regarding questions to investigate next, "if I happen to teach the same students next year, I'd like to know how much they transfer the strategies year to year, genre to genre, and subject to subject."

CONCLUSIONS AND FUTURE DIRECTIONS

We began this chapter by making a case for the importance of a focus on self-regulation, particularly SRL, in school. We believe such an emphasis is necessary to ensure the success of all students. However, we noted that teachers' awareness and implementation of SRL-promoting practices is not as widespread as researchers in this field might like it to be. The reason for this theory/research-to-practice gap likely is multifactorial. We focused on some of the limitations of researcher-driven models of intervention research, particularly the ways in which research findings often get communicated to teachers. Moreover, we agree that teachers' voices are absent in most intervention studies, and this is a weakness in research that seeks to change practice. We believe participatory approaches to research and PD hold promise in their potential to close, or at least narrow, theory/research-to-practice and practice-to-theory/research gaps.

In particular, we perceive that the main strengths of participatory approaches for teachers include active participation in the research and PD experience; opportunities to consider and then test new practices in their classrooms; and sustained support from colleagues and, ideally, knowledgeable and skilled facilitators (e.g., researchers who are also teacher educators). Randi and Corno (2005) observed that teachers involved in supportive, action-oriented approaches to PD succeeded in flexibly and effectively adapting educational innovations to suit the needs of their students, and our aforementioned examples suggest this was the case for the teachers participating in the TLTs Perry facilitated.

Also, we perceive that the emphasis that participatory approaches place on the social and situated nature of teachers' and students' learning is relevant for research and knowledge-building about SRL. Interventions often are designed for and implemented in quasi-controlled—decontextualized—environments which may not resemble all classrooms or prove effective with all learners. Advancing research and practice in SRL likely requires designing interventions that are sensitive to the specific characteristics of particular contexts and individuals. We perceive a need to move beyond a focus on fixing students, or teachers for that matter, to creating contexts in which all learners, including teachers and researchers, can develop SRL practices in and for diverse communities. Also, because meaningful shifts in practice do not occur overnight, we need to allow time for local innovations to work (Gersten et al., 2010).

We believe researchers can benefit from knowledge teachers have developed through practice. Advancing the teaching and researching of SRL likely depends on productive collaborations between researchers and teachers. Controlled experiments that emphasize fidelity of implementation may not be possible or desirable, and what counts as evidence may need to be considered: Are we open to new and varied sources of data? We also recognize the need for more research on whether and how these participatory PD efforts enhance teaching effectiveness and student learning (Gersten et al., 2010; Timperley et al., 2009). Currently, much of the evidence is anecdotal or from small N qualitative studies, often case studies. There is a need to study the efficacy of TLTs and other configurations on a larger scale, and to document teachers' development and its effects on student learning over time and from multiple perspectives/data sources (i.e., we need to expand beyond teacher reports/testimonials). This research and these data will bolster arguments that these seemingly resource-intensive approaches to PD are a wise expenditure from both a cost and people perspective.

REFERENCES

Bandura, A. (1986). *Social foundations of thought and action: A social cognitive theory*. Englewood Cliffs, NJ: Prentice Hall.

Blair, C., & Razza, R. P. (2007). Relating effortful control, executive function, and false belief understanding to emerging math and literacy ability in kindergarten. *Child Development, 78*, 647–663. doi:10.1111/j.1467-8624.2007.01019.x

British Columbia Ministry of Education. (2013). *BC performance standards*. Retrieved from http://www.bced.gov.bc.ca/perf_stands/

Brown, A. L., & Campione, J. C. (1994). Guided discovery in a community of learners. In K. McGilly (Ed.), *Classroom lessons: Integrating cognitive theory and classroom practice* (pp. 229–270). Cambridge, MA: MIT Press.

Brown, A. L., Campione, J. C., & Day, J. D. (1981). Learning to learn: On training students to learn from texts. *Educational Researcher, 10*(2), 14–21. doi:10.3102/0013189X010002014

Butler, D. L. (1995). Promoting strategic learning by postsecondary students with learning disabilities. *Journal of Learning Disabilities, 28*, 170–190. doi:10.1177/002221949502800306

Butler, D. L., & Cartier, S. (2004). Promoting effective task interpretation as an important work habit: A key to successful teaching and learning. *Teachers College Record, 106*, 1729–1758. doi:10.1111/j.1467-9620.2004.00403.x

Butler, D. L., Lauscher, H. N., Jarvis-Selinger, S., & Beckingham, B. (2004). Collaboration and self-regulation in teachers' professional development. *Teaching and Teacher Education, 20*, 435–455. doi:10.1016/j.tate.2004.04.003

Butler, D. L., & Schnellert, L. (2012). Collaborative inquiry in teacher professional development. *Teaching and Teacher Education, 28*, 1206–1220.

Cleary, T. J., & Zimmerman, B. J. (2004). Self-regulation empowerment program: A school-based program to enhance self-regulated and self-motivated cycles of student learning. *Psychology in the Schools, 41*, 537–550. doi:10.1002/pits.10177

Cleary, T. J., & Zimmerman, B. J. (2006). Teachers' perceived usefulness of strategy microanalytic assessment information. *Psychology in the Schools, 43*, 149–155.

Cochran-Smith, M., & Lytle, S. L. (1990). Research on teaching and teacher research: The issues that divide. *Educational Researcher, 19*, 2–11. doi:10.3102/0013189X019002002

Diamond, A., Barnett, W. S., Thomas, J., & Munro, S. (2007). Preschool program improves cognitive control. *Science, 318*, 1387–1388. doi:10.1126/science.1151148

Duffy, G. G. (2005). Developing metacognitive teachers: Visioning and the expert's changing role in teacher education and professional development. In S. E. Israel, C. C. Block, K. L. Bauserman, & K. Kinnucan-Welsch (Eds.), *Metacognition in literacy learning: Theory, assessment, instruction, and professional development* (pp. 299–314). Mahwah, NJ: Erlbaum.

Eisenberg, N., & Spinrad, T. L. (2004). Emotion-related regulation: Sharpening the definition. *Child Development, 75*, 334–339. doi:10.1111/j.1467-8624.2004.00674.x

Gersten, R., Dimino, J., Jayanthi, M., Kim, J. S., & Santoro, L. E. (2010). Teacher study group: Impact of the professional development model on reading instruction and student outcomes in first grade classrooms. *American Educational Research Journal, 47*, 694–739. doi:10.3102/0002831209361208

Graham, S., & Harris, K. R. (2003). Students with learning disabilities and the process of writing: A meta-analysis of SRSD studies. In H. L. Swanson, K. R. Harris, & S. Graham (Eds.), *Handbook of learning disabilities* (pp. 323–344). New York, NY: Guilford Press.

Hadwin, A. F., Järvelä, S., & Miller, M. (2011). Self-regulated, co-regulated, and socially shared regulation of learning. In B. J. Zimmerman & D. H. Schunk (Eds.), *Handbook of self-regulation of learning and performance* (pp. 65–84). New York, NY: Routledge.

Hadwin, A. F., & Winne, P. H. (2012). Promoting learning skills in undergraduate students. In M. J. Lawson & J. R. Kirby (Eds.), *Enhancing the quality of learning: Dispositions, instruction, and mental structures* (pp. 201–227). New York, NY: Cambridge University Press. doi:10.1017/CBO9781139048224.013

Halbert, J., & Kaser, L. (2013). *Spirals of inquiry: For equity and quality.* Vancouver, British Columbia, Canada: BC Principals and Vice Principals Association.

Harris, K. R., & Graham, S. (1999). Programmatic intervention research: Illustrations from the evolution of self-regulated strategy development. *Learning Disability Quarterly, 22*, 251–262. doi:10.2307/1511259

Hilliard, A., III. (1991). Do we have the will to educate all children? *Educational Leadership, 49*(1), 31–36.

Koellner, K., Jacobs, J., Borko, H., Schneider, C., Pittman, M. E., Eiteljorg, E., . . . Frykholm, J. (2007). The problem-solving cycle: A model to support the development of teachers' professional knowledge. *Mathematical Thinking and Learning, 9*, 273–303. doi:10.1080/10986060701360944

Lambert, L. (2002). A framework for shared leadership. *Educational Leadership*, 59, 37–40.

Lewin, K. (1948). *Resolving social conflicts: Selected papers on group dynamics*. Oxford, England: Harper.

Lyman, F. T. (1987). Think trix: A classroom tool for thinking in response to reading. *Reading Issues and Practices*, 4, 15–18.

McClelland, M. M., Morrison, F. J., & Holmes, D. L. (2000). Children at risk for early academic problems: The role of learning-related social skills. *Early Childhood Research Quarterly*, 15, 307–329. doi:10.1016/S0885-2006(00)00069-7

McIntyre, D. (2005). Bridging the gap between research and practice. *Cambridge Journal of Education*, 35, 357–382.

Nuthall, G. (2004). Relating classroom teaching to student learning: A critical analysis of why research has failed to bridge the theory-practice gap. *Harvard Educational Review*, 74, 273–306.

Palincsar, A. S. (1999). Response: A community of practice. *Teacher education and special education*, 22, 272–274. doi:10.1177/088840649902200408

Palincsar, A. S., Magnusson, S. J., Marano, N., Ford, D., & Brown, N. (1998). Designing a community of practice: Principles and practices of the GIsML community. *Teaching and Teacher Education*, 14, 5–19. doi:10.1016/S0742-051X(97)00057-7

Perry, N. E. (1998). Young children's self-regulated learning and contexts that support it. *Journal of Educational Psychology*, 90, 715–729. doi:10.1037/0022-0663.90.4.715

Perry, N. E. (2013). Classroom processes that support self-regulation in young children [Monograph]. *British Journal of Educational Psychology, Monograph Series II: Psychological Aspects of Education—Current Trends*, 10, 45–68.

Perry, N. E., Phillips, L., & Hutchinson, L. (2006). Mentoring student teachers to support self-regulated learning. *Elementary School Journal*, 106, 237–254. doi:10.1086/501485

Perry, N. E., VandeKamp, K. O., Mercer, L. K., & Nordby, C. J. (2002). Investigating teacher–student interactions that foster self-regulated learning. *Educational Psychologist*, 37, 5–15. doi:10.1207/S15326985EP3701_2

Perry, N. E., Walton, C., & Calder, K. (1999). Teachers developing assessments of early literacy: A community of practice project. *Teacher Education and Special Education*, 22, 218–233. doi:10.1177/088840649902200404

Ponitz, C. C., McClelland, M. M., Matthews, J. S., & Morrison, F. J. (2009). A structured observation of behavioral self-regulation and its contribution to kindergarten outcomes. *Developmental Psychology*, 45, 605–619. doi:10.1037/a0015365

Pressley, M. (1986). The relevance of the good strategy user model to the teaching of mathematics. *Educational Psychologist*, 21, 139–161. doi:10.1080/00461520.1986.9653028

Putnam, R. T., & Borko, H. (2000). What do new views of knowledge and thinking have to say about research on teacher learning? *Educational Researcher, 29*(1), 4–15.

Randi, J., & Corno, L. (2000). Teacher innovations in self-regulated learning. In M. Boekaerts, P. R. Pintrich, & M. Zeidner (Eds.), *Handbook of self-regulation* (pp. 651–685). San Diego, CA: Academic Press. doi:10.1016/B978-012109890-2/50049-4

Randi, J., & Corno, L. (2005). Teaching and learner variation. In P. Tomlinson, J. Dockrell, & P. Winne (Eds.), *Pedagogy—Teaching for learning [British Journal of Educational Psychology Monograph Series II: Psychological Aspects of Education—Current Trends]* (Vol. 3, pp. 47–69). Leicester, England: British Psychological Society.

Randi, J., & Corno, L. (2007). Theory into practice: A matter of transfer. *Theory Into Practice, 46,* 334–342. doi:10.1080/00405840701593923

Rimm-Kaufman, S. E., & Chiu, Y.-J. I. (2007). Promoting social and academic competence in the classroom: An intervention study examining the contribution of the responsive classroom approach. *Psychology in the Schools, 44,* 397–413. doi:10.1002/pits.20231

Rimm-Kaufman, S. E., Curby, T. W., Grimm, K. J., Nathanson, L., & Brock, L. L. (2009). The contribution of children's self-regulation and classroom quality to children's adaptive behaviors in the kindergarten classroom. *Developmental Psychology, 45,* 958–972. doi:10.1037/a0015861

Schumaker, J. B., Deshler, D. D., & Ellis, E. S. (1986). Intervention issues related to the education of LD adolescents. In J. K. Torgeson & B. Y. L. Wong (Eds.), *Psychological and educational perspectives on learning disabilities* (pp. 329–365). New York, NY: Academic Press.

Skinner, B. F. (1967). *Science and human behavior.* New York, NY: Free Press.

Spencer, S. S., & Logan, K. R. (2003). Bridging the gap: A school-based staff development model that bridges the gap from research to practice. *Teacher Education and Special Education, 26,* 51–62. doi:10.1177/088840640302600106

Tice, D. M., Baumeister, R. F., & Zhang, L. (2004). The role of emotion in self-regulation: Differing roles of positive and negative emotion. In P. Philippot & R. S. Feldman (Eds.), *The regulation of emotion* (pp. 213–226). Mahwah, NJ: Erlbaum.

Timperley, H. S., Parr, J. M., & Bertanees, C. (2009). Promoting professional inquiry for improved outcomes for students in New Zealand. *Professional Development in Education, 35,* 227–245. doi:10.1080/13674580802550094

Wehmeyer, M. L., Yeager, D., Bolding, N., Agran, M., & Hughes, C. (2003). The effects of self-regulation strategies on goal attainment for students with developmental disabilities in general education classrooms. *Journal of Developmental and Physical Disabilities, 15,* 79–91.

Wharton-McDonald, R., Pressley, M., & Hampston, J. M. (1998). Literacy instruction in nine first-grade classrooms: Teacher characteristics and student achievement. *Elementary School Journal, 99,* 101–128. doi:10.1086/461918

Wharton-McDonald, R., Pressley, M., Rankin, J., Mistretta, J., Yokoi, L., & Ettenberger, S. (1997). Effective primary-grades literacy instruction = balanced literacy instruction. *Reading Teacher, 50,* 518–521.

Winne, P. H., & Hadwin, A. F. (1998). Studying as self-regulated learning. In D. J. Hacker, J. Dunlosky, & A. C. Graesser (Eds.), *Metacognition in educational theory and practice* (pp. 277–304). Mahwah, NJ: Erlbaum.

Winne, P. H., & Perry, N. E. (2000). Measuring self-regulated learning. In M. Boekaerts, P. R. Pintrich, & M. Zeidner (Eds.), *Handbook of self-regulation* (pp. 531–566). San Diego, CA: Academic Press. doi:10.1016/B978-012109890-2/50045-7

Wong, B. Y. L. (1994). Instructional parameters promoting transfer of learned strategies in students with learning disabilities. *Learning Disability Quarterly, 17,* 110–119. doi:10.2307/1511181

Wong, B. Y. L., Harris, K. R., Graham, S., & Butler, D. L. (2003). Cognitive strategies instruction research in learning disabilities. In H. L. Swanson, K. R. Harris, & S. Graham (Eds.), *Handbook of learning disabilities* (pp. 383–402). New York, NY: Guilford Press.

Zimmerman, B. J. (1989). Models of self-regulated learning and academic achievement. In B. J. Zimmerman & D. H. Schunk (Eds.), *Self-regulated learning and academic achievement: Theory, research, and practice* (pp. 1–25). New York, NY: Springer-Verlag.

Zimmerman, B. J. (1990). Self-regulated learning and academic achievement: An overview. *Educational Psychologist, 25,* 3–17. doi:10.1207/s15326985ep2501_2

Zimmerman, B. J. (2002). Becoming a self-regulated learner: An overview. *Theory Into Practice, 41,* 64–70. doi:10.1207/s15430421tip4102_2

Zimmerman, B. J. (2008). Investigating self-regulation and motivation: Historical background, methodological developments, and future prospects. *American Educational Research Journal, 45,* 166–183. doi:10.3102/0002831207312909

Zimmerman, B. J., & Campillo, M. (2003). Motivating self-regulated problem solvers. In J. E. Davidson & R. J. Sternberg (Eds.), *The psychology of problem solving* (pp. 233–262). New York, NY: Cambridge University Press. doi:10.1017/CBO9780511615771.009

Zimmerman, B. J., & Schunk, D. H. (2011). Self-regulated learning and performance: An introduction and an overview. In B. J. Zimmerman & D. H. Schunk (Eds.), *Handbook of self-regulation of learning and performance* (pp. 1–12). New York, NY: Routledge.

11

CONTEXTS SUPPORTING SELF-REGULATED LEARNING AT SCHOOL TRANSITIONS

WENDY S. GROLNICK AND JACQUELYN N. RAFTERY-HELMER

For more than 20 years, there has been growing interest in self-regulated learning (SRL), or the extent to which students are active participants in their own education (Zimmerman, 1989, 2000). Self-regulated learners are not passive recipients of knowledge; instead, they are active and self-directed, and approach learning tasks with volition and agency. Most educators and parents would agree that facilitating SRL should be of the utmost priority and that there is a need to understand the contexts that promote SRL so that teachers and parents can best support students, especially during times of motivational risk.

In this chapter, we use self-determination theory (SDT; Deci & Ryan, 1985, 2000) to better understand SRL and its contextual determinants at key school transitions. We begin by describing SRL and its underlying motivational processes in the classroom and then delineate contexts that facilitate it. Notably, these motivational processes are not static, and particular points

http://dx.doi.org/10.1037/14641-012
Self-Regulated Learning Interventions With At-Risk Youth: Enhancing Adaptability, Performance, and Well-Being,
T. J. Cleary (Editor)
Copyright © 2015 by the American Psychological Association. All rights reserved.

of vulnerability for SRL may exist. We discuss why school transitions, in particular, may undermine SRL and its motivational underpinnings, and we provide evidence for the effects of supportive contexts at these transitions. In doing so, we emphasize the ways in which contexts and outcomes of SRL influence each other and the learner in a series of feedback loops. We end with recommendations for facilitating SRL in home and school contexts.

THEORETICAL FOUNDATIONS OF SELF-REGULATED LEARNING

General Overview and Underlying Processes

At some point, we all have witnessed a self-regulated learner. Proactive, self-regulated learners are problem solvers: They seek out information, take steps to master material, and persist when tasks are challenging. One way of conceptualizing the quality of participation in learning among these students is through the concept of engagement. Skinner, Kindermann, Connell, and Wellborn (2009) defined *engagement* as the "outward manifestation of motivation—namely energized, directed, and sustained action" (p. 225), which is reflected in one's cognitive, affective, and behavioral orientation toward learning. The self-regulated learner shows active participation, sustained attention, focus, and a propensity to set goals that exceed minimum requirements. Affectively, these students are enthusiastic about learning, find enjoyment and pleasure in classroom activities, and report satisfaction on completing challenging assignments. Their behavior is characterized by perseverance, persistence, determination, effort, and intensity.

Zimmerman's (1989) theory focuses on the strategies self-regulated learners use, which help them to transform their cognitive abilities (e.g., verbal or spatial aptitude) into knowledge or skill. These learning strategies include environmental structuring (e.g., arranging the physical setting to make learning easier), goal setting and planning, keeping records and monitoring achievement results, organizing and transforming instructional materials, rehearsing and memorizing material, reviewing records and educational material, seeking information, seeking social assistance, providing oneself with positive or negative consequences for success and failure experiences, and self-evaluating.

SRL does not simply begin during the school years; rudimentary SRL skills can be seen in younger children. Early abilities to be engaged and active in learning activities are in evidence when children can focus their attention, resist distractions, and adjust their emotional responses to participate in learning activities. Such skills have been discussed under the rubrics of executive functioning (EF) and emotion regulation. *Executive functioning* involves cognitive skills that are important for learning, such as the ability to shift one's focus and attention, resist distraction, and hold information in memory. *Emotion regulation* involves the ability to modulate emotional responses. Such skills have been associated with academic competence (Ursache, Blair, & Raver, 2012). Although neither the term EF nor *emotion regulation* is meant to reflect the more purposeful nature of Zimmerman's (1989) SRL strategies or the notion of academic engagement, the concepts overlap in that they all refer to skills that allow for active persistence in learning activities.

SRL is manifested during routine learning activities but also is reflected in children's response to academic challenges, such as difficult tasks, test taking, and experiences with failure that affect their cognitions and behavior. Indeed, SRL may be most necessary when such challenges arise. Thus, researchers interested in SRL have examined the coping strategies that students bring to bear so they are not disrupted by these types of stressful academic situations. Work on coping with failure (e.g., Raftery-Helmer & Grolnick, 2012) has suggested that for self-regulated or engaged learners, failure is merely part of the process of learning something that is challenging. Therefore, when challenged, self-regulated learners are likely to focus their attention on task mastery so that they may do better on future assignments: They actively problem solve and seek information to understand the failure and complete the task at hand. In contrast, other learners respond by rigidly focusing on the self, attempting to defensively restore internal experiences threatened by failure; thus, they are less focused on learning, tackling issues, or understanding material. Hence, even in the context of failure or negative feedback, self-regulated learners channel their effort into mastering the environment.

Because they entail new expectations and requirements, school transitions may involve many challenges to established routines and thus require adaptive and flexible SRL skills. How children negotiate these challenges includes a complex interaction between the SRL skills they bring and their new environments. This chapter focuses on such SRL using different conceptualizations, including engagement, direction of attention, and coping at key school transitions.

Researchers from a variety of theoretical perspectives have argued that underlying SRL are attitudes, beliefs, and motivational propensities that students have with regard to themselves and the world. Much work has highlighted the importance of two motivational beliefs for SRL: perceived control and perceived competence (i.e., beliefs in one's competence) or self-efficacy (i.e., beliefs in one's ability to cope). For instance, Zimmerman (1989) suggested that use of SRL strategies is instigated and sustained by perceptions of efficacy. Students reportedly select SRL strategies according to their perceptions of academic efficacy. Furthermore, in what has been referred to as a *self-oriented feedback loop* (Zimmerman, 1989, 2000), students monitor the effectiveness of these strategies for subsequent performance. If the strategies undermine performance, students' perceptions of self-efficacy will be negatively affected and will affect ongoing motivation and subsequent selection and use of learning strategies. Similarly, control-value theory (Pekrun, Frenzel, Goetz, & Perry, 2007) proposes that students who perceive academic outcomes as within their control are likely to use more active coping strategies, including task- and problem-focused strategies, when confronted with academic stressors. Feedback loops would suggest that, in using more active coping strategies, these students would experience enhanced perceived control or a sense of their own capacities to affect the environment.

In addition to perceived control/competence, many theories have posited that to engage in SRL, students must see learning as interesting or valuable for their own goals. Pekrun (2000) showed that, when confronted with academic stressors, students who perceived the value of the task (i.e., its importance) as high were more likely to use coping aimed at mastering the environment. Similarly, Eccles and colleagues (e.g., Eccles et al., 1983) proposed that achievement-related behaviors (e.g., persistence on difficult tasks, sustained effort during learning activities) are directly related to the importance or value that students attach to the achievement task. SDT, which is discussed in depth in the next section, includes a differentiated theory focusing on why students engage in schoolwork and homework. This theory suggests a continuum of autonomy for regulating school behavior ranging from doing so for purely external reasons (e.g., to avoid punishment) to autonomous regulation, which involves a sense of volition and willingness. It pulls together much of the previously reviewed work by positing universal needs that explain why processes, such as perceived control, perceived competence, and autonomy, are crucial for SRL.

Self-Determination Theory

SDT (Deci & Ryan, 1985) asserts that individuals have psychological needs for competence, relatedness, and autonomy. According to this perspective, the satisfaction of these needs is essential for well-being, whereas their thwarting results in a disturbance of functioning. The need for *competence* entails needing to feel effective in one's interactions with the environment and believing that one has the capacity to produce outcomes and to experience mastery. Individuals also have a primary need for *relatedness*: to feel connected, loved, and valued by others. People also have a need for *autonomy*: to feel volitional regarding their actions, and for behaviors to feel self-initiated rather than externally controlled (Ryan & Connell, 1989).

SDT connects these needs to the motivational processes that allow for SRL. Thus, it provides a framework for understanding why certain motivational beliefs and propensities set the stage for SRL. In particular, fulfillment of the need for competence is reflected in students' understanding about how to achieve success or avoid failure (perceived control) and their belief that they have the competencies to be successful. Autonomy needs are reflected in students' sense of volition for school activities and is indexed by initiating activities with a sense of agency or willingness. Such initiation is not an all-or-none phenomenon; types of regulation can be seen as varying along a continuum of autonomy. At the least autonomous end of this continuum, children engage in behaviors to avoid punishment, comply with externally imposed rules, or obtain a reward. This type of regulation is *external*. Children also may engage in activities because of self-imposed pressure or avoidance of negative affect, such as guilt or shame. This type of regulation is termed *introjected*. Both external and introjected regulation are forms of controlled or nonautonomous motivation, because students feel coerced or pressured to engage in school behaviors. Students also may engage in behaviors because of their perceived value or importance. This is *identified* regulation. For example, a student may complete extra math problems because he or she wants to understand geometry. Although completing these problems may not be fun, doing so stems from a personal goal and thus the student experiences it as volitional. At the most self-determined end of this continuum, students undertake school behaviors because they find them enjoyable, fun, or interesting. Students' experience of autonomy results in particular patterns of action: Students who are more autonomous show more enthusiastic, focused, and purposeful learning, or exemplify what it means to be self-regulated (Deci & Ryan, 2000).

Children's need for relatedness is satisfied when they feel a sense of connection and belonging, and that others care for them and treat them as important. Work from many traditions, including attachment theory (Bretherton, 1985), has proposed that when people have internal representations of themselves as lovable and others as sensitive and responsive, they are free to explore and master their environment. Empirical evidence has supported this proposal: Using self and teacher ratings of emotional and behavioral engagement, Furrer and Skinner (2003) found that children who reported a higher sense of relatedness were more engaged in school.

A number of theories have proposed that one's environment influences SRL and its motivational underpinnings (e.g., perceived competence/control), although many of these theories have not specified what types of environments may support or undermine SRL. Unlike these approaches, SDT (Deci & Ryan, 1985) delineates the social contexts that fuel SRL by connecting them to the three psychological needs. Thus, linked to these needs are three aspects of the environment presumed to be key in the development of SRL. In particular, SRL will be exhibited most when one's social context supports autonomy by providing autonomy support versus control, supports competence by providing structure, and supports relatedness by providing involvement. These supportive contexts are most crucial during school transitions, which may undermine the motivational components underlying SRL (i.e., perceived competence, perceived control, autonomous self-regulation), thus leaving needs unsatisfied.

Autonomy Support

Autonomy support versus control refers to caregivers' support for children's perspectives, point of view, autonomous initiations and problem solving at one end, to disregard for children's perspectives and goals at the other (Grolnick & Ryan, 1989). Autonomy support includes valuing children's thoughts and opinions, encouraging their initiations, providing choice, creating opportunities for children to provide input, and supporting children's interests. At the other extreme, controlling behavior ignores children's perspectives and pressures them toward specific outcomes, thus hindering their autonomy and causing them to feel coerced and externally regulated (Grolnick & Ryan, 1989).

Research has demonstrated a clear link between parental autonomy support and motivational propensities associated with SRL. For example, Grolnick and Ryan (1989) showed that, compared to parents who favored pressure, punishment, and controlling rewards, parents who supported autonomous problem-solving, provided choice, and engaged in joint decision making had children who more autonomously regulated learning behaviors. Ginsburg and Bronstein (1993) found that students from families that supported their autonomy showed higher achievement standards, initiated schoolwork more independently, were mastery oriented, and approached learning materials with curiosity, enthusiasm, and interest. In a similar study (Joussemet, Koestner, Lekes, & Landry, 2005), mothers who communicated behavioral standards in an autonomy-supportive way had 5-year-olds who listened attentively, set higher standards for their work, and used free time more productively. Grolnick, Ryan, and Deci (1991) found evidence in elementary school students that perceptions of maternal and paternal autonomy support were associated with children's perceived autonomy, perceptions of control, and perceptions of competence that, in turn, predicted achievement. More recent work has replicated these earlier findings that parental autonomy support robustly predicts students' self-regulation (e.g., Soenens & Vansteenkiste, 2005). Bronstein, Ginsburg, and Herrera (2005), for example, found that maternal autonomy support was associated with higher achievement, which, in turn, predicted greater subsequent perceived competence and intrinsic motivation (2 years later).

The association between autonomy-supportive parenting and self-regulation likely represents a bidirectional transaction such that parents may react to their child's self-regulation and competence with autonomy-supportive or controlling behavior (Grolnick & Ryan, 1989). Indeed, Bronstein et al. (2005) found that autonomy support predicted higher achievement that, subsequently, predicted greater autonomy support. Pomerantz and Eaton (2001) showed that elementary students' poor academic performance elicited more controlling behavior from mothers in the form of intrusive homework-checking and unsolicited help. Overall, empirical work has suggested that parental autonomy support contributes to children's self-regulation through a bidirectional process whereby autonomy support affects motivational processes that then affect parenting.

Evidence also exists that teacher autonomy support relates to children's motivation. Chirkov and Ryan (2001) found that, among U.S. and Russian high-school students, students' perceptions of parent and teacher autonomy support were related to greater autonomous motivation. More recently, Jang, Kim, and Reeve (2012) showed reciprocal effects of an autonomy-supportive teacher context. In particular, children who perceived more support for autonomy tended to feel their need for autonomy was met, which, in turn, predicted higher engagement. Higher levels of engagement then predicted more autonomy need satisfaction over time. Thus, students who are engaged may elicit more autonomy support from those around them, thus creating positive long-term trajectories of active school engagement.

Structure

Structured environments support competence by providing clear and consistent rules, expectations and guidelines, predictable consequences, and clear feedback about how to better meet expectations (Farkas & Grolnick, 2010), thus allowing children to anticipate outcomes and mobilize, direct, and sustain their academic efforts. In taking an active role in their learning, these students may be more able to make use of feedback or structure provided by the environment.

Compared with autonomy support, less research has addressed how structure is related to SRL. In one of the first studies that used an SDT conceptualization of structure, Grolnick and Ryan (1989) coded parent interviews for whether clear rules, expectations, and guidelines had been set in the home, and for parental consistency or adherence to those rules and expectations. Children whose homes were rated high in structure had a greater understanding of how to attain success and avoid failure in school and generally. Grolnick and Wellborn (1988) found that parental structure, conceptualized as clarity of expectations and predictability of consequences, was positively associated with perceived competence and negatively associated with maladaptive control beliefs (i.e., believing that success in school resulted from luck or powerful others). Similarly, using a self-report questionnaire, Skinner, Johnson, and Snyder (2005) found that parental structure was associated with higher perceived control, perceived competence, and engagement in school.

In our lab, we have examined parental structure in more depth; we have delineated specific components and examined how they relate to motivational outcomes. In particular, Farkas and Grolnick (2010) identified six components of structure: clear and consistent rules and expectations, predictability of consequences for action, information feedback, opportunities to meet expectations, provision of rationales for rules and expectations, and parental authority (i.e., whether parents take a leadership role in the home). Seventh- and eighth-grade students were interviewed about their homes with regard to homework and grades, and from those interviews, parents were rated on these components of structure. All structure components, except information feedback, were combined to form a structure composite, which was correlated with academic perceived control and perceived competence above and beyond the effects of parental autonomy support and involvement. In a second study, Grolnick, Raftery-Helmer, Marbell, Flamm, Cardemil, and Sanchez (2014) rated four components of structure from interviews of 160 sixth-grade children: clarity and consistency of rules and expectations, predictability of consequences, rationales provided, and parental authority. Similar to Farkas and Grolnick (2010), these authors found that parental provision of structure predicted academic perceived control. In a related study on children's academic coping, Raftery-Helmer and Grolnick (2012) found that sixth graders who experienced their parents as providing more structure were more likely to actively attempt to remedy the cause of a perceived school failure and less likely to report blaming the teacher or test, attempt not to think about the failure, and experience worry and anxiety. Tests of meditational models indicated that parental structure affected children's coping directly and through perceived control.

In addition to this new work on parental structure, researchers have begun to examine structure provided by teachers. Jang, Reeve, and Deci (2010) coded classrooms for three components of structure: whether students were provided with a plan of action, clear directions, and constructive feedback. These three components were combined to form a structure composite that related to children's classroom engagement. More empirical support is needed to clearly establish the link between teacher provision of structure and SRL and associated motivational processes.

Involvement

Involvement supports children's need for relatedness. Involvement is manifested in caregivers' provision of psychological resources, such as love and affection, and tangible resources, such as attention and time (Grolnick & Slowiaczek, 1994). High involvement communicates to a child that he or she belongs and is valued by others, whereas contexts that are not involved leave children feeling inconsequential, isolated, and insignificant.

An abundance of research has indicated the importance of parent involvement for student achievement, although fewer studies have examined its effects on motivational outcomes. Sanders (1998) found that students who reported that their parents encouraged their academic endeavors were more likely to value the importance of academic achievement for future success. In a more recent study, Fan and Williams (2010) found that parents' educational aspirations for their children and school-based involvement predicted student self-efficacy, engagement, and motivation. Studies also have shown that parent involvement is related to perceived competence and perceived value of academic effort (Marchant, Paulson, & Rothlisberg, 2001). Others (e.g., Gonzalez-DeHass, Willems, & Holbein, 2005) have shown that parent involvement facilitates students' sense of competence and perceptions of control, and helps them to take in educational values introduced by others and internalize them as their own. In a particularly illustrative study, Grolnick and Slowiaczek (1994) examined three types of parental involvement: behavioral (e.g., involvement in school events); cognitive–intellectual (e.g., exposing children to academically stimulating activities), and personal (showing interest and enthusiasm about learning). Relations existed between mother and father behavioral and cognitive–intellectual involvement and students' perceptions of control and competence. Results suggested a mediational model in which parent involvement affects achievement through perceived competence and control.

Research similarly has supported the importance of teacher involvement for student motivation and self-regulation. Birch and Ladd (1997) found reported closeness between teacher and student-predicted student engagement in the classroom. Voelkl (1995) similarly found that students who perceived their schools as warm showed greater classroom participation and higher achievement. Students who see their teachers as warm and affectionate also have been shown to display higher affective engagement in the classroom (e.g., Skinner & Belmont, 1993) and greater perceived competence (e.g., Skinner et al., 2009). Given the importance of autonomy support, structure, and relatedness in parents and teachers, it is important to examine how they relate to children's adjustment at key educational transitions.

SELF-REGULATED LEARNING AT SCHOOL TRANSITIONS: RESEARCH AND APPLICATIONS

Life transitions, such as starting a new job or entering a new school, involve substantial changes in the new environment in which individuals find themselves. The changes require adaptation, including adopting new roles and behaviors. Transitions offer opportunities for growth and development, but they also are points of potential vulnerability. Successful adaptation involves an interaction between what the individual brings and the qualities of the new environment (Bronfenbrenner, 1979). Individuals bring both their own characteristics (i.e., personality, skills, attitudes, perceptions) and more or less supportive resources (i.e., families, peers). Both factors can contribute to how children weather what may be stressful changes.

Different school transitions present distinct challenges to which children must adjust. The transition to school, for example, may be the first time children are exposed to structured learning environments and the expectations they entail. On the other hand, the change from elementary to middle school typically includes a new organizational structure with a larger and more bureaucratic school, more teachers, and a more diverse student body (Eccles & Midgley, 1989). The specific challenges introduced by school transitions must be considered in understanding their effects on SRL.

One way of understanding the effect of transitions is to consider how they affect need satisfaction. From an SDT perspective, when transitions undermine need satisfaction, they are likely to have disruptive effects. However, when they support need satisfaction, they are more likely to be salutary. A number of reasons exist to expect that transitions to a new school environment, particularly one that is extremely different from the previous one, will be disruptive. Consider the following potential challenges to the three needs discussed earlier: competence, relatedness, and autonomy.

First, an environment with a new organization and new rules and expectations will likely challenge children's sense of (and perhaps actual) competence. When rules, guidelines, and expectations change, children may have a difficult time understanding connections between their actions and their success and failure outcomes. That is, in the new environment, they may not know how to be successful and to avoid failure, thus perceived control and competence will be undermined. New schools may also disrupt a sense of relatedness. Established peer networks may be split up as students enter different schools. Students must form new relationships and achieve a new sense of connectedness with peers and teachers. Autonomy needs also may be challenged, especially when students perceive that environments are more controlling and allow less opportunity for autonomy. Furthermore, because experiencing autonomy or volition requires a backdrop of competence, discomfort with one's new role may challenge the ability to be autonomous with respect to tasks and behaviors.

Thus, from an SDT perspective, transitions may undermine the autonomy, competence, and relatedness required for SRL. Successful adaptation will be most likely when children bring the requisite skills and attitudes that enable them to take on new roles and to adapt. Furthermore, when environmental resources support their needs, they may more easily adapt. In the following section, we discuss three school transitions that present different challenges. We discuss how having attitudes and motivational propensities connected to greater self-regulation, (i.e., perceived competence, perceived control, and autonomous self-regulation) and need-satisfying environments (i.e., autonomy-supportive, structured, involved) may facilitate successful adaptation. Table 11.1 provides a summary of needs, contexts, and need-challenges posed by school transitions.

Transition to School

Entry into formal schooling may be the first time children encounter a structured classroom setting in which lessons are presented and children are expected to pay attention and focus on material. For children to successfully adapt to such a new setting, they must be able to control their impulses and negative emotions, and display motivation and attention. Children must be able to display at least rudimentary SRL skills. In the literature on young children, such skills often have been discussed as *self-regulation*, defined as the biological and behavioral mechanisms that enable the individual to manage arousal, attention, emotion, behaviors, and cognitions in an adaptive manner (e.g., Calkins & Howse, 2004).

Researchers who have examined self-regulatory abilities in young children have largely focused on two constructs: one cognitive, often termed *executive functioning*; and one more emotional, which has been termed *effortful control* (EC) or *emotion regulation*. *Executive functioning* has been defined as the "volitional control of thinking in purposeful goal-directed activities" (Ursache et al., 2012, p. 122) and refers to higher order cognitive processes that allow for effective learning (see Chapters 1 and 4, this volume). EF includes three components: the ability to hold information in working memory, the ability to resist interference and distraction from extraneous sources, and the ability to shift attention when required. EF is said to allow the child to obtain knowledge by remembering instructions, staying on task, and dealing with concepts and symbols (Best, Miller, & Jones, 2009). The second construct, emotion regulation, sometimes referred to as EC, involves the ability to modulate emotion through cognitive and behavioral strategies (see Chapters 6 and 7, this volume). When children are able to dampen down negative emotion, they are better able to

TABLE 11.1
Needs, Contexts, and Challenges to Needs Posed by School Transitions

Need	Motivational resources	Context	Transition to school	Challenge to need — Middle school	Challenge to need — High school
Autonomy	Autonomous self-regulation Emotion regulation	Autonomy support	—	Controlling school context Performance goals More normative comparison	Controlling school context Increased competition
Competence	Perceived control Perceived competence Self-efficacy Executive functioning	Structure	Expectations to sit, attend, stay on task	Larger school New organization Higher expectations	New, higher expectations More difficult material
Relatedness	Relational security	Involvement	New peers New teachers	New, diverse peer group Multiple teachers who may know children less well	New, diverse peer group Multiple teachers who may know children less well

follow rules in the classroom, engage in activities, and form positive relationships with teachers and peers (Eisenberg, Eggum, Sallquist, & Edwards, 2010). Emotion regulation is often considered to have a temperamental basis.

Research has supported the importance of EF and emotion regulation for successful adaptation to school. Executive functioning has been predictive of school readiness (e.g., Blair & Razza, 2007), subsequent academic achievement, and classroom behavior (Valiente, Lemery-Chalfant, & Swanson, 2010). The ability to regulate positive and negative emotions has been linked to high levels of achievement in early elementary math and reading and achievement on standardized tests in kindergarten (Graziano, Reavis, Keane, & Calkins, 2007). Children with more developed emotional competence, including better emotion regulation, have been found to be more engaged in the classroom, and teachers perceive them as more academically and socially competent than students with lower emotional competence (Denham, 2006). In a large, longitudinal study, Neuenschwander, Röthlisberger, Cimeli, and Roebers (2012) examined EF and EC in relation to adaptation to primary school. They found that EF at preschool predicted standardized achievement, grades, and learning-related behavior (assessed by teachers' ratings of children's persistence, attention, and self-reliance) at primary school. EC at preschool predicted learning behavior and grades. Moreover, the effect of EC on grades was mediated by learning behavior. In contrast, EF had both direct and indirect effects on achievement.

Given the significance of EF and EC, it is important to understand the contexts that facilitate these abilities. It is within children's early interactions with caregivers that they learn the strategies and skills to successfully modulate emotional and behavioral responses. From an SDT perspective, autonomy-supportive versus controlling, structured, and involved parenting should facilitate emotional and behavioral regulation. And research has supported this perspective, particularly for the construct of parental controlling interactions. For example, Calkins, Smith, Gill, and Johnson (1998), in a study of 2-year-olds, examined three aspects of emotion regulation: physiological reactivity, behavioral regulation (i.e., impulsivity vs. compliance), and emotion regulation (i.e., the use of distraction vs. focus on focal object during delay tasks). They also coded two aspects of mothers' interactive style: *maternal negative control*, which was the frequency of scolding, anger, and restricting the child's movements; and *maternal positive guidance*, which included the use of praise, demonstration of behavior, and feedback and suggestion, thus including both elements of involvement and structure. Analyses showed that more maternal negative control was associated with more time focusing on the focal object during the delay and less use of distraction. It also was associated with poorer vagal suppression (i.e., emotion regulation). Positive guidance was associated with more compliance.

In our own work (Grolnick, Kurowski, McMenamy, Rivkin, & Bridges, 1998), we examined the regulatory strategies mothers used to assist their 12-, 18-, 24-, and 32-month-old children during mildly frustrating delay situations and how use of these strategies was related to children's ability to regulate distress when on their own. Controlling for children's distress levels, mothers who more actively engaged children in alternative strategies in the delay situation had children who had more difficulty when on their own. Interestingly, it was not mothers' responses per se that were problematic but continuing them despite children's decreases in distress. Thus, mothers who responded to their children's distress, yet also allowed them opportunities to use their own capacities and strategies when not too upset, had children who were more successful at emotion regulation when on their own.

Successful emotion regulation involves not just the ability to modulate emotion but also to recognize and use emotion to guide behavior. Thus, suppressing emotion is at odds with the goal of emotion regulation. Some authors have discussed the importance of parenting in the development of such skills. In particular, it has been argued that parents who dismiss emotion in their children deprive them of the opportunity to learn about emotions in themselves and others. Lunkenheimer, Shields, and Cortina (2007) found that children of parents who tended to dismiss emotions showed poorer emotion regulation.

The results of these studies support the importance of self-regulation for children's successful transition to school. In addition, they highlight how contexts that provide structure (i.e., guidance, support) but also support children's autonomous attempts to discern and to regulate their emotions and behavior (i.e., support autonomy) are central to developing these capacities.

Transition to Middle School

The transition to middle school involves numerous changes to which children must adapt. Notably, children typically move from a smaller school with one teacher to a larger school with multiple teachers. In addition, the standards set by teachers are higher, as are the expectations that children will work more independently (Eccles et al., 1993). In recent years, many school districts have recognized the challenges that such a new organization entails and have worked to attenuate some of the negative effects by implementing smaller teams of teachers and students, which makes for a greater sense of cohesion. However, despite such changes, the new school organization still entails multiple changes to which children must adapt.

From an SDT perspective, these changes may affect children's adjustment to the extent that they impinge on need fulfillment. In particular, the new organization and expectations characterizing middle school may challenge children's sense of how to attain success and avoid failure, that is, their perceptions of control and their sense of competence. Furthermore, the fact that middle-school teachers tend to be more controlling (Eccles, Lord, & Midgley, 1991) it may be a challenge to a sense of autonomy. Relatedly, the goal structures of middle-school classrooms have been described as more performance oriented (i.e., focusing on performance relative to others as a measure of success) and less mastery oriented (i.e., focusing on developing knowledge or understanding with improvement as a goal; Midgley, Anderman, & Hicks, 1995). Performance goal orientations predict lower feelings of competence (Midgley & Urdan, 1995) and autonomy (Gurland & Grolnick, 2005). The new peers and multiple teachers with whom children need to form bonds may impinge on children's sense of relatedness.

Research has suggested that changes in children's self-concepts and motivation are consistent with these challenges. In particular, some studies have shown declines in academic self-concept at school transitions (e.g., Wigfield & Eccles, 2000), which suggests that such transitions challenge perceptions of competence. Consistent with the notion that transitions challenge relatedness, feelings of affiliation with teachers decrease across the transition (Schneider, Tomada, Normand, Tonci, & de Domini, 2008). Although some studies have found such detrimental effects, others have shown no changes in self-concept, motivation, or connection. Thus, it becomes important to understand who shows changes and what factors predict declines over the transition.

In our work, we have focused on how the home environment might buffer children from declines in self-regulation. In one study (Grolnick, Kurowski, Dunlap, & Hevey, 2000), we found that the more involved parents were in sixth grade, the less children decreased in perceived competence and reading grades over the transition. More maternal autonomy support at sixth grade was associated with lower increases in acting out and learning problems over the transition. Furthermore, children whose mothers increased in their autonomy support over the transition did not show the same negative declines in self-worth, control understanding, and reading grades that other children did. There also were buffering effects of changes in involvement on changes in self-worth and learning problems. Thus, strong evidence exists that both parental involvement and autonomy support play key roles in helping children adjust at the transition to middle school.

A second study of 160 sixth-grade children transitioning to middle school (Grolnick, Raftery-Helmer, Flamm, Marbell, & Cardemil, in press) focused on the effects of parental academic structure on changes in perceived competence, autonomous self-regulation, engagement, and grades. The study looked at the degree to which homes included academic structure, for example, provided clear and consistent guidelines, expectations, and consequences for homework and studying, and examined the extent to which this structure was provided in a way that supported rather than controlled children's autonomy. When structure was conveyed in an autonomy-supportive manner, parents involved children in establishing the guidelines, allowed for discussion of the rules, provided empathy when children did not want to follow the rules, and provided some choice in the way the rules/expectations were followed. Conversely, when structure was implemented in a more controlling manner, parents unilaterally created the rules, did not allow for discussion or did not provide empathy when children disagreed with the rules/expectations, and dictated how the children were to carry out the rules. Results showed that higher parental structure was associated with increases (i.e., lesser decreases) in perceived competence, engagement, and English grades across the transition. In addition, the more structure was implemented in an autonomy-supportive manner, the more perceived competence, and English grades increased (i.e., decreased less) across the transition. Autonomy-supportive structure also was associated with changes in children's regulation of their school behavior. Specifically, children from homes in which structure was implemented in a more autonomy-supportive manner were less likely to increase in their tendency to engage in schoolwork for external reasons (i.e., rewards and punishments) and increased more in their tendency to engage in school behaviors for more autonomous reasons. Furthermore, relations between structure and autonomy support of structure and English grades and engagement were mediated by perceived competence.

Our results also showed reciprocal effects over the transition: More autonomy support, structure, and involvement predicted higher engagement and higher engagement predicted increased provision of structure and involvement (Flamm & Grolnick, 2013). Thus, supportive parental environments both facilitate and respond to children's engagement.

Studies also have addressed facilitative contexts provided by teachers at the transition to middle school. Gutman and Midgley (2000) examined low-income children's perceptions of parents and schools as they transitioned to middle school. Results showed that students who perceived higher levels of parental involvement, teacher support, and school belonging at sixth grade had higher grade point averages in sixth grade, controlling for prior achievement.

Friedel, Cortina, Turner, and Midgley (2010) focused on the effects of the motivational context of the classroom for children's math self-concepts by measuring children's perceptions of their sixth- and seventh-grade classrooms' emphasis on performance versus mastery goals. A classroom emphasis on performance goals involves a focus on grades and a tendency to compare children's performance outcomes. By contrast, a focus on mastery involves emphasis on learning and finding new ways to solve problems and to reward for effort. Perceived increases in mastery goal emphasis following the transition resulted in higher self-efficacy beliefs in math, whereas increases in performance goal emphasis predicted decreased self-efficacy. Thus, evidence exists that a context that involves pressure and likely feels controlling undermines the feelings of competence and control so crucial to SRL.

Evidence also exists that the transition to middle school entails challenges to the competence, autonomy, and relatedness needs crucial for SRL. Home contexts that are involved, support children's autonomy, and provide structure (implemented in an autonomy-supportive manner) buffer children from decreases in perceived competence, autonomous self-regulation, and, ultimately engagement and grades. In addition, when school environments are experienced as supportive and as emphasizing mastery, children's academic self-concepts benefit.

Transition to High School

Although less research has focused on the transition to high school relative to the transition to formal schooling and middle school, increasing attention has been paid to this key transition (Benner, 2011). As with the middle-school transition, the transition to high school involves organizational and policy changes that may challenge children's feelings of competence and perceptions of control. Grading standards are typically higher, which creates more competition and pressure on students (Reyes, Gillock, Kobus, & Sanchez, 2000) and thus may undermine feelings of autonomy. The larger school size and more diverse student body result in students' losing contact with close friends and may require them to establish a new, supportive peer group. Such a disturbance in peer groups may have consequences for students' feelings of relatedness.

Although diversity exists in the outcomes of the transition in various studies focusing on different populations, some evidence has suggested that this transition can be disruptive. Studies have reported declines in students' motivation and interest in school, and in their perceptions of academic competence (Roderick, 1995). Furthermore, students tend to be less satisfied with teachers, viewing them as more strict and less supportive (Barber & Olsen, 2004). Students have described the school climate as less friendly and that they feel more anonymous. Barber and Olsen (2004) reported that students described lower classroom autonomy and higher perceived need for school organization (which indicates that they perceived less adequate structure) over the transition from eighth to ninth grade.

Given these potential difficulties, it is important to identify contexts that facilitate self-regulation. Reyes et al. (2000) examined the degree to which changes in students' self-perceptions, perceptions of social support, and academic performance at the transition to high school (eighth to ninth grade) predicted their status at the end of high school (i.e., actively attending school or having withdrawn from or dropped out of school). Students who were inactive at follow-up showed larger declines in grades, greater increases in upset with friends, and more upset with the school than those who were active at follow-up. In addition, those who were active at follow-up perceived themselves as more academically competent before the transition than those who were later inactive.

Barber and Olsen (2004) examined how perceptions of the school environment predicted changes in motivation and achievement across the transition to high school. Notably, they found that perceived support from teachers had the largest effect: Students who reported more decreases in teacher support increased in their levels of depression. Furthermore, there was one effect for school organization: Students who perceived a more organized school environment at the transition showed more participation in school activities over the transition. Perceived gains in classroom autonomy predicted more participation in school activities.

As with the middle-school transition, evidence exists that relationships with parents play a role in the transition to high school. Individuals whose parents monitored them more and were more involved in their academic and social lives experienced fewer disruptions and exhibited greater resilience following the high-school transition (Roderick, 2003). In addition, higher parent involvement—in particular, parents' grade and school attainment expectations—predicted higher teacher-rated student engagement from fall to spring of ninth grade (Chen & Gregory, 2009).

Thus, evidence suggests that supportive contexts may play a key role in students' self-regulation and achievement at the transition to high school. Although some might question the importance of parents to adolescents, who are often portrayed as more peer focused, research has supported the key role of parents' high expectations and involvement in their adolescents' lives for their successful adjustment.

IMPLICATIONS, RECOMMENDATIONS, AND FUTURE DIRECTIONS

Our review of the role of SRL for successful learning outcomes and that of supportive contexts at academic transitions suggests the importance of key stakeholders (i.e., educators, parents, communities) in focusing on helping children make successful academic transitions. The work shows that multiple contexts are important to facilitating successful adaptation.

Given that work on all three school transitions showed relations between home and school autonomy support, structure and involvement and SRL, it is a key task to identify transactional mechanisms in these relations. As discussed, contexts facilitate SRL, but SRL also provides feedback to the learner and to the context. For example, when children are engaged and use SRL strategies, teachers and parents may provide positive feedback that increases engagement and use of such strategies. When children engage in defensive coping strategies, such as blaming the teacher for their failures, the result may be that teachers display less warmth to students, thus decreasing students' sense of relatedness and undermining their motivation. When students engage in SRL, parents may be most likely to allow them autonomy, thus increasing their autonomous regulation of school behavior. Therefore, reciprocal relations exist between need-supportive contexts and self-regulation; more optimal contexts enhance the use of SRL strategies, and self-regulated learners receive more autonomy support, structure, and involvement compared with their disengaged peers. An interesting question would be whether these self-regulated learners also are better able to make use of need-satisfying conditions—being receptive to support for autonomy, competence, and relatedness. More research on the nature of these dynamic relations will help researchers and practitioners to intervene into maladaptive SRL cycles.

It also is important to tackle the barriers that may inhibit parents and teachers from providing need-supportive resources. Our earlier work (e.g., Grolnick, Benjet, Kurowski, & Apostoleris, 1997) showed that multiple factors, including stress, support, and parents' views of their own roles, affect levels of parent involvement. In addition, although teacher practices of involving parents can increase parent involvement, they tend to be most effective for the least stressed parents. Thus, schoolwide efforts that consider characteristics and circumstances of families will be necessary to increase involvement for all families.

Our work has shown that more economically stressed parents and those with lower education are less likely to implement the structure that provides consistency and support for competence at times of transitions. Again, outreach to all parents in culturally sensitive ways is required.

It is crucial that school efforts to involve parents help them to provide structure and involvement in ways that support rather than control their children's autonomy. Given the competitive nature of schools in the United States, parents may feel pressure to ensure that their children perform well. When pressured, they are more likely to push children and solve problems for them (Grolnick, Gurland, DeCourcey, & Jacob, 2002). Thus, efforts to involve parents must clarify the goals of homework (i.e., to build skills and self-reliance) and what their roles might be in relation to those goals.

Acknowledgment in the educational community of the pivotal role of transitions in determining educational pathways has led to some successful programs and interventions. Several programs designed to increase school readiness have focused on self-regulation. For example, the Chicago School Readiness Project (Raver et al., 2009), conducted in Head Start classrooms, focuses on increasing emotional and behavioral self-regulation skills by training teachers to improve the emotional climate of the classroom and lower teacher stress so that children can learn to manage challenging situations in a supportive environment. The project also helps teachers create predictable classroom routines and responses (i.e., structure) to facilitate self-regulation. Compared with children in a control group, treatment group children were higher in EF and rated by observers as showing greater attention and lower impulsivity.

One successful high-school transition program involved restructuring homerooms to ensure greater teacher support and lower student anonymity (Felner, Ginter, & Primavera, 1982). The intervention resulted in students' having more positive views of teachers, schools, and classrooms, and better grades and lower declines in self-concept. Smith (1997) demonstrated that students attending a high-school transition program that targeted adolescents, teachers, and parents did better academically than those who had no support systems or had only partial support systems.

The success of these and other transition programs illustrates the importance of educators' developing programs to help children navigate transitions. Beyond transitions, a need exists for classroom and school contexts, more generally, that will help children to persist and thrive as self-regulated learners. In particular, strategies such as finding room for choice, student voice, and discussion can help children feel autonomous. Providing opportunities for students to get to know school personnel more intimately, such as by assigning students mentors or advisors who see them frequently, can increase feelings of relatedness. Providing clear expectations and strategies to students at the start of activities and lessons can facilitate a sense of competence.

Although the research presented here provides evidence for the importance of autonomy-supportive, structured, and involved contexts at school transitions, much of it followed children for only 1 year or 2 years. It is important to determine whether contexts have enduring effects as children progress in their school careers and make the transition to the adult working world. Many studies have looked at only one context (e.g., teachers) and have focused on only one dimension (e.g., involvement). Studies that examine multiple contexts and multiple dimensions will help identify what might be most important to target. Clearly a focus on school transitions is an excellent step in ensuring that all students enter and stay on trajectories as self-regulated learners.

REFERENCES

Barber, B. K., & Olsen, J. A. (2004). Assessing the transition to middle and high school. *Journal of Adolescent Research, 19*, 3–30. doi:10.1177/0743558403258113

Benner, A. D. (2011). The transition to high school: Current knowledge, future directions. *Educational Psychology Review, 23*, 299–328. doi:10.1007/s10648-011-9152-0

Best, J. R., Miller, P. H., & Jones, L. L. (2009). Executive functions after age 5: Changes and correlates. *Developmental Review, 29*, 180–200. doi:10.1016/j.dr.2009.05.002

Birch, S. H., & Ladd, G. W. (1997). The teacher–child relationship and children's early school adjustment. *Journal of School Psychology, 35*, 61–79. doi:10.1016/S0022-4405(96)00029-5

Blair, C., & Razza, R. P. (2007). Relating effortful control, executive function, and false belief understanding to emerging math and literacy ability in kindergarten. *Child Development, 78*, 647–663. doi:10.1111/j.1467-8624.2007.01019.x

Bretherton, I. (1985). Attachment theory: Retrospect and prospect. *Monographs of the Society for Research in Child Development, 50*, 3–35. doi:10.2307/3333824

Bronfenbrenner, U. (1979). *The ecology of human development.* Cambridge, MA: Harvard University Press.

Bronstein, P., Ginsburg, G. S., & Herrera, I. S. (2005). Parental predictors of motivational orientation in early adolescence: A longitudinal study. *Journal of Youth and Adolescence, 34*, 559–575. doi:10.1007/s10964-005-8946-0

Calkins, S. D., & Howse, R. B. (2004). Individual differences in self-regulation: Implications for child adjustment. In P. Philippot & R. S. Feldman (Eds.), *The regulation of emotion* (pp. 302–332). Mahwah, NJ: Erlbaum.

Calkins, S. D., Smith, C. L., Gill, K. L., & Johnson, M. C. (1998). Maternal interactive style across contexts: Relations with emotional, behavioral, and physiological regulation during toddlerhood. *Social Development, 7*, 350–369. doi:10.1111/1467-9507.00072

Chen, W. B., & Gregory, A. (2009). Parental involvement as a protective factor during the transition to high school. *Journal of Educational Research, 103*, 53–62. doi:10.1080/00220670903231250

Chirkov, V. I., & Ryan, R. M. (2001). Parent and teacher autonomy-support in Russian and U.S. adolescents: Common effects on well-being and academic motivation. *Journal of Cross-Cultural Psychology, 32*, 618–635. doi:10.1177/0022022101032005006

Deci, E. L., & Ryan, R. M. (1985). *Intrinsic motivation and self-determination in human behavior.* New York, NY: Plenum Press. doi:10.1007/978-1-4899-2271-7

Deci, E. L., & Ryan, R. M. (2000). The "what" and "why" of goal pursuits: Human needs and the self-determination of behavior. *Psychological Inquiry, 11*, 227–268. doi:10.1207/S15327965PLI1104_01

Denham, S. (2006). Social–emotional competence as support for school readiness: What is it and how do we assess it? *Early Education and Development, 17,* 57–89. doi:10.1207/s15566935eed1701_4

Eccles, J. S., Adler, T. F., Futterman, R., Goff, S. B., Kaezala, C. M., Meece, J. L., & Midgeley, C. (1983). Expectations, values, and academic behaviors. In J. T. Spence (Ed.), *Perspectives on achievement and achievement motivation* (pp. 75–146). San Francisco, CA: Freeman.

Eccles, J. S., Lord, S., & Midgley, C. (1991). What are we doing to early adolescents? The impact of educational contexts on early adolescents. *American Journal of Education, 99,* 521–543. doi:10.1086/443996

Eccles, J. S., & Midgley, C. (1989). Stage/environment fit: Developmentally appropriate classrooms for young adolescents. In R. E. Ames & C. Ames (Eds.), *Research on motivation in education: Vol. 3, Goals and cognitions* (pp. 13–44). New York, NY: Academic Press.

Eccles, J. S., Wigfield, A., Midgley, C., Reuman, D., Mac Iver, D., & Feldlaufer, J. (1993). Negative effects of traditional middle schools on students' motivation. *Elementary School Journal, 93,* 553–574. doi:10.1086/461740

Eisenberg, N., Eggum, N. D., Sallquist, J., & Edwards, A. (2010). Relations of self-regulatory/control capacities to maladjustment, social competence, and emotionality. In R. H. Hoyle (Ed.), *Handbook of personality and self-regulation* (pp. 21–46). Oxford, England: Wiley-Blackwell. doi:10.1002/9781444318111.ch2

Fan, W., & Williams, C. M. (2010). The effects of parental involvement on students' academic self-efficacy, engagement and intrinsic motivation. *Educational Psychology, 30,* 53–74. doi:10.1080/01443410903353302

Farkas, M. S., & Grolnick, W. S. (2010). Examining the components and concomitants of parental structure in the academic domain. *Motivation and Emotion, 34,* 266–279. doi:10.1007/s11031-010-9176-7

Felner, R. D., Ginter, M., & Primavera, J. (1982). Primary prevention during school transitions: Social support and environmental structure. *American Journal of Community Psychology, 10,* 277–290. doi:10.1007/BF00896495

Flamm, E., & Grolnick, W. S. (2013, April). *Predicting student engagement across the transition to middle school: Prospective effects of parental involvement, structure and autonomy support.* Paper presented at Society for Research in Child Development, Seattle, WA.

Friedel, J. M., Cortina, K. S., Turner, J. C., & Midgley, C. (2010). Changes in efficacy beliefs in mathematics across the transition to middle school: Examining the effects of perceived teacher and parent goal emphases. *Journal of Educational Psychology, 102,* 102–114. doi:10.1037/a0017590

Furrer, C., & Skinner, E. (2003). Sense of relatedness as a factor in children's academic engagement and performance. *Journal of Educational Psychology, 95,* 148–162. doi:10.1037/0022-0663.95.1.148

Ginsburg, G. S., & Bronstein, P. (1993). Family factors related to children's intrinsic/extrinsic motivational orientation and academic performance. *Child Development, 64,* 1461–1474. doi:10.2307/1131546

Gonzalez-DeHass, A., Willems, P., & Holbein, M. (2005). Examining the relationship between parental involvement and student motivation. *Educational Psychology Review, 17,* 99–123. doi:10.1007/s10648-005-3949-7

Graziano, P. A., Reavis, R. D., Keane, S. P., & Calkins, S. D. (2007). The role of emotion regulation in children's early academic success. *Journal of School Psychology, 45,* 3–19. doi:10.1016/j.jsp.2006.09.002

Grolnick, W. S., Benjet, C., Kurowski, C. O., & Apostoleris, N. (1997). Predictors of parent involvement in children's schooling. *Journal of Educational Psychology, 89,* 538–548. doi:10.1037/0022-0663.89.3.538

Grolnick, W. S., Gurland, S. T., DeCourcey, W., & Jacob, K. (2002). Antecedents and consequences of mothers' autonomy support: An experimental investigation. *Developmental Psychology, 38,* 143–155. doi:10.1037/0012-1649.38.1.143

Grolnick, W. S., Kurowski, C. O., Dunlap, K. G., & Hevey, C. (2000). Parental resources and the transition to junior high. *Journal of Research on Adolescence, 10,* 465–488. doi:10.1207/SJRA1004_05

Grolnick, W. S., Kurowski, C. O., McMenamy, J. M., Rivkin, I. R., & Bridges, L. J. (1998). Mothers' strategies for regulating their toddlers' distress. *Infant Behavior & Development, 21,* 437–450. doi:10.1016/S0163-6383(98)90018-2

Grolnick, W. S., Raftery-Helmer, J. N., Flamm, E. S., Marbell, K., & Cardemil, E. V. (in press). Parental structure and the transition to middle school. *Journal of Research on Adolescence.*

Grolnick, W. S., Raftery-Helmer, J. N., Marbell, K. N., Flamm, E. S., Cardemil, E. V., & Sanchez, M. (2014). Parental provision of structure: Implementation, correlates, and outcomes in three domains. *Merrill-Palmer Quarterly, 60,* 355–384.

Grolnick, W. S., & Ryan, R. M. (1989). Parent styles associated with children's self-regulation and competence in school. *Journal of Educational Psychology, 81,* 143–154. doi:10.1037/0022-0663.81.2.143

Grolnick, W. S., Ryan, R. M., & Deci, E. L. (1991). The inner resources for school achievement: Motivational mediators of children's perceptions of their parents. *Journal of Educational Psychology, 83,* 508–517. doi:10.1037/0022-0663.83.4.508

Grolnick, W. S., & Slowiaczek, M. L. (1994). Parents' involvement in children's schooling: A multidimensional conceptualization and motivational model. *Child Development, 65,* 237–252. doi:10.2307/1131378

Grolnick, W. S., & Wellborn, J. (1988, April). *Parent influences on children's school-related self-system process.* Paper presented at the annual meeting of the American Educational Research Association, New Orleans, LA.

Gurland, S. T., & Grolnick, W. S. (2005). Perceived threat, controlling parenting, and children's achievement orientations. *Motivation and Emotion, 29,* 103–121. doi:10.1007/s11031-005-7956-2

Gutman, L. M., & Midgley, C. (2000). The role of protective factors in supporting the academic achievement of poor African American students during the middle school transition. *Journal of Youth and Adolescence, 29*, 223–249. doi:10.1023/A:1005108700243

Jang, H., Kim, E. J., & Reeve, J. (2012). Longitudinal test of self-determination theory's motivation mediation model in a naturally occurring classroom context. *Journal of Educational Psychology, 104*, 1175–1188. doi:10.1037/a0028089

Jang, H., Reeve, J., & Deci, E. L. (2010). Engaging students in learning activities: It's not autonomy support or structure but autonomy support and structure. *Journal of Educational Psychology, 102*, 588–600. doi:10.1037/a0019682

Joussemet, M., Koestner, R., Lekes, N., & Landry, R. (2005). A longitudinal study of the relationship of maternal autonomy support to children's adjustment and achievement in school. *Journal of Personality, 73*, 1215–1236. doi:10.1111/j.1467-6494.2005.00347.x

Lunkenheimer, E. S., Shields, A. M., & Cortina, K. S. (2007). Parental emotion coaching and dismissing in family interaction. *Social Development, 16*, 232–248. doi:10.1111/j.1467-9507.2007.00382.x

Marchant, G. J., Paulson, S. E., & Rothlisberg, B. A. (2001). Relations of middle school students' perceptions of family and school contexts with academic achievement. *Psychology in the Schools, 38*, 505–519. doi:10.1002/pits.1039

Midgley, C., Anderman, E., & Hicks, L. (1995). Differences between elementary and middle school teachers and students: A goal theory approach. *Journal of Early Adolescence, 15*, 90–113. doi:10.1177/0272431695015001006

Midgley, C., & Urdan, T. (1995). Predictors of middle school students' use of self-handicapping strategies. *Journal of Early Adolescence, 15*, 389–411. doi:10.1177/0272431695015004001

Neuenschwander, R., Röthlisberger, M., Cimeli, P., & Roebers, C. M. (2012). How do different aspects of self-regulation predict successful adaptation to school? *Journal of Experimental Child Psychology, 113*, 353–371. doi:10.1016/j.jecp.2012.07.004

Pekrun, R. (2000). A social-cognitive, control-value theory of achievement emotions. In J. Heckhausen (Ed.), *Motivational psychology of human development* (pp. 143–163). New York, NY: Elsevier. doi:10.1016/S0166-4115(00)80010-2

Pekrun, R., Frenzel, A. C., Goetz, T., & Perry, R. P. (2007). The control-value theory of achievement emotions: An integrative approach to emotions in education. In P. A. Schutz (Ed.), *Emotion in education* (pp. 13–36). San Diego, CA: Elsevier Academic Press. doi:10.1016/B978-012372545-5/50003-4

Pomerantz, E. M., & Eaton, M. M. (2001). Maternal intrusive support in the academic context: Transactional socialization processes. *Developmental Psychology, 37*, 174–186. doi:10.1037/0012-1649.37.2.174

Raftery-Helmer, J. R., & Grolnick, W. S. (2012). *Children's coping with academic failure: Relations with contextual and motivational resources supporting competence.* Unpublished manuscript, Clark University.

Raver, C. C., Jones, S. M., Li-Grining, C., Zhai, F., Metzger, M. W., & Solomon, B. (2009). Targeting children's behavior problems in preschool classrooms: A cluster-randomized controlled trial. *Journal of Consulting and Clinical Psychology, 77*, 302–316. doi:10.1037/a0015302

Reyes, O., Gillock, K. L., Kobus, K., & Sanchez, B. (2000). A longitudinal examination of the transition into senior high school for adolescents from urban, low-income status, and predominantly minority backgrounds. *American Journal of Community Psychology, 28*, 519–544. doi:10.1023/A:1005140631988

Roderick, M. (1995). School transitions and school dropout. In K. Wong (Ed.), *Advances in educational policy* (pp. 135–185). Greenwich, CT: JAI Press.

Roderick, M. (2003). What's happening to the boys? Early high school experiences and school outcomes among African American male adolescents in Chicago. *Urban Education, 38*, 538–607. doi:10.1177/0042085903256221

Ryan, R. M., & Connell, J. P. (1989). Perceived locus of causality and internalization: Examining reasons for acting in two domains. *Journal of Personality and Social Psychology, 57*, 749–761. doi:10.1037/0022-3514.57.5.749

Sanders, M. G. (1998). The effects of school, family, and community support on the academic achievement of African American adolescents. *Urban Education, 33*, 385–409. doi:10.1177/0042085998033003005

Schneider, B. H., Tomada, G., Normand, S., Tonci, E., & de Domini, P. (2008). Social support as a predictor of school bonding and academic motivation following the transition to Italian middle school. *Journal of Social and Personal Relationships, 25*, 287–310. doi:10.1177/0265407507087960

Skinner, E. A., & Belmont, M. J. (1993). Motivation in the classroom: Reciprocal effects of teacher behavior and student engagement across the school year. *Journal of Educational Psychology, 85*, 571–581. doi:10.1037/0022-0663.85.4.571

Skinner, E. A., Johnson, S., & Snyder, T. (2005). Six dimensions of parenting: A motivational model. *Parenting: Science and Practice, 5*, 175–235. doi:10.1207/s15327922par0502_3

Skinner, E. A., Kindermann, T. A., Connell, J. P., & Wellborn, J. G. (2009). Engagement as an organizational construct in the dynamics of motivational development. In K. Wentzel & A. Wigfield (Eds.), *Handbook of motivation in school* (pp. 223–245). Mahwah, NJ: Erlbaum.

Smith, J. B. (1997). Effects of eighth-grade transition programs on high school retention and experiences. *Journal of Educational Research, 90*, 144–152. doi:10.1080/00220671.1997.10543770

Soenens, B., & Vansteenkiste, M. (2005). Antecedents and outcomes of self-determination in three life domains: The role of parents' and teachers' autonomy support. *Journal of Youth and Adolescence, 34*, 589–604. doi:10.1007/s10964-005-8948-y

Ursache, A., Blair, C., & Raver, C. C. (2012). The promotion of self-regulation as a means of enhancing school readiness and early achievement in children at risk for school failure. *Child Development Perspectives, 6,* 122–128. doi:10.1111/j.1750-8606.2011.00209.x

Valiente, C., Lemery-Chalfant, K., & Swanson, J. (2010). Prediction of kindergartners' academic achievement from their effortful control and emotionality: Evidence for direct and moderated relations. *Journal of Educational Psychology, 102,* 550–560. doi:10.1037/a0018992

Voelkl, K. E. (1995). School warmth, student participation, and achievement. *Journal of Experimental Education, 63,* 127–138. doi:10.1080/00220973.1995.9943817

Wigfield, A., & Eccles, J. S. (2000). Expectancy-value theory of achievement motivation. *Contemporary Educational Psychology, 25,* 68–81. doi:10.1006/ceps.1999.1015

Zimmerman, B. J. (1989). A social cognitive view of self-regulated academic learning. *Journal of Educational Psychology, 81,* 329–339. doi:10.1037/0022-0663.81.3.329

Zimmerman, B. J. (2000). Self-efficacy: An essential motive to learn. *Contemporary Educational Psychology, 25,* 82–91. doi:10.1006/ceps.1999.1016

12

LEARNING TECHNOLOGIES AS SUPPORTIVE CONTEXTS FOR PROMOTING COLLEGE STUDENT SELF-REGULATED LEARNING

ANASTASIA KITSANTAS, NADA DABBAGH, SUZANNE E. HILLER, AND BRIAN MANDELL

In the past two decades, a substantial body of research has focused on testing the effectiveness of interventions tailored to engage students in self-regulation, a process in which an individual takes responsibility for his or her learning (Bembenutty, Cleary, & Kitsantas, 2013; Hofer & Yu, 2003; Kitsantas & Dabbagh, 2010; Kitsantas & Zimmerman, 2009). These interventions, which include how-to-learn courses and technological supports for freshman students, have shown considerable success in helping those students with transition and retention (Bednall & Kehoe, 2011; Hu & Ma, 2010; Kitsantas & Chow, 2007; Kitsantas & Dabbagh, 2010). Ongoing research has shown that learning technologies can serve as an important determinant in fostering self-regulation, particularly in online or blended courses (Kitsantas & Chow, 2007; Kitsantas & Dabbagh, 2010). *Self-regulation* is the degree to which students can proactively and independently set goals and select, implement, monitor, and evaluate the effectiveness of strategies to

http://dx.doi.org/10.1037/14641-013
Self-Regulated Learning Interventions With At-Risk Youth: Enhancing Adaptability, Performance, and Well-Being, T. J. Cleary (Editor)
Copyright © 2015 by the American Psychological Association. All rights reserved.

accomplish their goals (Zimmerman, 2008). Use of learning technologies can increase student interaction with faculty, who model and help students select viable strategies to accomplish their goals, and can be effective in engaging students in feedback loops which prompt learners to check the degree to which those strategies are facilitating their learning goals.

This chapter focuses on how learning technologies can help college students become responsible for their own learning by engaging in self-regulatory feedback loops. We provide an overview of the theory of self-regulation and illustrate how learning technologies can serve as self-regulated learning (SRL) contexts, with particular emphasis on how feedback loops may serve as a key mechanism for enhancing student learning in these contexts. We discuss how learning technologies enhance SRL and academic performance, and we underscore current technology systems that can engage students in self-regulatory feedback loops. We also present a case scenario that illustrates the developmental process of acquiring SRL skills using a multilevel approach, and we suggest future directions for research.

LEARNING TECHNOLOGIES AS CONTEXTS FOR ENHANCING SELF-REGULATED LEARNING FEEDBACK LOOPS

Theoretical Foundation

Self-regulation of learning includes three interrelated phases: forethought, performance, and self-reflection (Zimmerman, 2008, 2013). The first phase, *forethought*, contains key self-regulatory and motivational processes, such as strategic planning and goal-setting, and the learner's motivation, including self-efficacy beliefs to engage in a task, outcome expectancies, and task interest. An important distinction in goal setting is process- versus outcome-oriented goals (Zimmerman & Kitsantas, 1997). Research has shown that students who first focus on mastering and achieving process goals (e.g., goals that focus on gradual progression toward a given outcome) before shifting their attention to mastering and achieving outcome goals (e.g., goals that focus on the outcome itself) are more likely to attain stronger outcomes than students who focus solely on outcome goals. Furthermore, empirical evidence has indicated that students with higher self-efficacy are more likely to persist and succeed in completing a task (Zimmerman, 2008, 2013).

In the *performance* phase, students engage in completing the task at hand. Processes in this phase diverge into the two major categories of self-control strategies and self-observation. *Self-control* refers to major strategies that learners use during knowledge acquisition, such as mental imagery, task strategies, attention focusing, and self-instruction. *Self-observation* refers to metacognitive monitoring or physical record-keeping of a learner's performance (Zimmerman, 2013).

The *self-reflection* phase encompasses two major categories: self-evaluation and self-reactions. *Self-evaluation* involves comparing self-monitored outcomes with a goal, whereas *self-reactions* refer to the learner's satisfaction with outcomes and adaptive or defensive inferences, which are conclusions about how the learner needs to adjust his or her approach in subsequent learning efforts. It is in this phase that students reflect on their learning outcomes and make necessary changes to adjust their strategies. They then apply feedback from the self-reflection phase to make adaptive changes in the forethought and performance phases of learning. Findings stemming from at least a decade of research have provided support for these three phases of self-regulation: They have indicated that students' academic achievement is greatly influenced by the use of these processes in a cyclical manner (Zimmerman, 2008, 2013; Zimmerman & Schunk, 2011).

Research Supporting the Link Between Self-Regulated Learning and Learning Technologies

Research findings that have focused on college students have consistently shown that self-regulation influences college retention and achievement (Kitsantas, Winsler, & Huie, 2008; Lee, Choi, & Kim, 2013; see also Chapter 3, this volume). Given that self-regulation is amenable to teaching through intervention, a growing trend among universities is to offer first-year undergraduate students courses geared toward enhancing or developing self-regulation and motivation. For incoming freshman, successful transitions stem from a need to shift from past educational experiences that were based on preplanned instructional programs to independent learning in terms of self-directed planning, performing, and reflecting. Furthermore, collegiate courses necessitate more cognitive demands, and perhaps motivational and metacognitive challenges, than experiences in secondary education. For this reason, structured guidance from faculty based on consistent interaction and training in self-reflection is a pressing consideration (Wingate, 2007). Interventions implemented both at the course and program levels have focused on a variety of self-regulatory processes to assist students in developing independent skill sets (Bednall & Kehoe, 2011; Kitsantas & Dabbagh, 2004; Langley & Bart, 2008; Lizzio & Wilson, 2013).

Learning technologies play a critical role in SRL. Specifically, when learning technologies are deliberately used to support self-regulation, motivation, and engagement in online learning contexts, student academic performance significantly improves and students report more positive attitudes toward learning (Dabbagh & Kitsantas, 2013; Kitsantas & Chow, 2007;

Kitsantas & Dabbagh, 2010; Kramarski & Gutman, 2006; López-Morteo & López, 2007). For example, Nicol (2009) investigated how electronic feedback and assessment practices can be used to help first-year college students develop SRL skills and adjust to college-level academics. Students completed a series of weekly assignments. Model essays and answers to assignments enabled students to compare and self-assess their performance against the model examples and answers. In addition, the professors and course leaders provided motivational feedback electronically to students on task completion to help them develop a positive sense of efficacy. Results showed that, at the end of the course, participants reported increased levels of engagement and of intrinsic motivation. Nicol suggested that, given the range of learning technologies, professors can select and customize learning technologies to the needs of their specific class. For example, in a language course, students can be prompted to self-assess their learning through weekly online reading, writing, and listening self-assessments. Videos and online tutorials can serve as supplemental lecture tools.

Self-regulation needs to be cultivated in online settings for students to engage in self-regulation practices; it needs to go beyond reminding students to self-regulate their learning through e-mail messages. For example, Hodges and Kim (2010) investigated how e-mail messages that included self-regulation reminders influenced first-year college students' self-regulation, self-efficacy, and achievement in an online math course. The students in the course were assigned to three groups. The first group received general e-mail messages (i.e., e-mails sent to the group) with statements reminding students to engage in specific self-regulation strategies. The second group received personal e-mails from the professor that individually reminded them to engage in self-regulation strategies. The third group, the control group, did not receive any messages or reminders to engage in self-regulated practice. The course was separated into 11 weeks of instruction; each week, the professor focused on a specific self-regulation strategy. Results indicated that, at the end of the semester, the three groups did not differ in levels of achievement, self-efficacy, or self-regulation.

In contrast, Azevedo and Cromley (2004) found significant achievement differences between students who were trained (i.e., not simply reminded) to self-regulate while learning a complex topic with hypermedia technology and students who did not receive instruction on how to self-regulate their learning. In the intervention condition, undergraduate students received a 30-minute training session on self-regulation that included planning, monitoring, and other related processes. Following the training, students completed a hypermedia learning task on a sophisticated and complex topic (i.e., the circulatory system). The control students only completed the hypermedia learning task; they did not complete a self-regulation training session. Furthermore, a think-aloud protocol instructed students to verbalize their thinking and cognitions while engaging in the learning task. The results showed that intervention students were more able to learn complex topics with hypermedia technology than control students. Specifically, intervention students displayed a deeper conceptual understanding of the circulatory system than control students. Moreover, the results showed that intervention students had engaged in more SRL than students in the control condition; thus, ultimately, the intervention students outperformed the control students in the learning task.

Research has revealed that students who engage in SRL in online learning courses outperform their counterparts. For example, Puzziferro (2008) examined how student SRL strategies and self-efficacy for learning technologies influenced the academic performance of students enrolled in an undergraduate online course. Results showed that students who received higher final grades reported stronger time management strategies and engaged in more self-regulation techniques than students who received lower final grades. Furthermore, individuals who used rehearsal task strategies, metacognitive self-regulation, and time management expressed more satisfaction with their overall final grades than students who did not report high engagement in those processes. Self-efficacy for online learning technologies was not found to influence final grades.

In terms of student engagement in an online course, Sun and Rueda (2012) investigated the influence of self-regulation, situational interest, and computer self-efficacy on student behavioral, emotional, and cognitive engagement. The data revealed that self-regulation was the only variable that significantly predicted all three types of student engagement in the course. Computer self-efficacy was not a significant predictor of any of the engagement variables, whereas situational interest significantly related only to emotional engagement. Those findings indicate that self-regulation plays a key role in student academic success and in determining the level of motivation and engagement in online courses.

Overall, college instructors should leverage learning technologies to support and promote student self-regulation in online learning contexts. However, research indicates that college faculty experienced in online teaching do not deliberately use learning technologies to support student SRL (Dabbagh & Kitsantas, 2009). Faculty need pedagogical and technological guidance to develop strategies and practices that support and promote student self-regulation and engage students in cyclical self-regulatory feedback loops. Specifically, faculty members may benefit from training on how to use learning technologies within and outside existing technology platforms to design course assignments and learning activities that support task complexity. This type of curriculum design encompasses the capability to diagnose, guide, and evaluate different processes of self-regulation to better understand how self-regulation operates in an online or blended learning context (Kitsantas & Dabbagh, 2010). In the following section, we review the literature on existing technologically supported learning environments that promote SRL.

Illustration of Existing Technology Platforms

Several learning technology systems have been developed to engage students in self-regulation; examples include MetaTutor, gStudy, and Betty's Brain. Here, we describe these technologies and discuss their research implications on informing the design of a pedagogical framework that college faculty and instructors can use to support and promote student SRL in online and blended learning.

MetaTutor is a research-based learning tool that specifically targets and scaffolds self-regulatory processes to improve academic performance. The design of MetaTutor is based on research by Azevedo and colleagues that details how adaptive human scaffolding, which addresses SRL content and processes, enhances students' learning about challenging science topics with hypermedia (Azevedo, 2008; Azevedo, Johnson, Chauncey, & Graesser, 2011; Azevedo & Witherspoon, 2009). MetaTutor detects, models, traces, and fosters students' SRL about body systems, such as the circulatory, digestive, and nervous systems, as they explore a hypermedia learning environment (Azevedo et al., 2009). Several key SRL processes associated with learning gains form the basis of the SRL scaffolding provided by MetaTutor. The platform begins with a training session for users that is focused on SRL processes. After completing the training phase, learners begin to explore the hypermedia learning environment. During this phase, they are exposed to a learning goal, a list of subtopics determined by learner or teacher, and a communication dialogue window in which a pedagogical agent, "Mary the Monitor," assists them with preprogrammed prompts and scaffolds (Azevedo et al., 2009). These prompts on the user's screen support the deployment of key self-regulatory processes. Throughout the entire user learning experience, researchers collect a variety of other data to gain a greater understanding of the connection between self-regulatory processes and learning with hypermedia learning environments. One of the key objectives for MetaTutor is to create a system that seamlessly uses the collected data to provide the user with timely, specific, and strategic feedback during learning. The data might show that a student is using ineffective strategies, in which case the agent might provide feedback by alerting the learner to use a better learning strategy (e.g., summarizing a complex biological pathway instead of copying it verbatim). The user could use this feedback to improve his or her own learning choices and outcomes in the immediate learning environment but also in subsequent learning opportunities.

Declarative knowledge gains from pretest to posttest, more time spent planning and monitoring, and more thoughtful use of learning strategies were just some of the fruitful findings demonstrated by students as they learned with the help of MetaTutor (Azevedo et al., 2011). However, assessing SRL and providing the proper scaffolding to students remains a challenge for MetaTutor. Although MetaTutor collects limitless log file data and Mary the Monitor is able to redirect or prompt the learner with preprogrammed suggestions, evaluating what the user is doing and linking that information to how much he or she knows is a challenge. Nevertheless, MetaTutor represents an exciting step in the use of technology to assess, support, and guide the deployment and reflection of SRL processes during learning.

gStudy is a state-of-the-art technology support system that is designed for researching learning by providing tools and resources to help learners save and organize their actions as they explore topics and multimedia resources (Winne, Hadwin, Nesbit, Kumar, & Beaudoin, 2005). As learners explore the multimedia resource of their choice, the system collects trace data that are derived from signs and observable indicators, such as personal comments, diagrams, footnotes, asterisks, or summaries, regarding cognitive processes that individuals perform while engaging in learning activities (Torrano Montalvo & Gonzales Torres, 2004). When students underline, it is considered an observable indicator of their cognition, and researchers have labeled such indicators as traces (Winne, 1982). *Traces* represent a window into what the students are thinking about at a given instance during a learning task. These data points, which have been collected and analyzed in the case of gStudy, have the potential to provide feedback to students as they learn.

The trace data can drive internal discussions for the learners and can also be used for collaborative feedback. By using the log analyzer, a built-in aspect of gStudy, learners can review their own learning sequences by exploring words they have highlighted, concepts they have linked to other concepts, words they have taken notes on, and the location on the screen of all of those words (Winne et al., 2005). Learners may be able to uncover trends in their learning that may prompt them to change their behavior in future situations. gStudy provides learners with the ability to use open and guided chat tools that have the ability to share their learning kits (e.g., notes, glossaries, searches, concept maps) with teachers or classmates so they may receive feedback (Winne et al., 2005). gStudy seems to also allow users to visualize decisions in the form of the log-analyzer reports and how they have affected their learning performance by receiving feedback from their learning kits. Even though most of the inferences tend to be user generated, an entire feedback loop is embedded within gStudy so that users can engage and reflect on their own learning processes. By applying these data provided by gStudy, researchers and users can better understand how their study tactics affect learning. For example, Malmberg, Järvenoja, and Järvelä (2010) examined the log file trace data with elementary school students. The goal was to examine how students used study tactics while learning in science and whether frequent study tactic use was related to their achievement. The results showed that how the study tactic was performed made a difference in student learning and that frequent use of study tactics was not predictive of deep learning. gStudy represents a unique option for helping learners achieve a level of empowerment by providing data of their own learning processes, and feedback from peers and teachers to guide future learning opportunities.

Another technology-supported learning system, the Betty's Brain system, was designed by a team of researchers to demonstrate that students learn science better by monitoring someone else's learning (Leelawong & Biswas, 2008). The system uses a computer-based domain-independent teachable agent that students can teach to help them learn how to use SRL processes (Leelawong & Biswas, 2008). The Betty's Brain system is an example of a learning-by-teaching system in that the students get the chance to observe and analyze how teachable agents apply new knowledge to solve problems. In this process, they may learn to monitor their own knowledge creation. Betty's Brain system has been used to teach middle-school students about river systems. The students were responsible for teaching Betty using a concept map, querying Betty to see how much she has understood, and quizzing Betty with a provided test to see how well she would do on questions the students may not have considered. Throughout the process, a mentor agent, "Mr. Davis," is available to provide feedback about learning, teaching, and domain knowledge. Mr. Davis is also there to help users scaffold SRL processes for Betty.

Leelawong and Biswas (2008) explored what effect the Betty's Brain system has had on content acquisition and familiarity with SRL processes for a group of students in a fifth-grade science classroom. The researchers compared the results of three versions of the system: one in which the students were taught by an agent, one in which the students had to teach the agent without support, and one in which the students had to teach the agent with the support of feedback on SRL strategies, courtesy of Mr. Davis. Research demonstrated that both learning-by-teaching groups outperformed the group taught solely by the agent; of particular interest, though, was the finding that the learning-by-teaching group, aided by the SRL prompts, better prepared students for a future learning transfer test in a different science topic that was administered 7 weeks after the initial experiment (Leelawong & Biswas, 2008). That latter finding is important because it provides a tangible example of the feedback loop mechanism in action and demonstrates how the students used the feedback from a previous learning experience, grounded in SRL, to assist their content acquisition in a subsequent learning opportunity.

Although the literature describes several other technology-supported learning systems that focus on SRL, the aforementioned three systems demonstrate how learning technologies can be used to scaffold SRL, facilitate SRL, and incorporate feedback loops to improve a user's ability to know when and where to most effectively use certain SRL processes. Next, we present a single case scenario that illustrates the developmental process of acquiring SRL skills using a training model and a broad spectrum of learning technologies.

BUILDING SELF-EMPOWERING CYCLES OF LEARNING WITH LEARNING TECHNOLOGIES: A CASE STUDY APPLICATION

Self-regulated learners engage in forethought, performance, and self-reflection phases in a cyclical manner, and on the basis of ongoing feedback, they adjust their strategies to accomplish a goal. An important question, however, is, How can students learn to effectively engage in a cyclical feedback loop in which they set appropriate goals, select strategies, self-monitor the effectiveness of those strategies, and self-evaluate? Research has shown that students acquire mastery of SRL skills in four sequential levels—observation, emulation, self-control, and self-regulation—thus leading to a four-phase training model (Kitsantas, Zimmerman, & Cleary, 2000; Zimmerman, 2008). In the first level, *observation*, students observe the expert instructor performing a task or skill to be learned, whereas, during the *emulation* level, students enact the performance of the expert model in close proximity to the instructor, who offers guidance and support. The emulation level allows students to refine their performance of the task or skill using such feedback. During the *self-control* level, students engage in self-directed practice to achieve automaticity in task performance by comparing their practice efforts with personal standards acquired from the expert instructor performance. In the *self-regulation* phase, students shift their attention from processes to performance outcomes, and they learn to adapt their performance to other tasks. This four-level model of self-regulation development can be used as a training framework to help students become self-regulated learners who use a broad spectrum of learning technologies in which learners are prompted to engage in feedback loops (e.g., moving from forethought to performance to self-reflection) within each level (Zimmerman, 2013). Figure 12.1 demonstrates how the instructor can use this training model to support college student self-regulation through learning technologies.

```
┌─────────────────────────────────────────────────────────────────┐
│ Instructor identifies the learning task; determines the          │
│ processes, steps, or procedure associated with performing the    │
│ learning task; and then uses the four-phase training model.      │
└─────────────────────────────────────────────────────────────────┘
                              ↓
```

Phase 1: Observation

Enables students to think strategically before acting

- Instructor uses synchronous collaborative tools (e.g., whiteboard, chat session) or asynchronous tools (e.g., a webcast, podcast, video tools) to demonstrate or model the step-by-step process or procedure associated with performing the learning task.
- Student observes the instructor and begins to discriminate between strategies used to execute the task.

Phase 2: Emulation

Enables students to gather information about their learning behaviors and performance with the help of the instructor and peers

- Student uses synchronous collaborative tools (e.g., whiteboard, chat) or asynchronous tools (e.g., a webcast, podcast, video tools) to emulate or enact the task in the presence of the instructor and peers to receive feedback and coaching.
- Instructor coaches and provides encouragement and feedback, gradually fading this support based on student performance.

Phase 3: Self-Control

Enables students to focus on mastering the steps related to completing the learning task during practice episodes

- Student uses wikis, blogs, document-sharing technologies, and online bookmarking tools to practice performing the learning task on his or her own and monitors and rewards own progress.
- Instructor provides scaffolding for student self-monitoring through the commenting features of wikis and blogs and the collaborative editing and tagging features of document-sharing and online bookmaking technologies.

Phase 4: Self-Regulation

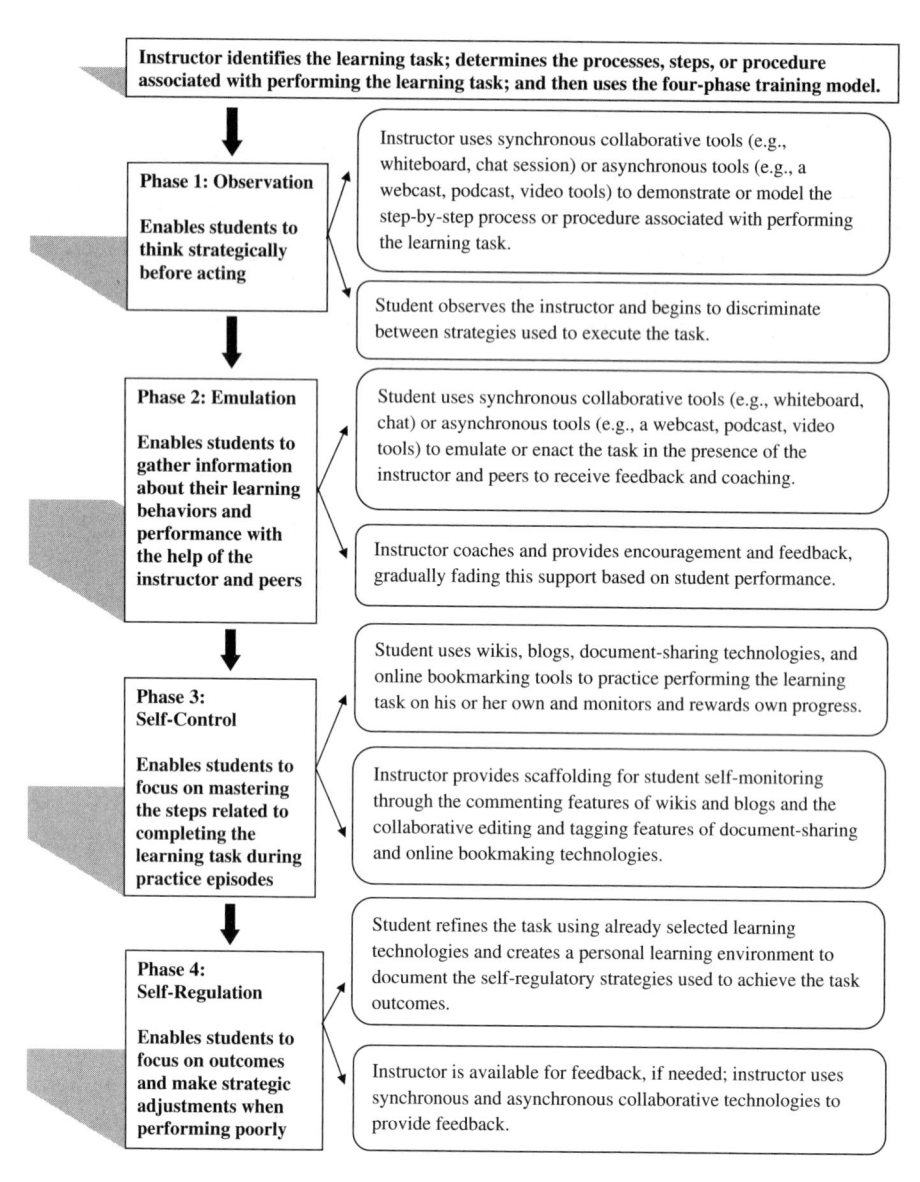

Enables students to focus on outcomes and make strategic adjustments when performing poorly

- Student refines the task using already selected learning technologies and creates a personal learning environment to document the self-regulatory strategies used to achieve the task outcomes.
- Instructor is available for feedback, if needed; instructor uses synchronous and asynchronous collaborative technologies to provide feedback.

Figure 12.1. Use of the training model to support college student self-regulation through learning technologies.

To effectively apply the four-level model in online learning contexts, instructors should first perform a task analysis to identify the specific processes or steps associated with the learning task. For example, an Introduction to Learning Theory course instructor, Mr. X, wants students to understand the differences between two epistemological orientations: objectivism and constructivism, and the types of learning environments that each supports. Mr. X begins to think about the best approach or instructional strategy to present these concepts to the students. He designs a learning activity or assignment called Compare and Contrast in which students, in teams of two, are asked to find a technology-supported learning environment that is extremely objectivist and a technology-supported learning environment that is extremely constructivist; and to use the course readings to justify why these technology-supported learning environments demonstrate the principles of the particular epistemology. The Compare and Contrast assignment also requires students to develop a narrated PowerPoint presentation that demonstrates the selected technology-supported learning environments and to justify their epistemological orientation. During the observation level of the training model, Mr. X prerecords a video lecture that describes the principles of objectivism and constructivism. He uses the assignment feature of Blackboard to provide the specific requirements of the Compare and Contrast assignment and a rubric of how it will be evaluated. Mr. X provides a resource area using Blackboard's resource feature and uploads exemplary examples of technology-supported learning environments and PowerPoint presentations that students in previous courses had used successfully to fulfill the requirements of the assignment. Thus, Mr. X is modeling the content and process involved, and is allowing students to vicariously experience the steps or procedure needed to complete the learning task. Mr. X schedules a live session on Blackboard Collaborate so that students can ask questions after they have viewed the prerecorded video and explored the assignment examples and resources.

In the emulation level, Mr. X creates virtual group areas for each team. Blackboard allows instructors to create group areas with several embedded features, such as file exchange, wikis, e-mail, tasks, collaboration, and discussion board, so that each team can use the features they choose as they begin collaborating to complete the assignment. Mr. X asks each team to create a table, using the course readings, that compares the principles of objectivism and constructivism along several variables and to upload that table to the group wiki. This activity engages students in enacting the task processes and allows the instructor to observe and monitor their performance, and to provide feedback as needed. Mr. X encourages the teams to post links to examples of technology-supported learning environments they have found in their wiki space and to post related questions. Thus, students are provided every opportunity to interact with the instructor and peers, and to seek help and clarification as they perform the task processes so they may become aware of the self-regulatory processes of goal-setting and task strategies.

In the third level of the self-regulatory training model, self-control, Mr. X asks students to begin developing the narrated PowerPoint presentation using the technology-supported learning environments they have identified and the table they created. He provides links to screencasting software that allows students to narrate PowerPoint presentations. Student teams use the collaboration feature of their group area to practice narration; they also use the file exchange to transfer PowerPoint files. At this level, students spend most of their time practicing the modeled behaviors on their own and focusing on mastering the task processes. Mr. X reminds students of the Compare and Contrast assignment evaluation rubric to ensure that students can accurately assess their performance. This directive helps students become metacognitively aware of their own learning processes and strategies. Furthermore, Mr. X assigns peer teams and asks each team to provide comments on at least two other team presentations using the assignment evaluation rubric. Mr. X transforms the text-based evaluation rubric into an online form that has input fields and a Likert scale, thereby facilitating peer feedback. Mr. X uses the online form to provide feedback on each team's final narrated presentation.

During self-regulation, the last level of the training model, students engage in learning independently and become proactive learners who focus primarily on outcomes and refine their learning strategies as needed. In the case of the Compare and Contrast assignment, students can now turn their attention to outcomes by reflecting on their overall performance and strategy approach based on the feedback they received from their peers and instructor. Mr. X posts both grades for each team in the grading area of Blackboard and written feedback about their students' overall performance on this learning task. Students have the opportunity again to respond to unsatisfactory outcomes and prepare for new learning tasks, set new goals, and, if necessary, replace their strategies with more effective ones. Overall, the four-level training model can be used to train students to become self-regulated learners in online and blended contexts. It enables students to engage in cyclical feedback loops in which they learn to set effective goals, keep track of their performance, self-evaluate, and adjust their strategies accordingly to accomplish their goals.

FUTURE DIRECTIONS AND CONCLUSIONS

As described in this chapter, the research base on SRL, higher education, and learning technologies contains rich studies on scaffolding platforms, conceptual frameworks, and an array of fixed and embedded assistive structures designed to foster the development and deployment of self-regulatory processes and skills. Current research is shifting toward social media and learning analytics as potentially promising learning technologies that support, promote, and focus on the cyclical nature of self-regulatory processes and subsequently increase student retention. *Social media* is a group of Internet-based applications that build on the ideological and technological foundations of Web 2.0 and turn communication into interactive dialogue by allowing the creation, exchange, and classification (i.e., tagging) of user-generated content (Kaplan & Haenlein, 2010). Social media includes resource- and media-sharing tools, such as Delicious, Pinterest, Flickr, and YouTube; blogging and microblogging platforms, such as WordPress, Blogger, and Twitter; collaborative editing and document-sharing workspaces such as PBworks and Google Sites; and social networking sites, such as Facebook and LinkedIn (Dabbagh & Reo, 2011; Kitsantas & Dabbagh, 2010).

Learning in the context of social media has become highly self-motivated, autonomous, and informal—and an integral part of the college experience. In addition, evidence exists that social media can facilitate the creation of personal learning environments (PLE) that help learners develop and apply SRL processes, such as setting appropriate personal goals, using task strategies to manage information, and engaging in self-monitoring and self-evaluation to progress to socially mediated knowledge and networked learning (Dabbagh & Kitsantas, 2013). For example, Dabbagh and Kitsantas (2013) found that blogs, microblogs, and social bookmarking tools are more useful for personal information management in PLE development, whereas wikis, cloud-based technologies, social networks, and social media-sharing tools are suitable for social interaction and collaboration. They also discovered that students perceived social media as particularly useful in supporting the self-regulation processes of goal setting, self-monitoring, help-seeking, and task strategies, but not as supportive in terms of the self-regulation processes of self-evaluation and time management. More research is needed, however, to determine how social media can be used to develop formal and informal learning spaces or experiences that start out as an individual learning platform or PLE and enable individual knowledge management and construction.

Furthermore, *learning analytics*, which is defined as the collection and analysis of learner-produced data to understand, predict, optimize, and advise student learning ("Learning Analytics and Knowledge," 2011), may be useful in helping students achieve their learning goals, particularly in the emulation, self-control, and self-regulation phases of this training model. Learning analytics represents one of the most exciting factors that potentially could affect education today. Learning analytics bases its analysis and conclusions on the various types of data stored in organizations' databases as a result of their information systems. The industry-accepted term for these large data sets is *big data*. In higher education, big data can be found—especially in the delivery of an online class—in the number of times a student creates a new blog, takes practice quizzes, accesses the online library, e-mails the professor, spends time on class resources, and logs in to the school's learning management system. Each of these interactions represents one data point that may clarify and potentially predict the individual's learning, and show trends in the class as a whole.

An example is Purdue University's Course Signals, a behaviorally based model that collects and analyzes data on past academic performance, interaction with the learning management system, and help-seeking behavior to provide students with a red, yellow, or green light to symbolize their current academic standing in a class (Pistilli & Arnold, 2010). A key feature of Course Signals is its capability to recognize patterns of struggling students and provide them with e-mail reminders and other strategies to correct their class progress before the end of the semester. Changes to a student's behavior automatically refreshes the color of his or her signal light, which means students are better able to see the connection between action and performance. Using a slightly different approach, Northern Arizona University's grade performance status, online academic early alert tool focuses on increasing instructor feedback and facilitating instructor–student interactions (Star & Collette, 2010). Grade performance status e-mail messages are prepackaged into four categories: attendance, grades, academic concerns, and positive feedback. The goals are to increase formal and informal instructor–student interactions, increase use of the student learning center, and decrease Ds and Fs in high D to F courses. In each of these learning analytic examples, the systems use data to inform students of their academic standing and direct them to assistance during the semester. These technologies harness the power of the feedback loop mechanism by allowing for informative and timely feedback to be immediately communicated with specific self-reflective strategies in place. Clearly, big data can be used to help solve or explain a variety of issues in higher education, particularly the design of adaptive online environments that can greatly improve retention. What is even more powerful and promising is examining how PLEs and learning analytics can work hand in hand to support self-empowered cycles of learning and enable students to become lifelong learners who are better prepared for educational and professional pursuits.

Researchers have consistently demonstrated that, regardless of factors such as gender, racial and or ethnic backgrounds, socioeconomic status, and academic domains, self-regulation continues to be one of the most potent predictors of academic achievement. As such, the implementation of systematic self-regulatory processes is a pivotal consideration in supporting students' learning and performance in college settings. With an increasingly diverse and unprecedented student population in the United States, at no time will the need for self-regulation instruction be more critical than in the first year of collegiate programs, particularly in remedial courses. The intersection of technological resources and self-regulation training is a viable approach to foster academic success for all students entering collegiate pathways.

REFERENCES

Azevedo, R. (2008). The role of self-regulation in learning about science with hypermedia. In D. Robinson & G. Schraw (Eds.), *Recent innovations in educational technology that facilitate student learning* (pp. 127–156). Charlotte, NC: Information Age.

Azevedo, R., & Cromley, J. G. (2004). Does training on self-regulated learning facilitate students' learning with hypermedia? *Journal of Educational Psychology, 96,* 523–535. doi:10.1037/0022-0663.96.3.523

Azevedo, R., Johnson, A., Chauncey, A., & Graesser, A. (2011). Use of hypermedia to assess and convey self-regulated learning. In B. J. Zimmerman & D. H. Schunk (Eds.), *Handbook of self-regulation of learning and performance* (pp. 102–119). New York, NY: Routledge.

Azevedo, R., & Witherspoon, A. M. (2009). Self-regulated use of hypermedia. In D. J. Hacker, J. Dunlosky, & A. C. Graesser (Eds.), *Handbook of metacognition in education* (pp. 319–339). New York, NY: Routledge.

Azevedo, R., Witherspoon, A., Graesser, A., McNamara, D., Chauncey, A., Siler, E., . . . Lintean, M. (2009). MetaTutor: Analyzing self-regulated learning in a tutoring system for biology. In V. Dimitrova, R. Mizoguchi, B. Du Boulay, & A. C. Graesser (Eds.), *Proceedings of the 14th International Conference on Artificial Intelligence in Education—Building Learning Systems That Care: From Knowledge Representation to Affective Modelling* (pp. 635–637). Amsterdam, The Netherlands: IOS Press.

Bednall, T. C., & Kehoe, E. J. (2011). Effects of self-regulatory instructional aids on self-directed study. *Instructional Science, 39,* 205–226. doi:10.1007/s11251-009-9125-6

Bembenutty, H., Cleary, T. J., & Kitsantas, A. (2013). *Applications of self-regulated learning applied across diverse disciplines: A tribute to Barry J. Zimmerman.* Charlotte, NC: Information Age.

Dabbagh, N., & Kitsantas, A. (2009). Exploring how experienced online instructors report using integrative learning technologies to support self-regulated learning. *International Journal of Technology in Teaching and Learning, 5,* 154–168.

Dabbagh, N., & Kitsantas, A. (2013). The role of social media in self-regulated learning. *International Journal of Web Based Communities, 9,* 256–273. doi:10.1504/IJWBC.2013.053248

Dabbagh, N., & Reo, R. (2011). Impact of Web 2.0 on higher education. In D. W. Surry, T. Stefurak, & R. Gray (Eds.), *Technology integration in higher education: Social and organizational aspects* (pp. 174–187). Hershey, PA: IGI Global.

Hodges, C. B., & Kim, C. (2010). Email, self-regulation, self-efficacy, and achievement in a college online mathematics course. *Journal of Educational Computing Research, 43,* 207–223. doi:10.2190/EC.43.2.d

Hofer, B. K., & Yu, S. L. (2003). Teaching self-regulated learning through a "learning to learn" course. *Teaching of Psychology, 30*(1), 30–33. doi:10.1207/S15328023TOP3001_05

Hu, S., & Ma, Y. (2010). Mentoring and student persistence in college: A study of the Washington State Achievers Program. *Innovative Higher Education, 35,* 329–341. doi:10.1007/s10755-010-9147-7

Kaplan, A. M., & Haenlein, M. (2010). Users of the world, unite! The challenges and opportunities of social media. *Business Horizons, 53,* 59–68. doi:10.1016/j.bushor.2009.09.003

Kitsantas, A., & Chow, A. (2007). College students perceived threat and preference for seeking help in traditional, distributed, and distance learning environments. *Computers & Education, 48,* 383–395. doi:10.1016/j.compedu.2005.01.008

Kitsantas, A., & Dabbagh, N. (2004). Using web-based pedagogical tools to support student self-regulation: What do teachers need to know? In C. Vrasidas & G. V. Glass (Eds.), *Current perspectives on applied information technologies: Preparing teachers to teach with technologies* (pp. 141–158). Charlotte, NC: Information Age.

Kitsantas, A., & Dabbagh, N. (2010). *Learning to learn with integrative learning technologies (ILT): A practical guide for academic success.* Greenwich, CT: Information Age.

Kitsantas, A., Winsler, A., & Huie, F. (2008). Self-regulation and ability predictors of academic success during college: A predictive validity study. *Journal of Advanced Academics, 20*(1), 42–68.

Kitsantas, A., & Zimmerman, B. J. (2009). College students' homework and academic achievement: The mediating role of self-regulatory beliefs. *Metacognition and Learning, 4,* 97–110. doi:10.1007/s11409-008-9028-y

Kitsantas, A., Zimmerman, B. J., & Cleary, T. (2000). The role of observation and emulation in the development of athletic self-regulation. *Journal of Educational Psychology, 92,* 811–817. doi:10.1037/0022-0663.92.4.811

Kramarski, B., & Gutman, M. (2006). How can self-regulated learning be supported in mathematical e-learning environments? *Journal of Computer Assisted Learning, 22*(1), 24–33. doi:10.1111/j.1365-2729.2006.00157.x

Langley, S. R., & Bart, W. M. (2008). Examining self-regulatory factors that influence the academic achievement motivation of underprepared college students. *Research & Teaching in Developmental Education, 25*(1), 10–22.

Learning analytics and knowledge: February 7–March 1, 2011. (2011). *First International Conference on Learning Analytics and Knowledge, 2011, in Banff, Alberta.* Retrieved from https://tekri.athabascau.ca/analytics/

Lee, Y., Choi, J., & Kim, T. (2013). Discriminating factors between completers of and dropouts from online learning courses. *British Journal of Educational Technology, 44,* 328–337. doi:10.1111/j.1467-8535.2012.01306.x

Leelawong, K., & Biswas, G. (2008). Designing learning by teaching agents: The Betty's Brain system. *International Journal of Artificial Intelligence in Education, 18,* 181–208.

Lizzio, A., & Wilson, K. (2013). Early intervention to support the academic recovery of first-year students at risk of non-continuation. *Innovations in Education and Teaching International, 50*, 109–120. doi:10.1080/14703297.2012.760867

López-Morteo, G., & López, G. (2007). Computer support for learning mathematics: A learning environment based on recreational learning objects. *Computers & Education, 48*, 618–641. doi:10.1016/j.compedu.2005.04.014

Malmberg, J., Järvenoja, H., & Järvelä, S. (2010). Tracing elementary school students' study tactic use in gStudy by examining a strategic and self-regulated learning. *Computers in Human Behavior, 26*, 1034–1042. doi:10.1016/j.chb.2010.03.004

Nicol, D. (2009). Assessment for learner self-regulation: Enhancing achievement in the first year using learning technologies. *Assessment & Evaluation in Higher Education, 34*, 335–352. doi:10.1080/02602930802255139

Pistilli, M. D., & Arnold, K. A. (2010). In practice: Purdue Signals—Mining real-time academic data to enhance student success. *About Campus, 15*(3), 22–24. doi:10.1002/abc.20025

Puzziferro, M. (2008). Online technologies self-efficacy and self-regulated learning as predictors of final grade and satisfaction in college-level online courses. *American Journal of Distance Education, 22*(2), 72–89. doi:10.1080/08923640802039024

Star, M., & Collette, L. (2010). GPS: Shaping student success one conversation at a time. *EDUCAUSE Quarterly, 33*(4), 15.

Sun, J. C.-H., & Rueda, R. (2012). Situational interest, computer self-efficacy and self-regulation: Their impact on student engagement in distance education. *British Journal of Educational Technology, 43*, 191–204. doi:10.1111/j.1467-8535.2010.01157.x

Torrano Montalvo, F., & Gonzales Torres, M. C. (2004). Self-regulated learning: Current and future directions. *Electronic Journal of Research in Educational Psychology, 2*(1), 1–34.

Wingate, U. (2007). A framework for transition: Supporting "learning to learn" in higher education. *Higher Education Quarterly, 61*(3), 391–405. doi:10.1111/j.1468-2273.2007.00361.x

Winne, P. H. (1982). Minimizing the black box problem to enhance the validity of theories about instructional effects. *Instructional Science, 11*, 13–28. doi:10.1007/BF00120978

Winne, P. H., Hadwin, A. F., Nesbit, J. C., Kumar, V., & Beaudoin, L. (2005). gStudy: A Toolkit for Developing Computer-Supported Tutorials and Researching Learning Strategies and Instruction (Version 2.0) [Computer software]. Burnaby, British Columbia, Canada: Simon Fraser University.

Zimmerman, B. J. (2008). Investigating self-regulation and motivation: Historical background, methodological developments, and future prospects. *American Educational Research Journal, 45*(1), 166–183. doi:10.3102/0002831207312909

Zimmerman, B. J. (2013). From cognitive modeling to self-regulation: A social cognitive career path. *Educational Psychologist, 48,* 135–147. doi:10.1080/0046152 0.2013.794676

Zimmerman, B. J., & Kitsantas, A. (1997). Developmental phases in self-regulation: Shifting from process goals to outcome goals. *Journal of Educational Psychology, 89,* 29–36. doi:10.1037/0022-0663.89.1.29

Zimmerman, B. J., & Schunk, D. H. (2011). Self-regulated learning and performance: An introduction and overview. In B. J. Zimmerman & D. H. Schunk (Eds.), *Handbook of self-regulation of learning and performance* (pp. 1–12). New York, NY: Routledge.

INDEX

Academic counseling, 72
Action research, 234–236. *See also* Teacher learning teams
Adaptive inferences, 145, 217
ADHD. *See* Attention-deficit/hyperactivity disorder
Administrators, school, 206
American Federation of Teachers, 45
American Lung Association, 189
Anderman, E., 265
Anger, 139, 163
Anxiety, 16. *See also* Emotion regulation interventions for youth anxiety
Assessment, 102–103, 216–217
Asthmatic individuals, self-regulation-based interventions for. *See* Self-regulation-based interventions for asthmatic individuals
Attention-deficit/hyperactivity disorder (ADHD), 15–38
  adult support of SRL for treatment of, 31–36
  assessment of, 16
  challenges with, 95
  child training in SRL strategies for children with, 28–31
  DSM criteria for, 16
  and executive functioning, 17–19, 103
  intervention process with, 16
  proposed training/intervention framework for treatment of, 27–36
  research support for SLR training/intervention approaches with, 19–27
  symptoms of, 16–17
Auditory processing disorder, 16
Autonomy, 77, 100, 254, 256–257, 259–261
Avoidance (emotion regulation), 162, 165–168
Azevedo, R., 280, 282

Bandura, A., 185, 210
Barber, B. K., 267, 268
Barkley, R. A., 18

Bartholomew, L. K., 184
Beare, P. L., 50–51
Beidel, D. C., 139
Berkes, J. L., 139
Berman, M. G., 18
Betty's Brain (learning technology), 282, 284–285
Birch, S. H., 259
Biswas, G., 284
Black, P., 102
Bratslavsky, E., 160
Brewer, G. A., 140
Bronstein, P., 256, 257
Brown, A. L., 233
Brownell, K. D., 49
Butler, D. L., 74, 91–93, 97, 101, 102

Calkins, S. D., 263
Campione, J. C., 233
Carmedil, E. V., 258
Cartier, S. C., 91, 93, 97, 101, 104
Carver, C. S., 160
Cavalier, A. R., 51
Center for Managing Chronic Disease, 189
CERT (Contextual Emotion Regulation Therapy for Childhood Depression), 162–163
Changing Results for Young Readers (CR4YRs), 236–244
Childhood depression. *See* Depression, childhood
Child training (ADHD treatment), 27–31
Chirkov, V. I., 257
Chorpita, B. F., 150
Chronic disease, 181, 185–189. *See also* Self-regulation-based interventions for asthmatic individuals
Cimeli, P., 263
Clark, Noreen M., 181
Classroom interaction, 211
Classroom Strategies Scale–Observer Form (CSS), 33
Cleary, T. J., 105, 209

Coaching (professional development), 209, 214
Cognitive–behavioral techniques
　to emotion regulation interventions for anxiety, 140–149
　for parent training, 35
Cognitive flexibility and reappraisal, 166–167
Coleman, M., 58
College students, motivationally disengaged. *See* Motivationally disengaged college students
Common Core state standards, 116
Competence, 254
Comprehension monitoring, 121–127
Computer simulation games, 184
Conditioning, 231–232
Connell, J. P., 252
Contextual Emotion Regulation Therapy for Childhood Depression (CERT), 162–163
Control, 71
Control-value theory, 254
Coping Cat program, 143, 144
Corno, L., 230, 233, 235, 245
Cortina, K. S., 266
Counseling, academic, 72
Course-based SRL interventions, 76–81
Course Signals model, 290
Course work, 73, 75–76
CR4YRs (Changing Results for Young Readers), 236–244
Cromley, J. G., 280
CSS (Classroom Strategies Scale–Observer Form), 33
Cycles of inquiry, 234

Dabbagh, N., 289
Daily Report Card (DRC), 33–34
Dart throwing techniques, 211
Deci, E. L., 258
Declarative knowledge, 78
Defensive inferences, 145
Depression, childhood
　ADHD comorbidity with, 16
　interventions for. *See* Emotion regulation interventions for childhood depression
　prevalence of, 157

"Detective thinking and questioning," 166
Diagnostic and Statistical Manual of Mental Disorders (DSM), 16
DiGangi, S. A., 52
Disease management, 181–182
Disengagement. *See* Motivationally disengaged college students
Disruptive behavior disorders, 16
Disruptive classroom behavior, self-management for reduction of. *See* Self-management for reduction of disruptive classroom behavior
Distal goals (ADHD treatment), 28
DRC (Daily Report Card), 33–34
DSM *(Diagnostic and Statistical Manual of Mental Disorders)*, 16

Eaton, M. M., 257
ECBT. *See* Emotion-focused cognitive behavioral therapy
Eccles, J., 254
EF. *See* Executive functioning
Effortful control, 261–263. *See also* Executive functioning
Electronic feedback, 184
Elementary school–middle school transitions, 264–267
ELLs. *See* English language learners
E-mail self-regulation reminders, 280
Emotion awareness and experiencing, 165–166
Emotion education, 164–165
Emotion exposure, 167–168
Emotion-focused cognitive behavioral therapy (ECBT), 143–146, 148–149, 151, 162
Emotion regulation, 138–139, 158–160, 253, 261–263. *See also* Executive functioning
Emotion regulation feedback loop, 161
Emotion regulation interventions for childhood depression, 157–173
　and anxiety, 157–158, 163
　case example, 168–171
　and cognitive flexibility/reappraisal, 166–167
　current research support for, 171–172

and emotion awareness/experiencing, 165–166
and emotion exposure, 167–168
future research directions, 172–173
relapse prevention with, 168
theoretical and research foundations, 159–162
UP-A as transdiagnostic model for, 158, 162–164
Emotion regulation interventions for youth anxiety, 137–152
cognitive–behavioral techniques for, 140–149
feedback in, 138
future research directions, 149–152
theoretical and research foundations for, 138–145
Emulation, 214, 285
Engagement, 49, 252. *See also* Motivationally disengaged college students
English language learners (ELLs), 113–130
areas of struggle for, 115
future directions for interventions with, 128–130
motivation in, 115–116
research-based applications of SRL for, 119–128
theoretical foundations of SRL for, 116–119
Executive functioning (EF)
with attention-deficit/hyperactivity disorder, 17–19, 103
components of, 252–253
defined, 261
and learning disabilities, 95–96, 103
and school transitions, 261–263
Exposure, 149
External factors of change, 188
External regulation, 254

Fan, W., 259
Fantuzzo, J. W., 46
Farkas, M. S., 258
Feedback. *See also* Feedback loop
defined, 5
electronic, 184
in emotion regulation interventions for anxiety, 138, 140, 142

in professional development, 213–215
self-oriented feedback loop, 253–254
in SRL interventions for learning disabilities, 102–103
student reflections on, 71
Feedback loop
and ADHD interventions, 19–20
and CBT interventions, 140–141
and chronic disease management, 187
and depression regulation, 160–162
for English language learners, 116, 129
and learning technologies, 278–285
and motivation disengagement, 71
overview, 5–6
and professional development, 210–211, 231
for reduction of disruptive classroom behavior, 46
and school transitions, 253–254
and self-management, 49
and technology, 285–287
in treatment of anxiety, 140–145
Ferretti, R. P., 51
Fizur, P., 142
Flamm, E. S., 258
Forethought
in ADHD interventions, 36
for motivationally disengaged college students, 77
in professional development, 218
in self-regulated learning, 4, 19, 70, 116, 140–142, 211, 278
in self-regulated learning microanalysis, 216
supporting, through structured teaching, 120–123
in treatment of ADHD, 28–29
Friedel, J. M., 266
Furrer, C., 255

Gagnon, F., 97
Gender differences, with ADHD, 16–17
General goals (ADHD treatment), 28–29
Gersten, R., 235
Giammarino, M., 97
Gill, K. L., 263
Ginsburg, G. S., 256

Goals
    in ADHD treatment, 28–29
    and emotion regulation, 160
    in learning disability interventions, 101, 105
    in professional development, 218–220
    in reading interventions, 121–122
    in self-regulated learning, 4, 70, 92, 116, 278
    student monitoring of, 94
    in teacher learning teams, 237
    in technology supports, 282
Goal-setting. *See* Goals
Graham, S., 95, 103
Grolnick, W. S., 258, 259
Gross, J. J., 159, 163
gStudy (learning technology), 282–284
Guided practice activities (professional development), 212
Gutman, L. M., 266

Hadwin, A., 92
Hallahan, D. P., 51–52
Han, S. S., 209
Harris, K. R., 95, 103
Harrison, J. P., 142
Hattie, J., 102
Herrera, I. S., 256
Hicks, L., 265
Hodges, A. E., 51
Hodges, C. B., 280
Hofer, B. K., 80
Hoff, A. L., 142
Hyperactivity, 16. *See also* Attention-deficit/hyperactivity disorder

Identified regulation, 254
Imagery techniques, 151
Impulsivity, 16. *See also* Attention-deficit/hyperactivity disorder
Institute of Education Science, 20
Internal factors of change, 188
Intrapersonal factors of change, 188
Introjected regulation, 254
In vivo exposure, 149

Jamestown and the Virginia Colony (Daniel Rosen), 121, 123
Jang, H., 257, 258

Järvelä, S., 284
Järvenoja, H., 284
Johnson, M. C., 263
Johnson, S., 258
Juniper, E. F., 189

Kanfer, F. H., 47–50, 52–55
Kaplan, S., 18
Kendall, P. C., 139, 142, 150
Kim, C., 280
Kim, E. J., 257
Kindermann, T. A., 252
Kitsantas, A., 289
Kneedler, R. D., 51–52
Kosiewicz, M. M., 51–52

Ladd, G. W., 259
Learners' engagement, 91
Learning analytics, 289–290
Learning disabilities, 89–107
    ADHD comorbidity with, 16
    analytic framework for understanding, 97–98
    and conceptualization of SRL, 90–93
    deficits with, 94–95
    executive functioning impairment with, 95–96
    and future directions for SLR-supportive interventions, 106–107
    and self-determination theory, 93–94
    SRL-supportive interventions and environments for, 98–106
Learning teams, 234. *See also* Teacher learning teams
Learning technologies for self-regulated learning, 277–290
    building self-empowering cycles of learning with, 285–288
    current research, 279–282
    examples of, 282–288
    future research directions, 288–290
    theoretical foundations for, 278–279
Learning through reading (LTR) activity, 92
Learning to Learn (L2L), 75–76
Leelawong, K., 284
Lewin, K., 234
Lezak, M. D., 18

Literacy learning. *See* English language learners
Lloyd, J. W., 51–52
Logan, K. R., 235
Long, J. H., 139

Maag, J. W., 52
MacArthur, C. A., 103
Malmberg, J., 284
Management, 71
Marbell, K., 258
Maternal negative control, 263
Maternal positive guidance, 263
Mathematics difficulties, 103–104
MBCT-C (mindfulness-based cognitive therapy for children), 143
McCall, C., 58
McCarl, J. J., 50–51
McFall, R. M., 47–48
Media, 211, 288–289. *See also* Learning technologies for self-regulated learning
Medication, ADHD, 34
Mentoring, 72
Metacognition, 91, 96, 211, 231, 232
MetaTutor, 282–283
Microanalysis (SRL model of professional development), 216–221
Middle school–high school transitions, 267–268
Midgley, C., 265, 266
Miller, S. D., 118
Mindfulness-based cognitive therapy for children (MBCT-C), 143
Mindfulness-based emotion awareness, 165
Model for management of chronic disease (MMCD), 185–189
Monitoring, 70–71, 77–78. *See also* Self-monitoring
   in ADHD interventions, 20
   chart used for, 30–31
   collaborative, 34
   comprehension, 121–127
   of goals, by students, 94
   in interventions for childhood depression, 170
Montague, M., 104
Morelen, D., 140

Motivation
   defined, 79
   in English language learners, 115–116
   with learning disabilities, 96
   in self-regulated learning models, 91, 231, 232
   in SRL strategies, 211
Motivationally disengaged college students, 67–83
   characteristics of and problems associated with, 68
   course-based SRL interventions for, 76–81
   future research directions, 81–83
   improving SRL for, 71–76
   SRL framework for understanding, 69–71
Murray, C., 94

Nakamura, B. J., 150
National Assessment of Educational Progress (NAEP), 115
National Research Center on Learning Disabilities (NRCLD), 95
National Research Council Synthesis, 206
Neuenschwander, R., 263
Nicol, D., 280
No Child Left Behind Act, 205
Northern Arizona University, 290
NRCLD (National Research Center on Learning Disabilities), 95
Nuthall, G., 235

Observation, 212, 214, 285. *See also* Self-observation
Olsen, J. A., 267, 268
Open Airways for Schools (OAS), 189, 196–197
Operant conditioning, 231–232
Outcome expectancy, 187
Outcome goals (ADHD treatment), 28

Parent training, 27, 34–36
Participatory frameworks (teacher learning teams), 234–244
   applications of, 236–244
   arguments in favor of, 235–236
   history of, 234–235

Partner reading, 127
PD training. *See* Professional development training
Pekrun, R., 254
Performance
   in professional development, 218
   in self-regulated learning, 4, 278
Performance control
   defined, 19
   as focus of research, 20, 37
   as interdependent with forethought and self-reflection, 211
   in interventions for ADHD, 29
   in self-regulated learning microanalysis, 220–221
Perry, N. E., 100, 233, 236
Personal learning environments (PLEs), 289
Pestle, S. L., 150
Peters-Burton, E. E., 217, 218, 220, 222
Pintrich, P. R., 79
Planning skills, 4–5
PLEs (personal learning environments), 289
Polite, K., 46
Pomerantz, E. M., 257
Professional development (PD) training, 205–222. *See also* Teacher learning teams
   challenges of, with teachers, 207–208
   increased focus on, 206
   SRL model of. *See* Self-regulated learning model of professional development training
Proximal goals (ADHD treatment), 28. *See also* Goals
Psychoeducation, 34–35
Purdue University, 290
Puzziferro, M., 281

Raftery-Helmer, J. N., 258
Randi, J., 230, 233, 235, 245
Reactivity of self-monitoring, 47–48
Reading comprehension, 114–116
Reading disabilities, 16, 95–96, 103–104
Reappraisal (emotion regulation), 160
Reeve, J., 257, 258
Reflection. *See* Self-reflection
Reid, R., 19–20
Reid, R. R., 95, 103
Relapse prevention, 168
Relatedness, 77, 254, 259
Response modulation (emotion regulation), 159
Rewards (self-reinforcement), 55
Reyes, O., 267–268
Rock, M., 95
Roebers, C. M., 263
Rosen, Daniel, 121
Röthlisberger, M., 263
Rueda, R., 281
Rumination (emotion regulation), 162, 165–167
Rutherford, R. B., 52
Ryan, R. M., 257

Sadness, 139, 163, 167. *See also* Depression, childhood
Safety behaviors, 164, 167, 168
Sanders, M. G., 259
Scaffolding activities (professional development), 212
Scheier, M. F., 161
Scheuermann, B., 58
Schnellert, L., 97, 101
School administrators, 206
School transitions, 251–270
   adaptation required for, 260
   from elementary school to middle school, 264–267
   for first-year college students, 279–280
   future research directions, 268–270
   from middle school to high school, 267–268
   research on, 260–268
   and theoretical foundations of self-regulated learning, 252–260
Schunk, D. H., 79, 118
SCL (strategic content learning), 105–106
SDT. *See* Self-determination theory
Self-control, 215, 278, 285
Self-determination theory (SDT), 93–94, 251, 254–259
Self-efficacy
   and anxiety disorders, 148

of English language learners, 118, 122
increase of, 77
and learning disabilities, 96
Self-empowering cycles of learning, 285–288
Self-esteem, 157
Self-evaluation
defined, 279
for reduction of disruptive classroom behavior, 52–54
in treatment of youth anxiety, 151
Self-instruction, 151
Self-management for reduction of disruptive classroom behavior, 45–60
case scenario, 56–58
completing the loop in, 56
future research directions, 58–60
research on, 46, 49–56
self-evaluation in, 52–54
self-monitoring in, 46–47, 50–52
self-reinforcement in, 55
theoretical foundations, 47–49
Self-monitoring
of emotional processes, 165
in emotional regulation, 160
in interventions for youth anxiety, 150
by motivationally disengaged college students, 77–78
in professional development, 218, 221
reactivity of, 47–48
for reduction of disruptive classroom behavior, 46–48, 50–52
in self-regulated learning models, 211
by students with learning disabilities, 102–103
Self-motivation beliefs, 140
Self-observation, 143, 187–188, 278–279
Self-oriented feedback loop, 253–254
Self-reactions, 279
Self-recording, 51–52
Self-reflection
in ADHD interventions, 34
in college students, 79–80
components of, 19
cues to engage in, 30
defined, 211
in interventions for youth anxiety, 144–145, 151–152
in professional development, 211, 218
in reading interventions for ELLs, 127–128
in self-regulated learning, 4, 71, 116, 140, 279
in self-regulated learning microanalysis, 216
and teacher learning teams, 231
in tutoring sessions, 74
Self-regulated empowerment program (SREP), 104–105
Self-regulated learning (SRL). *See also specific headings*
applications of, for English language learners, 119–128
definitions of, 4, 17, 90–91, 206
early development of, 232–233
link between self-determination theory and, 93–94
motivation in, 211
theoretical foundations of, 17–19, 67–71, 90–93, 116–119, 230–231, 252–260
Self-regulated learning (SRL) interventions
adult support of, as treatment for ADHD, 31–36
child training in, as treatment for ADHD, 28–31
course-based, 76–81
feedback in, for learning disabilities, 102–103
for learning disabilities, 98–106
research support for, with ADHD, 19–27
and teacher learning teams, 231–233
Self-regulated learning model of professional development training
future research directions, 221–222
instructional characteristics of, 212–216
microanalysis in, 216–221
rationale for using, 208–210
theoretical and empirical foundations of, 210–212

Self-Regulated Learning Training Institute, 213
Self-regulated strategy development (SRSD), 103–104
Self-regulation. *See also specific headings*
 defined, 17, 137, 261, 277
 overview, 71
 theoretical basis of, 182–183
 theoretical foundations of, 230–231
Self-regulation-based interventions for asthmatic individuals, 181–199
 case examples, 190–197
 future research directions, 197–199
 and model for management of chronic disease, 185–189
 theoretical foundations, 182–189
 types of, 183–185
 in urban contexts, 189–197
Self-reinforcement, 55
Self-satisfaction, 151
Self-verbalizations, 55
Shipman, K., 139
Simonian, S. J., 139
Situation modification (emotion regulation), 159
Skinner, E., 255
Skinner, E. A., 252, 258
Slowiaczek, M. L., 259
Smith, C. L., 263
Snyder, T., 258
Social-cognitive perspective. *See* Social-cognitive theory
Social-cognitive theory, 4, 19, 116, 197, 211
Social impairment, 157, 159
Social media, 288–289
Social phobia, 139
Socioconstructivist model of self-regulated learning, 91
Southam-Gerow, M. A., 139
Specific goals (ADHD treatment), 28–29
Spencer, S. S., 235
SREP (self-regulated empowerment program), 104–105
SRSD (self-regulated strategy development), 103–104
Standards (self-regulation concept), 160
Stimulant medication, 34

Strategic action
 with learning disabilities, 96, 101, 104–106
 phases of, 92
 in self-regulated learning models, 91, 231
Strategic content learning (SCL), 105–106
Strengths (self-regulation concept), 160
Structured environments, 257–259
Subjective units of distress (SUDS), 143
Sun, J. C.-H., 281
Suppression (emotion regulation), 159, 162
Suveg, C., 139, 140
Svobodny, L., 50–51

Task analysis, 140
Teacher learning teams (TLTs), 229–246
 case examples, 236–244
 future research directions, 245–246
 and intervention research on SRL, 231–233
 and participatory frameworks, 234–244
 and theoretical foundations of self-regulation and SRL, 230–231
Teacher professional development. *See* Professional development (PD) training
Teacher training, 27, 32–33. *See also* Professional development training
Technology, learning. *See* Learning technologies for self-regulated learning
Think-alouds, 123
Thomassin, K., 140
Thompson, R. A., 163
Tice, D. M., 160
Timperley, H., 102
Tiwari, S., 142
TLTs. *See* Teacher learning teams
Training
 for ADHD treatment, 27, 32–36
 professional development. *See* Professional development training
 for self-monitoring, 49

Transitions, school. *See* School transitions
Trout, A. L., 20
Turner, J. C., 266
Turner, S. M., 139
Tutoring, 72–74

Unified Protocol for the Treatment of Emotional Disorders in Adolescence (UP-A), 158, 162–164
Unified Protocol for the Treatment of Emotional Disorders in Children (UP-C), 163
United States History for Engaged Reading (USHER), 119–128

Voelkl, K. E., 259

Webber, J., 58
Weiss, B., 209
Wellborn, J. G., 252

Wharton-McDonald, R., 233
Wiliam, D., 102
Williams, C. M., 259
Winne, P. H., 92, 102
Wong, B., 96
Workshops, 73–75
Writing difficulties, 96, 103–104
Writing revision, 211
Written expression disorder, 16

Zeman, J., 139
Zimmerman, B. J.
   and definition of self-regulated learning, 4, 210–211
   and feedback loop, 116, 140
   and learning disabilities, 105
   and model for management of chronic disease, 185
   and self-regulated learning strategies, 252–254
   and strategic action, 92

ABOUT THE EDITOR

Timothy J. Cleary, PhD, is an associate professor in the Graduate School of Applied and Professional Psychology at Rutgers, The State University of New Jersey. He earned his bachelor's degree in psychology from Manhattan College, his master's degree and professional certification in school psychology from Queens College, and his doctorate in educational psychology from City University of New York Graduate School and University Center. Dr. Cleary's research interests include developing evidence-based self-regulation and motivation assessments and intervention programs for children, adolescents, and young adults. He has published extensively on a variety of self-regulation issues and has applied his work across academic, athletic, and clinical contexts. Dr. Cleary served as coeditor of a 2013 book, *Applications of Self-Regulated Learning Across Diverse Disciplines: A Tribute to Barry J. Zimmerman*.

Dr. Cleary has provided leadership in the scholarly community, serving on multiple editorial boards for top-tier journals as well as on the executive board of the Studying and Self-Regulated Learning Special Interest Group for American Educational Research Association for over 6 years. He frequently consults with schools and agencies on both national and international levels and specializes in translating self-regulation theory and research into applied practices for teachers, educators, and practitioners.